ROBERT BROWNING
AND
ELIZABETH BARRETT

The Courtship

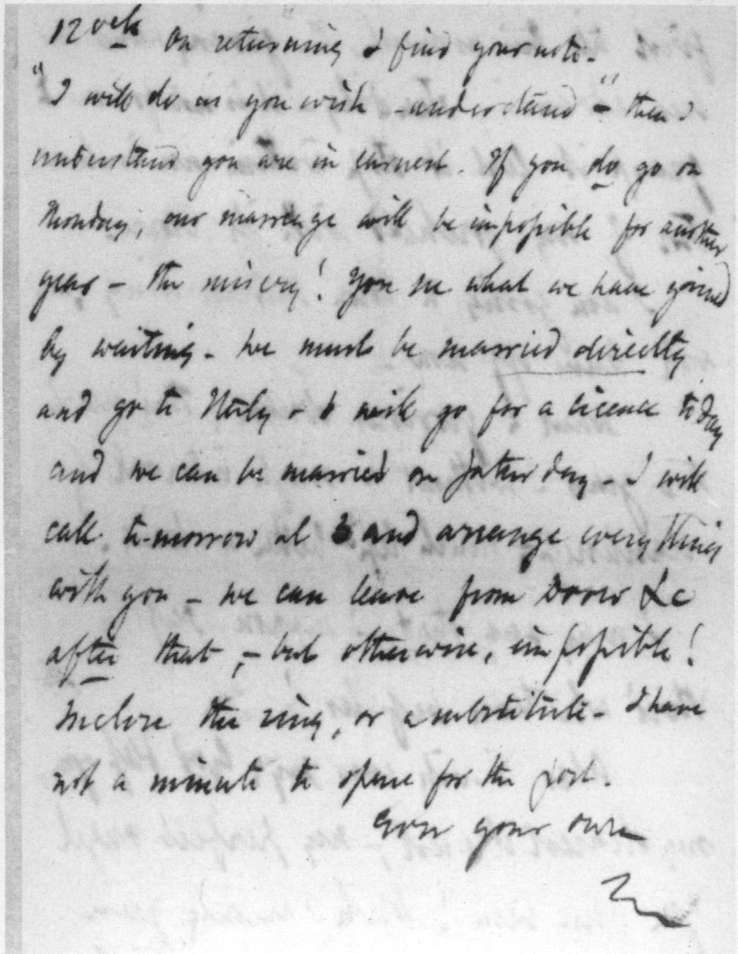
12 o'ck — On returning I find your note.
"I will do as you wish—understand"—then I
understand you are in earnest. If you *do* go on
Monday, our marriage will be impossible for another
year—the misery! You see what we have gained
by waiting. We must be *married directly*
and go to Italy—I will go for a licence today
and we can be married on Saturday—I will
call to-morrow at 3 and arrange everything
with you—we can leave from Dover &c
after that,—but otherwise, impossible!
Inclose the ring, or a substitute—I have
not a minute to spare for the post.
Ever your own
R

Moment of decision: Browning tells Elizabeth Barrett 'We must be *married directly* and go to Italy' (10 September 1846).

ROBERT BROWNING
AND
ELIZABETH BARRETT
The Courtship Correspondence 1845–1846

A Selection
Edited by
DANIEL KARLIN

Oxford   New York
OXFORD UNIVERSITY PRESS
1990

Oxford University Press, Walton Street, Oxford OX2 6DP

Oxford New York Toronto
Delhi Bombay Calcutta Madras Karachi
Petaling Jaya Singapore Hong Kong Tokyo
Nairobi Dar es Salaam Cape Town
Melbourne Auckland
and associated companies in
Berlin Ibadan

Oxford is a trade mark of Oxford University Press

First published 1989
First issued as an Oxford University Press paperback 1990

British Library Cataloguing in Publication Data
Browning, Robert, 1812–1889
The Courtship correspondence, 1845–1846.
1. Poetry in English. Browning, Robert, 1812–1889 Correspondence with
Browning, Elizabeth Barrett, 1806–1861 I. Title
II. Browning, Elizabeth Barrett, 1806–1861 III. Karlin, Daniel
821.8
ISBN 0–19–282753–7

Library of Congress Cataloging in Publication Data
Browning, Robert, 1812–1889.
[Correspondence. Selections]
The courtship correspondence, 1845–1846: a selection / Robert Browning
and Elizabeth Barrett; edited by Daniel Karlin.
p. cm.—(Oxford letters and memoirs)
Includes bibliographical references.
1. Browning, Robert, 1812–1889 Correspondence. 2. Browning,
Elizabeth Barrett, 1806–1861—Correspondence. 3. Poets.
English—19th century—Correspondence. 4. Love-letters.
I. Browning, Elizabeth Barrett, 1806–1861 II. Karlin, Daniel, 1953–
III. Title. IV. Series: Oxford letters & memoirs.
821'.8—dc20 PR4231.A43 1990 [B] 89–72141
ISBN 0–19–282753–7

Printed in Great Britain by
Richard Clay Ltd.
Bungay, Suffolk

ACKNOWLEDGEMENTS

I am grateful for grants from the British Academy and the Central Research Fund of the University of London, which enabled me to travel to Wellesley College, Massachusetts, to study the manuscripts of the Barrett–Browning letters. The letters are housed in the Special Poetry Collection of the Library of Wellesley College, Massachusetts, whose kind permission to use them I gratefully acknowledge. The frontispiece is reproduced with their permission. I should like to extend special thanks to the Special Collections Librarian Ms Anne Anninger, and her staff, for their kindness and help.

CONTENTS

INTRODUCTION   ix

NOTE ON THE TEXT   xvii

Calendar of letters and meetings   xxi

THE LETTERS   I

NOTES   334

INDEX   359

INTRODUCTION

WHEN their correspondence began in 1845 Robert Browning
was 32 years old, and Elizabeth Barrett 38. They were both,
though in different ways, disillusioned and disappointed
people. In the ten years since the encouraging reception of
Paracelsus Browning had seen his great poem *Sordello* heaped
with ridicule for its impenetrable obscurity, and had suffered
the more prolonged failure of his attempt to write for the
stage. His series of plays and poems *Bells and Pomegranates* was
being published in cheap paper pamphlets, paid for by his
father; he himself was still living with his parents and sister
in suburban New Cross, subject to the occasional taunts of
society acquaintances about his apparent unwillingess to earn
his living. The London literary set in which he moved and
dined and had his being was beginning to get on his nerves.
'Sir L. Bulwer has published a set of sing-songs', he wrote
with sour wit to his friend Alfred Domett, who had recently
emigrated to New Zealand, in July 1842. 'I read two, or one,
in a review, and thought them abominable. Mr Taylor's
affected, unreal putting together, called "Edwin the Fair", is
the flattest of fallen. . . . Dickens is back, and busy in "doing"
America for his next numbers—sad work.'[1] Browning's own
creativity was as strong and as resourceful as ever, but his
feelings about it were depressed and irritable. Elizabeth
Barrett, on the other hand, had just published a collection
(*Poems*, 2 vols., 1844) which raised her reputation to a point
which Browning was not to enjoy for over twenty years.
Together with the ambitious work at the head of the collection, *A Drama of Exile*, which starts where *Paradise Lost* ends,
went a series of intensely wrought, thoughtful sonnets, and a
number of sentimental lyrics and vigorous romantic ballads,
many of the latter with surprising twists in their conventional
fabric. (In one of the most popular of these ballads, 'Lady
Geraldine's Courtship', Browning was to read the flattering

---

[1] *Robert Browning and Alfred Domett*, ed. F. G. Kenyon (London: Smith, Elder,
1906), p. 41.

reference to himself which prompted his first letter.[2] But success seemed a cruel joke to Elizabeth Barrett, embroiled in a family plot partly of her own making but now too densely woven, it seemed, for her to find a way out. After the traumatic death by drowning of her brother Edward in 1840 her ambiguous illness worsened, she declined into downright invalidism, sustained by opium and the care (tender, complacent, sinister) of her family; her father prayed with her nightly, and she listened for the sound of his footstep on the stair as the greatest happiness in her life. Her invalidism answered, as she later saw it, to a sickness in the family itself which sheltered and oppressed her; and, though it is inevitably on the gloomy, ponderous, contorted figure of Edward Barrett Moulton Barrett that attention centres, we should not forget that the whole household at 50 Wimpole Street contributed to the 'morbid and desolate state' which Elizabeth Barrett describes in a letter written soon after her escape from it:

my family had been so accustomed to the idea of my living on and on in that room, that while my heart was eating itself, their love for me was consoled, and at last the evil grew scarcely perceptible. It was no want of love in them, and quite natural in itself: we all get used to the thought of a tomb; and I was buried, there was the whole.[3]

It was no want of love, but Browning's advent signalled a love of which Elizabeth Barrett was, indeed, in want, just as her presence allowed him to envisage a renewal of his own emotional and creative life. The letters tell a story of discovery, the discovery of a refuge and strength in each other which both Browning and Elizabeth Barrett had ceased to imagine possible, of the liberation of thwarted desires and energies. Not surprisingly, this story has taken on the form of a heroic myth of rescue and regeneration, but it is a myth we should

[2] The hero of the poem is reading to Lady Geraldine from the works of modern poets, among them 'from Browning some "Pomegranate," which, if cut deep down the middle, / Shows a heart within blood-tinctured, of a veined humanity'. Browning did not mention this compliment in his first letter to Elizabeth Barrett; but see letter RB 16 Nov., p. 155.

[3] *Letters of Elizabeth Barrett Browning*, ed. F. G. Kenyon, 2 vols. (London: Smith, Elder, 1897), i. 288.

consider with some scepticism, not least because of the problematic richness of the form in which it has been bequeathed to us. In the intensity of their *writerly* natures, and under the pressure of the peculiar circumstances of their courtship, Browning and Elizabeth Barrett wrote to each other incessantly and at prodigious length: 573 extant letters, one of the longest, fullest, most self-contained correspondences in English literary history. Of their ninety-one meetings in Elizabeth Barrett's room in Wimpole Street (the first time they met outside it was when they were married) we have few traces, and even those few are, of course, preserved in the letters. Are not the letters, then, the heart of the matter? Possessing them, do we not have privileged and intimate access to the relationship of which they were the medium?

The Special Collections room in the Library of Wellesley College, Massachusetts, is large, quiet, and comfortable. The furnishings are old-fashioned in appearance compared to the functional stacks of the main library outside. There are rare books in glass-fronted cases, and portraits of their authors on the walls. In this haven of conservation the temperature is stable, the light muted, the only writing allowed is in soft pencil: there is passion here, but it is a passion of scholarly respect. The letters of Robert Browning and Elizabeth Barrett are kept in separate boxes, and each letter is separate from the others in its own white wrapper.[4] The sheets are kept flat, not folded as they were when they were sent. The paper has stiffened and dried, in some cases acquiring a grainy sheen, in some a smooth, wax-like transparency, and the inks have faded to lighter or darker browns. The living enclosures—such as the yellow rose Browning sent to Elizabeth Barrett in his letter of 14 June 1845, or the unnamed flower she sent to him in her letter of 29 May 1846—have disappeared, and it is worth considering what else has vanished with them.

Browning had harsh words to say about the reading of 'real' letters—letters, that is, whose 'thoughts, feelings &

---

[4] The letters were bought by the London dealer Frank Sabin for £6,550 at the sale in 1913 of the estate of 'Pen' Browning, only child of Robert and Elizabeth Barrett Browning, who died intestate. They were given to Wellesley College in 1930 by Miss Caroline Hazard.

expressions', as he told Elizabeth Barrett 'move & live . . . in a self-imposed circle limiting the experience of two persons only': the presence of a 'third person', he insisted, 'breaks the line, so to speak, and lets in a whole tract of country on the originally inclosed spot'.[5] Clearly the 'originally inclosed spot', the 'self-imposed circle' of Browning's and Elizabeth Barrett's 'thoughts, feelings & expressions', is inaccessible to us: we cannot recover the sense of what these letters meant in the living privacy of their making and reading. They are no longer 'real letters', but, in the language of scholarship, 'holograph manuscripts'. We touch them and read them as 'third persons'. We do so, moreover, in an alien form, that of a 'correspondence': we read them one after another, in a sequence devoid of the times and seasons through which they were originally threaded; the eye jumps the gap between each, reduced to a date and the name of a day, and we do not have to wait for the arrival of the next letter. Suspense on the small scale is eliminated; so it is, too, on the larger scale of the story, since we know the outcome before we begin. Indeed the *correspondence* has a plot of which the *letters* themselves could not be aware, as the letters of a word cannot know the word they spell.

I emphasize these losses just because letters in general give so strong an impression of the texture of life 'as it happens'. Unlike most other forms of imaginative writing, they bear directly on their subject: a letter *is* an action or gesture, as well as the representation of one. Or rather (especially in a case such as that of the Browning–Barrett correspondence) a letter *was* an action; modern readers are just that, readers, and not participants, and unless we remember the necessary detachment of our position we will give ourselves the illusion of re-entering paradise lost—the 'originally inclosed spot' of the lovers' dialogue—and, at the same time, miss what the letters have really to offer us.

The story told by the letters is not, it must be emphasized, the raw material of events, but a treatment of those events, a representation—at times, we might even say a fiction.[6] Of

---

[5] Letter of 15 Feb. 1846, not included in this edition.

[6] The fiction making was especially necessary, and effective, in the matter of Elizabeth Barrett's relations with her father. See Karlin, pp. 3–8, 237–51.

course this does not mean that incidents and attitudes are deliberately falsified or invented. It is sober fact that Mr Barrett was resolutely opposed to any of his children marrying. This prohibition was not made in direct terms, but in the form of a principle that children should never marry without the consent of their father, with the unspoken clause that, in his case, the consent would never be forthcoming. In the face of this prohibition Browning and Elizabeth Barrett felt obliged to carry on their courtship clandestinely. The extent of Elizabeth Barrett's general correspondence with her numerous literary and personal friends disguised the nature of her correspondence with Browning, and her letters were posted by her sisters or her trusted maid Wilson; but the lovers were driven to conceal the frequency of their meetings, and pretended that the ones they acknowledged were mere exchanges of literary gossip. They were married in secret and eloped, and Mr Barrett did, indeed, renounce his daughter— to the extent of returning her letters unopened, and of forbidding her name to be mentioned for the rest of his life. If a 'myth' has grown up around these events it has had some excuse! But the process has been reductive, not enriching, and the letters themselves are more interesting than the tabloid version which has predominated from the first outbreak of gossip and which was fixed in the lurid colours of Rudolf Besier's *The Barretts of Wimpole Street*. And the letters contain their own myth: one which does not exactly conform to the apparent outline of the story. Both Browning and Elizabeth Barrett believed that, as Browning put it, 'there is no love but from beneath, far beneath,—that is the law of its nature'.[7] Obviously they could not each be inferior to the other—or could they? After all, as Imlac remarks in Johnson's *Rasselas*, 'Inconsistencies . . . cannot be right, but, imputed to man, they may both be true.' The letters show that Browning and Elizabeth Barrett came to terms with what each believed the other's delusion, as the price of the acceptance of their own 'true' insight. But each position of deference and devotion concealed a spring of creative strength. Browning needed to believe Elizabeth Barrett his personal and poetic mentor,

---

[7] Letter of 10 August. 1846, not included in this edition.

since his whole intellectual and emotional life was based on the resources and opportunities of secondariness and imperfection; Elizabeth Barrett, in turn, needed to believe the same of Browning, since the appearance of a figure who embodied and articulated power (she invariably characterizes Browning as a man and writer of compelling force) gave her the opportunity to seize power in her own life. Anticipating *Aurora Leigh*, she wrote to Browning in only her fifth letter that she was 'waiting for a story & I won't take one because I want to make one, & I like to make my own stories, because then I can take liberties with them in the treatment'.[8] The pleasure which the writer takes in such power is pre-eminent in the correspondence, where the lines of both Elizabeth Barrett's and Browning's 'stories' run parallel, diverge, intersect, and finally merge. 'I should like to write something in concert with you—how I would try!' Browning wrote to Elizabeth Barrett in an early letter.[9] He did: the correspondence is that text, written and performed 'in concert'.

The rhetoric of which both writers were masterly practitioners is displayed in every aspect of the letters, and it is always a rhetoric of awareness, both of self and others. 'Of course you are *self-conscious*—How could you be a poet otherwise?' wrote Elizabeth Barrett to Browning.[10] These were, in no pejorative sense, artful people, and the text they produced is true to their imaginative and expressive skills.

If, therefore, we must accept that we cannot read the letters in their original form, that certain kinds of authenticity simply have no shelf-life, we need not conclude that the letters are dumb and lifeless. Our loss is, in another direction, our gain: our detachment, the privilege of seeing both sides, and therefore of being able to witness the interplay of two acute and inventive minds. Browning and Elizabeth Barrett show themselves to be both expressive and responsive writers. Each was a mature, forceful individual, with habits of mind and style whose patterns are impressed in the fabric of the letters like a watermark in paper; at the same time they are each alert to the other's language, continually picking up and

---

[8] Letter EB 27 Feb., p. 28.
[9] Letter RB 3 May, p. 45.
[10] Letter EB 27 Feb., p. 29.

modifying each other's phrases and commenting on each other's rhetoric. This creative process, combining the strong individuality of the writers with their passionate and sensitive scrutiny of each other, is illuminated by the form in which we now possess the letters as it could not have been for the writers themselves.

The principal topic of this scrutiny is love, and I have chosen in the present selection to concentrate in both narrative and thematic terms on what the two writers have to say about their own love-relationship, and on the way they say it. In doing so, however, I am aware—and wish the reader to be aware—of what has had to be sacrificed. About half the letters are represented, and many of those only by short extracts, so that considerably less than half the text of the correspondence is reprinted here. The limitation of space has imposed a limitation of topic, if the volume was to have any continuity and shape and not consist of a miscellaneous and disconnected series of observations. Accordingly, the documentary side of the letters—their representation of the Victorian domestic, social, political, religious, and artistic 'scene'—has, with regret, been greatly circumscribed. Episodes such as Elizabeth Barrett's visit to the art collection of Samuel Rogers, or her reaction to the suicide of the painter Benjamin Robert Haydon (both in June 1846), could not have been given adequate treatment in terms either of the length of the letters themselves or the annotation which they would have required. Some impression of the range of reference of the whole correspondence may be gained from its opening sequence (from Browning's first letter to the episode of his abortive declaration of love in May 1845), which is presented virtually complete, and the reader must remember that subsequent letters are equally rich in this kind of material. It will also be seen, by comparing the selection with the full calendar of the letters on pp. xxi–xxviii, that the proportion of letters taken from, roughly, the first half of the courtship is greater than that from the second, because the material which I have judged to be of most interest comes from this period. I have placed the accent of the selection on the letters and passages where Browning's and Elizabeth Barrett's self-consciousness and consciousness of the other were at their sharpest and most intense: where the writers were lovers and the lovers writers.

NOTE ON THE TEXT

THE text of the letters has been freshly edited from the holograph manuscripts. I have referred also to the first edition (2 vols., London: Smith, Elder, 1899) and to Elvan Kintner's edition (see below). The manuscript has been silently emended in a few places, where the spelling and punctuation of the original would have been needlessly puzzling. Quotation marks have been made uniformly single, with double quotation marks reserved for inset speech. Apart from this, however, the idiosyncrasies and inconsistencies of both writers have been preserved. In particular, readers should note that Elizabeth Barrett frequently spelt days of the week without an initial capital, and that both she and Browning employed two points (..) where modern punctuation would have three points or a dash. In addition:

1. Deletions from and corrections to the manuscript, whether legible or not, have only been recorded when they have been judged to be critically interesting and important. Deletions are indicated by the use of angle brackets ⟨ ⟩; corrections are indicated in the notes.

2. The unconventional position of single words or passages (e.g. where a phrase has been inserted above the line) has not been noted; nor has the placing of parts of a letter (e.g. the writing of a postscript in the throat of the envelope). The position of greetings and valedictions has been regularized.

3. From early on in the correspondence, both Browning and Elizabeth Barrett abandoned the practice of formally dating their letters; they usually noted only the day of the week, and sometimes the time of day, except where marking a special occasion (New Year's day, or the anniversary of their first meeting). Where there is no date in the letter, it can almost always be established from the postmark. Unless the note of the day and time is of some interest, it has not been included in the text; the full date ascribed to each letter will be found in the heading. Where Browning or Elizabeth Barrett wrote more than one letter in a day, the date is

followed by a number in the brackets. A full list of letters is given in the Calendar, together with the dates of meetings; for Browning's notation of these meetings, see p. 55.

4. Italics indicate underlining; small capitals indicate double underlining.

5. Ellipses in the manuscript, of whatever length, are indicated by three spaced points (. . .); three closed points (...) indicates authorial punctuation. Where the text resumes with a new paragraph, the ellipses are placed at the end of the preceding paragraph; where the text resumes in mid-paragraph, the ellipses are placed after the paragraph indent. Where one or more complete paragraphs have been omitted from the beginning or end of a letter, the ellipses occupy a separate line; where a postscript has been omitted, the ellipses occupy a line below the signature.

People mentioned more than once in the letters are identified on their first appearance only, which can be found from the index.

The following short titles are used in the introduction and notes:

Hood	T. L. Hood (ed.), *Letters of Robert Browning* (London: John Murray, 1933).
Karlin	D. Karlin, *The Courtship of Robert Browning and Elizabeth Barrett* (Oxford: Clarendon Press, 1985).
Kelley and Hudson	P. Kelley and R. Hudson (eds.), *The Brownings' Correspondence* (Winfield: Wedgestone Press, 1984–).
Kelley and Hudson, *Checklist*	P. Kelley and R. Hudson, *The Brownings' Correspondence: A Checklist* (New York: The Browning Institute, and Winfield: Wedgestone Press, 1978).
Kenyon	F. G. Kenyon (ed.), *Letters of Elizabeth Barrett Browning*, 2 vols. (London: Smith, Elder, 1897).
Kintner	E. Kintner (ed.), *The Letters of Robert Browning and Elizabeth Barrett Barrett, 1845–1846*, 2 vols. (Cambridge, Mass.: Harvard University Press, 1969).

Pagination runs consecutively through both volumes: the volume number is therefore not given in references.

Landis
: P. Landis (ed.), *Letters of the Brownings to George Barrett*, (Urbana: University of Illinois Press, 1958).

McAleer
: E. C. McAleer (ed.), *Learned Lady: Letters from Robert Browning to Mrs. Thomas FitzGerald* (Cambridge, Mass.: Harvard University Press, 1966).

Maynard
: J. Maynard, *Browning's Youth* (Cambridge, Mass.: Harvard University Press, 1977).

Miller
: B. Miller (ed.), *Elizabeth Barrett to Miss Mitford* (London: John Murray, 1954).

CALENDAR OF LETTERS
AND MEETINGS

THE left-hand column lists the numbers of the letters in Kintner's edition, the right-hand column giving the page numbers for those letters which are reprinted in whole or in part in this edition. A query before the date usually implies that the letter was sent in a parcel, so that there is no envelope and postmark. There is one brief undated note or fragment in Elizabeth Barrett's hand which cannot be placed in the sequence of 573 extant letters; Kintner suggests the date 11 July 1846 and places it between nos. 452 and 453.

1845		page
1.	RB 10 Jan.	1
2.	EB 11 Jan.	2
3.	RB 13 Jan.	4
4.	EB 15 Jan.	5
5.	RB 27 Jan.	8
6.	EB 3 Feb.	10
7.	RB 11 Feb.	14
8.	EB 17 Feb.	17
9.	RB 26 Feb.	23
10.	EB 27 Feb.	26
11.	RB 1 Mar.	29
12.	EB 5 Mar.	30
13.	RB 11 Mar.	31
14.	EB 20 Mar.	33
15.	RB 31 Mar.	
16.	RB 15 Apr.	37
17.	EB 17 Apr.	38
18.	RB 30 Apr.	39
19.	EB 1 May	41
20.	RB 3 May	42
21.	EB 5–6 May	46
22.	EB 11 May	48
23.	RB 12 May	48
24.	RB 13 May	49
25.	EB 15 May	50
26.	RB 16 May	52
27.	EB 17 May	53
[Meeting 1: 20 May]		
28.	RB 20 May	55
29.	EB 21 May	56
[RB's missing letter ?22 May]		
30.	EB 23 May	57
31.	RB 24 May	59
32.	EB 25 May	62
33.	RB 26 May	65
34.	EB 26–7 May	66
35.	RB 28 May	
36.	EB 30 May	
[Meeting 2: 31 May]		
[Meeting 3: 5 June]		
37.	EB 6 June	67
38.	RB 7 June	
39.	RB 9 June	69
40.	EB 10 June	
[Meeting 4: 11 June]		
41.	EB 13 June	69
42.	RB 14 June	70
43.	EB 16 June	72
[Meeting 5: 18 June]		
44.	RB 19 June	74
45.	EB 19 June	74
46.	RB 22 June	75
47.	EB 23 June	76
48.	RB 24 June	
49.	EB 24 June	
50.	RB 25 June	

51.	EB 26 June	
52.	RB 27 June	
53.	EB 27 June	
[Meeting 6: 28 June]		
54.	EB 30 June	
55.	RB 1 July	76
56.	EB 2–3 July	77
[Meeting 7: 5 July]		
57.	RB 7 July	
58.	EB 7–8 July	80
59.	RB 9 July	81
[Meeting 8: 10 July]		
60.	EB. 11 July	81
61.	RB 13 July	83
62.	EB 16–17 July	85
[Meeting 9: 16 July]		
63.	RB ? 18 July	88
64.	EB 21 July	90
65.	RB 22 July	
[Meeting 10: 24 July]		
66.	EB 25 July	91
67.	RB 25 July	92
68.	EB 26–7 July	93
69.	RB 28 July	
[Meeting 11: 30 July]		
70.	RB 31 July	
71.	EB 31 July–1 Aug.	95
72.	RB 3 Aug.	96
[Meeting 12: 6 Aug.]		
73.	EB 8 Aug.	97
74.	RB 8 Aug.	98
75.	EB 8 Aug.	
76.	RB 10 Aug.	
77.	EB 11 Aug.	99
[Meeting 13: 12 Aug.]		
78.	RB 12 Aug.	99
79.	RB 13 Aug.	100
80.	RB 15 Aug.	100
81.	EB 16 Aug.	101
82.	EB 17 Aug.	
83.	RB 18 Aug.	
84.	EB 19 Aug.	
85.	RB 20 Aug.	
86.	RB 21 Aug.	
87.	EB 20–3 Aug.	103
[Meeting 14: 22 Aug.]		
[Meeting 15: 26 Aug.]		
88.	RB 27 Aug.	107
89.	EB 27 Aug.	107
90.	EB 29 Aug.	108
91.	RB 29 Aug.	
92.	RB 30 Aug.	109
93.	EB 31 Aug.–1 Sept.	110
[Meeting 16: 1 Sept.]		
94.	RB 2 Sept.	
95.	RB 2 Sept.	
96.	EB 4 Sept.	113
97.	RB 5 Sept.	
98.	EB 6 Sept.	
[Meeting 17: 8 Sept.]		
99.	EB 9 Sept.	113
100.	RB 11 Sept.	
101.	EB 11 Sept.	
[Meeting 18: 12 Sept.]		
102.	RB 13 Sept.	114
103.	EB 16 Sept.	117
104.	RB 16 Sept.	120
105.	EB 17 Sept.	123
106.	EB 17 Sept.	124
107.	RB 17 Sept.	125
108.	EB 18 Sept.	125
109.	RB 18 Sept.	126
110.	EB 19 Sept.	127
[Meeting 19: 22 Sept.]		
111.	EB. 23 Sept.	
112.	RB. 24 Sept.	
113.	EB 25 Sept.	127
114.	RB 25 Sept.	129
[Meeting 20: 26 Sept.]		
115.	EB 26 Sept.	132
116.	RB 27 Sept.	133
117.	EB 29 Sept.	134
[Meeting 21: 30 Sept.]		
118.	EB 1 Oct.	
119.	RB 2 Oct.	
[Meeting 22: 3 Oct.]		
120.	EB 4 Oct.	134
121.	RB 6 Oct.	
122.	EB 6 Oct.	
123.	EB 7 Oct.	135

124. RB 8 Oct.
[Meeting 23: 9 Oct.]
125. EB 10–11 Oct.   136
126. RB 12 Oct.   136
127. EB 11–13 Oct.   137
128. RB 14 Oct.   138
129. EB 14 Oct.
130. RB 15 Oct.
131. EB 15 Oct.   138
[Meeting 24: 16 Oct.]
132. EB 17 Oct.   139
133. RB 18 Oct.
134. RB 20 Oct.
[Meeting 25: 21 Oct.]
135. EB 21–2 Oct.   140
136. RB 23 Oct.   141
137. EB 23 Oct.   143
138. EB 24 Oct.   144
139. RB 27 Oct.   145
140. RB 28 Oct.
[Meeting 26: 28 Oct.]
141. EB ?29 Oct.
142. RB 29 Oct.   146
143. EB 31 Oct.   146
[Meeting 27: 3 Nov.]
144. RB 4 Nov.
145. EB 5 Nov.   148
146. RB 6 Nov.   149
147. EB 6 Nov.
[Meeting 28: 8 Nov.]
148. RB 9 Nov.   149
149. EB 10 Nov.   150
[Meeting 29: 13 Nov.]
150. EB 12–14 Nov.   151
151. RB 16 Nov.   154
152. EB 17 Nov.   157
[Meeting 30: 19 Nov.]
153. RB 20 Nov.
154. EB 20 Nov.
155. RB 21 Nov.
156. EB 22 Nov.
157. RB 23 Nov.   159
158. EB 24 Nov.   159
[Meeting 31: 25 Nov.]
159. EB 24–6 Nov.   160

160. RB 27 Nov.
161. RB 28 Nov.   161
162. EB 28–29 Nov.   162
163. EB 29 Nov.
[Meeting 32: 1 Dec.]
164. RB 2 Dec.   163
165. RB 3 Dec.
166. EB 2–3 Dec.
167. EB 4 Dec.   163
[Meeting 33: 6 Dec.]
168. RB 7 Dec.
169. EB 7–8 Dec.
170. RB 9 Dec.
171. EB 9 Dec.
[Meeting 34: 11 Dec.]
172. RB 12 Dec.   165
173. EB 12 Dec.   165
174. RB 15 Dec.
175. EB 15 Dec.   167
176. EB 16 Dec.
[Meeting 35: 17 Dec.]
177. EB 18–19 Dec.   168
178. RB 19 Dec.   170
179. RB 20 Dec.   170
180. EB 20 Dec.   171
181. RB 21 Dec.   172
[Meeting 36: 23 Dec.]
182. EB 21–4 Dec.   173
183. RB 25 Dec.   177
184. RB 27 Dec.
185. EB 27 Dec.
[Meeting 37; 29 Dec.]
186. EB 30 Dec.   178
187. RB 31 Dec.   179

1846

188   EB 1 Jan.   180
[Meeting 38: 3 Jan.]
189. RB 4 Jan.   181
190. EB 4–5 Jan.   182
191. RB 6 Jan.
192. RB 6–7 Jan.   184
193. EB 7 Jan.
[Meeting 39: 8 Jan.]
194. EB 9 Jan.

195. RB 9 Jan.
196. EB 10 Jan.   186
197. RB 10 Jan.
198. RB 11 Jan.   187
      [Meeting 40: 13 Jan.]
199. EB 13–14 Jan.   188
200. RB 14 Jan.   189
201. RB 15 Jan.   190
202. EB 15 Jan.   191
203. EB 15–16 Jan.   193
204. RB 17 Jan.
205. RB 18 Jan.   195
206. EB 18 Jan.   197
207. RB 19 Jan.   197
      [Meeting 41: 21 Jan.]
208. EB 21 Jan.   199
209. RB 22 Jan.   200
210. EB 22 Jan.
211. RB 23 Jan.
      [Meeting 42: 24 Jan.]
212. EB 24–5 Jan.
213. RB 25 Jan.   201
214. EB 26–7 Jan.   202
215. RB 27 Jan.
216. RB 28 Jan.   205
      [Meeting 43: 29 Jan.]
217. EB 30 Jan.   205
218. RB 31 Jan.   206
219. EB 30 Jan.
220. EB 30 Jan.–1 Feb.   207
      [Meeting 44: 3 Feb.]
221. RB 4 Feb.   209
222. EB 4 Feb.   210
223. RB 6 Feb.
224. RB 7 Feb.
225. RB 7 Feb.
226. EB 7 Feb.
227. RB 8 Feb.
      [Meeting 45: 9 Feb.]
228. EB 10 Feb.   211
229. RB 11 Feb.   212
230. EB 12 Feb.
231. RB 13 Feb.   213
      [Meeting 46: 14 Feb.]
232. EB 14–15 Feb.

233. RB 15 Feb.
234. RB 16 Feb.
235. EB 16 Feb.   214
236. EB 16 Feb.
237. RB 17 Feb.
      [Meeting 47: 18 Feb.]
238. RB 19 Feb.   214
239. EB 19 Feb.   215
240. EB 19 Feb.
241. RB 20 Feb.
242. EB 20 Feb.
243. RB 21 Feb.   215
      [Meeting 48: 23 Feb.]
244. EB 23 Feb.   216
245. RB 24 Feb.
246. RB 25 Feb.   218
247. EB 26 Feb.   220
248. RB 26 Feb.   220
249. EB 26 Feb.   221
250. RB 27 Feb.
      [Meeting 49, 28 Feb.]
251. EB 1 Mar.   222
252. RB 1 Mar.
253. RB 2 Mar.
254. EB 2 Mar.
255. RB 3 Mar.   223
256. EB 3 Mar.   225
257. RB 4 Mar.   227
      [Meeting 50, 5 Mar.]
258. EB 5 Mar.
259. RB 6 Mar.
260. EB 6 Mar.   227
261. RB 7 Mar.
      [Meeting 51, 9 Mar.]
262. EB. 10 Mar.   228
263. RB 10 Mar.
264. EB 10 Mar.   228
265. RB 11 Mar.   229
266. EB 12 Mar.
      [Meeting 52; 14 Mar.]
267. RB 12 Mar.
268. EB 15 Mar.
269. RB 15 Mar.   230
270. RB 16 Mar.
271. EB 16 Mar.   231

272. RB 17 Mar.   231
273. EB 17 Mar.
274. RB 18 Mar.
      [Meeting 53: 19 Mar.]
275. EB 20 Mar.
276. RB 21 Mar.
277. EB 21 Mar.
278. RB 22 Mar.
      [Meeting 54: 23 Mar.]
279. EB 24 Mar.
280. RB 24 Mar.   232
281. EB 24 Mar.   233
282. RB 25 Mar.
283. EB 25 Mar.
284. RB 26 Mar.
285. EB 26 Mar.
286. RB 27 Mar.
      [Meeting 55: 28 Mar.]
287. RB 29 Mar.
288. EB 29 Mar.
289. RB 30 Mar.   233
290. EB 30 Mar.
291. EB 30 Mar.
292. RB 31 Mar.
293. EB 31 Mar.
294. RB 1 Apr.
      [Meeting 56: 2 Apr.]
295. EB 3 Apr.
296. RB 3 Apr.
297. EB 3 Apr.
298. RB 4 Apr.
299. EB 5 Apr.   234
300. RB 5 Apr.   235
301. RB 6 Apr.
      [Meeting 57: 6 Apr.]
302. EB 7 Apr.
303. RB 7 Apr.
304. EB 7 Apr.
305. RB 8 Apr.
306. EB 8 Apr.   236
307. RB 9 Apr.   236
308. EB 9 Apr.
309. EB 10 Apr.
310. RB 10 Apr.
      [Meeting 58: 11 Apr.]

311. EB 12 Apr.   238
312. RB 12 Apr.
313. EB 13 Apr.
314. RB 14 Apr.   240
      [Meeting 59: 15 Apr.]
315. EB 16 Apr.
316. RB 16 Apr.
317. EB 16 Apr.
318. RB 17 Apr.
319. EB 17 Apr.
320. RB 18 Apr.
321. RB 19 Apr.   240
      [Meeting 60: 20 Apr.]
322. EB 21 Apr.   242
323. RB 21 Apr.
324. EB 21 Apr.
325. RB 22 Apr.   243
326. EB 22 Apr.
327. RB 23 Apr.
328. EB 23 Apr.
329. RB 24 Apr.
      [Meeting 61: 25 Apr.]
330. EB 26 Apr.
331. RB 26 Apr.
332. RB 27 Apr.
333. EB 27 Apr.
334. RB 28 Apr.
335. EB 28 Apr.
336. RB 29 Apr.
      [Meeting 62: 30 Apr.]
337. EB 1 May
338. RB 1 May   243
339. EB 1 May   244
340. RB 2 May
341. RB 3 May
      [Meeting 63: 4 May]
342. RB 5 May   244
343. EB 5 May   245
344. EB 5 May
345. RB 6 May
346. EB 6 May
347. RB 7 May
348. EB 7 May   246
349. RB 8 May
      [Meeting 64: 9 May]

350. EB 10 May
351. RB 10 May   247
352. RB 11 May
353. EB 11 May   248
354. RB 12 May
355. EB 12 May
356. RB 13 May
[Meeting 65: 14 May]
357. EB 15 May   249
358. RB 15 May
359. EB 15 May
360. RB 16 May
361. EB 16 May
362. RB 17 May
[Meeting 66: 18 May]
363. EB 19 May   250
364. RB 19 May   250
365. EB 19 May   251
366. RB 20 May   251
367. EB 20 May
368. RB 21 May
369. EB 21 May
370. EB 21 May
371. RB 22 May
[Meeting 67: 23 May
372. RB 24 May   253
373. EB 24 May   253
374. RB 25 May
375. RB 25 May
376. EB 25 May   254
377. RB 26 May
[Meeting: 68: 27 May]
378. EB 28 May
379. RB 28 May
380. EB 28 May
381. RB 29 May
382. EB 29 May   256
383. RB 30 May   257
384. EB 30 May
385. RB 31 May
[Meeting 69: 1 June]
386. EB 2 June
387. RB 2 June
388. EB 2 June
389. RB 3 June   257

390. EB 3 June   258
391. EB 3 June
392. RB 4 June
393. EB 4 June
394. RB 5 June
[Meeting 70: 6 June]
395. EB 7 June
396. RB 7 June
397. RB 8 June   258
398. EB 8 June
399. RB 9 June
400. EB 9 June
[Meeting 71: 11 June]
401. EB 12 June
402. RB 12 June   259
403. EB 12 June   260
404. RB 13 June
405. EB 13 June
406. RB 14 June
[Meeting 72: 15]
407. EB 16 June   261
408. RB 16 June   261
409. EB 16 June   261
410. EB 16 June
411. RB 17 June   263
412. EB 17 June
413. RB 18 June
414. EB 18 June
415. RB 19 June
[Meeting 73: 20 June]
416. RB 21 June
417. EB 21 June
418. RB 22 June
419. EB 22 June
420. RB 23 June
421. EB 23 June
422. RB 24 June
[Meeting 74: 25 June]
423. RB 26 June   264
424. EB 26 June
425. EB 26 June
426. RB 27 June
427. EB 27 June
[Meeting 75: 29 June]
428. RB 28 June

429.	EB 30 June	265
430.	RB 30 June	265
431.	EB 30 June	266
432.	RB 1 July	266
433.	EB 1 July	267
434.	RB 2 July	267
435.	EB 2 July	268
436.	EB 3 July	
437.	RB 3 July	
438.	EB 3 July	
439.	RB 4 July	
440.	EB 4 July	
441.	RB 5 July	
442.	EB 5 July	
443.	RB 6 July	
444.	EB 6 July	
445.	EB 7 July	
446.	RB 7 July	
447.	EB 7 July	
448.	RB 8 July	
[Meeting 76: 8 July]		
449.	RB 9 July	
450.	EB 9 July	286
451.	EB 9 July	
452.	RB 10 July	269
[Meeting 77: 11 July]		
453.	RB 12 July	
454.	EB 12 July	
455.	RB 13 July	
456.	EB 13 July	
[Meeting 78: 14 July]		
457.	EB 15 July	269
458.	RB 15 July	
459.	EB 15 July	
460.	RB 16 July	271
461.	EB 16 July	271
462.	RB 17 July	
463.	EB 17 July	
[Meeting 79: 18 July]		
464.	RB 19 July	
465.	EB 19 July	
466.	RB 20 July	
[Meeting 80: 21 July]		
467.	EB 22 July	
468.	RB 22 July	273

469.	EB 22 July	273
470.	RB 23 July	275
471.	EB 23 July	
472.	RB 24 July	
[Meeting 81: 25 July]		
473.	EB 26 July	276
474.	RB 26 July	
475.	RB 27 July	277
476.	EB 27 July	
[Meeting 82: 28 July]		
477.	EB 28 July	
478.	RB 29 July	278
479.	EB 29 July	278
480.	RB 30 July	279
481.	EB 30 July	
482.	RB 31 July	
[Meeting 83: 1 Aug.]		
483.	EB 2 Aug.	279
484.	RB 2 Aug.	
485.	RB 3 Aug.	281
486.	EB 3 Aug.	282
[Meeting 84: 4 Aug.]		
487.	EB 4 Aug.	
488.	RB 5 Aug.	
489.	EB 5 Aug.	
490.	RB 6 Aug.	
491.	EB 6 Aug.	
492.	RB 7 Aug.	
[Meeting 85: 8 Aug.]		
493.	RB 9 Aug.	
494.	EB 9 Aug.	
495.	RB 10 Aug.	
496.	EB 10 Aug.	283
[Meeting 86: 11 Aug.]		
497.	RB 12 Aug.	
498.	EB 12 Aug.	284
499.	EB 12 Aug.	
500.	RB 13 Aug.	284
[Meeting 87: 14 Aug.]		
501.	EB 15 Aug.	
502.	RB 15 Aug.	
503.	EB 15 Aug.	
504.	RB 16 Aug.	
505.	EB 16 Aug.	286
506.	RB 17 Aug.	

507.	EB 17 Aug.	
508.	RB 18 Aug.	
509.	EB 18 Aug.	
510.	RB 19 Aug.	
[Meeting 88: 20 Aug.]		
511.	EB 21 Aug.	286
512.	RB 21 Aug.	
513.	EB 21 Aug.	
514.	RB 22 Aug.	
515.	EB 22 Aug.	
516.	EB 23 Aug.	287
517.	RB 23 Aug.	
518.	RB 24 Aug.	288
519.	EB 24 Aug.	289
520.	RB 25 Aug.	
521.	EB 25 Aug.	
522.	EB 25 Aug.	
523.	RB 26 Aug.	289
524.	EB 26 Aug.	291
525.	EB 27 Aug.	
526.	RB 27 Aug.	292
527.	EB 27 Aug.	292
528.	RB 28 Aug.	293
529.	EB 28 Aug.	295
[Meeting 89: 29 Aug.]		
530.	EB 30 Aug.	296
531.	RB 30 Aug.	297
532.	RB 31 Aug.	
533.	EB 31 Aug.	299
534.	RB 1 Sept.	301
535.	EB 1 Sept.	301
536.	RB 2 Sept.	302
537.	EB 2 Sept.	303
538.	RB 3 Sept.	304
539.	RB 3 Sept.	
540.	EB 3 Sept.	305
541.	RB 4 Sept.	307
542.	EB 4 Sept.	309
543.	RB 5 Sept.	309
544.	EB 5 Sept.	310
545.	EB 6 Sept.	
546.	RB 6 Sept.	312
547.	EB 7 Sept.	313
548.	RB 7 Sept.	313
549.	EB 7 Sept.	314
550.	RB 8 Sept.	314
551.	EB 8 Sept.	
[Meeting 90: 9 Sept.]		
552.	EB 9 Sept.	315
553.	RB 10 Sept.	316
554.	RB 10 Sept.	
555.	EB 10 Sept.	318
[Meeting 91: 11 Sept.]		
[Marriage: 12 Sept.]		
556.	RB 12 Sept.	319
557.	EB 12 Sept.	320
558.	EB 13 Sept.	321
559.	RB 13 Sept.	323
560.	RB 14 Sept.	325
561.	EB 14 Sept.	326
562.	EB 14 Sept.	326
563.	RB 15 Sept.	
564.	EB 15 Sept.	328
565.	RB 16 Sept.	329
565.	RB 16 Sept.	330
566.	EB 16 Sept.	
567.	RB 17 Sept.	331
568.	RB 17 Sept.	
569.	EB 17 Sept.	
570.	EB 17 Sept.	
571.	EB 18 Sept.	
572.	RB 18 Sept.	331
573.	EB 18 Sept.	332

RB, *Friday 10 January 1845*

I love your verses with all my heart, dear Miss Barrett,—
and this is no off-hand complimentary letter that I shall
write,—whatever else, no prompt matter-of-course recognition of your genius and there a graceful and natural end of
the thing: since the day last week when I first read your
poems,° I quite laugh to remember how I have been turning
and turning again in my mind what I should be able to tell
you of their effect upon me—for in the first flush of delight I
thought I would this once get out of my habit of purely
passive enjoyment, when I do really enjoy, and thoroughly
justify my admiration—perhaps even, as a loyal fellow-
craftsman should, try and find fault and do you some little
good to be proud of hereafter!—but nothing comes of it all—
so into me has it gone, and part of me has it become, this
great living poetry of yours, not a flower of which but took
root and grew—oh, how different that is from lying to be
dried and pressed flat and prized highly and put in a book
with a proper account at top and bottom, and shut up and
put away .. and the book called a 'Flora,' besides! After all I
need not give up the thought of doing that, too, in time;
because even now, talking with whoever is worthy, I can give
a reason for my faith in one and another excellence, the fresh
strange music, the affluent language, the exquisite pathos and
true new brave thought—but in this addressing myself to
you, your own self, and for the first time, my feeling rises
altogether. I do, as I say, love these books with all my heart—
and I love you too: do you know I was once not very far from
seeing—really seeing you? Mr. Kenyon° said to me one
morning 'would you like to see Miss Barrett?'—then he went
to announce me,—then he returned .. you were too unwell—
and now it is years ago°—and I feel as at some untoward
passage in my travels—as if I had been close, so close, to
some world's-wonder in chapel or crypt, only a screen to push
and I might have entered, but there was some slight .. so it
now seems .. slight and just-sufficient bar to admission, and
the half-opened door shut, and I went home my thousands of
miles, and the sight was never to be!

Well, these Poems were to be—and this true thankful joy and pride with which I feel myself

> Yours ever faithfully,
> Robert Browning.

EB, *Saturday, 11 January 1845*

I thank you, dear Mr. Browning, from the bottom of my heart. You meant to give me pleasure by your letter—and even if the object had not been answered, I ought still to thank you. But it is thoroughly answered. Such a letter from such a hand! Sympathy is dear—very dear to me: but the sympathy of a poet & of such a poet, is the quintessence of sympathy to me! Will you take back my gratitude for it?— agreeing too that, of all the commerce done in the world, from Tyre to Carthage, the exchange of sympathy for gratitude is the most princely thing?

For the rest you draw me on with your kindness. It is difficult to get rid of people when you once have given them too much pleasure—*that* is a fact, & we will not stop for the moral of it. What I was going to say .. after a little natural hesitation .. is, that if ever you emerge without inconvenient effort from your 'passive state,' & will *tell* me of such faults as rise to the surface & strike you as important in my poems, (for of course, I do not think of troubling you with criticism in detail)—you will confer a lasting obligation on me, and one which I shall value so much, that I covet it at a distance. I do not pretend to any extraordinary meekness under criticism—and it is possible enough that I might not be altogether obedient to yours. But with my high respect for your power in your Art, your experience as an artist, it w^d be quite impossible for me to hear a general observation of yours on what appear to you my master-faults, without being the better for it hereafter in some way. I ask for only a sentence or two of general observation—and I do not ask even for *that*, so as to teaze you—but in the humble, low voice, which is so excellent a thing in women°—particularly when they go a-begging! The most frequent general criticism I receive, is, I think, upon the style .. 'if I *would* but change my style!'—But *that* is an objection (isn't it?) to the writer bodily? Buffon says, and every sincere writer must feel, that '*Le style c'est l'homme*'—: a fact, however, scarcely calculated to lessen the objection with certain critics.

Is it indeed true that I was so near to the pleasure and honour of making your acquaintance?—and can it be true that you look back upon the lost opportunity with any regret?—But, ... you know, .. if you had entered the 'crypt,' you might have caught cold, or been tired to death, & *wished* yourself 'a thousand miles off'—which w^d have been worse than travelling them. It is not my interest however to put such thoughts in your head about its' being 'all for the best—' and I would rather hope (as I do) that what I lost by one chance I may recover by some future one. Winters shut me up as they do dormouse's eyes: in the spring, *we shall see*: & I am so much better that I seem turning round to the outward world again. And in the meantime I have learnt to know your voice, not merely from the poetry but from the kindness in it. Mr. Kenyon often speaks of you—dear Mr. Kenyon!—who most unspeakably, or only speakably with tears in my eyes, .. has been my friend & helper, & my book's friend & helper! critic & sympathiser .. true friend of all hours! You know him well enough, I think, to understand that I must be grateful to him.

I am writing too much, notwithstanding,—and notwithstanding that I am writing too much, I will write of one thing more. I will say that I am your debtor, not only for this cordial letter & for all the pleasure which came with it, but in other ways, & those the highest: & I will say that while I live to follow this divine art of poetry, .. in proportion to my love for it & my devotion to it, I must be a devout admirer & student of your works. This is in my heart to say to you—& I say it.

And, for the rest, I am proud to remain | Your obliged & faithful

Elizabeth B. Barrett.

RB, *Monday, 13 January, 1845*

Dear Miss Barrett,

I just shall say, in as few words as I can, that you make me very happy, and that, now the beginning is over, I dare say I shall do better .. because my poor praise, number one, was nearly as felicitously brought out, as a certain tribute to no less a personage than Tasso, which I was amused with at Rome some weeks ago, in a neat pencilling on the plaster-wall by his tomb at Sant' Onofrio—'Alla cara memoria—di—(please fancy solemn interspaces and grave capital letters at the new lines)—di—Torquato Tasso—il Dottore Bernar-dini—offriva—il seguente Carme—*O tu*'° .. and no more, the good man, it should seem, breaking down with the overload of love here! But my 'O tu'—was breathed out most sincerely, and now you have taken it in gracious part, the rest will come after. Only,—and which is why I write now—it looks as if I have introduced some phrase or other about 'your faults' so cleverly as to give exactly the opposite meaning to what I meant—which was, that in my first ardour I had thought to tell you of *everything* which impressed me in your verses, down, even, to whatever 'faults' I could find—a good earnest, when I had got to *them*, that I had left out not much between: as if some Mr Fellows° were to say, in the overflow of his first enthusiasm of rewarded adventure, 'I will describe you all the outer life and ways of these Lycians, down to their very sandal-thongs'—whereto the be-corresponded one rejoins—'Shall I get next week, then, your Dissertation on sandal-thongs'? Yes, and a little about the 'Olympian Horses', and god-charioteers as well!

What 'struck me as faults,' were not matters on the removal of which, one was to have—poetry, or high poetry,—but the very highest poetry, so I thought,—and that, to universal recognition:—for myself, or any artist, in many of the cases there would be a positive loss of true, peculiar artists-pleasure .. for an instructed eye loves to see where the brush has dipped twice in a lustrous colour, has lain insistingly along a favorite outline, dwelt lovingly in a grand shadow—for these 'too muches' for the everybody's picture are so many helps to the making out the real painter's-picture, as he had it in his brain; and all of the Titian's Naples Magdalen° must have once been golden in its degree to justify that heap of hair in her hands .. the *only* gold effected now!

But about this soon—for night is drawing on and I go out—yet cannot, quiet at conscience, till I repeat (to *myself* .. for I never said it to you, I think) that your poetry must be, cannot but be, infinitely more to me than mine to you—for you *do* what I always wanted, hoped to do, and only seem now likely to do for the first time. You speak out, *you*,—I only make men & women speak—give you truth broken into prismatic hues, and fear the pure white light, even if it is in me: but I am going to try .. so it will be no small comfort to have your company just now,—seeing that when you have your men & women aforesaid, you are busied with them, whereas it seems bleak melancholy work, this talking to the wind (.. for I have begun)—yet I don't think I shall let *you* hear, after all, the savage things about Popes and imaginative religions that I must say.°

See how I go on and on to you,—I who, whenever now and then pulled, by the head and hair, into letter-writing, get sorrowfully on for a line or two, as the cognate creature urged on by stick and string, and then come down 'flop' upon the sweet haven of page one, line last, as serene as the sleep of the virtuous! You will never more, I hope, talk of 'the honor of my acquaintance'—but I will joyfully wait for the delight of your friendship, and the Spring, and my Chapel-sight after all!

Ever yours most faithfully
R. Browning.

For Mr. Kenyon—I have a convenient theory about *him*, and his otherwise quite unaccountable kindness to me—but 'tis quite night now, and they call me.

EB, *Wednesday, 15 January 1845*

Dear Mr. Browning
    The fault was clearly with me & not with you.
    When I had an Italian master, years ago, he told me that

there was an unpronounceable English word which absolutely expressed me, & which he w^d say in his own tongue, as he could not in mine, .. '*testa lunga*'°. Of course the signor meant *headlong*—and now I have had enough to tame me, & might be expected to stand still in my stall. But you see I do not. Headlong I was at first, & headlong I continue—precipitously rushing forward through all manner of nettles & briars instead of keeping the path,—guessing at the meaning of unknown words instead of looking into the dictionary .. tearing open letters, & never untying a string,—& expecting everything to be done in a minute, & the thunder to be as quick as the lightning. And so, at your half word I flew at the whole one, with all its possible consequences, & wrote what you read. Our common friend, as I think he is, Mr. Horne,° is often forced to entreat me into patience & coolness of purpose,—though his only intercourse with me has been by letter. And, by the way, you will be sorry to hear that during his stay in Germany *he* has been 'headlong,' (out of a metaphor) twice,—once, in falling from the Drachenfels, when he only just saved himself by catching at a vine,—and once quite lately, at Christmas, in a fall on the ice of the Elbe in skating, when he dislocated his left shoulder in a very painful manner. He is doing quite well I believe—but it was sad to have such a shadow from the German Christmas tree, & he a stranger.

In Art, however, I understand that it does not do to be headlong, but patient & laborious—& there is a love strong enough, even in me, to overcome nature. I apprehend what you mean in the criticism you just intimate, & shall turn it over & over in my mind until I get practical good from it. What no mere critic sees, but what you, an artist, know, is the difference between the thing desired & the thing attained, between the idea in the writer's mind, & the εἴδωλον° cast off in his work. All the effort .. the quickening of the breath & beating of the heart in pursuit, which is ruffling & injurious to the general effect of a composition; all which you call 'insistency,' & which many w^d call superfluity, & which *is* superfluous in a sense .. *you* can pardon, because you understand. The great chasm between the thing I say, & the thing

I would say, w^d be quite dispiriting to me, in spite even of such kindnesses as yours, if the desire did not master the despondency. 'Oh for a horse with wings!'—It is wrong of me to write so of myself—only you put your finger on the root of a fault, which has, to my fancy, been a little misapprehended. I do not *say everything I think* (as has been said of me by master-critics) but I *take every means to say what I think*, which is different!—or I fancy so!

In one thing however you are wrong. Why sh^d you deny the full measure of my delight & benefit from your writings? I could tell you why you should not. You have in your vision two worlds—or to use the language of the schools of the day, you are both subjective & objective° in the habits of your mind. You can deal both with abstract thought, & with human passion in the most passionate sense. Thus, you have an immense grasp in Art; and no one at all accustomed to consider the usual forms of it, could help regarding with reverence & gladness the gradual expansion of your powers. Then you are 'masculine' to the height—and I, as a woman, have studied some of your gestures of language & intonation wistfully, as a thing beyond me far! & the more admirable for being beyond.

Of your new work I hear with delight. How good of you to tell me. And it is not dramatic in the strict sense, I am to understand .. (am I right in understanding so?) and you speak in your own person 'to the winds'? no—but to the thousand living sympathies which will awake to hear you. A great dramatic power may develop itself otherwise than in the formal drama; and I have been guilty of wishing, before this hour, (for reasons which I will not thrust upon you after all my tedious writing) that you w^d give the public a poem unassociated directly or indirectly with the stage, for a trial on the popular heart. I reverence the drama, but—

But I break in on myself out of consideration for you. I might have done it you will think, before. I vex your 'serene sleep of the virtuous' like a nightmare. Do not say .. 'no'—I am *sure* I do! As to the vain parlance of the world, I did not talk of the 'honor of your acquaintance' without a true sense of honor, indeed,—but I shall willingly exchange it all, .. (&

now, if you please, at this moment, for fear of worldly mutabilities) for the 'delight of your friendship'.

Believe me, therefore, dear Mr Browning | Faithfully yours
                                                                  & gratefully,
                                                    Elizabeth B Barrett.

For Mr. Kenyon's kindness, as *I* see it .. no 'theory' will account. I class it with mesmerism for that reason.

RB, *Monday, 27 January, 1845*

                                                            Monday Night.
Dear Miss Barrett,

Your books lie on my table here, at arm's length from me, in this old room where I sit all day: and when my head aches° or wanders or strikes work, as it now and then will, I take my chance for either green covered volume, as if it were so much fresh trefoil to feel in one's hands this winter-time,—and round I turn, and, putting a decisive elbow on three or four half-done-with 'Bells'° of mine, read, read, read—and just as I have shut up the book and walked to the window, I recollect that you wanted me to find faults there, and that, in an unwise hour, I engaged to do so. Meantime, the days go by (the whitethroat is come and sings now) and as I would not have you 'look down on me from your white heights'° as promise breaker, evader, or forgetter, if I could help .. and as, if I am very candid & contrite, you may find it in your heart to write to me again .. who knows? .. I shall say at once that the said faults cannot be lost, must be *somewhere*, and shall be faithfully brought you back whenever they turn up,—as people tell one of missing matters. I am rather exacting, myself, with my own gentle audience, and get to say spiteful things about them when they are backward in their dues of appreciation—but really, *really*—could I be quite sure that anybody as good as .. I must go on, I suppose, and say .. as myself, even, were honestly to feel towards me as I do, towards the writer of Bertha, and the Drama, and the

Duchess, and the Page° and—the whole two volumes, I should be paid after a fashion, I know.

One thing I can do .. pencil, if you like, and annotate, and dissertate upon what I love most and least—I think I can do it, that is.

Here an odd memory comes—of a friend who,—volunteering such a service to a sonnet-writing somebody, gave him a taste of his quality in a side-column of short criticisms on sonnet the First, and—starting off the beginning three lines with, of course, 'bad, worse, worst'—made, by a generous mintage of words to meet the sudden run on his epithets, 'worser, worserer, worserest' pay off the second terzet in full .. no 'badder, badderer, badderest' fell to the *Second's* allowance, and 'worser' &c. answered the demands of the Third— 'worster, worsterer, worsterest' supplied the emergency of the Fourth; and, bestowing his last 'worserestest and worstestest' on lines 13 and 14, my friend (slapping his forehead like an emptied strong-box) frankly declared himself bankrupt and honourably incompetent, to satisfy the reasonable expectations of the rest of the series.

What an illustration of the law by which opposite ideas suggest opposite, and contrary images come together!

See now, how, of that 'Friendship' you offer me (and here Juliet's word° rises to my lips)—I feel sure once and for ever—I have got already, I see, into this little pet-hand writing of mine (not any one else's) which scratches on as if theatrical copyists (ah me!) and BRADBURY AND EVANS'° READER were not! But you shall get something better than this nonsense one day, if you will have patience with me .. hardly better, tho', because this does me real good, gives real relief, to write. After all, you know nothing, next to nothing of me, and that stops me. Spring is to come, however!

If you hate writing to me as I hate writing to nearly everybody, I pray you never write: if you do, as you say, care for anything I have done,—I will simply assure you, that meaning to begin work in deep earnest, BEGIN without affectation, God knows—I do not know what will help me more than hearing from you,—and therefore, if you do not so

very much hate it, I know I *shall* hear from you .. and very
little more about your 'tiring me.'

Ever yours faithfully,
Robert Browning.

EB, *Monday, 3 February 1845*

Why how could I hate to write to you, dear Mr. Browning?
Could you believe in such a thing? If nobody likes writing to
everybody (except such professional letter writers as you & I
are *not*—) yet everybody likes writing to somebody—& it w^d
be strange and contradictory if I were not always delighted
both to hear from *you* and to write to *you* .. this talking upon
paper being as good a social pleasure as another, when our
means are somewhat straightened. As for me, I have done
most of my talking by the post of late years—as people shut
up in dungeons, take up with scrawling mottos on the walls.
Not that I write to many in the way of regular correspondence, as our friend Mr. Horne predicates of me in his
romances°(—which is mere romancing!—) but that there are
a few who will write & be written to by me, without a sense
of injury. Dear Miss Mitford, for instance—you do not know
her, I think, personally, although she was the first to tell me
(when I was very ill & insensible to all the glories of the world
except poetry) of the grand scene in Pippa Passes,°—*she* has
filled a large drawer in this room with delightful letters, heart-
warm & soul-warm, .. driftings of nature (if sunshine c^d drift
like snow)—& which if they sh^d ever fall the way of all writing
.. into print, w^d assume the folio shape, as a matter of course,
& take rank on the lowest shelf of libraries, with Benedictine
editions of the Fathers, κ.τ.λ. [etc.] I write this to you to show
how I can have pleasure in letters, and never think them too
long, nor too frequent, nor too illegible from being written in
little 'pet hands'. I can read any M.S. except the writing on the
pyramids. And if you will only promise to treat me 'en bon
camarade', .. without reference to the conventionalities of
'ladies & gentlemen,' taking no thought for your sentences,

(nor for mine)—nor for your blots, (nor for mine) nor for your blunt speaking (nor for mine), nor for your badd speling, (nor for mine)—and—if you agree to send me a blotted thought whenever you are in the mind for it, & with as little ceremony & less legibility than you would think it necessary to employ towards your printer .. why *then*, I am ready to sign & seal the contract, and to rejoice in being 'articled' as your correspondent. Only *don't* let us have any constraint, any ceremony! *Don't* be civil to me when you feel rude,—nor loquacious, when you incline to silence,—nor yielding in the manners, when you are perverse in the mind. See how out of the world I am! Suffer me to profit by it in almost the only profitable circumstance, .. & let us rest from the bowing & the courtesying, you & I, on each side. You will find me an honest man on the whole, if rather hasty & prejudging .. which is a different thing from prejudice at the worst. And we have great sympathies in common, & I am inclined to look up to you in many things, & to learn as much of everything as you will teach me. On the other hand you must prepare yourself to forbear & to forgive—will you? While I throw off the ceremony, I hold the faster to the kindness.

Is it true, as you say, that I 'know so little' of you? And is it true as others say, that the productions of an artist do not partake of his real nature, .. that in the minor sense, man is not made in the image of God? It is *not* true, to my mind—& therefore it is not true that I know little of you, except in as far as it is true (which I believe) that your greatest works are to come. Need I assure you that I shall always hear with the deepest interest every word you will say to me of what you are doing or about to do? I hear of the 'old room' & the 'bells lying about,' with an interest .. which you may guess at, perhaps. And when you tell me besides, .. of *my poems being there;* & of your caring for them so much beyond the tide-mark of my hopes, .. the pleasure rounds itself into a charm, & prevents its own expression. Overjoyed I am with this cordial sympathy—but it is better, I feel, to try to justify it by future work, than to thank you for it now. I think,—if I may dare to name myself with you in the poetic relation,—that we both have high views of the art we follow, and stedfast purpose in the pursuit of it—& that we should not, either of *us*, be likely to be thrown from the course, by the casting of any Atalanta-ball° of speedy popularity. But I do not know, I cannot guess, .. whether you are liable to be pained deeply by hard criticism & cold neglect, .. such as original writers like yourself, are too often exposed to—or whether the love of Art is enough for you, & the exercise of Art the filling joy of your life. Not that praise must not always, of necessity, be delightful to the artist,—but that it may be redundant to his content. Do you think so? or not? It appears to me that poets who, like Keats, are highly susceptible to criticism, must be jealous, in their own persons, of the future honour of their works. Because if a work is worthy, honour must follow it—though the worker should not live to see that following or overtaking. Now, is it not enough that the work be honoured—enough I mean, for the worker? And is it not enough to keep down a poets ordinary wearing anxieties, to think, that if his work be worthy it will have honour, &, if not, that 'Sparta must have nobler sons than he'?° I am writing nothing applicable, I see, to anything in question—but when one falls into a favorite train of thought, one indulges oneself in thinking on. I began by thinking & wondering what sort of artistic constitution you had—being determined, as you may observe (with a sarcastic smile at the impertinence!), to set about knowing as much as possible of you immediately. Then you spoke of your 'gentle audience'—(*you began*!) & I who know that you have not one but many enthusiastic admirers, the 'fit & few' in the intense meaning, yet not the *diffused* fame which will come to you presently,—wrote on, down the margin of the subject, till I parted from it altogether. But, after all, we are on the proper matter of sympathy. And after all, & after all that has been said & mused upon the 'natural ills,' the anxiety, & wearing out experienced by the true artist, .. is not the *good* immeasurably greater than the *evil*? Is it not great good, & great joy? For my part, I wonder sometimes .. I surprise myself wondering, .. how without such an object & purpose of life, people find it worth while to live at all. And, for happiness .. why my only idea of happiness, as far as my personal enjoyment is concerned, (but I have been straightened in some respects & in comparison with the majority of livers!) lies deep in poetry

& its associations. And then, the escape from pangs of heart
& bodily weakness, .. when you throw off *yourself* .. what you
feel to be *yourself*, .. into another atmosphere & into other
relations, where your life may spread its wings out new, &
gather on every separate plume, a brightness from the sun of
the sun!—Is it possible that imaginative writers sh^d be so
fond of depreciating & lamenting over their own destiny?
Possible, certainly—but reasonable, not at all—& grateful,
less than anything!

My faults, my faults—Shall I help you? Ah—you see them
too well, I fear. And do you know that *I* also, have something
of your feeling about 'being about to *begin*'—or I should dare
to praise you for having it. But in you, it is different—it is, in
you, a virtue. When Prometheus had recounted a long list of
sorrows to be endured by Io, & declared at last that he was
μηδέπω ἐυ προοιμίοις,° poor Io burst out crying. And when
the author of 'Paracelsus' & the 'Bells & Pomegranates' says
that he is only 'going to begin,' we may well (to take 'the
opposite idea' as you write) rejoice & clap our hands. Yet I
believe that, whatever you may have done, you *will* do what
is greater. It is my faith for you.

And how I sh^d like to know what poets have been your
sponsors, 'to promise & vow' for you,—and whether you have
held true to early tastes, or leapt violently from them—&
what books you read, & what hours you write in. How curious
I could prove myself!—if it isn't proved already.

But this is too much indeed—past all bearing, I suspect.
Well—but if I ever write you again, .. I mean, if you wish
it,—it may be in the other extreme of shortness. So do not
take me for a born heroine of Richardson, or think that I sin
always to this length! else,—you might indeed repeat your
quotation from Juliet .. which I guessed at once—& of
course.

> 'I have no joy in this contract to-day!
> It is too unadvised, too rash & sudden.'°

Ever faithfully yours
Elizabeth B Barrett.

RB, *Tuesday, 11 February, 1845*

Dear Miss Barrett,

People would hardly ever tell falsehoods about a matter, if they had been let tell truth in the beginning—for it is hard to prophane one's very self, and nobody who has, for instance, used certain words and ways to a mother or a father *could* .. even if by the devil's help he *would* .. reproduce or mimic them with any effect to anybody else that was to be won over; and so, if 'I love you' were always outspoken when it might be, there would, I suppose, be no fear of its desecration at any after time: but lo! only last night, I had to write, on the part of Mr Carlyle, to a certain ungainly foolish gentleman who keeps back from him, with all the fussy impotence of stupidity (not bad feeling, alas; for *that* we could deal with) a certain MS letter of Cromwell's which completes the collection now going to press°—and this long-ears had to be 'dear Sir'd' and 'obedient servanted' till I *said* (to use a mild word) 'Commend me to the sincerities of this kind of thing'! When I spoke of you knowing little of me, one of the senses in which I meant so was this .. that I would not well vowel-point my common-place letters and syllables with a masoretic° *other* sound and sense, make my 'dear' something intenser than 'dears' in ordinary, and 'yours ever' a thought more significant than the run of its like; and all this came of your talking of 'tiring me,' 'being too curious,' &c. &c. which I should never have heard of had the plain truth looked out of my letter with its unmistakeable eyes: *now*, what you say of the 'bowing,' and convention that is to be, and *tant de façons* [the many formalities] that are not to be, helps me once and for ever—for have I not a right to say simply that, for reasons I know, for other reasons I don't exactly know, but might if I chose to think a little, and for still other reasons, which, most likely, all the choosing and thinking in the world would not make me know, I had rather hear from you than see anybody else—never you care, dear noble Carlyle, nor you, my own friend Alfred over the sea,° nor a troop of true lovers!—Are not these fates written? There! Don't you answer this, please, but, mind it is on record, and now then, with a lighter conscience I shall

begin replying to your questions. First then,—what I have
printed gives *no* knowledge of me—it evidences abilities of
various kinds, if you will—and a dramatic sympathy with
certain modifications of passion .. *that* I think: but I never
have begun, even, what I hope I was born to begin and
end,—'R.B. a poem.' And, next, if I speak (and, God knows,
feel) as if what you have read were sadly imperfect demonstrations of even mere ability, it is from no absurd vanity, tho' it
might seem so—these scenes and song-scraps *are* such mere
and very escapes of my inner power, which lives in me like
the light in those crazy Mediterranean phares I have watched
at sea—wherein the light is ever revolving in a dark gallery,
bright and alive, and only after a weary interval leaps out, for
a moment, from the one narrow chink, and then goes on with
the blind wall between it and you; and, no doubt, *then*,
precisely, does the poor drudge that carries the cresset set
himself most busily to trim the wick—for don't think I want
to say I have not worked hard—(this head of mine knows
better)—but the work has been *inside*, and not when at stated
times I held up my light to you—and, that there is no self-
delusion here, I would prove to you, (and nobody else) even
by opening this desk I write on, and showing what stuff, in
the way of wood, I *could* make a great bonfire with, if I might
only knock the whole clumsy top off my tower!—Of course,
every writing body says the same, so I gain nothing by the
avowal; but when I remember how I have done what was
published, and half done what may never be, I say with some
right, you can know but little of me. Still, I *hope* sometimes,
tho' phrenologists will have it that I *cannot*, and am doing
better with this darling 'Luria'°—so safe in my head, and a
tiny slip of paper I cover with my thumb!

Then you inquire about my 'sensitiveness to criticism,' and
I shall be glad to tell you exactly—because I have, more than
once, taken a course you might else not understand. I shall
live always,—that is for me—I am living here this 1845, that
is for London. I write from a thorough conviction that it is
the duty of me, and, with the belief that, after every drawback
& shortcoming, I do my best, all things considered—that is
for *me*, and, so being, the not being listened to by one human
creature would, I hope, in nowise affect me. But of course I

must, if for merely scientific purposes, know all about this
1845, its ways and doings, and something I do know,—as
that for a dozen cabbages, if I pleased to grow them in the
garden here, I might demand, say, a dozen pence at Covent
Garden Market,—and that for a dozen scenes, of the average
goodness, I may challenge as many plaudits at the theatre
close by; and a dozen pages of verse, brought to the Rialto
where verse-merchants most do congregate,° ought to bring
me a fair proportion of the Reviewers' gold-currency, seeing
the other traders pouch their winnings, as I do see: well,
when they won't pay me for my cabbages, nor praise me for
my poems, I may, if I please, say 'more's the shame,' and bid
both parties 'decamp to the crows,'° in Greek phrase, and
YET go very lighthearted back to a garden-full of rose-trees,
and a soul-full of comforts; if they had bought my greens I
should have been able to buy the last number of 'Punch,' and
go thro' the toll-gate of Waterloo Bridge, and give the blind
clarionet-player a trifle, and all without changing my gold—
if they had taken to my books, my father and mother would
have been proud of this and the other 'favourable critique,'
and .. at least so folks hold .. I should have to pay Mr Moxon
less by a few pounds—whereas .. but you see! Indeed, I force
myself to say ever and anon, in the interest of the market-
gardeners regular, and Keats's proper,—'it's nothing to
you,—critics & hucksters, all of you, if I *have* this garden and
this conscience,—I might go die at Rome, or take to gin and
the newspaper, for what *you* would care'! So I don't quite lay
open my resources to everybody. But it does so happen, that
I have met with much more than I could have expected in
this matter of kindly and prompt recognition. I never wanted
a real set of good hearty praisers—and no bad reviewers .. I
am quite content with my share. No—what I laughed at in
my 'gentle audience' is a sad trick the real admirers have of
admiring at the wrong place—enough to make an apostle
swear! *That* does make me savage,—*never* the other kind of
people: why, think now: take your own 'Drama of Exile' and
let *me* send it to the first twenty men & women that shall
knock at your door to-day and after—of whom the first five
are—the Postman, the seller of cheap sealing-wax, Mr Hawk-
ins Junr, the Butcher for orders, and the Tax gatherer,—will

you let me, by Cornelius Agrippa's assistance°, force these
five and their fellows to read, and report on, this Drama—
and, when I have put these faithful reports into fair English,
do you believe they would be better than, if as good, as, the
general run of Periodical criticisms? Not they, I will venture
to affirm. But then,—once again, I get these people together
and give them your book, and persuade them, moreover, that
by praising it, the Postman will be helping its author to divide
Long Acre into two beats, one of which she will take with half
the salary and all the red collar,—that the sealing wax-vendor
will see red wafers brought into vogue, and so on with the
rest—and won't you just wish for your Spectators and
Observers and Newcastle-upon-Tyne-Hebdomadal Mercu-
ries back again! You see the inference—I do sincerely esteem
it a perfectly providential and miraculous thing that they are
so well-behaved in ordinary, these critics; and for Keats and
Tennyson to 'go softly all their days'° for a gruff word or two
is quite inexplicable to me, and always has been. Tennyson
reads the 'Quarterly' and does as they bid him,° with the
most solemn face in the world—out goes this, in goes that, all
is changed, and ranged .. Oh me!—

Out comes the sun, in comes the 'Times' and Eleven strikes
(it *does*) aleady, and I have to go to Town, and I have no
alternative but that this story of the Critic and Poet, 'the Bear
and fiddle,' should 'begin but break off in the middle'°—yet I
do not—nor will you henceforth, I know, say, 'I vex you, I
am sure, by this lengthy writing'—mind that spring is
coming, for all this snow; and know me for yours ever
faithfully,

R Browning.

I don't dare—yet I will—ask *can* you read this? Because I
could write a little better, but not so fast. Do you keep writing
just as you do now!

EB, *Monday, 17 February, 1845*

Dear Mr. Browning
   To begin with the end (which is only characteristic of the
perverse like myself), I assure you I read your handwriting

as currently as I could read the clearest type from font. If I had practised the art of reading your letters all my life, I couldn't do it better. And then I approve of small M.S. upon principle. Think of what an immense quantity of physical energy must go to the making of those immense sweeping handwritings achieved by some persons .. Mr. Landor° for instance, who writes as if he had the sky for a copybook & dotted his *i*'s in proportion. People who do such things sh^d wear gauntlets,—yes, and have none to wear,—or they wouldn't waste their strength so. People who write .. by profession .. shall I say? .. never should do it .. or what will become of them when most of their strength retires into their head & heart, (as is the case with some of us & may be the case with all) & when they have to write a poem twelve times over, as Mr. Kenyon says I should do if I were virtuous? Not that I do it. Does anybody do it, I wonder? Do *you*, ever? From what you tell me of the trimming of the light, I imagine not. And besides, one may be laborious as a writer, without copying twelve times over. I believe there are people who will tell you in a moment what three times six is, without 'doing it' on their fingers; and in the same way one may work one's verses in one's head quite as laboriously as on paper—I maintain it. I consider myself a very patient, laborious writer—though dear Mr. Kenyon laughs me to scorn when I say so. And just see how it could be otherwise. If I were netting a purse I might be thinking of something else & drop my stitches,—or even if I were writing verses to please a popular taste, I might be careless in it. But the pursuit of an Ideal acknowledged by the mind, *will* draw & concentrate the powers of the mind—and Art, you know, is a jealous god & demands the whole man .. or woman. I cannot conceive of a sincere artist who is also a careless one—though one may have a quicker hand than another, in general,—& though all are liable to vicissitudes in the degree of facility .. & to entanglements in the machinery, notwithstanding every degree of facility. You may write twenty lines one day—or even three like Euripides in three days°—and a hundred lines in one more day: & yet on the hundred, may have been expended as much good work, as on the twenty & the three. And also, as you say, the lamp is trimmed behind the wall—

and the act of utterance is the evidence of forgone study still
more than it is the occasion of study. The deep interest with
which I read all that you had the kindness to write to me of
yourself, you must trust me for, as I find it hard to express it.
It is sympathy in one way, and interest every way! And now,
see! Although you proved to me with admirable logic that, for
reasons which you know & reasons which you don't know, I
couldn't possibly know anything about you, .. though that is
all true .. & proven (which is better than true) I really did
understand of you before I was told, exactly what you told
me. Yes—I did indeed. I felt sure that as a poet you fronted
the future—& that your chief works, in your own apprehension, were to come. Oh—I take no credit of sagacity for it,—
as I did not long ago to my sisters & brothers, when I
professed to have knowledge of all their friends whom I never
saw in my life, by the image coming with the name: & threw
them into shouts of laughter by giving out all the blue eyes &
black eyes & hazel eyes & noses Roman & Gothic ticketted
aright for the Mr. Smiths & Miss Hawkinses, .. & hit the
bull's eye & the true features of the case, ten times out of
twelve. But *you* are different. *You* are to be made out by the
comparative anatomy system. You have thrown out fragments
of *os* .. *sublime* .. indicative of soul-mammothism—and you
live to develop your nature, .. *if* you live. That is easy &
plain. You have taken a great range—from those high faint
notes of the mystics which are beyond personality .. to
dramatic impersonations, gruff with nature, 'Gr-r- you
swine';° & when these are throw into harmony, as in a
manner they are in 'Pippa Passes' (which I could find in my
heart to covet the authorship of, more than any of your
works,—), the combinations of effect must always be striking
& noble—and you must feel yourself drawn on to such
combinations more and more. But I do not, you say, know
yourself .. you. I only know abilities & faculties. Well, then!
teach me yourself .. you. I will not insist on the knowledge—
and, in fact, you have not written the R. B. poem yet—your
rays fall obliquely rather than directly straight. I see you only
in your moon. Do tell me all of yourself that you can & will ..
before the R. B. poem comes out. And what is *Luria*? A poem
and not a drama? I mean, a poem not in the dramatic form?

Well! I have wondered at you sometimes, not for daring, but for bearing to trust your noble works into the great mill of the 'rank, popular' play-house, to be ground to pieces between the teeth of vulgar actors & actresses. I, for one, would as soon have 'my soul among lions'.° 'There is a fascination in it' says Miss Mitford—& I am sure there must be, to account for it. Publics in the mass are bad enough; but to distil the dregs of the public & baptise oneself in that acrid moisture, where can be the temptation—I could swear by Shakespeare, as was once sworn 'by those dead at Marathon,' that I do not see where. I love the drama too. I look to our old dramatists as to our Kings & princes in poetry. I love them through all the deeps of their abominations. But the theatre in those days, was a better medium between the people & the poet; and the press in those days was a less sufficient medium than now. Still the poet suffered by the theatre even then; & the reasons are very obvious.

How true—how true .. is all you say about critics. My convictions follow you in every word. And I delighted to read your views of the poet's right aspect towards criticism—I read them with the most complete appreciation & sympathy. I have sometimes thought that it would be a curious & instructive process, as illustrative of the wisdom & apprehensiveness of critics, if anyone would collect the critical soliloquies of every age touching its own literature, (as far as such may be extant) and *confer* them with the literary product of the said ages. Professor Wilson° has begun something of the kind apparently, in his initiatory paper of the last Blackwood number on critics, beginning with Dryden—but he seems to have no design in his notice—it is a mere critique on the critic. And then, he sh^d have begun earlier than Dryden— earlier even than Sir Philip Sydney, who in the noble 'Discourse on Poetry,'° gives such singular evidence of being stone-critic-blind to the gods who moved around him. As far as I can remember, he saw even Shakespeare but indifferently. Oh—it was in his eyes, quite an unillumed age, that period of Elizabeth which *we* see full of suns! and few can see what is close to the eyes though they run their heads against it: the denial of contemporary genius is the rule rather than the exception. No one counts the eagles in the nest, till there is a

rush of wings—and lo! they are flown. And here we speak of
understanding men, such as the Sidneys and the Drydens. Of
the great body of critics you observe rightly, that they are
better than might be expected of their badness—only the fact
of their *influence* is no less undeniable than the reason why
they should not be influential. The brazen kettles will be
taken for oracles all the world over. But the influence is for
to-day, for this hour—not for to-morrow & the day after—
unless indeed as you say, the poet do himself perpetuate the
influence by submitting to it. Do you know Tennyson? that
is, with a face to face knowledge? I have great admiration for
him. In execution, he is exquisite,—and, in music, a most
subtle weigher out to the ear, of fine airs. That such a poet
sh^d submit blindly to the suggestions of his critics, (I do not
say that suggestions from without may not be accepted with
discrimination sometimes, to the benefit of the acceptor)
blindly & implicitly to the suggestions of his critics, .. is much
as if Babbage° were to take my opinion & undo his calculating
machine by it. Napoleon called poetry '*science creuse* [hollow
science]'—which, although he was not scientific in poetry
himself, is true enough. But anybody is qualified, according
to everybody, for giving opinions upon poetry. It is not so in
chymistry and mathematics. Nor is it so, I believe, in whist
and the polka. But then these are more serious things.

Yes—and it does delight me to hear of your 'garden full of
roses and soul full of comforts'. You have the right to both—
you have the key to both. You have written enough to live by,
though only beginning to write, as you say of yourself. And
this reminds me to remind you that when I talked of coveting
most the authorship of your 'Pippa', I did not mean to call it
your finest work (you might reproach me for *that*) but just to
express a personal feeling. Do you know what it is to covet
your neighbour's poetry?—not his fame, but his poetry?—I
dare say not. You are too generous. And, in fact, beauty is
beauty, and, whether it comes by our own hand or another's,
blessed be the coming of it! *I*, besides, feel *that*. And yet—and
yet, I have been aware of a feeling within me which has
spoken two or three times to the effect of a wish, that I had
been visited with the vision of 'Pippa', before you—and
confiteor tibi [I confess to you]—I confess the baseness of it.

The conception is to my mind, most exquisite & altogether original—and the contrast in the working out of the plan, singularly expressive of various faculty.

Is the poem under your thumb, emerging from it? and in what metre? May I ask such questions?

And does Mr. Carlyle tell you that he has forbidden all 'singing' to this perverse & froward generation°, which should work & not sing? And have you told Mr. Carlyle that song is work, and also the condition of work?—I am a devout sitter at his feet—and it is an effort to me to think him wrong in anything—and once when he told me to write prose & not verse,° I fancied that his opinion was I had mistaken my calling, .. a fancy which in infinite kindness & gentleness he stooped immediately to correct. I never shall forget the grace of that kindness—but then! For *him* to have thought ill of *me*, would not have been strange—I often think ill of myself, as God knows. But for Carlyle to think of putting away even for a season, the poetry of the world, was wonderful, and has left me ruffled in my thoughts ever since. I do not know him personally at all. But as his disciple I ventured (by an exceptional motive) to send him my poems, and I heard from him as a consequence. 'Dear & noble' he is indeed—and a poet unaware himself; all but the sense of music. You feel it so—do you not? And the 'dear sir' has let him have the 'letter of Cromwell,' I hope,—and satisfied 'the obedient servant'? The curious thing in this world is not the stupidity, but the upper-handism of the stupidity. The geese are in the Capitol, and the Romans in the farm-yard°—and it seems all quite natural that it should be so, both to geese & Romans!

But there are things you say, which seem to me supernatural, .. for reasons which I know & for reasons which I don't know. You will let me be grateful to you, .. will you not? You must, if you will or not. And also .. I would not wait for more leave, .. if I could but see your desk .. as I do your death's heads and the spider-webs appertaining:°—but the soul of Cornelius Agrippa fades from me.

Ever faithfully yours
Elizabeth B Barrett.

RB, *Wednesday, 26 February 1845*

Wednesday morning—Spring!
Real warm Spring, dear Miss Barrett, and the birds know
it; and in Spring I shall see you, surely see you .. for when did
I once fail to get whatever I had set my heart upon?—as I
ask myself sometimes, with a strange fear.

I took up this paper to write a great deal: now, I don't
think I shall write much—'I shall see you,' I say!

That 'Luria' you enquire about, shall be my last play .. for
it is but a play, woe's me! I have one done here—'A Soul's
Tragedy,' as it is properly enough called, but *that* would not
do to end with—(end I will)—and Luria is a Moor, of
Othello's country, and devotes himself to something he thinks
Florence, and the old fortune follows—all in my brain, yet,
but the bright weather helps and I will soon loosen my
Braccio and Puccio—(a pale discontented man)—and Tibur-
zio (the Pisan, good true fellow, this one), and Domizia the
Lady .. loosen all these on dear foolish (ravishing must his
folly be)—golden-hearted Luria, all these with their worldly-
wisdom, and Tuscan shrewd ways,—and, for me, the misfortune is, I sympathise just as much with these as with him,—
so there can no good come of keeping this wild company any
longer, and 'Luria' and the other sadder ruin of one Chiappino,—these got rid of, I will do as you bid me, and .. but
first I have some Romances and Lyrics, all dramatic, to
dispatch, and *then*, I shall stoop of a sudden under and out of
this dancing ring of men & women hand in hand; and stand
still awhile, should my eyes dazzle,—and when that's over,
they will be gone and you will be there, *pas vrai?*—For, as I
think I told you, I always shiver involuntarily when I look ..
no, glance .. at this First Poem of mine to be. *Now*—I call
it—what, upon my soul,—for a solemn matter it is—what is
to be done *now*, believed *now*,—so far as it has been revealed
to me—solemn words, truly,—and to find myself writing
them to any one else! Enough now.

I know Tennyson 'face to face,'—no more than that. I
know Carlyle and love him—know him so well, that I would
have told you he had shaken that grand head of his at singing,

so thoroughly does he love and live by it. When I last saw
him, a fortnight ago, he turned, from I don't know what other
talk, quite abruptly on me with, 'Did you never try to write a
Song? Of all things in the world, *that* I should be proudest to
do.' Then came his definition of a song—then, with an
appealing look to Mrs. C.,—'I always says that some day "*in
spite of nature and my stars*" I shall burst into a song' (he is not
mechanically 'musical,'—he meant, and the music is the
poetry, he holds, and should enwrap the thought as Donne
says 'an amber-drop enwraps a bee'),° and then he began to
recite an old Scotch song, stopping at the first rude couplet—
'The beginning words are merely to set the tune, they tell
me'—and then again at the couplet about—or, to the effect
that—give me (but in broad Scotch) 'give me but my lass, I
care not for my cogie.' '*He says,*' quoth Carlyle magisteri-
ally,—'that if you allow him the love of his lass, you may take
away all else,—even his cogie, his cup or can, and he cares
not'—just as a professor expounds Lycophron.° And just
before I left England, six months ago, did not I hear him
croon, if not certainly sing, 'Charlie is my darling' ('my
darling' with an adoring emphasis)—and then he stood back,
as it were, from the song, to look at it better, and said 'How
must that notion of ideal wondrous perfection have impressed
itself in this old Jacobite's "young Cavalier"—("They go to
save their land—and the *young Cavalier!*")—when I who care
nothing about such a rag of a man, cannot but feel as he felt,
in speaking his words after him!' After saying which, he would
be sure to counsel everybody to get their heads clear of all
singing!—Don't let me forget to clap hands—we got the
letter, dearly bought as it was by the 'Dear Sirs,' &c and
insignificant scrap as it proved—but still it is got, to my
encouragement in diplomacy.

Who told you of my sculls and spider webs°—Horne? Last
year I petted extraordinarily a fine fellow, (a *garden* spider,—
there was the singularity,—the thin clever-even-for a spider-
sort, and they are *so* 'spirited and sly,' all of them—this kind
makes a long cone of web, with a square chamber of vantage
at the end, and there he sits loosely and looks about)—a great
fellow that housed himself, with real gusto, in the jaws of a
great scull, whence he watched me as I wrote .. and I

remember speaking to Horne about his good points. Phrenologists° look gravely at that great scull, by the way, and hope, in their grim manner, that its owner made a good end. It looks quietly, now, out at the green little hill behind. I have no little insight to the feelings of furniture, and treat books and prints with a reasonable consideration—how some people use their pictures, for instance, is a mystery to me—very revolting all the same: portraits obliged to face each other for ever,—prints put together in portfolios, .. my Polidoro's perfect Andromeda° along with 'Boors Carousing by Ostade',°—where I found her,—my own father's doing, or I would say more.

And when I have said I like 'Pippa' better than anything else I have done yet, I shall have answered all you bade me. And now may *I* begin questioning? No,—for it is all a pure delight to me, so that you do but write. I never was without good, kind, generous friends and lovers, so they say—so they were and are—perhaps they came at the wrong time—I never wanted them,—though that makes no difference in my gratitude, I trust—but I know myself—surely—and always have done so—for is there not somewhere the little book I first printed when a boy, with John Mill, the metaphysical head, *his* marginal note that 'the writer possesses a deeper self-consciousness than I ever knew in a sane human being'°— So I never deceived myself much, nor called my feelings for people other than they were; and who has a right to say, if I have not, that I had, but I said that, supernatural or no. Pray tell me, too, of your present doings and projects, and never write yourself 'grateful' to me who *am* grateful, very grateful to you,—for none of your words but I take in earnest—and tell me if Spring *be not* coming, come—and I will take to writing the gravest of letters—because this beginning is for gladness' sake like Carlyles song-couplet. My head aches a little, to-day, too, and, as poor dear Kirke White said to the moon, from his heap of mathematical papers, 'I throw aside the learned sheet,—I cannot choose but gaze she looks so— mildly sweet'°—out on the foolish phrase, but there's hard rhyming without it!

Ever yours faithfully,
Robert Browning.

EB, *Thursday, 27 February 1845*

Yes, but, dear Mr. Browning, I want the spring according to the new 'style'° (mine), & not the old one of you & the rest of the poets. To me unhappily, the snowdrop is much the same as the snow—it feels as cold underfoot: and I have grown sceptical about 'the voice of the turtle',° the east winds blow so loud. April is a Parthian with a dart—& May (at least the early part of it) a spy in the camp. *That* is my idea of what you call spring,—mine, in the *new style!* A little later comes my spring,—and indeed after such severe weather, from which I have just escaped with my life, I may thank it for coming at all. How happy you are, to be able to listen to the 'birds,' without the commentary of the east wind,—which, like other commentaries, spoils the music. And how happy I am to listen to you, when you write such kind open-hearted letters to me!—I am delighted to hear all you say to me of yourself, & 'Luria,' & the spider, & to do him no dishonour in the association, of the great teacher of the age, Carlyle, who is also yours & mine. He fills the office of a poet—does he not? .. by analyzing humanity back into its elements, to the destruction of the conventions of the hour. That is—strictly speaking .. the office of the poet,—is it not?—and he discharges it fully,—and with a wider intelligibility perhaps as far as the contemporary period is concerned, than if he did forthwith 'burst into a song'.

But how I do wander!—I meant to say, and I will call myself back to say, that spring will really come some day I hope & believe, & the warm settled weather with it, and that then I shall be probably fitter for certain pleasures than I can appear even to myself, now.

And, in the meantime, I seem to see 'Luria' instead of you,—I have visions & dream dreams. And the 'Soul's Tragedy', which sounds to me like the step of a ghost of an old Drama! & you are not to think that I blaspheme the Drama, dear Mr. Browning; or that I ever thought of exhorting you to give up the 'solemn robes' & tread of the buskin.° It is the theatre which vulgarizes these things,—the modern theatre in which we see no altar!—where the thymele° is replaced by the caprice of a popular actor. And also, I have a fancy that your great dramatic power would work more clearly & audibly in the less definite mould—but you ride your own faculty as Oceanus did his seahorse, 'directing it by your will';° and woe to the impertinence which w^d dare to say 'turn this way'—or 'turn from that way'—it should not be MY impertinence. Do not think I blaspheme the Drama. I have gone through 'all such reading as should never be read,' (that is, by women!) through my love of it on the contrary. And the dramatic faculty is strong in you—& therefore, as 'I speak unto a wise man, judge what I say'.°

For myself & my own doings, you shall hear directly what I have been doing, & what I am about to do. Some years ago, as perhaps you may have heard—(but I hope not .. for the fewer who hear of it the better ..) Some years ago, I translated or rather *undid* into English, the Prometheus of Aeschylus. To speak of this production moderately (not modestly) it is the most miserable of all miserable versions of the class. It was completed (in the first place) in thirteen days—the iambics thrown into blank verse, the lyrics into rhymed octosyllabics & the like—and the whole together, as cold as Caucasus, & as flat as the nearest plain. To account for this, the haste may be something—but if my mind had been properly awakened at the time, I might have made still more haste & done it better. Well!—the comfort is, that the little book was unadvertised & unknown, & that most of the copies (through my entreaty of my father) are shut up in the wardrobe of his bedroom. If ever I get well I shall show my joy by making a bondfire of them. In the meantime, the recollection of this sin of mine, has been my nightmare & daymare, too, & the sin has been the 'Blot on my escutcheon.'° I could look in nobody's face, with a 'Thou canst not say I did it'°—I know, I did it. And so I resolved to wash away the transgression, and translate the tragedy over again. It was an honest straightforward proof of repentance,—was it not? and I have completed it, except the transcription & last polishing. If Aeschylus stands at the foot of my bed now, I shall have a little breath to front him. I have done my duty by him, not indeed according to his claims, but in proportion to my faculty. Whether I shall ever publish or not (remember) remains to be considered—that is a different side of the subject. If I do, it *may* be in a magazine .. or .. but this is another ground. And then, I have in my head to associate with the version, .. a monodram of my own—not a long poem, .. but a monologue of Aeschylus° as he sate a blind exile on the flats of Sicily and recounted the past to his own soul, just before the eagle cracked his great massy skull with a stone.

But my chief *intention* just now is the writing of a sort of novel-poem°—a poem as completely modern as 'Geraldine's Courtship,'° running into the midst of our conventions, & rushing into drawing-rooms & the like 'where angels fear to tread';—& so, meeting face to face & without mask, the Humanity of the age, & speaking the truth as I conceive of it, out plainly. That is my intention. It is not mature enough yet to be called a plan. I am waiting for a story—& I won't take one—because I want to make one, & I like to make my own stories, because then I can take liberties with them in the treatment.

Who told me of your skulls & spiders? Why, couldn't I know it without being told? Did Cornelius Agrippa know nothing without being told? Mr. Horne—never spoke it to my ears—(I never saw him face to face in my life, although we have corresponded for long & long—) & he never wrote it to my eyes. Perhaps he does not know that I know it. Well, then! if I were to say that *I heard it from you yourself*, .. how would you answer? AND IT WAS SO. Why, are you not aware that these are the days of Mesmerism & clairvoyance? are you an infidel? I have believed in your skulls for the last year, for my part.

And I have some sympathy in your habit of feeling for chairs & tables. I remember, when I was a child & wrote poems in little clasped books, I used to kiss the books & put them away tenderly because I had been happy near them, & take them out by turns when I was going from home, to cheer them by the change of air & the pleasure of the new place. This, not for the sake of the verses written in them, & not for the sake of writing more verses in them, but from pure gratitude. Other books I used to treat in a like manner—and to talk to the trees & the flowers, was a natural inclination—

but between me & that time, the cypresses grow thick & dark.°

Is it true that your wishes fulfil themselves?—And when they *do*, are they not bitter to your taste—do you not wish them *un*fulfilled? Oh—this life, this life! There is comfort in it, they say, & I almost believe—but the brightest place in the house, is the leaning out of the window!—at least, for me.

Of course you are *self-conscious*—How c^d you be a poet otherwise? Tell me.

Ever faithfully yours
E. B. B.

And was the little book written with Mr. Mill, pure meta-physics, or what?

RB, *Saturday, 1 March 1845*

Dear Miss Barrett—I seem to find of a sudden—.. surely I knew before .. anyhow, I *do* find now,—that with the octaves on octaves of quite new golden strings you enlarged the compass of my life's harp with, there is added, too, such a tragic chord—that which you touched, so gently, in the beginning of your letter I got this morning—'just escaping' &c But if my truest heart's wishes avail, as they have hitherto done, you shall laugh at East winds yet, as I do! See now: this sad feeling is so strange to me, that I must write it out, *must*— and you might give me great, the greatest pleasure for years and yet find me as passive as a stone used to wine-libations, and as ready in expressing my sense of them but when I am pained, I find the old theory of the uselessness of communi-cating the circumstances of it, singularly untenable. I have been 'spoiled' in this world—to such an extent, indeed, that I often *reason out* .. make clear to myself .. that I might very properly .. so far as myself am concerned .. take any step that would peril the whole of my future happiness—because the past is gained, secure, and on record; and, tho' not another of the old days should dawn on me, I shall not have lost my life, no!—Out of all which you are—please—to make a sort of sense, if you can, so as to express that I have been deeply struck to find a new real unmistakable sorrow along with these as real but not so new joys you have given me—

. . . And pray you not to 'lean out of the window' when my own foot is only on the stair—do wait a little for

Yours ever,
RB.

EB, *Wednesday, 5 March 1845*

But I did not mean to strike a 'tragic chord': indeed I did not! Sometimes one's melancholy will be uppermost & sometimes one's mirth,—the world goes round, you know—& I suppose that in that letter of mine the melancholy took the turn. As to 'escaping with my life,' it was just a phrase—at least it did not signify more than that the sense of mortality, & discomfort of it, is peculiarly strong with me when east winds are blowing & waters freezing. For the rest, I am *essentially better*, & have been for several winters,—and I feel as if it were intended for me to live & not die, & I am reconciled to the feeling.

. . . you are not to think,—whatever I may have written or implied,—that I lean either to the philosophy or affectation which beholds the world through darkness instead of light, & speaks of it wailingly. Now, may God forbid that it sh^d be so with me. I am not desponding by nature—and after a course of bitter mental discipline & long bodily seclusion, I come out with two learnt lessons, (as I sometimes say & oftener feel) .. the wisdom of cheerfulness—& the duty of social intercourse. Anguish has instructed me in joy—and solitude in society— it has been a wholesome & not unnatural reaction. And altogether, I may say that the earth looks the brighter to me in proportion to my own deprivations: the laburnum trees & rose trees are plucked up by the roots—but the sunshine is in their places—and the root of the sunshine is above the storms. What we call Life is a condition of the soul—and the soul must improve in happiness & wisdom, except by its own

fault. These tears in our eyes—these faintings of the flesh, ..
will not hinder such improvement!

And I do like to hear testimonies like yours, to *happiness*—
& I feel it to be a testimony of a higher sort than the obvious
one. Still, it is obvious too that you have been spared up to
this time, the great natural afflictions, against which we are
nearly all called, sooner or later, to struggle & wrestle—or
your step would not be 'on the stair' quite so lightly. And so,
we turn to you, dear Mr. Browning, for comfort & gentle
spiriting! Remember that as you owe your unscathed joy to
God, you should pay it back to this world. And I thank you
for some of it already. . . .

How kind you are!—how kindly & gently you speak to
me!—Some things you say are very touching, & some,
surprising—& although I am aware that you unconsciously
exaggerate what I can be to you, yet it is delightful to be
broad awake & think of you as my friend.

May God bless you.

Faithfully yours,
Elizabeth B Barrett.

RB, *Tuesday, 11 March 1845*

Your letter made me so happy, dear Miss Barrett, that I
have kept quiet this while: is it too great a shame if I begin to
want more good news of you, and to say so?—Because there
has been a bitter wind ever since. Will you grant me a great
favour? Always when you write, tho' about your own works,
not Greek plays merely, put me in—*always*—a little official
bulletin-line that shall say 'I am better'—or 'still better'—
will you? That is done, then—and now, what do I wish to tell
you first? The Poem you propose to make, for the times,—the
fearless fresh living work, you describe,—is the *only* Poem to
be undertaken now by you or anyone that *is* a Poet at all,—
the only reality, only effective piece of service to be rendered
God and man—it is what I have been all my life intending to
do, and now shall be much, much nearer doing, since you will
be along with me. And you *can* do it, I know and am sure—

so sure, that I could find in my heart to be jealous of your stopping in the way even to translate the Prometheus; tho' the accompanying monologue will make amends, too—

. . . You think .. for I must get to *you* .. that I 'unconsciously exaggerate what you are to me'—now, you don't know what *that* is, nor can I very well tell you, because the language with which I talk to myself of these matters is spiritual Attic,° and 'loves contractions' as grammarians say; but I read it myself, and well know what it means .. that's why I told you I was self-conscious,—I meant that I never yet mistook my own feelings, one for another—there! Of what use is talking? Only, do you stay here with me in the 'House' these few short years. Do you think I shall see you in two months, three months? I may travel, perhaps. So you have got to like society, and would enjoy it, you think? For me, I always hated it,—have put up with it these six or seven years past lest by foregoing it I should let some unknown good escape me, in the true time of it, and only discover my fault when too late,—and now, that I have done most of what is to be done, *any* lodge in a garden of cucumbers° for me! I don't even care about reading now—the world,—and pictures of it—rather than writings about the world! but you must read books in order to get words and forms for 'the public' if you *write*, and *that* you needs must do, if you fear God. I have no pleasure in writing myself—none, in the mere act,—tho' all pleasure in the sense of fulfilling a duty—whence, if I have done my real best, judge how heartbreaking a matter must it be to be pronounced a poor creature by Critic This and acquaintance the other. But I think you like the operation of writing as I should like that of painting or making music, do you not? After all, there is a great delight in the heart of the thing,—and use and forethought have made me ready at all times to set to work—but—I don't know why—my heart sinks whenever I open this desk, and rises when I shut it. Yet but for what I have written you would never have heard of me—and *thro'* what you have written, not properly *for* it, I love and wish you well! Now, will you remember what I began my letter by saying—how you have promised to let me know if my well wishing takes effect, and if you still continue better? And not even .. (since we are learned in magnanimity ..) don't even tell me that or anything else, if it teases you,—but wait your own good time, and know me for .. if these words were but my own, and fresh-minted for this moment's use! ..

Yours ever faithfully
R Browning.

EB, *Thursday, 20 March 1845*

Whenever I delay to write to you dear Mr. Browning, it is not, be sure, that I take my 'own good time' but submit to my own bad time. It was kind of you to wish to know how I was, & not unkind of me to suspend my answer to your question—for indeed I have not been very well, nor have had much heart for saying so. This implacable weather!—this east wind that seems to blow through the sun & moon! who can be well in such a wind? Yet for me, I should not grumble. There has been nothing very bad the matter with me, as there used to be—I only grow weaker than usual, & learn my lesson of being mortal, in a corner—and then all this must end!—April is coming. There will be both a May & a June if we live to see such things .. & perhaps, after all, we may. And as to seeing *you* besides, I observe that you distrust me—& that perhaps you penetrate my morbidity & guess how when the moment comes to see a living human face to which I am not accustomed, I shrink & grow pale in the spirit—Do you?—You are learned in human nature, & you know the consequences of leading such a secluded life as mine .. notwithstanding all my fine philosophy about social duties & the like—well—if you have such knowledge or if you have it not, I cannot say—but I do say that I will indeed see you when the warm weather has revived me a little, & put the earth 'to rights' again so as to make pleasures of the sort possible. For if you think that I shall not *like* to see you—— you are wrong, for all your learning. But I shall be afraid of you at first—though I am not, in writing thus. You are Paracelsus°—and I am a recluse with nerves that have been all broken on the rack, & now hang loosely, .. quivering at a step and breath.

And what you say of society draws me on to many comparative thoughts of your life & mine. You seem to have drunken of the cup of life full, with the sun shining on it. I have lived only inwardly,—or with *sorrow*, for a strong emotion. Before this seclusion of my illness, I was secluded still—& there are few of the youngest women in the world who have not seen more, heard more, known more, of society, than I, who am scarcely to be called young now. I grew up in the country .. had no social opportunities, .. had my heart in books & poetry, .. & my experience, in reveries. My sympathies drooped towards the ground like an untrained honeysuckle—& but for *one* .. in my own house .. but of this I cannot speak. It was a lonely life—growing green like the grass around it. Books & dreams were what I lived in—& domestic life only seemed to buzz gently around, like the bees about the grass. And so time passed, & passed—and afterwards, when my illness came & I seemed to stand at the edge of the world with all done, & no prospect (as appeared at one time) of ever passing the threshold of one room again,—why then, I turned to thinking with some bitterness (after the greatest sorrow of my life had given me room & time to breathe) that I had stood blind in this temple I was about to leave, .. that I had seen no Human nature .. that my brothers & sisters of the earth were *names* to me, .. that I had beheld no great mountain or river— nothing in fact .. I was as a man dying who had not read Shakespeare .. & it was too late!—do you understand? And do you also know what a disadvantage this ignorance is to my art. Why if I live on & yet do not escape from this seclusion, do you not perceive that I labour under signal disadvantages .. that I am, in a manner, as a *blind poet?*— Certainly, there is a compensation to a degree. I have had much of the inner life—& from the habit of selfconsciousness & selfanalysis, I make great guesses at Human Nature in the main. But how willingly I would as a poet exchange some of this lumbering, ponderous helpless knowledge of books, for some experience of life & man, for some ...

But all grumbling is a vile thing. We should all thank God for our measures of life, & think them enough for each of us. I write so, that you may not mistake what I wrote before in relation to society, although you do not see from my point of view,—& that you may understand what I mean fully when I say, that I have lived all my chief *joys*, & indeed nearly all emotions that go warmly by that name & relate to myself personally, in poetry & in poetry alone. Like to write? Of course, of course, I do. I seem to live while I write—it is life, for me. Why what is to live? Not to eat & drink & breathe, .. but to feel the life in you down all the fibres of being, passionately & joyfully. And thus, one lives in composition surely .. not always .. but when the wheel goes round & the procession is uninterrupted. Is it not so with you? oh—it must be so. For the rest, there will be necessarily a reaction; &, in my own particular case, whenever I see a poem of mine in print, or even smoothly transcribed, the reaction is most painful. The pleasure, . the sense of power,. without which I could not write a line, .. is gone in a moment, & nothing remains but disappointment & humiliation. I never wrote a poem which you could not persuade me to tear to pieces if you took me at the right moment! I have a *seasonable* humility, I do assure you.

How delightful to talk about oneself—but as you 'tempted me & I did eat,'° I entreat your longsuffering of my sin—& ah—if you would but sin back so in turn!—You & I seem to meet in a mild contrarious harmony .. as in the 'si .. no .. si .. no' of an Italian duet. I want to see more of men—& you have seen too much, you say. I am in ignorance, & you, in satiety. 'You don't even care about reading now.' Is it possible? And I am as 'fresh' about reading, as ever I was— as long as I keep out of the shadow of the dictionaries & of theological controversies, & the like. Shall I whisper it to you under the memory of the last rose of last summer ... *I am very fond of romances* .. yes!—and I read them not only as some wise people are known to do, for the sake of the eloquence here & the sentiment there, & the graphic intermixtures here & there, .. but for the story!—just as little children would, sitting on their Papa's knee. My childish love of a story never wore out with my love of plumbcake—& now there is not a hole in it. I make it a rule, for the most part, to read all the romances that other people are kind enough to write—& woe to the miserable wight who tells me how the third volume endeth.

Have you in you any surviving innocence of this sort? or do you call it idiocy?—If you do, I will forgive you, only smiling to myself, I give you notice, with a smile of superior .. pleasure! Mr. Chorley° made me quite laugh the other day by recommending Mary Howitt's 'Improvisatore,'° with a sort of deprecating reference to the *descriptions* in the book—just as if I never read a novel, .. *I!*—I wrote a confession back to him which made him shake his head perhaps—& now I confess to *you*, unprovoked. I am one who could have forgotten the plague, listening to Boccaccio's stories,—& I am not ashamed of it. I do not even 'see the better part,' I am so silly.

Ah—you tempt me with a grand vision of Prometheus!°—*I*, who have just escaped with my life, after treading Milton's ground°—you would send me to Aeschylus's. No—*I do not dare*. And besides ... I am inclined to think that we want new *forms* .. as well as thoughts—The old gods are dethroned. Why should we go back to the antique moulds .. classical moulds, as they are so improperly called. If it is a necessity of Art to do so, why then those critics are right who hold that Art is exhausted & the world too worn out for poetry. I do not, for my part, believe this: & I believe the so called necessity of Art to be the mere feebleness of the artist. Let us all aspire rather to *Life*—& let the dead bury their dead. If we have but courage to face these conventions, to touch this low ground, we shall take strength from it instead of losing it; & of that, I am intimately persuaded. For there is poetry *everywhere* .. the 'treasure' (see the old fable) lies all over the field.° And then Christianity is a worthy *myth*, & poetically acceptable.

I had much to say to you ... but am ashamed to take a step into a new sheet. If you mean 'to travel,' why, I shall have to miss you—do you really mean it? How is the play going on? & the poem? May God bless you!

Ever & truly yours,

E. B. B.

. . .

RB, *Tuesday, 15 April 1845*

I heard of you, dear Miss Barrett, between a Polka and a Cellarius° the other evening, of Mr Kenyon: how this wind must hurt you! And yesterday I had occasion to go your way—pass, that is, Wimpole Street, the end of it,—and, do you know, I did not seem to have leave from you to go down it yet, much less count number after number till I came to yours,—much least than less, look up when I did come there. So I went on to a viperine she-friend of mine who, I think, rather loves me she does so hate me, and we talked over the chances of certain other friends who were to be balloted for at the 'Athenaeum' last night,—one of whom, it seems, was in a fright about it—'to such little purpose' said my friend—'for he is so inoffensive—now, if one were to style *you* that!'—'Or you'—I said—and so we hugged ourselves in our grimness like tiger-cats. . . .

Monday—Last night when I could do nothing else I began to write to you, such writing as you have seen—strange! The proper time & season for good sound sensible & profitable forms of speech—when ought it to have occurred, and how did I evade it in these letters of mine? For people begin with a graceful skittish levity, lest you should be struck all of a heap with what is to come, and *that* is sure to be the stuff and staple of the man, full of wisdom and sorrow,—and then again comes the fringe of reeds and pink little stones on the other side, that you may put foot on land, and draw breath, and think what a deep pond you have swum across. But *you* are the real deep wonder of a creature,—and I sail these paper-boats on you rather impudently. But I always mean to be very grave one day,—when I am in better spirits and can go *fuori di me*.

And one thing I want to persuade you of, which is, that all you gain by travel is the discovery that you have gained nothing, and have done rightly in trusting to your innate ideas—or not rightly in distrusting them, as the case may be: you get, too, a little .. perhaps a considerable, good, in finding the world's accepted *moulds* every where, into which you may run & fix your own fused metal,—but not a grain Troy-

weight do you get of new gold, silver or brass. After this, you
go boldly on your own resources, and are justified to yourself,
that's all. Three scratches with a pen, even with this pen,—
and you have the green little Syrenusae where I have sate
and heard the quails sing.° One of these days I shall describe
a country I have seen in my soul only, fruits, flowers, birds
and all. *Perhaps if she falls in love with him?*

Ever yours, dear Miss Barrett,

R. Browning

EB, *Thursday, 17 April 1845*

If you did but know dear Mr. Browning how often I have
written .. not this letter I am about to write, but another
better letter to you, .. in the midst of my silence, .. you w^d not
think for a moment that the east wind, with all the harm it
does to me, is able to do the great harm of putting out the
light of the thought of you to my mind,—for this, indeed, it
has no power to do. I had the pen in my hand once to
write,—& why it fell out, I cannot tell you. And you see, ..
all your writing will not change the wind! You wished all
manner of good to me one day as the clock struck ten,—yes,
& I assure you I was better that day—& I must not forget to
tell you so though it is so long since. And *therefore*, I was
logically bound to believe that you had never thought of me
since .. unless you thought east winds of me! *That* was quite
clear; was it not?—or w^d have been,—if it had not been for
the supernatural conviction, I had above all, of your kindness,
which was too large to be taken in the hinge of a syllogism.
In fact I have long left off thinking that logic proves anything—it *doesn't*, you know.

But your Lamia° has taught you some subtle 'viperine'
reasoning & *motiving*, for the turning down one street instead
of another. It was conclusive. *jealousy*

Ah—but you will never persuade me that I am the better,
or as well, for the thing that I have not. We look from different
points of view, & yours is the point of attainment. Not that
you do not truly say that, when all is done, we must come

home to place our engines, & act by our own strength. I do not want material as material,—no one does. But every life requires a full experience, a various experience—& I have a profound conviction that where a poet has been shut from most of the outward aspects of life, he is at a lamentable disadvantage. Can you, speaking for yourself, separate the results in you from the external influences at work around you, that you say so boldly that you get nothing from the world? You do not *directly*, I know—but you do indirectly & by a rebound. Whatever acts upon you, becomes *you*—& whatever you love or hate, whatever charms you or is scorned by you, acts on you & becomes *you*. Have you read the 'Improvisatore'? or will you?—The writer seems to feel, just as I do, the good of the outward life,—and he is a poet in his soul. It is a book full of beauty & had a great charm to me.

As to the Polkas and Cellariuses, .. I do not covet them of course .. but what a strange world you seem to have, to me at a distance—what a strange husk of a world! How it looks to me like mandarin-life or something as remote; nay, not mandarin-life but mandarin *manners*, .. life, even the outer life, meaning something deeper, in my account of it. As to dear Mr. Kenyon I do not make the mistake of fancying that many can look like him or talk like him or *be* like him. I know enough to know otherwise. When he spoke of me he sh^d have said that I was better notwithstanding the east wind. It is really true—I am getting slowly up from the prostration of the severe cold, & feel stronger in myself.

. . .

RB, *Wednesday, 30 April 1845*

Wednesday Morning.

If you did but know, dear Miss Barrett, how the 'full stop' after 'Morning' just above, has turned out the fullest of stops,—and how for about a quarter of an hour since the ink dried I have been reasoning out the why & wherefore of the stopping, the wisdom of it, and the folly of it, ..

—By this time you see what you have got in me—You ask

me questions, 'if I like novels,'—'if the Improvisatore is not
good,' 'if travel and sightseeing do not effect this and that for
one,' and 'what I am devising—play or poem,'—and I shall
not say I could not answer at all manner of lengths—but, let
me only begin some good piece of writing of the kind, and ..
no, you shall have it, have what I was going to tell you stops
such judicious beginnings,—in a parallel case, out of which
your ingenuity shall, please, pick the meaning: There is a
story of D'Israeli's, an old one, with an episode of strange
interest, or so I found it years ago,—well, you go breathlessly
on with the people of it, page after page, till at last the end
must come, you feel—and the tangled threads draw to one,
and an out-of-door feast in the woods helps you .. that is,
helps them, the people, wonderfully on,—and, lo, dinner is
done, and Vivian Grey is here, and Violet Fane there,—and
a detachment of the party is drafted off to go catch butterflies,
and only two or three stop behind. At this moment, Mr
Somebody, a good man and rather the lady's uncle, 'in
answer to a question from Violet, drew from his pocket a
small, neatly written manuscript, and, seating himself on an
inverted wine-cooler, proceeded to read the following brief
remarks upon the characteristics of the Maeso-gothic literature'—this ends the page,—which you don't turn at once!
But when you *do*, in bitterness of soul, turn it, you read—'On
consideration, I' (Ben, himself) 'shall keep them for Mr
Colburn's New Magazine'—and deeply you draw thankful
breath!° (Note, this 'parallel case' of mine is pretty sure to
meet the usual fortune of my writings—you will ask what it
means,—and this it means, or should mean, all of it, instance
and reasoning and all,—that I am naturally earnest, in
earnest about whatever thing I do, and little able to write
about one thing while I think of another)—

I think I will really write verse to you some day: *this* day, it
is quite clear I had better give up trying.

No, spite of all the lines in the world, I will make an end of
it, as Ophelia with her swan's-song,—for it grows too absurd.
But remember that I write letters to nobody but you, and
that I want method and much more. That book you like so,

the Danish novel, must be full of truth & beauty, to judge from the few extracts I have seen in Reviews. That a Dane should write so, confirms me in an old belief—that Italy is stuff for the use of the North, and no more: pure Poetry there is none, nearly as possible none, in Dante even—materials for Poetry in the pitifullest romancist of their thousands, on the contrary—strange that those great wide black eyes should stare nothing out of the earth that lies before them! Alfieri,° with even grey eyes, and a life of travel, writes you some fifteen tragedies as colourless as salad grown under a garden glass with matting over it—as free, that is, from local colouring, touches of the soil they are said to spring from,— think of 'Saulle,' and his Greek attempts!

I expected to see Mr Kenyon, at a place where I was last week, but he kept away. Here is the bad wind back again, and the black sky. I am sure I never knew till now whether the East or West or South were the quarter to pray for—But surely the weather was a little better last week, and you, were you not better? And do you know—but it's all self-flattery I believe,—still I cannot help fancying the East wind does *my* head harm too!

Ever yours faithfully,
R Browning.

EB, *Thursday, 1 May 1845*

People say of you & of me, dear Mr. Browning, that we love the darkness & use a sphinxine idiom in our talk,—& really you do talk a little like a sphinx in your argument drawn from Vivian Grey. Once I sate up all night to read Vivian Grey,—but I never drew such an argument from him. Not that I give it up (nor *you* up) for a mere mystery. Nor that I can '*see what you have got in you*,' from a mere guess. But just observe! If I ask questions about novels, is it not because I want to know how much elbow-room there may be for our sympathies .. & whether there is room for my loose sleeves, & the lace lappets, as well as for my elbows,—& because I want to see *you* by the refracted lights as well as by the direct ones,—& because I am willing for you to know *me* from the beginning, with all my weaknesses & foolishnesses, .. as they are accounted by people who say to me 'no one would ever think, without knowing you, that you were so & so.' . . .

Indeed .. I do assure you .. I never for a moment thought of 'making conversation' about the Improvisatore or novels in general, when I wrote what I did to you. I might, to other persons .. perhaps. Certainly not to *you*. I was not dealing round from one pack of cards to you & to others. That's what you meant to reproach me for, you know—& of that, I am not guilty at all. I never could think of 'making conversation' in a letter to *you*—never. Women are said to partake of the nature of children—& my brothers call me 'absurdly childish' sometimes: & I am capable of being childishly 'in earnest' about novels, & straws, & such 'puppydogs tails' as my Flush's!° Also I write more letters than you do, .. I write in fact almost as you pay visits, .. & one has to 'make conversation' in turn, of course. *But*—give me something to vow by— whatever you meant in the Vivian Grey argument, you were wrong in it! & you never can be much more wrong—which is a comfortable reflection.

Yet you leap very high at Dante's crown—or you do not leap, .. you simply extend your hand to it, & make a rustling among the laurel-leaves, which is somewhat prophane. Dante's poetry only materials for the northern rhymers!—I must think of that .. if you please .. before I agree with you. Dante's poetry seems to come down in hail, rather than in rain—but count me the drops congealed in one hailstone! Oh! the 'Flight of the Duchess'—do let us hear more of her!° Are you (I wonder) ... not a 'self-flatterer,' .. but .. a flatterer.

Ever yours
E.B.B.

RB, *Saturday, 3 May 1845*

Now shall you see what you shall see—here shall be 'sound speech not to be reproved,'°—for this morning you are to know that the soul of me has it all her own way, dear Miss

Barrett, this green cool nine-in-the morning time for my
chestnut-tree over there, and for me who only coaxed my
good-natured—(really)—body up, after its three-hours night-
rest on condition it should lounge, or creep about, incognito
and without consequences—and so it shall, all but my right-
hand which is half-spirit and 'cuts' its poor relations, and
passes itself off for somebody (that is, some soul) and is
doubly active & ready on such occasions—Now I shall tell
you all about it, first what last letter meant, and then more.
You are to know, then, that for some reason, that looked like
an instinct, I thought I ought not to send shaft on shaft,
letter-plague on letter, with such an uninterrupted clanging ..
that I ought to wait, say a week at least, having killed all your
mules for you, before I shot down your dogs: but not being
exactly Phoibos Apollon,° you are to know further that when
I *did* think I might go modestly on, .. ὤμοι [alas], let me get
out of this slough of a simile, never mind with what dislocation
of ancles! Plainly, from waiting and turning my eyes away
(not from *you*, but from you in your special capacity of being
written-to, not spoken-to) when I turned again you had
grown—formidable somehow—tho' that's not the word,—
nor are you the person, either,—it was my fortune, my
privilege of being your friend this one way, that it seemed a
shame for me to make no better use of than by taking it up
with talk about books and I don't know what: write what I
will, you would read for once, I think—well, then,—what I
shall write shall be—something on this book, and the other
book, and my own books, and Mary Howitt's books, and at
the end of it—goodbye, and I hope here is a quarter of an
hour rationally spent. So the thought of what I should find in
my heart to say, and the contrast with what I suppose I ought
to say .. all these things are against me. But this is very
foolish, all the same, I need not be told—and is part & parcel
of an older—indeed primitive folly of mine, which I shall
never wholly get rid of, of desiring to do nothing when I
cannot do all; seeing nothing, getting, enjoying nothing, where
there is no seeing & getting & enjoying *wholly*—. . . Now you
see how I came to say some nonsense (I very vaguely think
what) about Dante—some desperate splash I know I made
for the beginning of my picture, as when a painter at his wits'

end and hunger's beginning, says 'Here shall the figures hand
be'—and spots *that* down, meaning to reach it naturally from
the other end of his canvass,—and leaving off tired, there you
see the spectral disjoined thing, and nothing between it and
rationality: I intended to shade down and soften off and put
in and leave out, and, before I had done, bring Italian Poets
round to their old place again in my heart, giving new praise
if I took old,—anyhow Dante is *out* of it all, as who knows but
I, with all of him in my head and heart? But they do fret one,
those tantalizing creatures, of fine passionate class, with such
capabilities, and such a facility of being made pure mind of.
And the special instance that vexed me, was that a man of
sands and dogroses and white rock and green sea-water just
under, should come to Italy where my heart lives, and
discover the sights and sounds .. certainly discover them. And
so do all Northern writers; for take up handfuls of sonetti,
rime, poemetti, doings of those who never did anything else,—
and try and make out, for yourself, what .. say, what flowers
they tread on, or trees they walk under,—as you might bid
them, those tree & flower loving creatures, pick out of *our*
North poetry a notion of what *our* daisies and harebells and
furze bushes and brambles are—'Odorose fiorette, rose porporine, bianchissimi gigli.'°—And which of you eternal triflers
was it called yourself 'Shelley' and so told me years ago that
in the mountains it was a feast 'when one should find those
globes of deep red gold—Which in the woods the strawberry-
tree doth bear, Suspended in their emerald atmosphere,'° so
that when my Mule walked into a sorb-tree, not to tumble
sheer over Monte Calvano,° and I felt the fruit against my
face, the little ragged bare-legged guide fairly laughed at my
knowing them so well—'Niursi—sorbi!' [Yes, sir—sorb
apples!] No, no,—does not all Naples-bay and half Sicily,
shore and inland, come flocking once a year to the Piedigrotta
fête only to see the blessed King's Volanti,° or livery servants
all in their best, as tho' heaven opened? and would not I
engage to bring the whole of the Piano [Plain] (of Sorrento)
in likeness to a red velvet dressing gown properly spangled
over, before the priest that held it out on a pole had even
begun his story of how Noah's son Shem, the founder of
Sorrento, threw it off to swim thither, as the world knows he

did? Oh, it makes one's soul angry, so enough of it.—But never enough of telling you—bring all your sympathies, come with loosest sleeves and longest lace-lappets, and you and yours shall find 'elbow room,' oh, shall you not! For never did man woman or child, Greek, Hebrew, or as Danish as our friend, like a thing, not to say love it, but I liked and loved it, one liking neutralizing the rebellious stir of its fellow, so that I do'n't go about now wanting the fixed stars before my time,—this world has not escaped me, thank God,—and—what other people say is the best of it, may not escape me after all, tho' until so very lately I made up my mind to do without it—perhaps, on that account, and to make fair amends to other people,—who, I have no right to say, complain without cause. I have been surprised, rather, with something not unlike illness of late—I have had a constant pain in the head for these two months, which only very rough exercise gets rid of, and which stops my 'Luria' and much beside. I thought I never could be unwell. Just now all of it is gone, thanks to polking all night and walking home by broad daylight to the surprise of the thrushes in the bush here. And do you know I said 'this must *go*, cannot mean to stay, so I will not tell Miss Barrett why this & this is not done,'—but I mean to tell you all, or more of, the truth, because you call me 'flatterer'—so that my eyes widened again! I, and in what? And of whom, pray? not of *you*, at all events,—of whom then? *Do* tell me, because I want to stand well with you—and am quite in earnest there. And 'The Flight of the Duchess,' to leave nothing out, is only the beginning of a story written some time ago, and given to poor Hood in his emergency° at a day's notice,—the true stuff and story is all to come, the '*Flight*,' and what you allude to is the mere introduction—but the Magazine has passed into other hands and I must put the rest in some 'Bell' or other—is is one of my Dramatic Romances—so is a certain 'Saul' I should like to show you one day—an ominous liking,—for nobody ever sees what I do till it is printed. But as you *do* know the printed little part of me, I should not be sorry if, in justice, you knew all I have *really* done,—written in the portfolio there,—tho' that would be far enough from *this* me, that writes to you now. I should like to write something in concert with you—how I would try!

. . . let me tell you that I am going to see Mr Kenyon on the 12 inst.—that you do not tell me how you are, and that yet if you do not continue to improve in health, I shall not see you—not—not—not—what 'knots' to untie! Surely the wind that sets my chestnut-tree dancing, all its baby-cone-blossoms, green now, rocking like fairy castles on a hill in an earthquake,—that is south west, surely! God bless you, and me in that. And do write to me soon, and tell me who was the 'flatterer,' and how he never was

Yours
RB.

EB, *Monday, 5–Tuesday, 6 May 1845*

Monday—& Tuesday.

So when wise people happen to be ill, they sit up till six o'clock in the morning & get up again at nine? Do tell me how Lurias can ever be made out of such ungodly imprudences. If the wind blows east or west, where can any remedy be, while such evil deeds are being committed? And what is to be the end of it? And what is the reasonableness of it in the meantime, when we all know that thinking, dreaming, creating people like yourself, have two lives to bear instead of one, & therefore ought to sleep more than others, .. throwing over & buckling in that fold of death, to stroke the life-purple smoother. You have to live your own personal life, & also Luria's life—& therefore you sh^d sleep for both. It is logical indeed—& rational, .. which logic is not always,—and if I had 'the tongue of men & of angels',° I would use it to persuade you. Polka, for the rest, may be good,—but sleep is better. I think better of sleep than I ever did, now that she will not easily come near me except in a red hood of poppies.° And besides, .. praise your 'goodnatured body' as you like, .. it is only a seeming goodnature! Bodies bear malice in a terrible way, be very sure—! appear mild & smiling for a few short years, and then, .. out with a cold steel,—& the soul *has it*, 'with a vengeance,' .. according to the phrase! You will not persist, (—will you?—) in this experimental homicide. Or tell me if you will, that I may do some more teazing. It really, really is wrong. Exercise is one sort of rest & you feel relieved by it—and sleep is another: one being as necessary as the other.

This is the first thing I have to say. The next is a question. *What do you mean about your manuscripts .. about 'Saul' & the portfolio?* ... I get half bribed to silence by the very pleasure of fancying. But if it could be possible that you should mean to say you would show me ... Can it be? or am I reading this 'Attic contraction' quite the wrong way? You see I am afraid of the difference between flattering myself & being flattered,—the fatal difference. And now will you understand that I sh^d be too overjoyed to have revelations from the 'Portfolio,' .. however incarnated with blots & pen-scratches, .. to be able to ask impudently of them now?—Is that plain?

It must be, .. at any rate, .. that if *you* would like to 'write something together' with me, *I* should like it still better. I should like it for some ineffable reasons. And I should not like it a bit the less for the grand supply of jests it w^d administer to the critical Board of Trade about visible darkness, multiplied by two, mounting into palpable obscure.°

. . .

Yes—you are going to Mr. Kenyon's on the 12th—& yes,—my brother & sister are going to meet you & your sister there one day to dinner. Shall I have courage to see you soon, I wonder! If you ask me, I must ask myself. But oh, this make-believe May—it cant be May after all! If a south-west wind sate in your chestnut tree, it was but for a few hours—the east wind 'came up this way' by the earliest opportunity of succession. ... the English spring-winds have excelled themselves in evil this year; & I have not been down stairs yet.—*But* I am certainly stronger & better than I was—that is undeniable—& I *shall* be better still. You are not going away soon—are you? In the meantime you do not know what it is to be .. a little afraid of Paracelsus. So right about the Italians! & the 'rose porporine' which made me smile. How is the head?

Ever yours
E. B. B.

Is the 'Flight of the Duchess' in the portfolio? Of course you must ring the Bell. That poem has a strong heart in it, to begin so strongly. Poor Hood! And all those thoughts fall mixed together. May God bless you.

EB, *Sunday, 11 May 1845*

Sunday—in the last hour of it—

May I ask how the head is? just under the bay? Mr. Kenyon was here today & told me such bad news that I cannot sleep tonight (although I did think once of doing it) without asking such a question as this, dear Mr. Browning.

Let me hear how you are—will you? and let me hear (if I can) that it was prudence or some unchristian virtue of the sort, & not a dreary necessity, which made you put aside the engagement for Tuesday—for Monday. I had been thinking so of seeing you on Tuesday .. with my sister's eyes—for the first sight.

And now if you have done killing the mules & the dogs, let me have a straight quick arrow for myself, if you please. Just a word, to say how you are. I ask for no more than a word, lest the writing should be hurtful to you.

May God bless you always.

Your friend
EBB.

RB, *Monday, 12 May 1845*

My dear, own friend, I am quite well now, or next to it—but this is how it was,—I have gone out a great deal of late, and my head took to ringing such a literal alarum that I wondered what was to come of it; and at last, a few evenings ago, as I was dressing for a dinner somewhere, I got really bad of a sudden, and kept at home to my friend's heartrending disappointment—Next morning I was no better—and it struck me that I should be really disappointing dear kind Mr

Kenyon, and wasting his time, if that engagement, too, were broken with as little warning,—so I thought it best to forego all hopes of seeing him, at such a risk. And that done, I got rid of every other promise to pay visits for next week and next, and told everybody, with considerable dignity, that my London season was over for this year, as it assuredly is—and I shall be worried no more, and let walk in the garden, and go to bed at ten o'clock, and get done with what is most expedient to do, and my 'flesh shall come again like a little child's,'° and one day, oh the day, I shall see you with my own, own eyes .. for, how little you understand me; or rather, your self,—if you think I would dare see you, without your leave, that way! Do you suppose that your power of giving & refusing ends when you have shut your room-door? Did I not tell you I turned down another street, even, the other day, and why not down your's? And often as I see Mr. Kenyon, have I ever dreamed of asking any but the merest conventional questions about you; your health, and no more?

I will answer your letter, the last one, to-morrow—I have said nothing of what I want to say.

Ever yours
RB.

RB, *Tuesday, 13 May 1845*

Did I thank you with any effect in the lines I sent yesterday, dear Miss Barrett? I know I felt most thankful, and, of course, began reasoning myself into the impropriety of allowing a 'more' or a 'most' in feelings of that sort towards you. I am thankful for you, all about you—as, do you not know?

Thank you, from my soul. . . .

'If you ask me, I must ask myself'—that is, when I am to see you—I will *never* ask you! You do *not* know what I shall estimate that permission at,—nor do I, quite—but you do— do not you? know so much of me as to make my 'asking' worse than a form—I do not 'ask' you to write to me—not *directly* ask, at least.

I will tell you—I ask you *not* to see me so long as you are unwell, or ⟨mistrustful of⟩

No, no, that is being too grand! Do see me when you can, and let me not be only writing myself

> Yours
> RB.

A kind, so kind, note from Mr Kenyon came—we, I & my sister, are to go in June instead .. I shall go nowhere till then; I am nearly well—all save one little wheel in my head that keeps on its

Sostenuto

—That you are better I am most thankful.

'Next letter' to say how you must help me with all my new Romances and Lyrics, and Lays & Plays, and read them and heed them and end them and mend them!

EB, *Thursday, 15 May 1845*

But how 'mistrustfulness'? And how 'that way'? What have I said or done, *I*, who am not apt to be mistrustful of anybody & sh^d be a miraculous monster if I began with *you*? What can I have said, I say to myself again & again.

One thing, at any rate, I have done, 'that way' or this way! I have made what is vulgarly called a 'piece of work' about little; or seemed to make it. Forgive me. I am shy by nature:— & by position & experience, .. by having had my nerves shaken to excess, & by leading a life of such seclusion, .. by these things together & by others besides, I have appeared shy & ungrateful to you. Only not mistrustful. You could not mean to judge me so. Mistrustful people do not write as I write, .. surely! for wasn't it a Richelieu or Mazarin (or who?) who said that with five lines from anyone's hand, he c^d take off his head for a corollary?° I think so.

Well!—but this is to prove that I am not mistrustful, & to say, that if you care to come to see me you can come,—&

that it is my gain (as I feel it to be) & not yours, whenever
you do come. You will not talk of having come afterwards I
know, because although I am 'fast bound' to see one or two
persons this summer (besides yourself, whom I receive of
choice & willingly,—) I *cannot* admit visitors in a general
way—& putting the question of health quite aside, it w^d be
unbecoming to lie here on a sofa & make a company-show of
an infirmity, & hold a beggar's hat for sympathy—I sh^d
blame it in another woman—& the sense of it has had its
weight with me sometimes.

For the rest, .. when you write that '*I* do not know how you
w^d *value* &c *not yourself quite,*' you touch very accurately on the
truth, .. & *so* accurately in the last clause, that to read it,
made me smile, 'tant bien que mal' [for good or ill]. Certainly
you cannot 'quite know,' or know at all, whether the least
straw of pleasure can go to you from knowing me otherwise
than on this paper—& I, for my part, 'quite know' my own
honest impression dear Mr. Browning, that none is likely to
go to you. There is nothing to see in me,—nor to hear in
me—I never learnt to talk as you do in London,—although I
can admire that brightness of carved speech in Mr. Kenyon
& others. If my poetry is worth anything to any eye,—it is
the flower of me. I have lived most & been most happy in it,
& so it has all my colours; the rest of me is nothing but a
root, fit for the ground & the dark. And if I write all this
egotism, .. it is for shame,—& because I feel ashamed° of
having made a fuss about what is not worth it,—& because
you are extravagant in caring so for a permission, which will
be nothing to you afterwards. Not that I am not touched by
your caring so at all!—I am deeply touched now,—& presently, .. I shall understand. Come then. There will be truth &
simplicity for you in any case,—& a friend. And do not
answer this—I do not write it as a flytrap for compliments.
Your spider would scorn me for it too much.

Also .. as to the how & when. You are not well now, & it
cannot be good for you to do anything but be quiet & keep
away that dreadful musical note in the head. I entreat you
not to think of coming until *that* is all put to silence satisfac-
torily. When it is done, .. you must choose whether you w^d
like best to come with Mr. Kenyon or to come alone—& if

you w^d come alone, you must just tell me on what day, & I will see you on any day unless there sh^d be an unforseen obstacle, .. any day after two, or before six. And my sister will bring you up stairs to me,—& we will talk,—or *you* will talk,—& you will try to be indulgent, & like me as well you can. If, on the other hand, you w^d rather come with Mr. Kenyon, you must wait, I imagine, till June,—because he goes away on Monday & is not likely immediately to return— no, on Saturday, tomorrow.

In the meantime, why I sh^d be '*thanked*,' is an absolute mystery to me—but I leave it!

You are generous & impetuous,—*that*, I can see & feel,— and so far from being of an inclination to mistrust you or distrust you, I do profess to have as much faith in your full, pure loyalty, as if I had known you personally as many years as I have appreciated your genius. Believe this of me—for it is spoken truly.

  . . .

RB, *Friday, 16 May 1845*

My friend is not 'mistrustful' of me, no, because she don't fear I shall make mainprize of the stray cloaks & umbrellas down-stairs, or turn an article for 'Colburn's'° on her sayings & doings up-stairs,—but, spite of that, she does mistrust .. *so* mistrust my common sense,—nay, uncommon and dramatic- poet's sense, if I am put on asserting it!—all which pieces of mistrust I could detect, and catch struggling, and pin to death in a moment, and put a label on, with name, genus and species, just like a horrible entomologist; only I won't, because the first visit of the Northwind will carry the whole tribe into the Red Sea°—and those horns and tails and scalewings are best forgotten altogether. And now will I say a cutting thing and have done: have *I* trusted *my* friend so,—or said even to myself, much less to her, she is even as—'Mr Simpson' who desireth the honour of the acquaintance of Mr B. whose admirable works have long been his, Simpson's, especial solace in private—and who accordingly is led to that personage by a mutual friend—Simpson blushing as only adorable ingenuousness can, and twisting the brim of his hat like a sailor giving evidence. Whereupon Mr B. beginneth by remarking that the rooms are growing hot—or that he supposes Mr S. has not heard if there will be another adjournment of the House tonight—whereupon Mr S. looketh up all at once, brusheth the brim smooth again with his sleeve, and takes to his assurance once more, in something of a huff, and after staying his five minutes out for decency's sake, noddeth familiarly an adieu, and spinning round on his heel ejaculateth mentally—'Well, I *did* expect to see something different from that little yellow commonplace man .. and, now I come to think, there *was* some precious trash in that book of his.'—Have *I* said 'so will Miss Barrett ejaculate'?

⟨And, remember, before you call any wish of mine extravagant, that I⟩

⟨You will⟩

Dear Miss Barrett, I thank you for the leave you give me, and for the infinite kindness of the way of giving it. I will call at 2 on Tuesday—not sooner, that you may have time to write should any adverse circumstances happen .. not that they need inconvenience you, because .. what I want particularly to tell you for now and hereafter,—do not mind my coming in the least, but,—should you be unwell, for instance,—just send or leave word, and I will come again, and again, and again—my time is of *no* importance, and I have acquaintances thick in the vicinity.

Now if I do not seem grateful enough to you, *am* I so much to blame? ⟨Don't forget to let me say that⟩ You see it is high time you *saw* me, for I have clearly written myself *out!*

Ever yours,
R. B.

EB, *Saturday, 17 May 1845*

I shall be ready on tuesday I hope,—but I hate & protest against your horrible 'entomology.' Beginning to explain, w^d thrust me lower & lower down the circles of some sort of an

'Inferno'; only with my dying breath I w^d maintain that I never could, consciously or unconsciously, mean to distrust you,—or, the least in the world, to Simpsonize you. What I said, ... it was *you* that put it into my head to say it—for certainly, in my usual disinclination to receive visitors, such a feeling does not enter. There, now!—There, I am a whole 'giro' lower! Now, you will say perhaps that I distrust *you*, & nobody else! .. So it is best to be silent, & bear all the 'cutting things' with resignation!—*that* is certain.

Still I must really say, under this dreadful incubus-charge of Simpsonism, .. that you, who know everything, or at least make awful guesses at everyone in one's feelings & motives, & profess to be able to pin them down in a book of classified inscriptions, .. should have been able to understand better, or misunderstand less, in a matter like this—Yes! I think so. I think you sh^d have made out the case in some such way as it was in nature—viz. that you had lashed yourself up to an exorbitant wishing to see me, .. (you who could see, every day, people who are a hundredfold & to all social purposes, my superiors!—) because I was unfortunate enough to be shut up in a room & silly enough to make a fuss about opening the door,—& that I grew suddenly abashed by the consciousness of this. How different from a distrust of *you!*— how different!—

Ah—if, after this day, you ever see any interpretable sign of distrustfulness in me, you may be 'cutting' again, & I will not cry out. In the meantime here is a fact for your 'entomology.' I have not so much *distrust*, as will make a *doubt*, as will make a *curiosity* for next Tuesday. Not the simplest modification of *curiosity* enters into the state of feeling with which I wait for tuesday—: and if you are angry to hear me say so, .. why, you are more unjust than ever.

(Let it be three instead of two—if the hour be as convenient for yourself.)

Before you come, try to forgive me for my 'infinite kindness' in the manner of consenting to see you. Is it 'the cruellest cut of all' when you talk of infinite kindness, yet attribute such villainy to me? Well!—but we are friends till tuesday—& after, perhaps!

Ever yours
EBB.

If on Tuesday you should be not well *pray do not come*—Now,
that is my request to your kindness.

> [Browning's first visit took place as arranged. He made
> a note of the visit, and the time it lasted, on the front of
> the envelope of Elizabeth Barrett's most recent letter (17
> May). The note reads:
>
> > + Tuesday, May 20, 1845
> > 3–4½ p.m.
>
> Subsequent visits (with one exception: see pp. 164–5)
> were similarly recorded. The significance of the cross at
> the beginning, which (sometimes slightly modified)
> appears in almost every note of a meeting, is not known.
> Visits are henceforward noted editorially.]

RB, *Tuesday, 20 May 1845*

Tuesday Ev^e

I trust to you for a true account of how you are—if tired, if
not tired, if I did wrong in any thing,—or, if you please, *right*
in anything—(only, not one more word about my 'kindness',
which, to get done with, I will grant is excessive)—but, let us
so arrange matters if possible,—and why should it not be?—
that my great happiness, such as it will be if I see you, as this
morning,° from time to time,—may be obtained at the cost of
as little inconvenience to you as we can contrive. For one
instance—just what strikes me—they all say here I speak
very loud—(a trick caught from having often to talk with a
deaf relative of mine).° And did I stay too long?
I will tell *you* unhesitatingly of such 'corrigenda'—nay, I
will again say, do not humiliate me—do *not* again,—by
calling me 'kind,' in that way.
I am proud & happy in your friendship—now and ever
May God bless you!
R. B.

EB, *Wednesday, 21 May 1845*

Indeed there was nothing wrong—how could there be? And there was everything right—as how sh^d there not be? And as for the 'loud speaking,' I did not hear any!—and, instead of being worse, I ought to be better for what was certainly (to speak it, or be silent of it,) happiness & honour to me yesterday.

Which reminds me to observe that you are so restricting our vocabulary, as to be ominous of silence in a full sense, presently. First, one word is not to be spoken—and then, another is not. And why? Why deny me the use of such words as have natural feelings belonging to them—and how can the use of such be 'humiliating' to YOU? If my heart were open to you, you c^d see nothing offensive to you in any thought there or trace of thought that has been there—but it is hard for you to understand ... what my mental position is after the peculiar experience I have suffered, & what a τί ἐμοὶ καὶ σοί° sort of feeling is irrepressible from me to you, when, from the height of your brilliant happy sphere, you ask, as you did ask, for personal intercourse with me. What words but 'kindness' .. but 'gratitude'—but I will not in any case be *un*kind, & *un*grateful, & do what is displeasing to you. And let us both leave the subject with the words—because we perceive in it from different points of view,—we stand on the black & white sides of the shield,—& there is no coming to a conclusion.

But you will come really on tuesday—& again, when you like & can together—& it will not be more 'inconvenient' to me to be pleased, I suppose, than it is to people in general—will it, do you think? Ah—how you misjudge!—Why it must obviously & naturally be delightful to me to receive you here when you like to come, & it cannot be necessary for me to say so in set words—believe it of

Your friend
EBB.

[Browning's next letter—written either on Wednesday evening or Thursday morning—is the only one missing from the correspondence: Elizabeth Barrett returned it to him, and he destroyed it. It undoubtedly contained a declaration of love, but not a proposal of marriage, given Elizabeth Barrett's remark that she is 'disobeying' Browning in mentioning his letter, and Browning's own belief, at the time, that she was permanently disabled (see letter RB 18 Sept., p. 126). The likeliest is that, stung by Elizabeth Barrett's repeated insistence that he, not she, was the benefactor in their relationship, Browning proclaimed his love for her and his desire to devote his life to her. For a full discussion of this episode, see Karlin, pp. 77–85.]

EB, *Friday, 23 May 1845*

Friday Evening.
I intended to write to you last night & this morning, & could not,—you do not know what pain you give me in speaking so wildly—And if I disobey you my dear friend, in speaking, (I for my part) of your wild speaking, I do it, not to displease you, but to be in my own eyes & before God, a little more worthy, or less unworthy, of a generosity from which I recoil by instinct & at the first glance, yet conclusively,—& because my silence w^d be the most disloyal of all means of expression, in reference to it. Listen to me then in this. You have said some intemperate things ... fancies—which you will not say over again, nor unsay, but *forget at once, & for ever, having said at all*,—& which (so) will die out between *you & me alone*, like a misprint between you and the printer. And this you will do *for my sake* who am your friend,—(& you have none truer)—& this I ask, because it is a condition necessary to our future liberty of intercourse. You remember—surely you do,—that I am in the most exceptional of positions; & that, just *because of it*, I am able to receive you as I did on Tuesday; and that, for me to listen to 'unconscious exaggerations', is as unbecoming to the humilities of my position, as unpropitious (which is of more consequence) to the prosperities of yours—Now, if there sh^d be one word of answer

attempted to this,—or of reference; *I must not .. I* WILL *not see you again*—& you will justify me later in your heart .. So for my sake you will not say it—I think you will not—& spare me the sadness of having to break through an intercourse just as it is promising pleasure to me,—to me who have so many sadnesses & so few pleasures. You will—! & I need not be uneasy—& I shall owe you that tranquillity, as one gift of many—For, that I have much to receive from you in all the free gifts of thinking, teaching master-spirits, .. *that*, I know!—it is my own praise that I appreciate you, as none can more. Your influence & help in poetry will be full of good & gladness to me—for with many to love me in this house, there is no one to judge me .. *now*. Your friendship & sympathy will be dear and precious to me all my life, if you indeed leave them with me so long or so little. Your mistakes in me .. which *I* cannot mistake (—& which have humbled me by too much honoring—) I put away gently, & with grateful tears in my eyes,—because *all that hail* will beat down & spoil crowns as well as 'blossoms.'

If I put off next Tuesday to the week after—I mean your visit, .. shall you care much?—For the relations I named to you, are to be in London next week: & I am to see one of my aunts whom I love,° & have not met since my great affliction—& it will all seem to come over again, & I shall be out of spirits & nerves. On tuesday week you can bring a tomahawk & do the criticism, & I shall try to have my courage ready for it—Oh, you will do me so much good—and Mr. Kenyon calls me 'docile' sometimes I assure you; when he wants to flatter me out of being obstinate—and in good earnest, I believe I shall do everything you tell me. The Prometheus is done—but the monodram is where it was—& the novel, not at all. But I think of some half promises half given, about something I read for 'Saul'—& the Flight of the Duchess—where is she?

You are not displeased with me? *No—that* w^d be hail & lightning together—I do not write as I might, of some words of yours—but you know that I am not a stone, even if silent like one. And if in the *un*silence, I have said one word to vex you, pity me for having had to say it—and for the rest, may

God bless you far beyond the reach of vexation from my words or my deeds!

Your friend in grateful regard,
EBB.

RB, *Saturday, 24 May 1845*

Don't you remember I told you, once on a time, that you 'knew nothing of me'? whereat you demurred—but I meant what I said, & knew it was so. To be grand in a simile, for every poor speck of a Vesuvius or a Stromboli in my microcosm there are huge layers of ice and pits of black cold water—and I make the most of my two or three fire-eyes, because I know by experience, alas, how these tend to extinction—and the ice grows & grows—still this last is true part of me, most characteristic part, *best* part perhaps, and I disown nothing—only,—when you talked of '*knowing* me'!— Still, I am utterly unused, of these late years particularly, to dream of communicating anything about *that* to another person (all my writings are purely dramatic as I am always anxious to say) that when I make never so little an attempt, no wonder if I *bungle* notably—'language,' too, is an organ that never studded this heavy head of mine. Will you not think me very brutal if I tell you I could almost smile at your misapprehension of what I meant to write?—Yet I *will* tell you, because it will undo the bad effect of my thoughtlessness, and at the same time exemplify the point I have all along been honestly earnest to set you right upon .. my real inferiority to you; just that and no more. I ⟨spoke⟩ wrote to you, in an unwise moment, on the spur of being again 'thanked,' and, unwisely writing just as if thinking to myself, said what must have looked absurd enough as seen apart from the horrible counterbalancing never-to-be-written *rest of me*—by the side of which, could it be written & put before you, my note would sink to its proper & relative place, and become a mere 'thank you for your good opinion—which I assure you is far too generous,—for I really believe you to be my superior in many respects, and feel uncomfortable till *you* see that, too—since I hope for your sympathy & assistance, and frankness is everything in such a case.' I do assure you, that had you read my note, *only* having '*known*' so much of me as is implied in having inspected, for instance, the contents, merely, of that fatal and often-referred-to 'portfolio' there (Dii meliora piis!)—° you would see in it, (the note not the portfolio) the blandest utterance ever mild gentleman gave birth to: but I forgot that one may make too much noise in a silent place by playing the few notes on the 'ear piercing fife' which, in Othello's regimental band, might have been thumped into decent subordination by his 'spirit stirring drum'°—to say nothing of gong and ophicleide. Will you forgive me, on promise to remember for the future, and be more considerate? Not that you must too much despise me, neither; nor, of all things, apprehend I am attitudinizing à la Byron, and giving you to understand unutterable somethings, longings for Lethe and all that—far from it! I never committed murders, and sleep the soundest of sleeps—but 'the heart is desperately wicked,'° that is true, and tho' I dare not say 'I know' mine, yet I have had signal opportunities, I who began life from the beginning, and can forget nothing (but names, and the date of the battle of Waterloo,) and have known good & wicked men and women, gentle & simple, shaking hands with Edmund Kean and Father Mathew, you and—Ottima!° Then, I had a certain faculty of self-consciousness, years, years ago, at which John Mill wondered,° and which ought to be improved by this time, if constant use helps at all—and, meaning, on the whole, to be a Poet, if not *the* Poet .. for I am vain and ambitious some nights,—I do myself justice, and dare call things by their names to myself, and say boldly, this I love, this I hate, this I would do, this I would not do, under all kinds of circumstances,—and talking (thinking) in this style *to myself*, and beginning, however tremblingly, in spite of conviction, to write in this style *for myself*—on the top of the desk which contains my 'Songs of the Poets—No. 1. M.P.,'° I wrote—what you now forgive, I know! Because I am, from my heart, sorry that by a foolish fit of inconsideration I should have given pain for a minute to you, towards whom, on every account, I would rather soften and 'sleeken every word—as to a bird'° .. (and, not such a bird as my black self that go

screeching about the world for 'dead horse'—corvus
(picus)—Mirandola!)° I, too, who have been at such pains to
acquire the reputation I enjoy in the world,—(ask Mr
Kenyon,) & who dine, and wine, and dance and enhance the
company's pleasure till they make me ill and I keep house, as
of late: Mr Kenyon, (for I only quote where you may verify if
you please) *he* says my common sense strikes him, and its
contrast with my muddy metaphysical poetry! And so it shall
strike you—for tho' I am glad that, since you *did* misunderstand me, you said so, and have given me an opportunity of
doing by another way what I wished to do in *that*,—yet, if
you had *not* alluded to my writing, as I meant you should not,
you would have certainly understood *something* of its drift
when you found me next Tuesday precisely the same quiet
(no, for I feel I speak too loudly, in spite of your kind
disclaimer, but—) the same mild man-about-town you were
gracious to, the other morning—for, indeed, my own way of
worldly life is marked out long ago, as precisely as yours can
be, and I am set going with a hand, winker-wise, on each side
of my head, and a directing finger before my eyes, to say
nothing of an instinctive dread I have that a certain whip-
lash is vibrating somewhere in the neighbourhood in playful
readiness! So 'I hope here be proofs,' to Dogberry's satisfac-
tion° that, first, I am but a very poor creature compared to
you and entitled by my wants to look up to you,—all I meant
to say from the first of the first—and that, next, I shall be too
much punished if, for this piece of mere inconsideration, you
deprive me, more or less, or sooner or later, of the pleasure of
seeing you,—a little over boisterous gratitude for which,
perhaps, caused all the mischief! The reasons you give for
deferring my visit next week are too cogent for me to
dispute—that is too true—and, being now & henceforward
'on my good behaviour,' I will at once cheerfully submit to
them, if needs must—but should your mere kindness and
forethought, as I half suspect, have induced you to take such
a step, you will now smile, with me, at this new and very
unnecessary addition to the 'fears of me' I had got so
triumphantly over in your case! Wise man, was I not, to
clench my first favorable impression so adroitly .. like a recent
Cambridge worthy, my sister heard of; who, being on his

theological (or rather, scripture-historical) examination, was asked by the Tutor, who wished to let him off easily, 'who was the first King of Israel?'—'Saul' answered the trembling youth. 'Good!' nodded approvingly the Tutor. 'Otherwise called *Paul*,' subjoined the youth in his elation! Now I have begged pardon, and blushingly assured you *that* was only a slip of the tongue, and that I did really *mean* all the while, (Paul or no Paul), the veritable son of Kish, he that owned the asses, and found listening to the harp the best of all things for an evil spirit!° Pray write me a line to say, 'Oh .. if *that's* all!' and remember me for good (which is very compatible with a moment's stupidity) and let me not for one fault, (and that the only one that shall be), lose *my pleasure* .. for your friendship I am sure I have not lost—

God bless you, my dear friend!

R Browning°

And, by the way, will it not be better, as co-operating with you more effectually in your kind promise to forget the 'printer's error' in my blotted proof, to send me back that same 'proof,' if you have not inflicted proper and summary justice on it? When Mephistopheles last came to see us in this world outside here, he counselled sundry of us 'never to write a letter,—and never to burn one'—do you know that? But I never mind what I am told! Seriously, I am ashamed .. I shall next ask a servant for my boots in the 'high fantastical'° style of my own 'Luria'!

EB, *Sunday, 25 May 1845*

I owe you the most humble of apologies dear Mr. Browning, for having spent so much solemnity on so simple a matter, & I hasten to pay it,—confessing at the same time (as why sh^d I not?) that I am quite as much ashamed of myself as I ought to be, which is not a little. You will find it difficult to believe me perhaps when I assure you that I never made such a mistake (I mean of over-seriousness to indefinite compliments) no, never in my life before—indeed my sisters have often jested with me (in matters of which they were cognizant) on my supernatural indifference to the superlative degree in general, as if it meant nothing in grammar. I usually know well that 'boots' may be called for in this world of ours, just as you called for yours,—& that to bring 'Bootes',° were the vilest of mal à propos-ities. Also, I sh^d have understood 'boots' where you wrote it, in the letter in question,—if it had not been for *the relation of two things* in it—& now I perfectly seem to see HOW I mistook that relation,—('*seem to see*,'— because I have not looked into the letter again since your last night's commentary, & will not—) inasmuch as I have observed before in my own mind, that a good deal of what is called obscurity in you, arises from a habit of very subtle association,—so subtle, that you are probably unconscious of it, .. and the effect of which is to throw together on the same level & in the same light, things of likeness & unlikeness—till the reader grows confused as I did, & takes one for another. I may say however, in a poor justice to myself, that I wrote what I wrote so unfortunately, *through reverence for you*, & not at all from vanity on my own account .. although I do feel palpably while I write these words here & now, that I might as well leave them unwritten,—for that no man of the world who ever lived in the world, (not even *you*) could be expected to believe them, though said, sung, & sworn.

For the rest, it is scarcely an apposite moment for you to talk, even 'dramatically,' of my 'superiority' to you, .. unless you mean, which perhaps you do mean, my superiority in *simplicity*—&, verily, to some of the 'adorable ingenuousness,' sacred to the shade of Simpson, I may put in a modest claim, .. '& have my claim allowed.' 'Pray do not mock me'° I quote again from your Shakespeare to you who are a dramatic poet, .. & I will admit anything that you like, (being humble just now)—even that I DID NOT KNOW YOU. I was certainly innocent of the knowledge of the 'ice & cold water' you introduce me to, and am only just shaking my head, as Flush w^d, after a first wholesome plunge—Well—if I do not know you, I shall learn, I suppose, in time. I am ready to try humbly to learn—& I may perhaps—if you are not done in Sanscrit, which is too hard for me, ... notwithstanding that I had the pleasure yesterday to hear, from America, of my profound skill in 'various languages less known than Hebrew'!—a liberal paraphrase on Mr. Horne's large fancies on the like subject,° & a satisfactory reputation in itself—as long as it is not necessary to deserve it. So I here enclose to you your letter back again, as you wisely desire,—although you never c^d doubt, I hope, for a moment, of its safety with me in the completest of senses: and then, from the heights of my superior .. stultity, & other qualities of the like order, .. I venture to advise you .. however (to speak of the letter critically, & as the dramatic composition it is,—) it is to be admitted to be very beautiful, & well worthy of the rest of its kin in the portfolio, .. 'Lays of the poets,' or otherwise, ... I venture to advise you to burn it at once. And then, my dear friend, I ask you (having some claim) to burn at the same time the letter I was fortunate enough to write to you on friday, & this present one—don't send them back to me,—I hate to have letters sent back—but burn them for me & never mind Mephistopheles. After which friendly turn, you will do me the one last kindness of forgetting all this exquisite nonsense, & of refraining from mentioning it, by breath or pen, TO ME OR ANOTHER. Now I trust you so far—! You will put it with the date of the battle of Waterloo—& I, with every date in chronology; seeing that I can remember none of them. And we will shuffle the cards, & take patience, & begin the game again, if you please—& I shall bear in mind that you are a dramatic poet, which is not the same thing, by any means, with *us* of the primitive simplicities, who dont tread on cothurns° nor shift the mask in the scene. And I will reverence you both as 'a poet' & as '*the* poet,'—because it is no false 'ambition,' but a right you have—& one which those who live longest, will see justified to the uttermost .. In the meantime I need not ask Mr. Kenyon if you have any sense, because I have no doubt that you have quite sense enough— & even if I had a doubt, I shall prefer judging for myself without interposition; which I can do, you know, as long as you like to come & see me. And you can come this week if you do like it—because our relations dont come till the end of it, it appears—not that I made a pretence 'out of kindness' .. pray dont judge me so outrageously—but if you like to come .. not on tuesday .. but on wednesday at three oclock, I shall be very glad to see you,—& I, for one, shall have forgotten everything by that time,—being quick at forgetting my own faults usually. If wednesday does not suit you, I am not sure that I *can* see you this week—but it depends on circumstances. Only dont think yourself *obliged* to come on wednesday. You know I *began* by entreating you to be open & sincere with me—& no more—I *require* no 'sleekening of every word' or of any word. I love the truth & can bear it— whether in word or deed—& those who have known me longest w^d tell you so fullest. Well!—May God bless you. We shall know each other some day perhaps—and I am

always & faithfully your friend
EBB—

RB, *Monday, 26 May 1845*

Nay—I *must* have last word—as all people in the wrong desire to have—and then, no more of the subject. You said I had given you *great pain*—so long as I stop *that*, think anything of me you choose or can! But *before* your former letter came, I saw the pre-ordained uselessness of mine: speaking is to some *end*, (apart from foolish self-relief,—which, after all, I can do without)—and where there is *no* end—you see! or, to finish characteristically—since the offering to cut off one's right-hand to save anybody a headache, is in vile taste, even for our melodrames, seeing that it was never yet believed in on the stage or off it,—how much worse to really make the ugly chop, and afterwards come sheepishly in, one's arm in a black sling, and find that the delectable gift had changed aching to nausea! There! And now, 'exit, promptside, nearest door, Luria'—and enter RB—next Wednesday,—as boldly as he suspects most people do just after they have been soundly frightened!

I shall be most happy to see you on the day & at the hour you mention.

God bless you, my dear friend,
RB.

EB, *Monday–Tuesday, 26–27 May 1845*

Monday Morning.

You will think me the most changeable of all the change-able,—but indeed it is *not* my fault that I cannot as I wished, receive you on wednesday. There was a letter this morning,— and our friends not only come to London but come to this house on tuesday (tomorrow) to pass two or three days, until they settle in an hotel for the rest of the season. Therefore, you see, it is doubtful whether the two days may not be three, & the three days four, .. but if they go away in time, & if saturday sh^d suit you, I will let you know by a word; & you can answer by a yea or nay. While they are in the house, I must give them what time I can—& indeed, it is something to dread altogether.

Tuesday.

I send you the note I had begun before receiving yours of last night, & also a fragment from Mrs. Hedley's herein enclosed,° a full & complete certificate, .. that you may know .. quite *know*, .. what the real & only reason of the obstacle to wednesday is. On saturday perhaps, or on monday more certainly, there is likely to be no opposition, .. at least not on the 'côté *gauche*'° (*my* side!) to our meeting—but I will let you know more.

For the rest, we have both been a little unlucky, there's no denying, in overcoming the embarrassments of a first acquaintance—but suffer me to say as one other last word, (*& quite, quite the last this time!*) in case there sh^d have been anything approaching, however remotely, to a distrustful or unkind tone in what I wrote on sunday, (& I have a sort of consciousness that in the process of my selfscorning I was not in the most sabbatical of moods perhaps—) that I do recall & abjure it, & from my heart entreat your pardon for it, & profess, notwithstanding it, neither to 'choose' nor 'to be able' to think otherwise of you than I have done, .. as of one MOST

generous and MOST loyal,—for that if I chose, I could not,—
& that if I could, I should not choose.

Ever & gratefully your friend,

E. B. B.

. . .

[Meeting 2: Saturday, 31 May 3.00–5.00 p.m.
Meeting 3: Thursday, 5 June 3.00–4.30 p.m.]

EB, *Friday, 6 June 1845*

When I see all you have done for me in this Prometheus, I
feel more than half ashamed both of it & of me for using your
time so, & forced to say in my own defence (not to you but
myself) that I never thought of meaning to inflict such work
on you who might be doing so much better things in the
meantime both for me & for others—because, you see, it is
not the mere reading of the ms., but the 'comparing' of the
text, & the melancholy comparisons between the English and
the Greek . . . Yet as you have done it for me—for me who
expected a few jottings down with a pencil & a general
opinion,—it is of course of the greatest value, besides the
pleasure & pride which come of it; & I must say of the
translation, (before putting it aside for the nonce), that the
circumstance of your paying it so much attention & seeing
any good in it, is quite enough reward for the writer & quite
enough motive for self-gratulation, if it were all torn to
fragments at this moment—which is a foolish thing to say
because it is so obvious, & because you w^{d} know it if I said it
or not.

And while you were doing this for me, you thought it
unkind of me not to write to you,—yes, and you think me at
this moment the very princess of apologies & excuses &
depreciations & all the rest of the small family of distrust .. or
of hypocrisy .. who knows? Well!—but you are wrong ..
wrong .. to think so; & you will let me say one word to show
where you are wrong, .. not for you to controvert, .. because

it must relate to myself especially, & lies beyond your
cognizance, & is something which *I must know best* after all.
And it is, .. that you persist in putting me into a false position,
with respect to *fixing days* & the like, & in making me feel
somewhat as I did when I was a child, & Papa used to put
me up on the chimney piece & exhort me to stand up straight
like a hero, which I did, straighter & straighter, and then
suddenly 'was 'ware' (as we say in the ballads) of the wall's
growing alive behind me & extending two stony hands to
push me down that frightful precipice to the rug, where the
dog lay .. dear old Havannah, .. & where he & I were likely
to be dashed to pieces together & mix our uncanonised bones.
Now my present false position .. which is not the chimney
piece's, .. is the necessity you provide for me in the shape of
my having to name this day, or that day, .. & of your coming
because I name it, & of my having to think & remember that
you come because I name it. Through a weakness, perhaps,
or morbidness, or ⟨apathy⟩ one knows not how to define it, I
cannot help being uncomfortable in having to do this,—it is
impossible. Not that I distrust *you*—you are the last in the
world I could distrust: and then (although you may be
sceptical) I am naturally given to trust .. to a fault .. as some
say—or to a sin, as some reproach me:—& then again, if I
were ever such a distruster, it could not be of you. But if you
knew me—! I will tell you! if one of my brothers omits coming
to this room for two days, .. I never ask why it happened! if
my own father omits coming up stairs to say 'good night', I
never say a word,—& not from indifference. Do try to make
out these readings of me as a 'dixit Casaubonus,'°—& dont
throw me down as a corrupt text!—nor convict me for an
infidel which I am not. On the contrary I am grateful &
happy to believe that you like to come here; & even if you
came here as a pure act of charity & pity to me, as long as
you CHOSE TO COME I should not be too proud to be grateful
& happy still. I could not be proud to *you*, & I hope you will
not fancy such a possibility, which is the remotest of all. Yes,
& I am anxious to ask you to be wholly generous & leave off
such an interpreting philosophy as you made use of yesterday,
& forgive me when I beg you to fix your own days for coming
for the future. Will you?

   . . .

RB, *Monday, 9 June 1845*

. . . I begin by promising cheerfully to do all you bid me about naming days &c. I do believe we are friends now & for ever,—there can be no reason, therefore, that I should cling tenaciously to any one or other time of meeting, as if, losing that, I lost everything—and, for the future, I will provide against sudden engagements, outrageous weather &c to your heart's content. Nor am I going to except against here & there a little wrong I could get up .. as when you *imply* from my 'quick impulses' & the like .. no, my dear friend—for I seem sure I shall have quite, quite time enough to do myself justice in your eyes—let time show!

Perhaps I feel none the less sorely, when you 'thank' me for such company as mine, that I cannot avoid confessing to myself that it would not be so absolutely out of my power, perhaps, to contrive really & deserve thanks in a certain acceptation; I *might* really *try*, at all events, and amuse you a little better, when I do have the opportunity,—and I *do not*— but there is the thing! It is all of a piece—I *do not* seek your friendship in order to do you good—any good—only to do myself good. Tho' I *would*, God knows, do that too—

Enough of this!—

. . .

[Meeting 4: Wednesday, 11 June 3.00–5.00 p.m.]

EB, *Friday, 13 June 1845*

Yes, the poem° *is* too good in certain respects for the prizes given in colleges .. (where all the pure parsley goes naturally to the rabbits) .. & has a great deal of beauty here & there in image & expression. Still I do not quite agree with you that it reaches the Tennyson standard any wise; & for the blank verse, I cannot for a moment think it comparable to one of the grand passages in Oenone, & Arthur & the like. In fact I seem to hear more in that latter blank verse than you do, .. to hear not only a 'mighty line' as in Marlowe, but a noble full orbicular wholeness in complete passages—which always struck me as the mystery of music & great peculiarity in Tennyson's versification,—inasmuch as he attains to these complete effects without that shifting of the pause practised by the masters, .. Shelley & others. A 'linked music' .. in which there are no links .. !—*that*, you w^d take to be a contradiction; & yet something like that, my ear has always seemed to perceive; & I have wondered curiously again & again how there could be so much union & no fastening. Only of course it is not model versification—& for dramatic purposes, it must be admitted to be bad.

Which reminds me to be astonished for the second time how you c^d think such a thing of me as that I wanted to read only your lyrics .. or that I 'preferred the lyrics' .. or something barbarous in that way? You don't think me 'ambidexter,' or 'either-handed' .. & both hands open for what poems you will vouchsafe to me,—& yet if you w^d let me see anything you may have in a readable state by you .. the Flight of the Duchess .. or act or scene of the Soul's tragedy, .. I shall be so glad & grateful to you! Oh—if you change your mind & choose to be 'bien prié,'° I will grant it is your right, & begin my liturgy directly. But this is not teazing .. (in the intention of it!—)—and I understand all about the transcription, & the inscrutableness of rough copies . . .

The sun shines so that nobody dares complain of the East wind—& indeed I am better altogether ..

May God bless you, my dear friend!—

EBB

. . .

RB, *Saturday, 14 June 1845*

When I ask my wise self what I really do remember of the Prize-poem—the answer is—both of Chapman's lines a-top, quite worth any prize for their quoter—then, the good epithet of 'green Europe' contrasting with Africa—then, deep in the piece, a picture of a Vestal in a vault, where I see a dipping & winking lamp plainest, and last of all the ominous 'all was dark' that dismisses you:° I read the poem many years ago, and never since—tho' I have an impression that the versification is good—yet from your commentary I see I must have said a good deal more in its praise than that. But have you not discovered by this time that I go on talking with my thoughts away?

I know, I have always been jealous of my own musical faculty (I can write music).—Now that I see the uselessness of such jealousy, and am for loosing & letting it go, it may be cramped possibly. Your music is more various & exquisite than any modern writer's to my ear. One should study the mechanical part of the art, or nearly all that there is to be studied—for the more one sits and thinks over the creative process, the more it confirms itself as 'inspiration' nothing more or less. Or, at worst, you write down old inspirations, what you remember of them—but with *that* it begins: 'Reflection' is exactly what it names itself—a *re*-presentation, in scattered rays from every angle of incidence, of what first of all became present in a great light, a whole one. So tell me how these lights are born, if you can! But I can tell anybody how to make melodious verses—let him do it therefore—it should be exacted of all writers.

You do not understand what a new feeling it is for me to have someone who is to like my verses or I shall not ever like them after! So far differently was I circumstanced of old, that I used rather to go about for a subject of offence to people; writing ugly things in order to warn the ungenial & timorous off my grounds at once. I shall never do so again, at least! As it is, I will bring all I dare, in as great quantities as I can—if not next time, after then—certainly. I must make an end, print this Autumn my last four 'Bells,' Lyrics, Romances, The Tragedy & Luria, and then go on with a whole heart to my own Poem—indeed, I have just resolved not to begin any new song, even, till this grand clearance is made—I will get the Tragedy transcribed to bring—

'To bring!' Next Wednesday—if you knew how happy you

make me! may I not say *that*, my dear friend, when I feel it from my soul?

I thank God that you are better: do pray make fresh endeavours to profit by this partial respite of the weather! All about you must urge that: but even from my distance some effect might come of such wishes. But you *are* better—look so & speak so!

God bless you.
RB

You let 'flowers be sent you in a letter,'° every one knows, and this hot day draws out our very first yellow rose—eccola! [look at it!]

EB, *Monday, 16 June 1845*

Yes, I quite believe as you do that what is called the 'creative process' in works of Art, is just inspiration & no less ... And is it not true that your inability to analyze the mental process in question, is one of the proofs of the fact of inspiration?—as the gods were known of old by not being seen to move their feet, .. coming & going in an equal sweep of radiance.—And still more wonderful than the first transient great light you speak of .. & far beyond any work of *re*flection, except in the pure analytical sense in which you use the word, .. appears that gathering of light on light upon particular points, as you go (in composition) step by step, till you get intimately near to things, & see them in a fulness & clearness, & an intense trust in the truth of them which you have not in any sunshine of noon (called *real*!) but which you have *then* .. & struggle to communicate—: an ineffectual struggle with most writers (oh, how ineffectual!) & when effectual, issuing in the 'Pippa passes's', & other master pieces of the world.

You will tell me what you mean exactly by being jealous of your own music? You said once that you had had a false notion of music, or had practised it according to the false notions of other people: but did you mean besides that you ever had meant to despise music altogether—because *that*, it is hard to set about trying to believe of you indeed. And then, you *can* praise my verses for music?—Why, are you aware that people blame me constantly for wanting harmony .. from Mr. Boyd who moans aloud over the indisposition of my 'trochees' .. to no less a person than Mr. Tennyson, who said to somebody who repeated it, that in the want of harmony lay the chief defect of the poems .. 'although it might verily be retrieved, as he c^d fancy that I had a[n] ear by nature.' Well—but I am pleased that you sh^d praise me—right or wrong—I mean, whether I am right or wrong in being pleased! . . . Only there's a flattery so far beyond praise .. even YOUR praise—as where you talk of your verses being liked &c &c, & of your being happy to bring them here, .. that it is scarcely a lawful weapon; and see if the Madonna may not signify so much to you!—Seriously, .. you will not hurry too uncomfortably, or uncomfortably at all, about the transcribing? Another day, you know, will do as well—& patience is possible to me, if not 'native to the soil.'

Also I am behaving very well in going out into the noise,— not quite out of doors yet, on account of the heat—& I am better as you say, without any doubt at all, & stronger—only my looks are a little deceitful,—& people are apt to be heated & flushed in this weather, one hour, to look a little more ghastly an hour or two after. Not that it is not true of me that I am better, mind!—Because I am.

The 'flower in the letter' was from one of my sisters—from Arabel (though many of these poems are *ideal* .. will you understand?) & your rose came quite alive & fresh, though in act of dropping its beautiful leaves because of having to come to me instead of living on in your garden, as it intended. But I thank you—for this, & all, my dear friend.

EBB

[Meeting 5: Wednesday, 18 June 3.00–4.30 p.m.]

RB, *Thursday, 19 June 1845*

When I next see you, do not let me go on & on to my confusion about matters I am more or less ignorant of, but always ignorant. I tell you plainly I only trench on them, and intrench in them, from gaûcherie, pure and respectable—I should certainly grow instructive on the prospects of hay-crops and pasture-land, if deprived of this resource. And now here is a week to wait before I shall have any occasion to relapse into Greek literature when I am thinking all the while, 'now I will just ask simply, what flattery there was' &c &c which, as I had not courage to say then, I keep to myself for shame now. This I will say, then—wait and know me better, as you will one long day at the end.

. . .

EB, *Thursday, 19 June 1845*

If on Greek literature or anything else it is your pleasure to cultivate a reputation for ignorance, I will respect your desire—& indeed the point of the deficiency in question being far above my sight I am not qualified either to deny or assert the existence of it,—so you are free to have it all your own way.

About the 'flattery' however, there is a difference,—& I must deny a little having ever used such a word .. as far as I can recollect, & I have been trying to recollect, .. as that word of flattery. Perhaps I said something about your having vowed to make me vain by writing this or that of my liking your verses & so on—& perhaps I said it too lightly .. which happened because when one doesn't know whether to laugh or to cry, it is far best, as a general rule, to laugh. But the serious truth is that it was all nonsense together what I wrote, & that, instead of talking of your making me vain, I sh^d have talked (if it had been done sincerely) of your humbling me— inasmuch as nothing does humble anybody so much as being lifted up too high. You know what vaulting Ambition did

once for himself?° and when it is done for him by another, his
fall is still heavier. And one moral of all this general philosophy is, that if when your poems come, you persist in giving
too much importance to what I may have courage to say of
this or of that in them, you will make me a dumb critic & I
shall have no help for my dumbness. . . .

Upon second or third thoughts, isn't it true that you are a
little suspicious of me? .. suspicious at least of my
suspiciousness?

RB, *Sunday, 22 June 1845*

And if I am 'suspicious of your suspiciousness,' who gives
cause, pray? The matter was long ago settled, I thought,
when you first took exception to what I said about higher &
lower, and I consented to this much—that you should help
seeing, if you could, our true intellectual & moral relation
each to the other, so long as you would allow *me* to see what
is there, fronting me. . . .

But I have a restless head to-day and so let you off easily.
Well, you ask me about it, that head, and I am not justified
in being positive when my Doctor is dubious—as for the
causes, they are neither superfluity of study, nor fancy, nor
care, nor any special naughtiness that I know how to amend.
So if I bring you 'nothing to signify' on Wednesday .. tho' I
hope to do more than that .. you will know exactly why it
happens. I will finish & transcribe the 'Flight of the Duchess'
since you spoke of that first.

I am truly happy to hear that your health improves still.

For me, going out does me good—reading, writing, &,—
what is odd,—infinitely most of all, *sleeping* do me the
harm,—never any very great harm.

And all the while I am yours ever
RB.

EB, *Monday, 23 June 1845*

I had begun to be afraid that I did not deserve to have my questions answered, .. & I was afraid of asking them over again. But it is worse to be afraid that you are not better at all in any essential manner (after all your assurances) & that the medical means have failed so far. Did you go to somebody who knows anything?—because there is no excuse, you see, in common sense, for not having the best & most experienced opinion when there is a choice of advice—& I am confident that that pain sh^d not be suffered to go on without something being done. What I said about *nerves*, related to what you had told me of your mother's suffering & what you had fancied of the relation of it to your own—& not that I could be thinking about imaginary complaints—I wish I could. Not (either) that I believe in the relation .. because such things are not hereditary .. are they?—& the bare coincidence is improbable.—Well, but,—I wanted particularly to say this—*Don't bring the Duchess with you on wednesday.* I shall not expect anything, I write distinctly to tell you—& I would far far rather that you did not bring it. You see it is just as I thought—for that whether too much thought or study did or did not bring on the illness, .. yet you admit that reading & writing increase it .. as they w^d naturally do any sort of pain in the head—therefore if you will but be in earnest & try to get well *first*, we will do the 'Bells' afterwards, & there will be time for a whole peal of them, I hope & trust, before the winter.

. . .

[Meeting 6: Saturday, 28 June 3.00–4.15 p.m.]

RB, *Tuesday, 1 July 1845*

How are you—may I hope to hear soon?
I don't know exactly what possessed me to set my next day so far off as Saturday—as it was said, however, so let it be.

And I will bring the rest of the 'Duchess'—four or five hundred lines,—'heu, herba mala crescit'—(as I once saw mournfully pencilled on a white wall at Asolo)°—but will you tell me if you quite remember the main of the *first* part—(*parts* there are none except in the necessary process of chopping-up to suit the limits of a magazine—& I gave them as much as I could transcribe at a sudden warning)—because, if you please, I can bring the whole,—of course. . . .

An old French friend of mine,° a dear foolish, very French heart & soul, is coming presently—his poor brains are whirling with mesmerism in which he believes, as in all other unbelief. He & I are to dine alone (—I have not seen him these two years)—and I shall never be able to keep from driving the great wedge right thro' his breast and, descending lower, from riveting his two foolish legs to the wintry chasm,°—for I that stammer and answer at hap-hazard with you, get proportionately valiant & voluble with a mere cupful of Diderot's rinsings,—and a man into the bargain.
. . .

EB, *Wednesday, 2–Thursday, 3 July 1845*

Yes—I know the first part of the 'Duchess' & have it here—& for the rest of the poem, dont mind about being very legible, or even legible in the usual sense; & remember how it is my boast to be able to read all such manuscript writing as never is read by people who dont like caviare.° Now you wont mind?—really I rather like blots than otherwise—being a sort of patron-saint of all manner of untidyness .. if Mr. Kenyon's reproaches (of which there's a stereotyped edition) are justified by the fact—& he has a great organ of order, & knows 'disorderly persons' at a glance, I suppose. But you wont be particular with *me* in the matter of transcription?— *that* is what I want to make sure of.

Talking of poetry I had a newspaper 'in help of social & political progress' sent to me yesterday from America— addressed to .. just my name .. *poetess, London!* Think of the simplicity of those wild Americans in 'calculating' that 'people in general' here in England, know what a poetess is!

And talking of poetesses, I had a note yesterday (again) which quite touched me .. from Mr. Hemans—Charles .. the son of Felicia°—written with so much feeling, that it was with difficulty I could say my perpetual 'no' to his wish about coming to see me. His mother's memory is surrounded to him, he says, 'with almost a divine lustre'—& 'as it cannot be to those who knew the writer alone & not the woman'. Do you not like to hear such things said? and is it not better than your tradition about Shelley's son?° & is it not pleasant to know that that poor noble purehearted woman, the Vittoria Colonna of our country, sh^d be so loved & comprehended by some .. by one at least .. of her own house?—Not that, in naming Shelley, I meant for a moment to make a comparison—there is not equal ground for it. Vittoria Colonna does not walk near Dante—no. And if you promised never to tell Mrs. Jameson° .. nor Miss Martineau ... ° I would confide to you perhaps my secret profession of faith—which is .. which is .. that let us say & do what we please & can .. there *is* a natural inferiority of mind in women—of the intellect .. not by any means, of the moral nature—& that the history of Art & of genius testifies to this fact openly. Oh—I would not say so to Mrs. Jameson for the world! I believe I was a coward to her altogether—for when she denounced carpet work as 'injurious to the mind,' because it led the workers into 'fatal habits of reverie,' I defended the carpet work as if I were striving *pro aris et focis*,° (*I*, who am so innocent of all that knowledge!) & said not a word for the poor reveries which have frayed away so much of silken time for me, .. & let her go away repeating again & again .. 'oh, but *you* may do carpet work with impunity—*you*! *because* you can be writing poems all the while'!—

Think of people making poems & rugs at once. There's complex machinery for you!

I told you that I had a sensation of cold blue steel from her eyes!—And yet I really liked & like & shall like her. She is very kind I believe—& it was my mistake—& I correct my impressions of her more & more to perfection, as *you* tell me who know more of her than I.

Only I sh^d not dare, .. *ever*, .. I think .. to tell her that I
believe women .. all of us in a mass .. to have minds of quicker
movement, but less power & depth .. & that we are under
your feet, because we can't stand upon our own. Not that we
sh^d either be quite under your feet!—so you are not to be too
proud, if you please—& there is certainly some amount of
wrong—: but it never will be righted in the manner & to the
extent contemplated by certain of our own prophetesses .. nor
ought to be, I hold in intimate persuasion. One woman
indeed now alive .. & only *that* one down all the ages of the
world .. seems to me to justify for a moment an opposite
opinion—that wonderful woman George Sand,° who has
something monstrous in combination with her genius, there
is no denying at moments—(for she has written one book,
Leila, which I could not read, though I am not easily turned
back—) but whom, in her good & evil together, I regard with
infinitely more admiration than all other women of genius
who are or have been. Such a colossal nature in every way—
with all that breadth & scope of faculty which women want—
magnanimous, & loving the truth & loving the people—and
with that 'hate of hate'° too, which you extol—so eloquent &
yet earnest as if she were dumb—so full of a living sense of
beauty, & of noble blind instincts towards an ideal purity—
& so proving a right even in her wrong. . . .

But belief in mesmerism is not the same thing as general
unbelief—to do it justice—now is it? It may be super-belief
as well. Not that there is not something ghastly & repelling to
me in the thought of Dr. Elliotson's great boney fingers°
seeming to 'touch the stops' of a whole soul's harmonies—as
in phreno-magnetism. And I sh^d have liked far better than
hearing & seeing *that*, to have heard *you* pour the 'cupful of
Diderot's rinsings,' out,—& indeed I can fancy a little that
you & how you c^d do it—& break the cup too afterwards!
. . .

[Meeting 7: Saturday, 5 July 3.00–4.30 p.m.]

EB, *Monday, 7–Tuesday, 8 July 1845*

Well—I have really been out,—and am really alive after it—which is more surprising still—alive enough I mean, to write even *so*, tonight. But perhaps I say so with more emphasis, to console myself for failing in my great ambition of getting into the Park & of reaching Mr. Kenyon's door° just to leave a card there vaingloriously, .. all which I did fail in, & was forced to turn back from the gates of Devonshire Place. The next time it will be better perhaps—& this time there was no fainting nor anything very wrong .. not even cowardice on the part of the victim—(be it recorded!) for one of my sisters was as usual in authority & ordered the turning back just according to her own prudence & not my selfwill. Only you will not, any of you, ask me to admit that it was all delightful—pleasanter work than what you wanted to spare me in taking care of your roses on saturday!—don't ask *that*, & I will try it again presently.

I ought to be ashamed of writing this I- and me-ism—but since your kindness made it worth while asking about, I must not be overwise & silent on my side.

Tuesday.

Was it fair to tell me to write though, & be silent of the Duchess—& when I was sure to be so delighted,—& *you knew it? I* think not indeed. And, to make the obedience possible, I go on fast to say that I heard from Mr. Horne a few days since & that *he* said—'your envelope reminds me of' .. *you*, he said .. & so, asked if you were in England still, & meant to write to you. . . . And when he was in Germany, I remember, .. writing just as your first letter came, .. that I mentioned it to him, & was a little frankly proud of it!—but since, your name has not occurred once—not once, certainly!—& it is strange. ... Only he *cant* have heard of your having been here, & it *must* have been a chance-remark—altogether!—taking an imaginary emphasis from my evil conscience perhaps.

. . .

RB, *Wednesday, 9 July 1845*

You are all that is good & kind: I am happy and thankful the beginning (and worst of it) is over and so well. The Park, & Mr. Kenyon's all in good time—and your sister was most prudent—and you mean to try again—God bless you!—all to be said or done—but, as I say it, no vain word.

No doubt it was a mere chance-thought, and *à-propos de bottes* of Horne—neither he or any other *can* know or even fancy how it is: indeed, tho' on other grounds I should be all so proud of being known for your friend by everybody, yet there's no denying the deep delight of playing the Eastern Jew's part here in this London—they go about, you know by travel-books, with the tokens of extreme destitution & misery, and steal by blind ways & bye-paths to some blank dreary house, one obscure door in it—which being well shut behind them, they grope on thro' a dark corridor or so, and then, a blaze follows the lifting a curtain or the like, for they are in a palace-hall with fountains and lights and marble and gold,— of which the envious are never to dream! And I, too, love to have few friends, and to live alone, and to see you from week to week—Do you not suppose I am grateful? . . .

To-morrow then: only—(and that is why I would write) do, do *know* me for what I am and treat me as I deserve in that *one* respect, and GO OUT, without a moment's thought or care, if to-morrow should suit you—leave word to that effect and I shall be glad as if I saw you or more—*reasoned* gladness, you know. Or you can write—tho' that is not necessary at all,—do think of all this!

I am yours ever, dear friend,
RB

[Meeting 8: Thursday, 10 July 3.00–4.30 p.m.]

EB, *Friday, 11 July 1845*

You understand that it was not a resolution passed in favour of formality, when I said what I did yesterday about not going out at the time you were coming—surely you do,—

whatever you might signify to a different effect,—If it were
necessary for me to go out every day, or most days even, it w^d
be otherwise—but as it is, I may certainly keep the day you
come, free from the fear of carriages, let the sun shine its best
or worst,—without doing despite to you or injury to me—
and that's all I meant to insist upon indeed & indeed. You
see, Jupiter tonans [thundering] was good enough to come
today on purpose to deliver me—one evil for another!—for I
confess with shame & contrition, that I never wait to enquire
whether it thunders to the left or the right, to be frightened
most ingloriously. Isn't it a disgrace to anyone with a
pretension to poetry? Dr. Chambers,° a part of whose office it
is, Papa says, 'to reconcile foolish women to their follies,' used
to take the side of my vanity—& discourse at length on the
passive obedience of some nervous systems to electrical influences—but perhaps my faintheartedness is besides traceable
to a half-reasonable terror of a great storm in Herefordshire,
.. where great storms most do congregate,—(such storms!)
round the Malvern hills, those mountains of England. We
lived four miles from their roots, thro' all my childhood &
early youth, in a Turkish house my father built himself,
crowded with minarets & domes, & crowned with metal
spires & crescents, to the provocation (as people used to
observe) of every lightning of heaven. Once a storm of storms
happened, & we all thought the house was struck—& a tree
was so really, within two hundred yards of the windows while
I looked out—the bark, rent from the top to the bottom ..
torn into long ribbons by the dreadful fiery hands, & dashed
out into the air, over the heads of other trees, or left twisted
in their branches—torn into shreds in a moment, as a flower
might be, by a child!—Did you ever see a tree after it has
been struck by lightning? The whole trunk of that tree was
bare & peeled—& up that new whiteness of it, ran the finger-
mark of the lightning in a bright beautiful rose-colour—(none
of your roses brighter or more beautiful!—) the fever-sign of
the certain death—Though the branches themselves were for
the most part untouched, & spread from the peeled trunk in
their full summer foliage,—the birds singing in them three
hours afterwards! And, in that same storm, two young women
belonging to a festive party were killed on the Malvern hills—

each, sealed to death in a moment with a sign on the chest which a common seal w^d cover—only the sign on them was not rose-coloured as on our tree .. but black as charred wood. So I get 'possessed' sometimes with the effects of these impressions—& so does one, at least, of my sisters, in a lower degree—and oh!—how amusing & instructive all this is to you! When my father came into the room today & found me hiding my eyes from the lightning, he was quite angry & called 'it disgraceful to anybody who had ever learnt the alphabet'—to which I answered humbly that 'I knew it was'—but if I had been impertinent, I MIGHT have added that wisdom does not come by the alphabet but in spite of it? Don't you think so in a measure? ... There's a profane question—& ungrateful too .. after the Duchess—I except the Duchess & her peers—& be sure she will be the world's Duchess & received as one of your most striking poems. Full of various power the poem is .. I cannot say how deeply it has impressed me—but though I want the conclusion, I don't *wish* for it; and in this, am reasonable for once!! You will not write & make yourself ill—will you? or read Sybil° at unlawful hours even? Are you better at all?—What a letter! & how very foolishly today I am

yours
EBB.

RB, *Sunday, 13 July 1845*

... your father must pardon me for holding most firmly with Dr Chambers—his theory is quite borne out by my own experience, for I have seen a man it were foolish to call a coward, a great fellow too, all but die away in a thunderstorm, though he had quite science enough to explain why there was really no immediate danger at all—whereupon his younger brother suggested that he should just go out and treat us to a repetition of Franklin's experiment with the cloud and the kite—a well-timed proposition which sent the Explainer down with a white face into the cellar. What a grand sight your tree was—*is*, for I see it—My father has a print of a tree so struck—torn to ribbons, as you describe—but the rose-mark is striking and new to me: we had a good storm on our last voyage, but I went to bed at the end, as I thought—and only found there had been lightning next day by the bare poles under which we were riding: but the finest mountain fit of the kind I ever saw has an unfortunately ludicrous association: it was at Possagno, among the Euganean Hills, and I was at a poor house in the town—an old woman was before a little picture of the Virgin, and at every fresh clap, she lighted, with the oddest sputtering muttering mouthful of prayer imaginable, an inch of guttery candle, which, the instant the last echo had rolled away, she as constantly blew out again for saving's sake—having, of course, to *light the smoke* of it, about an instant after that: the expenditure in wax at which the elements might be propitiated, you see, was a matter for curious calculation: I suppose I ought to have bought the whole taper for some four or five centesimi (100 of which make 8d English) and so kept the countryside safe for about a century of bad weather: Leigh Hunt tells you a story he had from Byron, of kindred philosophy in a Jew who was surprised by a thunderstorm while he was dining on bacon—he tried to eat between-whiles, but the flashes were as pertinacious as he, so at last he pushed his plate away, just remarking with a compassionate shrug, 'All this fuss about a piece of pork!' By the way, what a characteristic of an Italian *late* evening is Summer-lightning—it hangs in broad slow sheets, dropping from cloud to cloud, so long in dropping and dying off. The 'bora,' which you only get at Trieste, brings wonderful lightning—you are in glorious June-weather, fancy, of an evening, under green shock-headed acacias, so thick and green, with the cicalas stunning you above, and all about you men, women, rich & poor, sitting standing & coming & going—and thro' all the laughter & screaming & singing the loud clink of the spoons against the glasses, the way of calling for fresh 'sorbetti'—for all the world is at open-coffee-house at such an hour—when suddenly there is a stop in the sunshine, a blackness drops down, then a great white column of dust drives strait on like a wedge, and you see the acacia heads snap off, now one, then another—and all the people scream 'la bora, la bora'!—and you are caught up in their whirl and landed in some interior, the man with the guitar on one side of you, and the boy with a cageful of little brown owls for sale, on the other—meanwhile, the thunder claps, claps, with such a persistence, and the rain, for a finale, falls in a mass, as if you had knocked out the whole bottom of a huge tank at once—then there is a second stop—out comes the sun—somebody clinks at his glass, all the world bursts out laughing, and prepares to pour out again,—but *you*, the stranger, *do* make the best of your way out, with no preparation at all; whereupon you infallibly put your foot (and half your leg) into a river, really that, of rainwater—that's a *Bora* (and that comment of yours, a justifiable pun!) Such things you get in Italy, but better, better, the best of all things you do not (*I* do not) get there. And I shall see you on Wednesday, please remember, and bring you the rest of the poem—that you should like it, gratifies me more than I will try to say, but then, do not you be tempted by that pleasure of pleasing which I think is your besetting sin—may it not be?—and so cut me off from the other pleasure of being profited: as I told you, I like so much to fancy that you see, and will see, what I do as *I* see it, while it is doing, as nobody else in the world should, certainly,—even if they thought it worth while to want—but when I try and build a great building I shall want you to come with me and judge it and counsel me before the scaffolding is taken down, and while you have to make your way over hods of mortar & heaps of lime, and trembling tubs of size, and those thin broad whitewashing brushes I always had a desire to take up and bespatter with.

. . .

[Meeting 9: Wednesday, 16 July 3.00–4.15 p.m.]

EB, *Wednesday, 16–Thursday, 17 July 1845*

I suppose nobody is ever expected to acknowledge his or her 'besetting sin'—it w^d be unnatural—& therefore you will not be surprised to hear me deny the one imputed to me for

mine. I deny it quite & directly. And if my denial goes for
nothing, which is but reasonable, .. I might call in a great
cloud of witnesses,° .. a thundercloud, .. (talking of storms!)
& even seek no further than this table for a first witness,—
this letter,° I had yesterday, which calls me .. let me see how
many hard names .. 'unbending,' .. 'disdainful,' .. 'cold
hearted,' .. 'arrogant,' .. yes, 'arrogant, as women always are
when men grow humble' .. there's a charge against all possible
& probable petticoats beyond mine & through it! Not that
either they or mine deserve the charge—we do not,—to the
lowest hem of us!—for I don't pass to the other extreme,
mind, & adopt besetting sins 'over the way' & in antithesis.
It's an undeserved charge, & unprovoked!—& in fact, the
very flower of selflove selftormented into ill temper; & shall
remain unanswered, for *me*, ... & *should*, .. even if I could
write mortal epigrams, as your Lamia speaks them. Only it
serves to help my assertion that people in general who know
something of me, my dear friend, are not inclined to agree
with you in particular, about my having an 'over-pleasure in
pleasing,' for a besetting sin. . . . And then I have a pretension
to speak the truth like a Roman, even in matters of literature,
where Mr. Kenyon says falseness is a fashion—& really &
honestly I should not be afraid .. I sh^d have no reason to be
afraid, .. if all the notes & letters written by my hand for
years & years about presentation copies of poems & other
sorts of books, were brought together & 'conferred,' as they
say of manuscripts, before my face—I sh^d not shrink & be
ashamed. Not that I always tell the truth as I see it—*but* I
never do speak falsely with intention & consciousness,—
never—& I do not find that people of letters are sooner
offended than others are, by the truth told in gentleness;—I
do not remember to have offended anyone in this relation, &
by these means. Well!—but *from me to you*,—it is all different,
you know—you must know how different it is. I can tell you
truly what I think of this thing & of that thing in your
'Duchess'—but I must of a necessity hesitate & fall into
misgiving of the adequacy of my truth, so called. To judge at
all of a work of yours, I must *look up to it*,—& *far up*—because
whatever faculty *I* have is included in our faculty, & with a
great rim all round it besides! And thus, it is not at all from

an over-pleasure in pleasing *you*, nor at all from an inclination to depreciate myself, that I speak & feel as I do & must on some occasions—it is simply the consequence of a true comprehension of you & of me—& apart from it, I sh^d not be abler, I think, but less able, to assist you in anything. I do wish you w^d consider all this reasonably, & understand it as a third person would in a moment, & consent not to spoil the real pleasure I have & am about to have in your poetry, by nailing me up into a false position with your gold headed nails of chivalry, which wont hold to the wall through this summer. Now you will not answer this?—you will only understand it & me—& that I am not servile but sincere,— but earnest—but meaning what I say—& when I say I am afraid .. you will believe that I am afraid,—and when I say I have misgivings, .. you will believe that I have misgivings— you will *trust* me so far, & give me liberty to breathe & feel naturally .. according to my own nature. Probably or certainly rather, I have one advantage over you .. one, of which women are not fond of boasting—that of *being older by years*—for the Essay on Mind, which was the first poem published by me,— (& rather more printed than published after all) the work of my earliest youth, half childhood half womanhood, was published in 1826 I see—& if I told Mr. Kenyon not to let you see that book, it was not for the date, but because Coleridge's daughter° was right in calling it a mere 'girl's exercise',—because it is just *that* & no more, .. no expression whatever of my nature as it ever was .. pedantic, & in some things, pert, .. & such as altogether, & to do myself justice, (which I w^d fain do of course) I was not in my whole life. Bad books are never like their writers, you know—& those under-age books are generally bad. Also I have found it hard work to *get into expression*, though I began rhyming from my very infancy, much as you did, (& this, with no sympathy near to me—I have had to do without sympathy in the full sense—) & even in my Seraphim days,° my tongue clove to the roof of my mouth .. from leading so conventual recluse a life, perhaps—& all my better poems were written last year, the very best being to come, if there sh^d be any life or courage to come—: I scarcely know. Sometimes, .. it is the real truth, .. I have haste to be done with it all. It is the real truth; however to say so may be an ungrateful return for your kind & generous words .. which I DO feel gratefully, let me otherwise feel as I will, .. or must. But then you know you are liable to such prodigious mistakes about besetting sins & even besetting virtues—to such a set of small delusions, that are sure to break one by one, like other bubbles, as you draw in your breath, .. as I see by the light of my own star, my own particular star, the star I was born under, the star *Wormwood* .. on the opposite side of the heavens from the constellations of 'the Lyre & the Crown'.° In the meantime, it is difficult to thank you, or *not* to thank you, for all your kindnesses . . .

Do bring all the Hood poems° of your own—inclusive of the 'Tokay' . . . The Duchess is past speaking of here—but you will see how I am delighted. And we must make speed,— only taking care of your head .. for I heard to-day that Papa & my aunt are discussing the question of sending me off either to Alexandria or Malta for the winter. Oh—it is quite a passing talk & thought, I dare say!—and it w^d not *be* in any case, until September or October; tho' in every case, I suppose, *I* should not be much consulted .. & all cases and places w^d seem better to me (if I were) than Madeira which the physicians used to threaten me with long ago. So take care of your headache & let us have the 'Bells' rung out clear before the summer ends—& pray dont say again anything about clear consciences or unclear ones, in granting me the privilege of reading your manuscripts—which is all clear privilege to me, with pride & gladness waiting on it.

. . .

RB, *? Friday, 18 July 1845*°

I shall just say, at the beginning of a note as at the end, I am yours *ever*, and not till summer ends & my nails fall out, and my breath breaks bubbles,—ought you to write thus having restricted me as you once did, and do still? You tie me like a Shrove-Tuesday fowl to a stake and then pick the thickest cudgel out of your lot, and at my head it goes—I

wonder whether you remembered having predicted exactly
the same horror once before. 'I was to see you—and you were
to understand'—*Do* you? do you understand,—my own
friend—with that superiority in years, too! For I confess to
that—you need not throw that in my teeth .. as soon as I
read your 'Essay on Mind'—(which of course I managed to
do about 12 hours after Mr K.'s positive refusal to keep his
promise, and give me the book) from preface to the Vision of
Fame at the end, and reflected on my own doings about that
time,—1826,—I did indeed see, and wonder at, your advance
over me in years—what then? I have got nearer you considerably—(if only nearer—) since then,—and prove it by the
remarks I make at favorable times—such as this, for instance,
which occurs in a poem you are to see°—written some time
ago—which advises nobody who thinks nobly of the Soul, to
give, if he or she can help, such a good argument to the
materialist as the owning that any great choice of that Soul,
which it is born to make and which—(in its determining, as
it must, the whole future course and impulses of that soul)—
which must endure for ever, even tho' the object that induced
the choice should disappear)—owning, I say, that such a
choice may be scientifically determined and produced, at any
operator's pleasure, by a definite number of ingredients, so
much youth, so much beauty, so much talent &c &c with the
same certainty and precision that another kind of operator
will construct you an artificial volcano with so much steel
filings and flower of sulphur and what not: there is more in
the soul than rises to the surface and meets the eye; whatever
does *that*, is for this world's immediate uses; and were this
world *all*, *all* in us would be producible and available for use,
as it *is* with the body now—but with the soul, what is to be
developed *afterward* is the main thing, and instinctively asserts
its rights—so that when you hate (or love) you shall not be
so able to explain 'why' ('You' is the ordinary creature enough
of my poem—*he* might not be so able).

There, I will write no more. You will never drop *me* off the
golden hooks, I dare believe—and the rest is with God—
whose finger I see every minute of my life. Alexandria! Well,
and may I not as easily ask leave to come 'to-morrow at the
Muezzin' as next Wednesday at 3?

God bless you—do not be otherwise than kind to this letter which it costs me pains, great pains to avoid writing better, as truthfuller—this you get is not the first begun. Come, you shall not have the heart to blame me; for, see, I will send all my sins of commission with Hood—blame *them*, tell me about them, and meantime let me be, dear friend,

yours
RB

EB, *Monday, 21 July 1845*

But I never *did* strike you or touch you—& you are not in earnest in the complaint you make—& this is really all I am going to say today. What I said before was wrung from me by words on your part, which you know far too well how to speak so as to make them go deepest, & which sometimes it becomes impossible or overhard to bear without deprecation:—as when, for instance, you talk of being 'grateful' to *me!!*—Well! I will try that there shall be no more of it—no more provocation of generosities—& so, (this once) as you express it, I 'will not have the heart to blame' you . . .

. . . But I leave my sins & yours gladly, to get into the Hood poems which have delighted me so—& first to the St. Praxed's which is of course the finest & most powerful .. & indeed full of the power of life .. & of death. It has impressed me very much. Then the 'Angel & child,' with all its beauty & significance!—and the 'Garden Fancies' .. some of the stanzas about the name of the flower, with such exquisite music in them, & grace of every kind—& with that beautiful & musical use of the word 'meandering,' which I never remember having seen used in relation to *sound* before. It does to mate with your '*simmering* quiet' in Sordello, which brings the summer air into the room as sure as you read it.° Then I like your burial of the pedant *so* much!—you have quite the damp smell of funguses & the sense of creeping things through & through it. And the Laboratory is hideous as you meant to make it:—only I object a little to your tendency .. which is almost a habit .. & is very observable in this poem I think, ..

of making lines difficult for the reader to read .. see the opening lines of this poem.° Not that music is required everywhere, nor in *them* certainly, but that the uncertainty of rhythm throws the reader's mind off the *rail* .. & interrupts his progress with you & your influence with him. Where we have not direct pleasure from rhythm, & where no peculiar impression is to be produced by the changes in it, we sh^d be encouraged by the poet to *forget it altogether*; should we not? I am quite wrong perhaps—but you see how I do not conceal my wrongnesses where they mix themselves up with my sincere impressions. And how c^d it be that no one within my hearing ever spoke of these poems? Because it is true that I never saw one of them—never!—except the Tokay, which is inferior to all; & that I was quite unaware of your having printed so much with Hood—or at all, except this Tokay, & this Duchess! The world is very deaf & dumb, I think—but in the end, we need not be afraid of its not learning its lesson.
. . .

[Meeting 10: Thursday, 24 July 3.00–4.15 p.m.]

EB, *Friday, 25 July 1845*

Are you any better to-day? & will you say just the truth of it? & not attempt to do any of the writing which does harm— nor of the reading even, which may do harm—and something does harm to you, you see—& you told me not long ago that you knew how to avoid the harm .. now did you not? & what could it have been last week which you did not avoid & which made you so unwell? Beseech you not to think that I am going to aid & abet in this wronging of yourself, for I will not indeed—& I am only sorry to have given you my querulous queries° yesterday .. & to have omitted to say in relation to them, too, how they were to be accepted in any case as just passing thoughts of mine for *your* passing thoughts, .. some right, it may be .. some wrong, it must be .. & none, insisted on even by the thinker!—just impressions, & by no means pretending to be judgments—now WILL you understand?

Also, I intended (as a proof of my fallacy) to strike out one or two of my doubts before I gave the paper to you—so *whichever strikes you as the most foolish of them, of course must be what I meant to strike out*—(there's ingenuity for you!—) The poem did, for the rest, as will be suggested to you, give me the very greatest pleasure, & astonish me in two ways .. by the versification, mechanically considered,—& by the successful evolution of pure beauty from all that roughness & rudeness of the son of the boar-pinner—successfully evolved, without softening one hoarse accent of his voice.

. . .

RB, *Friday, 25 July 1845*

You would let me *now*, I dare say, call myself grateful to you—yet such is my jealousy in these matters,—so do I hate the material when it puts down, (or tries,) the immaterial in the offices of friendship,—that I could almost tell you I was *not* grateful, and try if that way I could make you see the substantiality of those other favours you refuse to recognize, and reality of the other gratitude you will not admit. But truth is truth, and you are all generosity, and will draw none but the fair inference, so I thank you as well as I can for this *also*—this last kindness. And you know its value, too—how if there were another *you* in the world, who had done all you have done and whom I merely admired for that,—if such an one had sent me such a criticism, so exactly what I want and can use and turn to good,—you know how I would have told you, my *you* I saw yesterday, all about it,—and been sure of your sympathy and gladness:—but the two in one!

For the criticism itself, it is all true, except the overrating— all the suggestions are to be adopted, the improvements accepted: I so thoroughly understand your spirit in this, that, just in this beginning, I should really like to have found some point in which I could coöperate with your intention, and help my work by disputing the effect of any alteration proposed, if it ought to be disputed—*that* would answer your purpose exactly as well as agreeing with you,—so that the benefit to me were apparent; but this time I cannot dispute one point—All is for best.

So much for this 'Duchess'—which I shall ever rejoice in—wherever was a bud, even, in that strip of May-bloom, a live musical bee hangs now—I shall let it lie, (my poem) till just before I print it; and then go over it, alter at the places, and do something for the places where I (really) wrote anyhow, almost, to get done. It is an odd fact, yet characteristic of my accomplishings one and all in this kind, that of *the poem*, the real conception of an evening (two years ago; fully) of *that*, not a line is written,—tho' perhaps, after all, what I am going to call the accessories in the story are real though indirect reflexes of the original idea, and so supersede properly enough the necessity of its personal appearance,—so to speak: but, as I conceived the poem, it consisted entirely of the Gipsy's description of the life the Lady was to lead with her future Gipsy lover—a *real* life, not an unreal one like that with the Duke—and as I meant to write it, all their wild adventures would have come out and the insignificance of the former vegetation have been deducible only—as the main subject has become now—of course it comes to the same thing, for one would never show half by half like a cut orange—

. . .

EB, *Saturday, 26–Sunday, 27 July 1845*

You say too much indeed in this letter which has crossed mine—& particularly as there is not a word in it of what I most wanted to know & want to know .. *how you* are .. for you must observe, if you please, that the very paper you pour such kindness on, was written after your own example & pattern, when, in the matter of my Prometheus, (such different wearying matter!) you took trouble for me & did me good. Judge from this, if even in inferior things, there can be gratitude from you to me!—or rather, do not judge—but listen when I say that I am delighted to have met your wishes in writing as I wrote; only that you are surely wrong in refusing to see a single wrongness in all that heap of weedy thoughts, & that when you look again, you must come to the admission of it. One of the thistles is the suggestion about the line

'Was it singing, was it saying,'

which you wrote so, & which I proposed to amend by an intermediate 'or'. Thinking of it at a distance, it grows clear to me that you were right, & that there should be and must be no 'or' to disturb the listening pause. Now *sh^d* there?° . . .

Sunday.

I wrote so much yesterday & then went out, not knowing very well how to speak or how to be silent (is it better today?) of some expressions of yours .. & of your interest in me— which are deeply affecting to my feelings—whatever else remains to be said of them. And you know that you make great mistakes . . . & may not be quite right besides as to my getting well '*if I please!*' .. which reminds me a little of what Papa says sometimes when he comes into this room unexpectedly & convicts me of having dry toast for dinner, & declares angrily that obstinacy & dry toast have brought me to my present condition, & that if I *pleased* to have porter & beefsteaks instead, I sh^d be as well as ever I was, in a month! .. But where is the need of talking of it? What I wished to say was this—that if I get better or worse .. as long as I live & to the last moment of life, I shall remember with an emotion which cannot change its character, all the generous interest & feeling you have spent on me—*wasted* on me I was going to write—but I would not provoke any answering—& in one obvious sense, it need not be so. I never shall forget these things, my dearest friend; nor remember them more coldly. God's goodness!—I believe in it, as in His sunshine here— which makes my head ache a little, while it comes in at the window, & makes most other people gayer—it does *me* good too in a different way. And so, may God bless you! & me in this .. just this, .. that I may never have the sense, .. intolerable in the remotest apprehension of it, .. of being, in any way, directly or indirectly, the means of ruffling your smooth path by so much as one of my flint-stones!

. . .

[Meeting 11: Wednesday, 30 July 3.00–3.45 p.m.]

EB, *Thursday, 31 July–Friday 1 August 1845*

. . . you must trust me,—& refrain as far as you can from accusing me of an over-love of Eleusinian mysteries when I ask you to say just as little about your visits here & of me as you find possible, .. *even to Mr. Kenyon*—.. as *to every other person whatever*. As you know .. & yet more than you know ... I am in a peculiar position—& it does not follow that you should be ashamed of my friendship or that I should not be proud of yours, if we avoid making it a subject of conversation in high places, or low places. . . .

And talking of Italy & the cardinals, and thinking of some cardinal points you are ignorant of, did you ever hear that I was one of

> 'those schismatiques
> of Amsterdam°

whom yr Dr. Donne w^d have put into the dykes?—unless he meant the Baptists, instead of the Independents, the holders of the Independent church principle. No—not '*schismatical*,' I hope—hating as I do from the roots of my heart, all that rending of the garment of Christ, which Christians are so apt to make the daily week-day work of this Christianity so called—& caring very little for most dogmas & doxies in themselves—too little, as people say to me sometimes, (when they send me 'New Testaments' to learn from, with very kind intentions—) & believing that there is only one church in heaven & earth, with one divine High Priest to it,—let exclusive religionists build what walls they please & bring out what chrisms—But I used to go with my father always, when I was able, to the nearest dissenting chapel of the congregationalists—from liking the simplicity of that praying & speaking without books—& a little too from disliking the theory of state churches. There is a narrowness among the dissenters which is wonderful,—an arid, grey Puritanism in the clefts of their souls: but it seems to me clear that they know what the 'liberty of Christ' *means*, far better than those do who call themselves 'churchmen'; & stand altogether as a body, on higher ground.

. . .

RB, *Sunday, 3 August 1845*

... For the other matter,—the talk of my visits,—it is
impossible that any hint of them can ooze out of the only
three persons in the world to whom I ever speak of them—
my father, mother and sister—to whom my appreciation of
your works is no novelty since some years, and whom I made
comprehend exactly your position and the necessity for the
absolute silence I enjoined respecting the permission to see
you: you may depend on them,—and Miss Mitford is in your
keeping, mind,—and dear Mr. Kenyon, if there should be
never so gentle a touch of 'garrulous God-innocence'° about
those kind lips of his. Come, let me snatch at *that* clue out of
the maze, and say how perfect, absolutely perfect, are those
three or four pages in the 'Vision' which present the Poets—
a line, a few words, and the man there,—one twang of the
bow and the arrowhead in the white—Shelley's 'white ideal
all statue-blind' is—perfect,—how can I coin words? And
dear deaf old Hesiod—and—all, all are perfect, perfect! But
'the Moon's regality will hear no praise'—well then, will she
hear blame? Can it be you, my own you past putting away,
you are a schismatic and frequenter of Independent Dissenting
Chapels? And you confess this to *me*—whose father and
mother went this morning to the very Independent Chapel
where they took me, all those years back, to be baptized—
and where they heard, this morning, a sermon preached by
the very minister who officiated on that other occasion! Now
will you be particularly encouraged by this successful instance
to bring forward any other point of disunion between us that
may occur to you? Please do not—for so sure as you begin
proving that there is a gulf fixed between us, so sure shall I
end proving that ... Anne Radcliffe° avert it! .. that you are
just my sister: not that I am much frightened, but there are
such surprizes in novels! ... for my Bells, Mr. Chorley tells
me there is no use in the world of printing them before
November at earliest—and by that time I shall get done with
these Romances and certainly one Tragedy (*that* could go to
press next week)—in proof of which I will bring you, if you
let me, a few more hundreds of lines next Wednesday: but,

'my poet,' if I would, as is true, sacrifice all my works to do your fingers, even, good—what would I not offer up to prevent you staying ... perhaps to correct my very verses .. perhaps read and answer my very letters .. staying the production of more Berthas and Caterinas and Geraldines,° more great and beautiful poems of which I shall be—how proud! ... for, observe, you have not done .. yes, the Prometheus, no doubt .. but with that exception *have* you written much lately, as much as last year when 'you wrote all your best things' you said, I think? Yet you are better now than then. Dearest friend, *I* intend to write more, and very likely be praised more, now I care less than ever for it, but still more do I look to have you ever before me, in your place, and with more poetry and more praise still, and my own heartfelt praise ever on the top, like a flower on the water. . . .

[Meeting 12: Wednesday, 6 August 3.00–4.30 p.m.]

EB, *Friday, 8 August 1845*

. . .

And I am to be made to work very hard,—am I?—But you should remember that if I did as much writing as last summer, I should not be able to do much else, .. I mean, to go out & walk about .. for really I think I *could* manage to read your poems & write as I am writing now, with ever so much head-work of my own going on at the same time. But the bodily exercise is different   & I do confess that the novelty of living more in the outer life for the last few months that I have done for years before, makes me idle & inclined to be idle—& everybody is idle sometimes—even *you* perhaps—are you not? For me, you know, I do carpet-work .. ask Mrs. Jameson—& I never pretend to be in a perpetual motion of mental industry. Still it may not be quite as bad as you think: I have done some work since Prometheus—only it is nothing worth speaking of & not a part of the romance-poem which is to be some day if I live for it .. lyrics for the most part, which lie written illegibly in pure Aegyptian—oh, there is time enough, & too much perhaps! & so let me be idle a little now, & enjoy your poems while I can. It is pure enjoyment & must be— but you do not know how much, or you would not talk as you do sometimes .. so wide of any possible application.

And do *not* talk again of what you would 'sacrifice' for ME. If you affect me by it, which is true, you cast me from you farther than ever in the next thought—*That* is true.

The poems .. yours .. which you left with me .. are full of various power & beauty & character, & you must let me have my own gladness from them in my own way.

Now I must end this letter. Did you go to Chelsea & hear the divine philosophy?

Tell me the truth always .. will you? I mean such truths as may be painful to me *though* truths ...

> May God bless you, ever dear friend.
>
> EBB

RB, *Friday, 8 August 1845*

. . .

I sent you the last of our poor roses this morning— considering that I fairly owed that kindness to them.

Yes, I went to Chelsea and found dear Carlyle alone—his wife is in the country where he will join her as soon as his book's last sheet returns corrected and fit for press—which will be at the month's end about—He was all kindness and talked like his own self while he made me tea—and, after- ward, brought chairs into the little—yard, rather than garden—and smoked his pipe with apparent relish; at night he would walk as far as Vauxhall Bridge on my way home.

If I used the word 'sacrifice,' you do well to object—I can imagine nothing ever to be done by me worthy such a name.

. . .

EB, *Monday, 11 August 1845*

. . .

I am very glad you went to Chelsea—& it seemed finer afterwards, on purpose to make room for the divine philosophy. Which reminds me (the going to Chelsea) that my brother Henry confessed to me yesterday, with shame & confusion of face, to having mistaken & taken your umbrella for another belonging to a cousin of ours then in the house. He saw you .. without conjecturing, just at the moment, who you were. Do *you* conjecture sometimes that I live all alone here like Mariana in the moated Grange?° It is not quite so—: but where there are many, as with us, every one is apt to follow his own devices—& my father is out all day & my brothers & sisters are in & out, & with too large a public of noisy friends for me to bear, .. & I see them only at certain hours, .. except, of course, my sisters. And then as you have 'a reputation' & are opined to talk generally in blank verse, it is not likely that there sh^d be much irreverent rushing into this room when you are known to be in it.

. . .

[Meeting 13: Tuesday, 12 August 3.00–4.30 p.m.]

RB, *Tuesday, 12 August 1845*

What can I say, or hope to say to you when I see what you do for me?°

—*This*—for myself, (nothing for *you!*)—*this*, that I think the great, great good I get by your kindness strikes me less than that kindness.

. . .

EB, *Wednesday, 13 August 1845*

. . .

But do not, I ask it of you, speak of my 'kindness' .. my kindness!—mine! It is 'wasteful & ridiculous excess' and misapplication to use such words of me.

. . .

RB, *Friday, 15 August 1845*

Do you know, dear friend, it is no good policy to stop up all the vents of my feeling, nor leave one for safety's sake, as you will do, let me caution you never so repeatedly; I know, quite well enough, that your 'kindness' is not *so* apparent, even, in this instance of correcting my verses, as in many other points—but on such points, you lift a finger to me and I am dumb. .. am I not to be allowed a word here neither?

—I remember,—in the first season of German Opera here,° when 'Fidelio's' effects were young—going up to the gallery in order to get the best of the last chorus,—get its oneness, which you do—and, while perched there an inch under the ceiling, I was amused with the enormous enthusiasm of an elderly German (we thought,—I and a cousin of mine)— whose whole body broke out in billows, heaved and swayed in the perfection of his delight, hands, head, feet, all tossing and striving to utter what possessed him: well—next week, we went again to the Opera, and again mounted at the proper time, but the crowd was greater, and our mild greatfaced white haired red cheeked German was not to be seen—not at first—for as the glory was at its full,—my cousin twisted me round and made me see an arm, only an arm, all the body of its owner being amalgamated with a dense crowd on each side, before, and—not behind because they, the crowd, occupied the last benches, over which we looked—and this arm waved and exulted as if 'for the dignity of the whole body,'—relieved it of its dangerous accumulation of repressed excitability: when the crowd broke up all the rest of the man disengaged itself by slow endeavours, and there stood our friend confessed—as we were sure!

—Now, you would have bade him keep his arm quiet? 'Lady Geraldine, you *would!*'° . . .

There lies Consuelo°—done with!

I shall tell you frankly that it strikes me as precisely what in conventional language with the customary silliness is styled a *woman's*-book, in its merits & defects,—and supremely timid in all the points where one wants and has a right to expect, some *fruit* of all the pretence and George Sand*ism*: there are occasions when one does say, in the phrase of her school, 'que la Femme parle'! . . .

The Accessories are not the Principal, the adjuncts—the essence, nor the ornamental incidents the book's self, so what matters it if the portraits are admirable—the descriptions eloquent, (eloquent, there it is—that is her characteristic,— what she *has* to speak, she *speaks out*, speaks volubly *forth*, too well, inasmuch as you say, advancing a step or two, 'And now speak as completely *here*'—and she says nothing)—but all *that*, another could do, as others have done—but 'la femme qui parle' [woman who speaks]—Ah, that, is this all? So I am not George Sand's—she teaches me nothing—I look to her for nothing—

I am ever yours, dearest friend. How I write to you—page on page! But Tuesday—who could wait till then! Shall I not hear from you?

God bless you ever
R.B.

EB, *Saturday, 16 August 1845*

. . . my dear friend, it was not the expression, but the thing expressed, I cried out against—the exaggeration in your mind. I am sorry when I write that what you do not like— but I have instincts & impulses too strong for me when you say things which put me into such a miserably false position in respect to you—as for instance, when in this very last letter (oh, I *must* tell you!) you talk of my 'correcting your

verses'!!!—My correcting your verses!!!—Now is *that* a thing
for you to say?—And do you really imagine that if I kept that
happily imagined phrase in my thoughts, I should be able to
tell you one word of my impressions from your poetry, ever,
ever again?—Do you not see at once what a disqualifying, &
paralysing phrase it must be, of simple necessity? . . .

As to 'Consuelo' I agree with nearly all that you say of it,—
though George Sand, we are to remember, is greater than
Consuelo & not to be depreciated according to the defects of
that book, nor classified as 'femme qui parle', .. she who is
man & woman together,—judging her by the standard of
even that book in the nobler portions of it. . . . Altogether, the
book is a sort of rambling Odyssey, a female Odyssey, if you
like, but full of beauty & nobleness, let the faults be where
they may. And then, I like those long, long books, one can
live away into .. leaving the world & above all oneself, quite
at the end of the avenue of palms—quite out of sight & out of
hearing!—Oh, I have felt something like *that* so often—so
often!—*you* never felt it, & never will, I hope—
 . . .

[Meeting 14: Friday, 22 August, 3.00–4.30 p.m.]

EB, *Wednesday, 20–Saturday, 23 August 1845*

 . . .

Friday.

I was writing you see before you came—& now I go on in
haste to speak 'off my mind' some things which are on it.
First .. of yourself,—how can it be that you are unwell again,
.. & that you should talk (now did you not?—did I not hear
you say so?) of being 'weary in your soul' .. YOU? What
should make *you*, dearest friend, weary in your soul; or out of
spirits in any way?—Do .. tell me .. I was going to write
without a pause—and almost I might, perhaps, .. even as one
of the two hundred of your friends, .. almost I might say out
that 'Do tell me.' Or is it (which I am inclined to think most
probable,—) that you are tired of a same life and want

change?—it may happen to anyone sometimes, & is independent of your will & choice, you know—& I know, & the whole world knows: & would it not therefore be wise of you, in that case, to fold your life new again & go abroad at once? What can make you weary in your soul, is a problem to me. You are the last from whom I should have expected such a word. And you did say so I *think*, I *think* that it was not a mistake of mine. And *you*, .. with a full liberty, & the world in your hand for every purpose & pleasure of it!—Or is it that, being unwell, your spirits are affected by *that*? But then you must be more unwell than you like to admit—. And I am teazing you with talking of it .. am I not?—and being disagreeable is only one third of the way towards being useful, it is good to remember in time.

And then the next thing to write off my mind is .. that you must not, you must not, make an unjust opinion out of what I said today. I have been uncomfortable since, lest you should—& perhaps it would have been better if I had not said it apart from all context in that way,—only that you could not long be a friend of mine without knowing & seeing what so lies on the surface. But then, .. as far as I am concerned, .. no one cares less for a 'will' than I do .. (& this though I never had one, .. in clear opposition to your theory which holds generally nevertheless) for a will in the common things of life. Every now & then there must of course be a crossing & vexation—but in one's mere pleasures & fantasies, one w^d rather be crossed & vexed a little than vex a person one loves .. & it is possible to get used to the harness & run easily in it at last—& there is a side-world to hide one's thoughts in, & 'carpet-work' to be immoral on in spite of Mrs. Jameson, .. & the word 'literature' has, with me, covered a good deal of liberty as you must see .. real liberty which is never enquired into—& it has happened throughout my life by an accident (as far as anything is accident) that my own sense of right & happiness on any important point of overt action, has never run contrariwise to the way of obedience required of me .. while in things not exactly *overt*, I & all of us are apt to act sometimes up to the limit of our means of acting, with shut doors & windows & no waiting for cognizance or permission. Ah—& that last is the worst of it all perhaps—! to be forced into concealments from the heart naturally nearest to us—& forced away from the natural source of counsel & strength!—and then, the disingenuousness—the cowardice—the 'vices of slaves'!—And everyone you see .. all my brothers, .. constrained *bodily* into submission .. apparent submission at least .. by that worst & most dishonoring of necessities, the necessity of *living*: everyone of them all, except myself, being dependent in money-matters on the inflexible will .. do you see? But what you do NOT see, what you *cannot* see, is the deep tender affection behind & below all those partriarchal ideas of governing grownup children 'in the way they *must* go!'—and there never was (under the strata) a truer affection in a father's heart .. no, nor a worthier heart in itself .. a heart loyaller & purer, & more compelling to gratitude & reverence, than his, as I see it!—The evil is in the system—& he simply takes it to be his duty to rule, & to make happy according to his own views of the propriety of happiness—he takes it to be his duty to rule like the Kings of Christendom, by divine right. But he loves us through & through it—& *I*, for one, love *him!*—& when, five years ago, I lost what I loved best in the world beyond comparison & rivalship ... far better than himself as he knew .. for everyone who knew *me* could not choose but know what was my first & chiefest affection .. when I lost *that*, .. I felt that he stood the nearest to me on the closed grave .. or by the unclosing sea .. I do not know which nor could ask. And I will tell you that not only he has been kind & patient & forebearing to me through the tedious trial of this illness (far more trying to standers by than you have an idea of perhaps) but that he was generous & forbearing in that hour of bitter trial, & never reproached me as he might have done & as my own soul has not spared .. never once said to me then or since, that if it had not been for *me*, the crown of his house w^d not have fallen. He *never did* .. & he might have said it, & more—& I could have answered nothing. Nothing, except that I had paid my own price .. & that the price I paid was greater than his loss .. his!! For see how it was—& how, 'not with my hand but heart' I was the cause or occasion of that misery—& though not with the intention of my heart but with its weakness, yet the *occasion*, any way!

They sent me down you know to Torquay—Dr. Chambers saying that I could not live a winter in London .. The worst ..—what people call the worst—was apprehended for me at that time. So I was sent down with my sister, to my aunt there—and he, my brother whom I loved so,° was sent too, to take us there & return. And when the time came for him to leave me, *I*, to whom he was the dearest of friends & brothers in one .. the only one of my family who ... Well, but I cannot write of these things; & it is enough to tell you that he was above us all, better than us all, & kindest & noblest & dearest to *me* beyond comparison, any comparison, as I said—& when the time came for him to leave me *I*, weakened by illness, could not master my spirits or drive back my tears—& my aunt kissed them away instead of reproving me as she should have done; & said that *she* would take care that I should not be grieved .. *she!* .. and so she sate down & wrote a letter to Papa to tell him that he would 'break my heart' if he persisted in calling away my brother—As if hearts were broken *so!* I have thought bitterly since that my heart did not break for a good deal more than *that!*—And Papa's answer was—burnt into me, as with fire, it is—that 'under such circumstances he did not refuse to suspend his purpose, but that he considered it to be *very wrong in me to exact such a thing*.' So there was no separation *then*: & month after month passed—& sometimes I was better & sometimes worse—& the medical men continued to say that they w^d not answer for my life .. they! .. if I were agitated—& so there was no more talk of a separation. And once *he* held my hand, .. how I remember! & said that he 'loved me better than them all & that he *would not* leave me .. till I was well,' he said!—how I remember *that!* And ten days from that day the boat had left the shore which never returned,—never—& he *had* left me!— gone! For three days we waited—& I hoped while I could— oh, that awful agony of three days! And the sun shone as it shines today, & there was no more wind than now; & the sea under the windows was like this paper for smoothness—& my sisters drew the curtains back that I might see for myself how smooth the sea was, & how it could hurt nobody—& other boats came back one by one.

Remember how you wrote in your Gismond°

'What says the body when they spring
Some monstrous torture-engine's whole
Strength on it? No more says the soul—!'

and you never wrote anything which *lived* with me more than
that. It is such a dreadful truth. But you knew it for truth, I
hope, by your genius, & not by such proof as mine—I, who
could not speak or shed a tear, but lay for weeks & months
half conscious half unconscious, with a wandering mind, &
too near to God under the crushing of His hand, to pray at
all. I expiated my weak tears before, by not being able to shed
then, one tear—and yet they were forbearing—& no voice
said 'You have done this'.

Do not notice what I have written to you my dearest friend.
I have never said so much to a living being—I never *could*
speak or write of it. I asked no question from the moment
when my last hope went: & since then, it has been impossible
for me to speak what was in me. I have borne to do it today
& to you, but perhaps if you were to write—so do not let this
be noticed between us again—*do not!*—And besides there is
no need—! I do not reproach myself with such acrid thoughts
as I had once—I *know* that I would have died ten times over
for *him*, & that therefore though it was wrong of me to be
weak, & I have suffered for it and shall learn by it I hope,—
remorse is not precisely the word for me—not at least in its full
sense. Still you will comprehend from what I have told you
how the spring of life must have seemed to break within me
then;—& how natural it has been for me to loathe the living
on—& to lose faith (even without the loathing) to lose faith
in myself .. which I have done on some points utterly. It is
not from the cause of illness—no. And you will comprehend
too that I have strong reasons for being grateful to the
forbearance. .. It would have been *cruel*, you think, to reproach
me. Perhaps so!—yet the kindness & patience of the desisting
from reproach, are positive things all the same.

Shall I be too late for the post, I wonder? Wilson° tells me
that you were followed up stairs yesterday (I write on
saturday this latter part) by somebody whom you probably
took for my father. Which is Wilson's idea—& I hope not
yours. No—it was neither father nor other relative of mine—
but an old friend in rather an ill temper.°

And so goodbye until tuesday. Perhaps I shall .. not .. hear from you tonight. Dont let the tragedy or aught else do you harm—will you?—& try not to be 'weary in your soul' any more—& forgive me this gloomy letter I half shrink from sending you, yet will send——

May God bless you.

EBB.

[Meeting 15: Tuesday, 26 August 3.00–4.10 p.m.]

RB, *Wednesday, 27 August 1845*

On the subject of your letter,—quite irrespective of the injunction in it,—I would not have dared speak; now, at least: But I may permit myself, perhaps, to say I am *most* grateful, *most grateful*, dearest friend, for this admission to participate, in my degree, in these feelings. There is a better thing than being happy in your happiness; I feel, now that you teach me, it is so. I will write no more now,—tho' that sentence of 'what you are *expecting*,—that I shall be tired of you &c,'—tho' I *could* blot that out of your mind for ever by a very few words *now*,—for you *would believe* me at this moment, close on the other subject:—but I will take no such advantage—I will wait.

I have many things (indifferent things, after those) to say; will you write, if but a few lines, to change the associations for that purpose? Then I will write too.—

May God bless you,—in what is past and to come! I pray that from my heart,

being yours

R B

EB, *Wednesday, 27 August 1845*

But your Saul° is unobjectionable as far as I can see, my dear friend. He was tormented by an evil spirit—but how, we are not told .. & the consolation is not obliged to be definite,

.. is it? A singer was sent for as a singer—& all that you are called upon to be true to, are the general characteristics of David the chosen, standing between his sheep & his dawning hereafter, between innocence & holiness, & with what you speak of as the 'gracious gold locks' besides the chrism of the prophet, on his own head—and surely you have been happy in the tone & spirit of these lyrics .. broken as you have left them. Where is the wrong in all this? For the right & beauty, they are more obvious—& I cannot tell you how the poem holds me & will not let me go until it blesses me .. & so, where are the 'sixty lines' thrown away? I do beseech you .. you who forget nothing, .. to remember them directly, & to go on with the rest .. *as* directly (be it understood) as is not injurious to your health. The whole conception of the poem, I like .. & the execution is exquisite up to this point—& the sight of Saul in the tent, just struck out of the dark by that sunbeam, 'a thing to see' .. not to say that afterwards when he is visibly 'caught in his pangs' like the king serpent, .. the sight is grander still. How could you doubt about this poem...

At the moment of writing which, I receive your note. Do *you* receive my assurances from the deepest of my heart that I never did otherwise than 'BELIEVE' *you* .. never did nor shall do .. & that you completely misinterpreted my words if you drew another meaning from them. Believe *me* in this—will you? I could not believe *you* any more for anything you could say, now or hereafter—and so do not avenge yourself on my unwary sentences by remembering them against me for evil. I did not mean to vex you .. still less to suspect you—indeed I did not!—

. . .

EB, *Friday, 29 August 1845*

I do not hear,—& come to you to ask the alms of just one line, having taken it into my head that something is the matter. It is not so much exactingness on my part, as that you spoke of meaning to write as soon as you received a note of mine .. which went to your five minutes afterwards .. which is three days ago, or will be when you read this. Are you not well—or what? Though I have tried & *wished* to remember having written in the last note something very or even a little offensive to you. I fail in it and go back to the worse fear . . . I took for granted yesterday that you had gone out as before— but tonight it is different—& so I come to ask you to be kind enough to write one word for me by some post tomorrow. Now remember .. I am not asking for a letter—but for a *word* .. or line strictly speaking—

Ever yours, dear friend,

EBB.

RB, *Saturday, 30 August 1845*

Can you understand me *so*, dearest friend, after all? Do you see me,—when I am away, or with you,—'taking offence' at words, 'being vexed' at words, or deeds of yours,—even if I could not immediately trace them to their source of entire, pure kindness—, as I have hitherto done in every smallest instance?

I believe in *you* absolutely, utterly. I believe that when you bade me, that time, be silent,—that such *was* your bidding, and I was silent—dare I say I think you did not know at that time the power I have over myself, that I could sit & speak & listen as I have done since—Let me say now—*this only once*— that I loved you from my soul, and gave you my life, so much of it as you would take,—and all that is *done*, not to be altered now: it was, in the nature of the proceeding, wholly indepen- dent of any return on your part: I will not think on extremes you might have resorted to:—as it is, the assurances of your friendship, the intimacy to which you admit me, *now*,—make the truest, deepest joy of my life—a joy I can never think fugitive while we are in life, because I KNOW, as to me, I *could* not willingly displease you,—while, as to you, your goodness and understanding will always see to the bottom of involun- tary or ignorant faults—always help me to correct them. I have done now: if I thought you were like other women I have known, I should say so much—but—(my first & last word—I *believe* in you!)—what you could and would give me, of your affection, you would give nobly and simply and *as* a giver—you would not need that I tell you—(*tell* you!)—what would be supreme happiness to me in the event—however distant—

I repeat .. I call on your justice to remember, on your intelligence to believe .. that this is merely a more precise stating the *first subject*; to put an end to any possible misunderstanding—to prevent your henceforth believing that because I *do not write*, from thinking too deeply of you, I am offended, vexed &c &c. I will never recur to this—nor shall you see the least difference in my manner next Monday: it is indeed, always before me .. how I know nothing of you and yours: but I think I ought to have spoken when I did—and to speak clearly .. or more clearly what I do—as it is my pride and duty to fall back, now, on the feeling with which I have been in the meantime—yours

God bless you—
R. B.

Let me write a few words to lead into Monday—and say, you have probably received my note. I am much better—with a little headache, which is all, and fast going this morning: of yours you say nothing—I trust you see your .. dare I say .. your *duty* in the Pisa affair,° as all else *must* see it—shall I hear on Monday? And my Saul that you are so lenient to!

Bless you ever—

EB, *Sunday, 31 August–Monday, 1 September 1845*°

I did not think you were angry—I never said so. But you might reasonably have been wounded a little, if you had suspected me of blaming you for any bearing of yours towards myself—& this was the amount of my fear, .. or rather hope .. since I conjectured most that you were not well. And after all you did think .. do think .. that in some way or for some moment I blamed you, disbelieved you, distrusted you—or

why this letter? How have I provoked this letter? Can I
forgive myself, for having even seemed to have provoked it?—
& will you believe me that if for the past's sake you sent it, it
was unnecessary, & if for the future's, irrelevant? Which I say
from no want of sensibility to the words of it—your words
always make themselves felt—but in fulness of purpose not to
suffer you to hold to words because they have been said, nor
to say them as if to be holden by them. Why if a thousand
more such words were said by you to me, how could they
operate upon the future or present, supposing me to choose to
keep the possible modification of your feelings, as a probability, in my sight & yours?—Can you help my sitting with the
doors all open if I think it right?—I do attest to you .. while I
trust you, as you must see, in word & act,—& while I am
confident that no human being ever stood higher or purer in
the eyes of another, than you do in mine, .. that you would
still stand high & remain unalterably my friend, if the
probability in question became a fact, as now at this moment.
And this I must say, since you have said other things: & this
alone, which *I* have said, concerns the future, I remind you
earnestly.

My dearest friend—you have followed the most generous
of impulses in your whole bearing to me—& I have recognized & called by its name, in my heart, each one of them.
Yet I cannot help adding that, of us two, yours has not been
quite the hardest part, .. I mean, to a generous nature like
your own, to which every sort of nobleness comes easily. Mine
has been more difficult—& I have sunk under it again &
again: & the sinking & the effort to recover the duty of a lost
position, may have given me an appearance of vacillation and
lightness, unworthy at least of *you*, & perhaps of both of us.
Notwithstanding which appearance, it was right & just (only
just) of you, to believe in me—in my truth—because I have
never failed to you in it, nor been capable of *such* failure:—the
thing I have said, I have meant .. always: & in things I have
not said, the silence has had a reason somewhere different
perhaps from where you looked for it. . . . You wrote once to
me .. oh, long before May & the day we met—that you 'had
been so happy, you should be now justified to yourself in
taking any step most hazardous to the happiness of your

life—'° but if you were justified, c^d *I* be therefore justified in abetting such a step,—the step of wasting, in a sense, your best feelings ... of emptying your water gourds into the sand?—What I thought then I think now—just what any third person knowing you, w^d think, I think & feel. I thought too, at first, that the feeling on your part was a mere generous impulse, likely to expend itself in a week perhaps—It affects me & has affected me, very deeply—more than I dare attempt to say .. that you sh^d persist so—& if sometimes I have felt, by a sort of instinct, that after all you w^d not go on to persist & that (being a man you know) you might mistake a little, unconsciously, the strength of your own feeling,—you ought not to be surprised,—when I felt it was more advantageous & happier for you that it *should* be so—*In any case*, I shall never regret my own share in the events of this summer, & your friendship will be dear to me to the last. You know I told you so—not long since. And as to what you say otherwise, you are right in thinking that I would not hold by unworthy motives in avoiding to speak what you had any claim to hear. But what could I speak that w^d not be unjust to you—? Your life! .. if you gave it to me & I put my whole heart into it; what should I put but anxiety, & more sadness than you were born to? What could I give you, which it would not be ungenerous to give? Therefore we must leave this subject—& I must trust you to leave it without one word more; (too many have been said already—but I could not let your letter pass quite silently .. as if I had nothing to do but to receive all as matter of course *so!*) while you may well trust *me* to remember to my life's end, as the grateful remember,— & to feel, as those do who have felt sorrow, (for where these pits are dug, the water will stand) the full price of your regard. May God bless you my dearest friend. I shall send this letter after I have seen you, & hope you may not have expected to hear sooner.

Ever yours
EBB—

[Meeting 16: Monday, 1 September 3.00–4.30 p.m.]

EB, *Thursday, 4 September 1845*

. . .

People complain of Dr. Chambers & call him rough & unfeeling—neither of which *I* ever found him for a moment,— & I like him for his truthfulness, which is the nature of the man, though it is essential to medical morality never to let a patient think himself mortal while it is possible to prevent it, & even Dr. Chambers may incline to this on occasion. Still he need not have said all the good he said to me on saturday— he *used* not to say any of it; & he must have thought some of it: &, any way, the Pisa-case is strengthened all round by his opinion & injunction, so that all my horror & terror at the thoughts of his visit, (& it's really true that I w^d rather *suffer* to a certain extent than be *cured* by many of those doctors!) had some compensation.

. . .

[Meeting 17: Monday, 8 September 3.00–4.30 p.m.]

EB, *Tuesday, 9 September 1845*

. . . thank your sister for me & from me for all her kindness about the flowers. Now you will not forget? you must not .. When I think of the repeated trouble she has taken week after week, & all for a stranger, I must think again that it has been very kind—& I take the liberty of saying so moreover .. *as I am not thanking you.* Also these flowers of yesterday which yesterday you disdained so, look full of summer & are full of fragrance, & when they seem to say that it is not September, I am willing to be lied to just *so.* For I wish it were not September. I wish it were July .. or November .. two months before or after: & that this journey were thrown behind or in front .. anywhere to be out of sight. You do not know the courage it requires to hold the intention of it fast through what I feel sometimes—if it (the courage) had been prophes- ied to me only a year ago, the prophet w^d have been laughed to scorn. Well!—but I want you to see George's letter, & how he and Mrs. Hedley, when she saw Papa's note of consent to me, gave unhesitating counsel. Burn it when you have read it. It is addressed to me .. which you will doubt from the address of it perhaps .. seeing that it goes βα .. ϱβαϱίζων.° We are famous in this house for what are called nic-names .. though a few of us have escaped rather by a caprice than a reason: and I am never called anything else (never at all) except by the nom de *paix* which you find written in the letter, .. proving as Mr. Kenyon says, that I am just 'half a Ba-by' .. no more nor less:—and in fact the name has that precise definition. Burn the note when you have read it.

. . .

[Meeting 18: Friday, 12 September 3.00–5.00 p.m.]

RB, *Saturday, 13 September 1845*

Now, dearest, I will try and write the little I shall be able, in reply to your letter of last week—and first of all I have to intreat you, now more than ever, to help me and understand from the few words the feelings behind them—(I should *speak* rather more easily, I think—but I dare not run the risk: and I know, after all, you will be just & kind where you can.) I have read your letter again & again: I will tell you—no, not *you*, but any imaginary other person, who should hear what I am going to avow; I would tell that person most sincerely there is not a particle of fatuity, shall I call it, in that avowal; cannot be, seeing that from the beginning and at this moment I never dreamed of winning your *love* .. I can hardly write this word, so incongruous & impossible does it seem,—such a change of our places does it imply—nor, next to that, tho' long after, *would* I, if I *could*, supplant one of any of the affections that I know to have taken root in you—*that* great & solemn one, for instance .. I feel that if I could get myself *remade*, as if turned to gold, I WOULD not even then desire to become more than the mere setting to *that* diamond you must always wear: the regard and esteem you now give me, in this letter, and which I press to my heart & bow my head upon, is all I can take & all too embarrassing, using *all* my gratitude: and yet, with that contented pride in being infinitely your debtor as it is, bound to you for ever as it is,—when I read your letter with all the determination to be just to us both; I dare not so far withstand the light I am master of, as to refuse seeing that whatever is recorded as an objection to your disposing of that life of mine I would give you—has reference to some supposed good in that life which your accepting it would destroy—(of which fancy I shall speak presently)—I say, wonder as I may at this, I cannot but find it there, surely there: I could no more 'bind *you* by words,' than you have bound me, as you say—but if I misunderstood you, one assurance to that effect will be but too intelligible to me— but, as it *is*, I have difficulty in imagining that while one of so many reasons, which I am not obliged to repeat to myself, but which any one easily conceives; while *any one* of those reasons would impose silence on me *for ever*—(for, as I observed, I love you as you now are, and *would* not remove one affection that is already part of you,)—*would* you, being able to speak *so*, only say that *you* desire not to put 'more sadness than I was born to,' into my life?— that you 'could give me only what it were ungenerous to give'?

Have I your meaning here? In so many words, is it on *my* account that you bid me 'leave the subject'? I think if it were so, I would for once call my advantages round me—I am not what your generous self-forgetting appreciation would some- times make me out—but it is not since yesterday, nor ten nor twenty years before, that I began to look into my own life, and study its end, and requirements, what would turn to its good or its loss—and I *know*, if one may know anything, that to make that life yours and increase it by the union with yours, would render me *supremely happy*, as I said, and say, and feel. My whole suit to you is, in that sense, *selfish*—not that I am ignorant that *your* nature would most surely attain happiness in being conscious that it made another happy— but *that best, best end of all*, would, like the rest, come from yourself, be a reflection of your own gift.

Dearest, I will end here—words, persuasions & arguments,—if they were at my service I would not use them—I believe in you, altogether have faith in you—in you I will not think of insulting by trying to reassure you on one point which certain phrases in your letter might at first glance seem to imply—you do not understand me to be living and labouring and writing (and *not* writing) in order to be successful in the world's sense? I even convinced the people *here* what was my true 'honorable position in society' &c. &c. . . .

'Tell me what I have a claim to hear': I can hear it, and be as grateful as I was before and am now—your friendship is my pride and happiness. If you told me your love was already bestowed elsewhere, and that it was in my power to serve you *there*, to serve you there would still be my pride and happiness. I look on, and on over the prospect of my love: it is all *on*wards,—and all possible forms of unkindness .. I quite laugh to think how they are *behind* .. cannot be encountered in the route we are traveling! I submit to you and will obey you implicitly .. obey what I am able to conceive of your least desire, much more of your expressed wish—But it was necessary to make this avowal, among other reasons, for one which the world would recognize too—My whole scheme of life, (with its wants, material wants at least, closely cut down,) was long ago calculated—and it supposed *you*, the finding such an one as you, utterly impossible—because in calculating one goes upon *chances*, not on providence—how could I expect you? So for my own future way in the world I have always refused to care—any one who can live a couple of years & more on bread and potatoes as I did once on a time, and who prefers a blouse and a blue shirt (such as I now write in) to all manner of dress and gentlemanly appointment, and who can, if necessary, groom a horse not so badly or at all events would rather do it all day long than succeed Mr Fitzroy Kelly° in the Solicitor Generalship, .. such an one need not very much concern himself beyond considering the lilies how they grow:° but now I see you near this life, all changes—and at a word, I will do all that ought to be done . . .

Take the sense of all this, I beseech you, dearest—all you shall say will be best—I am yours—

Yes—Yours ever—God bless you for all you have been, and are, and will certainly be to me, come what He shall please—!

RB.

EB, *Tuesday, 16 September 1845*

I scarcely know how to write what is to be written nor indeed why it is to be written & to what end. I have tried in vain—& you are waiting to hear from me. I am unhappy enough even where I am happy—but ungrateful nowhere—& I thank you from my heart—profoundly from the depths of my heart .. which is nearly all I can do.

One letter I began to write & asked in it how it could become me to speak at all if '*from the beginning & at this moment you never dreamed of*' .. & there, I stopped & tore the paper, .. because I felt that you were too loyal & generous, for me to bear to take a moment's advantage of the same, & bend down the very flowering branch of your generosity (as it might be) to thicken a little the fence of a woman's caution & reserve. You will not say that you have not acted as if you 'dreamed' .. & I will answer therefore to the general sense of your letter & former letters, & admit at once that I *did* state to you the difficulties most difficult to myself .. though not all .. & that if I had been worthier of you I should have been proportionably less in haste to 'bid you leave that subject'. I do not understand how you can seem at the same moment to have faith in my integrity & to have doubt whether all this time I may not have felt a preference for another .. which you are ready 'to serve,' you say. Which is generous in you—but in *me*, where were the integrity? Could you really hold me to be blameless? & do you think that true-hearted women act usually so? Can it be necessary for me to tell you that I could not have acted so, & did not? And shall I shrink from telling you besides .. you who have been generous to me & have a right to hear it .. & have spoken to me in the name of an affection & memory most precious & holy to me, in this same letter .. that, neither now nor formerly, has any man been to my feelings what you are .. & that if I were different in some respects & free in others by the providence of God, I would accept the great trust of your happiness, gladly, proudly, & gratefully; & give away my own life & soul to that end. I *would* do it .. *not, I do,* .. observe! it is a truth without a consequence,—only meaning that I am not all stone—only proving that I am not likely to consent to help you in wrong against yourself. You see in me what is not .. *that*, I know: & you overlook in me what is unsuitable to you .. *that* I know, & have sometimes told you. Still, because a strong feeling from some sources is self-vindicating & ennobling to the object of it, I will not say that, if it were proved to me that you felt this for me, I would persist in putting the sense of my own unworthiness between you & me—not being heroic you know, nor pretending to be so. But something worse than even a sense of unworthiness, GOD has put between us!—& judge yourself if to beat your thoughts against the immovable marble of it, can be anything but pain & vexation of spirit, waste & wear of spirit to you .. judge!—The present is here to be seen .. speaking for itself!—& the best future you can imagine for me, what a precarious thing it must be .. a thing for making burdens out of .. only not for your carrying; as I have vowed to my own soul. As dear Mr. Kenyon said to me today in his smiling kindness .. 'In ten years you may be strong perhaps'—or 'almost strong'! that being the encouragement of my best friends!—What would he say, do you think, if he could know or guess .. ! what *could* he say but that you were .. a poet!—& I .. still worse!—*Never* let him know or guess!—

And so if you are wise & would be happy (and you have excellent practical sense after all & should exercise it) you must leave me—these thoughts of me, I mean .. for if we might not be true friends for ever, I sh^d have less courage to say the other truth. But we may be friends always .. & cannot be so separated, that your happiness, in the knowledge of it, will not increase mine. And if you will be persuaded by me, as you say, you will be persuaded *thus* .. & consent to take a resolution & force your mind at once into another channel. Perhaps I might bring you reasons of the class which you tell me 'would silence you for ever'. I might certainly tell you that my own father if he knew that you had written to me *so*, & that I had answered you .. *so*, even .. would not forgive me at the end of ten years—& this, from none of the causes mentioned by me here & in no disrespect to your name & your position .. though he does not over value poetry even in his daughter, & is apt to take the world's measures of the means of life .. but for the singular reason that he never *does* tolerate in his family (sons or daughters) the development of one class of feelings. Such an objection I could not bring to you of my own will—it rang hollow in my ears—perhaps I thought even too little of it:—& I brought to you what I thought much of, & cannot cease to think much of equally. Worldly thoughts, these are not at all, nor have been: there need be no soiling of the heart with any such:—& I will say, in reply to some words of yours, that you cannot despise the gold & gauds of the world more than I do, & should do even if I found a use for them. And if I *wished* to be very poor, in the world's sense of poverty, I *could not*, with three or four hundred a year of which no living will can dispossess me. And is not the chief good of money the being free from the need of thinking of it? It seems so to me.

The obstacles then are of another character, & the stronger for being so. Believe that I am grateful to you—*how* grateful, cannot be shown in words nor even in tears .. grateful enough to be truthful in all ways. You know I might have hidden myself from you—but I would not: & by the truth told of myself, you may believe in the earnestness with which I tell the other truths—of you .. & of this subject. The subject will not bear consideration—it breaks in our hands. But that God is stronger than we, cannot be a bitter thought to you but a holy thought .. while He lets me, as much as I can be anyone's, be only yours

EBB.

RB, *Tuesday, 16 September 1845*

I do not know whether you imagine the precise effect of your letter on me—very likely you do, and write it just for that—for I conceive *all* from your goodness: but before I tell you what is that effect, let me say in as few words as possible what shall stop any fear,—tho' only for a moment and on the outset,—that you have been misunderstood,—that the goodness *outside*, and round and over all, hides all or any thing: I understand you to signify to me that you see, at this present, insurmountable obstacles to that .. can I speak it .. entire gift, which I shall own, was, while I dared ask it, above my hopes .. an. wishes, even, so it seems to me .. and yet could not but be asl ed, so plainly was it dictated to me, by something quite out of those hopes & wishes .. will it help me to say that once in this Aladdin-cavern I knew I ought to stop for no heaps of jewel-fruit on the trees from the very beginning, but go on to the lamp, *the* prize, the last and best of all? Well, I understand you to pronounce that at present you believe this gift impossible—and I acquiesce entirely—I submit wholly to you,— repose on you in all the faith of which I am capable: those obstacles are solely for *you* to see and to declare .. had *I* seen them, be sure I should never have mocked you or myself by affecting to pass them over .. what *were* obstacles, I mean: but you *do* see them, I must think,—and perhaps they strike me the more from my true, honest unfeigned inability to imagine what they are,—not that I shall endeavour: after what you *also* apprise me of, I know and am joyfully confident that if ever they cease to be what you now consider them, you who see now *for me*, whom I implicitly trust in to see for me,—you will *then*, too, see and remember me, and how I trust, and shall then be still trusting: and until you so see, and so inform me, I shall never utter a word—for that would involve the vilest of implications. I thank God—I *do* thank him, that in this whole matter I have been, to the utmost of my power, not unworthy of his introducing you to me, in this respect that, being no longer in the first freshness of life, and having for many years now made up my mind to the impossibility of loving any woman .. having wondered at this in the beginning,

and fought not a little against it, having acquiesced in it at
last, and accounted for it all to myself, and become, if
anything, rather proud of it than sorry .. I say, when real
love, making itself at once recognized as such, *did* reveal itself
to me at last, I *did* open my heart to it with a cry—nor care
for its overturning all my theory—nor mistrust its effect upon
a mind set in ultimate order, so I fancied, for the few years
more—nor apprehend in the least that the new element
would harm what was already organized without its help: nor
have I, either, been guilty of the more pardonable folly, of
treating the new feeling after the pedantic fashions and
instances of the world .. I have not spoken when *it* did not
speak, because 'one' might speak, or has spoken, or *should*
speak, and 'plead' and all that miserable work which, after
all, I may well continue proud that I am not called to
attempt: *here* for instance, and *now* .. 'one' should despair; but
'try again' first, and work blindly at removing those obstacles
(—if I saw them, I should be silent, and only speak when a
month hence, ten years hence, I could bid you look where
they *were*)—and 'one' would do all this, not for the *play-
acting's* sake, or to 'look the character' .. (*that* would be
something quite different from folly ..) but from a not
unreasonable anxiety lest by too sudden a silence, too complete an acceptance of your will; the earnestness and endur-
ance and unabatedness .. the *truth*, in fact, of what had already
been professed should get to be questioned—But I believe
that you believe me—and now that all is clear between us I
will say, what you will hear, without fearing for me or
yourself, that I am utterly contented .. ('grateful' I have done
with .. it must go—) I accept what you give me, what those
words deliver to me, as—not all I asked for .. as I said .. but
as more than I ever hoped for,—*all*, in the best sense, that I
desire. That phrase in my letter which you objected to,—and
the other—may stand, too—I never attempted to declare,
describe my feeling for you—one word of course stood for it
all .. but having to put down some one *point*, so to speak, of
it—you could not wonder if I took any extreme one *first* ..
never minding all the untold portion that *led up* to it, made it
possible and natural—it is true, 'I could not dream of *that*'—
that I was eager to get the horrible notion away from never

so flitting a visit to you, that you were thus and thus to me *on condition* of my proving just the same to you—just as if we had waited to acknowledge that the moon lighted us till we ascertained within these two or three hundred years that the earth happens to light the moon as well! But I felt that, and so said it:—now you have declared what I should never have presumed to hope—and I repeat to you that I, with all to be thankful for to God, am most of all thankful for this the last of his providences .. which is no doubt, the natural and inevitable feeling, could one always see clearly. Your regard for me is *all* success—let the rest come, or not come. . . .

One final word on the other matters—the 'worldly matters'—I shall own I alluded to them rather ostentatiously, because,—because *that would be* the *one* poor sacrifice I could make you—one I would cheerfully make,—but a sacrifice, and the only one; this careless 'sweet habitude of living'—this absolute independence of mine, which, if I had it not, my heart woud starve and die for, I feel—and which I have fought so many good battles to preserve,—for that has happened, too—this light rational life I lead, and know so well that I lead,—this I could give up for nothing less than—what you know—but I *would* give it up, not for you merely, but for those whose disappointment might re-act on you—and I should break no promise to myself—the money getting would not be for the sake of *it*; 'the labour not for that which is nought'—indeed the necessity of doing this, if at all, *now*, was one of the reasons which make me go on to that *last request of all* .. at once,—one must not be too old, they say, to begin their ways: but, in spite of all the babble, I feel sure that whenever I make up my mind to that, I can be rich enough and to spare—because along with what you have thought *genius* in me, is certainly talent, what the world recognizes as such . . .

So, now, dearest—let me once think of that, and of you as my own, my dearest—this once—dearest, I have done with words for the present: I will wait: God bless you and reward you—I kiss your hands *now*—this is my comfort, that if you accept my feeling as all but *un*expressed now,—more and more will become spoken—or understood, that is—we both live on—you will know better *what* it was, how much and manifold, what one little word had to give out.

God bless you—

Your
RB

. . .

EB, *Wednesday, 17 September 1845 (1)*

Wednesday Morning.

I write one word just to say that it is all over with Pisa,—which was a probable evil when I wrote last, & which I foresaw from the beginning—being a prophetess, you know. I cannot tell you now how it has all happened—*only do not blame me*, for I have kept my ground to the last, & only yield when Mr. Kenyon & all the world see there is no standing. I am ashamed almost of having put so much earnestness into a personal matter—I spoke face to face & quite firmly—so as to pass with my sisters for the 'bravest person in the house' without contestation.

Sometimes it seems to me as if it *could not* end so—I mean, that the responsibility of such a negative must be re-considered .. & you see how Mr. Kenyon writes to me. Still, as the matter lies, .. no Pisa!—And, as I said before, my prophetic instincts are not likely to fail, such as they have been from the beginning.

If you wish to come, it must not be until saturday at soonest. I have a headache & am weary at heart with all this vexation—& besides there is no haste now: & when you do come, IF *you do*, I will trust to you not to recur to one subject, which must lie where it fell .. must!

. . .

EB, *Wednesday, 17 September 1845 (2)*

Wednesday evening.

But one word before we leave the subject,—& then to leave it finally,—but I cannot let you go on to fancy a mystery anywhere, in obstacles or the rest. You deserve at least a full frankness,—& in my letter I meant to be fully frank. I even told you what was an absurdity, so absurd that I should far rather not have told you at all, only that I felt the need of telling you all: and no mystery is involved in that, except as an 'idiosyncrasy' is a mystery. But the 'insurmountable' difficulty is for you & everybody to see, .. & for me to feel, who have been a very byword among the talkers, for a confirmed invalid through months & years, & who, even if I were going to Pisa & had the best prospects possible to me, should yet remain liable to relapses & stand on precarious ground to the end of my life. Now that is no mystery for the trying of 'faith',—but a plain fact, which neither thinking nor speaking can make less a fact. But DON'T let us speak of it.

I must speak however (before the silence) of what you said and repeat in words for which I gratefully thank you—& which are *not* 'ostentatious' though unnecessary words—for, if I were in a position to accept sacrifices from you, I would not accept *such* a sacrifice .. amounting to a sacrifice of duty & dignity as well as of ease & satisfaction .. to an exchange of higher work for lower work .. & of the special work you are called to, for that which is work for anybody. I am not so ignorant of the right uses & destinies of what you have & are. . . .

And for all the rest I thank you—believe that I thank you .. & that the feeling is not so weak as the word. That *you* should care at all for *me* has been a matter of unaffected wonder to me from the first hour until now—& I cannot help the pain I feel sometimes, in thinking that it would have been better for you if you never had known me—May God turn back the evil of me!—Certainly I admit that I cannot expect you .. just at this moment .. to say more than you say, .. & I shall try to be at ease in the consideration that you are as accessible to the 'unicorn' now as you ever could be at any

former period of your life. And here I have done. I had done
living, I thought, when you came & sought me out!—and
why? & to what end? *That*, I cannot help thinking now.
Perhaps just that I may pray for you—which were a sufficient
end. If you come on saturday I trust to you to leave this
subject untouched, .. as it must be indeed henceforth.

I am yours
EBB.

No word more of Pisa—I shall not go, I think.

RB, *Wednesday, 17 September 1845*

Words!—it was written I should hate and never use them
to any purpose. I will not say one word here—very well
knowing neither word nor deed avails—from *me*.

My letter will have reassured you on the point you seem
undecided about—whether I would speak &c.

. . .

EB, *Thursday, 18 September 1845*

. . .

Papa has been walking to & fro in this room, looking
thoughtfully & talking leisurely—& every moment I have
expected I confess, some word (that did not come) about
Pisa. Mr. Kenyon thinks it cannot end so—& I do sometimes—& in the meantime I do confess to a little 'savageness'
also—at heart!—All I asked him to say the other day, was
that he was not displeased with me—& *he wouldn't*; & for me
to walk across his displeasure spread on the threshold of the
door, & moreover take a sister & brother with me, & do such
a think for the sake of going to Italy & securing a personal
advantage, were altogether impossible, obviously impossible!—So poor Papa is quite in disgrace with me just now—if
he would but care for *that!*——

. . .

RB, *Thursday, 18 September 1845*

But *you*, too, will surely want, if you think me a rational creature, *my* explanation—without which all that I have said & done would be pure madness, I think—it *is* just 'what I see' that I *do* see,—or rather it has proved, since I first visited you, that the reality was infinitely worse than I know it to be .. for at and after the writing of *that first letter*, on my first visit, I believed—thro' some silly or misapprehended talk, collected at second hand too—that your complaint was of quite another nature—a spinal injury irremediable in the nature of it:— had it been *so*—now speak for *me*, for what you hope I am, and say how *that* should affect or neutralize what you *were*, what I wished to associate with myself in you? But *as you now are*—! then if I had married you seven years ago, and this visitation came now first, I should be 'fulfilling a pious duty,' I suppose, in enduring what could not be amended—a pattern to good people in not running away .. for where were *now* the use and the good & the profit and—

I desire in this life, (with very little fluctuation for a man & too weak a one), to live and just write out certain things which are in me, and so save my soul. I would endeavour to do this if I were forced to 'live among lions' as you once said°—but I should best do this if I lived quietly with myself and with you—that you cannot dance like Cerito° does not materially disarrange this plan—nor that I might—(beside the perpetual incentive and sustainment and consolation) get, over and above the main reward, the incidental, particular and unexpected happiness of being allowed when not working to rather occupy myself with watching you, than with certain other pursuits I might be otherwise addicted to—*this*, also, does not constitute an obstacle, as I see obstacles—

But *you* see them—and I see *you*, and know my first duty and do it resolutely if not cheerfully.

As for referring again, till leave by word or letter—you will see.

And very likely, the tone of this letter even will be misunderstood—because I studiously cut out all vain words, protesting &c!—No—will it?

. . .

EB, *Friday, 19 September 1845*

It is not 'misunderstanding' you to know you to be the most generous & loyal of all in the world—you overwhelm me with your generosity—only while you see from above & I from below, we cannot see the same thing in the same light. Moreover, if we DID, I should be more beneath you in one sense, than I am. Do me the justice of remembering this whenever you recur in thought to the subject which ends here in the words of it.

. . .

[Meeting 19: Monday, 22 September 3.00–4.30 p.m.]

EB, *Thursday, 25 September 1845*

I have spoken again,—& the result is that we are in precisely the same position,—only with bitterer feelings on one side. If I go or stay they *must* be bitter: words have been said that I cannot easily forget, nor remember without pain— & yet I really do almost smile in the midst of it all, to think how I was treated this morning as an undutiful daughter because I tried to put on my gloves .. for there was no worse provocation. At least he complained of the undutifulness & rebellion (! ! !) of everyone in the house—& when I asked if he meant that reproach for ME, the answer was that he meant it for all of us, one with another. And I could not get an answer. He would not even grant me the consolation of thinking that I sacrificed what I supposed to be a good, to HIM. I told him that my prospects of health seemed to me to depend on taking this step, but that through my affection for him, I was ready to sacrifice those to his pleasure if he exacted it—only it was necessary to my self satisfaction in future years, to understand definitely that the sacrifice *was* exacted by him & *was* made to him, .. & not thrown away blindly & by a misapprehension. And he would not answer *that*. I might do my own way, he said—*he* would not speak—*he* would not say that he was not displeased with me, nor the contrary:—I had better do what I liked:—for his part, he washed his hands of me altogether—

And so I have been very wise—witness how my eyes are swelled with annotations & reflections on all this! The best of it is that now George himself admits I can do no more in the way of speaking, .. I have no spell for charming the dragons, .. & allows me to be passive & enjoins me to be tranquil, and not 'make up my mind' to any dreadful exertion for the future. Moreover he advises me to go on with the preparations for the voyage & promises to state the case himself at the last hour to the 'highest authority'; & judge finally whether it be possible for me to go with the necessary companionship. And it seems best to go to Malta on the 3rd of October—if at all .. from steam-packet reasons .. without excluding Pisa .. remember .. by any means.

Well!—& what do you think? Might it be desirable for me to give up the whole? Tell me. I feel aggrieved of course & wounded—& whether I go or stay that feeling must last—I cannot help it. But my spirits sink altogether at the thought of leaving England *so*—& then I doubt about Arabel & Stormie .. & it seems to me that I *ought not* to mix them up in a business of this kind where the advantage is merely personal to myself. On the other side, George holds that if I give up & stay even, there will be displeasure just the same, .. & that, when once gone, the irritation will exhaust & smooth itself away—which however does not touch my chief objection. Would it be better .. more *right* .. to give it up? Think for me. Even if I hold on to the last, at the last I shall be thrown off— *that* is my conviction. But .. shall I give up *at once?* Do think for me—

And I have thought that if you like to come on friday instead of saturday .. as there is the uncertainty about next week, .. it w^d divide the time more equally: but let it be as you like & according to circumstances as you see them. Perhaps you have decided to go at once with your friends— who knows? I wish I could know that you were better to-day—May God bless you.

Ever yours,
E. B. B.

RB, *Thursday, 25 September 1845*

You have said to me more than once that you wished I might never know certain feelings *you* had been forced to endure: I suppose all of us have the proper place where a blow should fall to be felt most—and I truly wish *you* may never feel what I have to bear in looking on, quite powerless, and silent, while you are subjected to this treatment, which I refuse to characterize—so blind is it *for* blindness. I think I ought to understand what a father may exact—and a child should comply with—and I respect the most ambiguous of love's caprices if they give never so slight a clue to their all-justifying source: did I, when you signified to me the probable objections .. you remember what .. to myself, my own happiness,—did I once allude to .. much less argue against, or refuse to acknowledge those objections? For I wholly sympathize, however it go against me, with the highest, wariest, pride & love for you, and the proper jealousy and vigilance they entail—but now, and here, the jewel is not being over guarded, but ruined, cast away,—and whoever is privileged to interfere should do so in the possessor's own interest—all common sense interferes—all rationality against absolute no-reason at all .. and you ask whether you ought to obey this no-reason?—I will tell you: all passive obedience and implicit submission of will and intellect is by far too easy, if well considered, to be the course prescribed by God to Man in this life of probation—for they *evade* probation altogether, tho' foolish people think otherwise: chop off your legs, you will never go astray,—stifle your reason altogether and you will find it is difficult to reason ill: 'it is hard to make these sacrifices'! Not so hard as to lose the reward or incur the penalty of an Eternity to come; 'hard to effect them, then, and go through with them'—*not* hard, when the leg is to be *cut off*—that it is rather harder to keep it quiet on a stool, I know very well—the partial indulgence, the proper exercise of one's faculties, there is the difficulty and problem for solution, set by that Providence which might have made the laws of Religion as indubitable as those of vitality, and revealed the article of belief as certainly as that condition, for instance, by

which we breathe so many times in a minute to support life:
but there is no reward proposed for the feat of breathing, and
a great one for that of believing—consequently there must go
a great deal more of voluntary effort to this latter than is
implied in the getting absolutely rid of it at once, by adopting
the direction of an infallible church, or private judgment of
another—for all our life is some form of religion, and all our
action some belief, and there is but one law, however modified, for the greater and the less—In your case I do think you
are called upon to do your duty to yourself,—that is, to God
in the end: your own reason should examine the whole matter
in dispute by every light which can be put in requisition; and
every interest that appears to be affected by your conduct
should have its utmost claims considered—your father's in
the first place; and that interest, not in the miserable limits of
a few days' pique or whim in which it would seem to express
itself,—but in its whole extent .. the *hereafter* which all
momentary passion prevents him seeing .. indeed, the *present*
on either side which everyone else must see—and this examination made, with whatever earnestness you will, I do think
and am sure that on its conclusion you should *act*, in
confidence that a duty has been performed .. *difficult*, or how
were it a duty? Will it *not* be infinitely harder to act so than to
blindly adopt his' pleasure, and die under it? Who can *not* do
that?

I fling these hasty rough words over the paper, fast as they
will fall—knowing to whom I cast them, and that any sense
they may contain or point to, will be caught and understood
and presented in a better light: the hard thing .. this is all I
want to say .. is to act on one's own best conviction—not to
abjure it and accept another's will, and say '*there* is my plain
duty'—easy it is, whether plain or no!

How 'all changes!' When I first knew you,—you know
what followed. I supposed you to labour under an incurable
complaint—and, of course, to be completely dependent on
your father for its commonest alleviations; the moment after
that inconsiderate letter, I reproached myself bitterly with the
selfishness apparently involved in any proposition I might
then have made—for tho' I have never been at all frightened

of the world, nor mistrustful of my power to deal with it, and get my purpose out of it if once I thought it worth while, yet I could not but feel the consideration, of *what* failure would *now* be, paralyse all effort even in fancy: when you told me lately that 'you could never be poor'—all my solicitude was at an end—I had but myself to care about, and I told you, what I believed and believe, that I can at any time amply provide for that, and that I could cheerfully & confidently undertake the removing *that* obstacle. Now again the circumstances shift—and you are in what I should wonder at as the veriest slavery—and I who *could* free you from it, I am here scarcely daring to write .. tho' I know you must feel for me and forgive what forces itself from me .. what retires so mutely into my heart at your least word .. what *shall not* be again written or spoken, if you so will .. that I should be made happy beyond all hope of expression by—Now while I *dream*, let me once dream! I would marry you now and thus—I would come when you let me, and go when you bade me—I would be no more than one of your brothers—'*no more*'—that is, instead of getting to-morrow for Saturday, I should get Saturday as well—two hours for one—when your head ached I should be *here*. I deliberately choose the realization of that dream (—of sitting simply by you for an hour every day) rather than of any other, excluding you, I am able to form for this world, or any world I know—And it will continue but a dream.

God bless my dearest EBB—
RB.

You understand that I see you to-morrow, Friday, as you propose.

I am better—thank you—and will go out to-day.

You know what I am, what I would speak, and all I would do.

[Meeting 20: Friday, 26 September 3.00–4.30 p.m.]

EB, *Friday, 26 September 1845*

Friday evening.

I had your letter late last night, everyone almost, being out of the house by an accident, so that it was left in the letterbox, and if I had wished to answer it before I saw you, it had scarcely been possible.

But it will be the same thing—for you know as well as if you saw my answer, what it must be, what it cannot choose but be, on pain of sinking me so infinitely below not merely your level but my own, that the depth cannot bear a glance down. Yet, though I am not made of such clay as to admit of my taking a base advantage of certain noble extravagances, (& that I am not I thank God for your sake) I will say, I must say, that your words in this letter have done me good & made me happy, .. that I thank & bless you for them, .. & that to receive such a proof of attachment from YOU, not only overpowers every present evil, but seems to me a full and abundant amends for the merely personal sufferings of my whole life. When I had read that letter last night I *did* think so. I looked round & round for the small bitternesses which for several days had been bitter to me—& I could not find one of them. The tear-marks went away in the moisture of new, happy tears. Why how else could I have felt? how else do you think I could?—How would any woman have felt .. who could feel at all .. hearing such words said (though 'in a dream' indeed) by such a speaker?—

And now listen to me in turn. You have touched me more profoundly than I thought even *you* could have touched me—my heart was full when you came here today. Henceforward I am yours for everything but to do you harm—and I am yours too much, in my heart, ever to consent to do you harm in that way—. If I could consent to do it, not only should I be less loyal .. but in one sense, less yours. I say this to you without drawback & reserve, because it is all I am able to say, & perhaps all I *shall* be able to say. However this may be, a promise goes to you in it that none except God & your will, shall interpose between you & me, .. I mean, that if He should free me within a moderate time from the trailing chain of this weakness, I will then be to you whatever at that hour you shall choose .. whether friend or more than friend .. a friend to the last in any case. So it rests with God & with you. Only in the meanwhile you are most absolutely free .. 'unentangled' (as they call it) by the breadth of a thread—& if I did not know that you considered yourself so, I would not see you any more, let the effort cost me what it might. You may force me to *feel:* .. but you cannot force me to *think* contrary to my first thought .. that it were better for you to forget me at once in one relation. And if better for *you*, can it be bad for *me?*—which flings me down on the stone-pavement of the logicians.

And now if I ask a boon of you,° will you forget afterwards that it ever was asked?—I have hesitated a great deal; but my face is down on the stone-pavement—no—I will not ask today—It shall be for another day—& may God bless you on this & on those that come after, my dearest friend.

RB, *Saturday, 27 September 1845*

Think for me, speak for me, my dearest, *my own!* You that are all great-heartedness and generosity, do that one more generous thing!

God bless you for
RB

What can it be you ask of me?—'a boon'—once my answer to *that* had been the plain one—but now .. when I have better experience of—

No, now I have BEST experience of how you understand my interests; that at last we *both* know what is my true good— so ask, ask! *My own, now!* For there it is!—oh, do not fear I am *'entangled'*—my crown is loose on my head, not nailed there—my pearl lies in my hand—I may return it to the sea, if I will!

What is it you ask of me, this first asking?

EB, *Monday, 29 September 1845*

Then *first* .. first,—I ask you not to misunderstand. Because we do not .. no, we do not .. agree (but disagree) as to 'what is your true good' .. but disagree, & as widely as ever indeed.

The other asking shall come in its season .. some day before I go if I go. It only relates to a restitution—and you cannot guess it if you try .. so dont try!—and perhaps you cant grant it if you try—and I cannot guess. . . .

DON'T think too hardly of poor Papa. You have his wrong side .. his side of peculiar wrongness .. to you just now. When you have walked round him you will have other thoughts of him.

. . .

[Meeting 21: Tuesday, 30 September 3.00–4.30 p.m.]
Meeting 22: Friday, 3 October 3.00–4.30 p.m.]

EB, *Saturday, 4 October 1845*

Tuesday is given up in full council. The thing is beyond doubting of as George says & as you thought yesterday. And then George has it in his head to beguile the Duke of Palmella° out of a smaller cabin, so that I might sail from the Thames on the twentieth—and whether he succeeds or not, I humbly confess that one of the chief advantages of the new plan if not the very chief (as *I* see it) is just in the *delay*.

Your spring-song° is full of beauty as you know very well— & 'that's the wise thrush,' so characteristic of you (& of the thrush too) . . . And now when you come to print these fragments, would it not be well if you were to stoop to the vulgarism of prefixing some word of introduction, as other people do, you know, .. a title .. a name? You perplex your readers often by casting yourself on their intelligence in these things—and although it is true that readers in general are stupid & cant understand, it is still more true that they are lazy & wont understand .. & they dont catch your point of sight at first unless you think it worth while to push them by the shoulders & force them into the right place. Now these fragments .. you mean to print them with a line between .. & not one word at the top of it .. now don't you?—And then people will read

'Oh, to be in England'

& say to themselves .. 'Why who is this? .. who's out of England?' Which is an extreme case of course,—but you will see what I mean .. & often I have observed how some of the very most beautiful of your lyrics have suffered just from your disdain of the usual tactics of writers in this one respect.

. . .

EB, *Tuesday, 7 October 1845*

. . .

Be sure that I shall be 'bold' when the time for going comes—& both bold & capable of the effort. I am desired to keep to the respirator & the cabin for a day or two, while the cold can reach us, .. & midway in the bay of Biscay some change of climate may be felt, they say. There is no sort of danger for me; except that I shall *stay in England*. And why is it that I feel tonight more than ever almost, as if I should stay in England? Who can tell? *I* can tell one thing. IF I stay, it will not be from a failure in my resolution—*that will* not be— *shall* not be. Yes—& Mr. Kenyon & I agreed the other day that there was something of the tigress-nature very distinctly cognizable under what he is pleased to call my 'Ba-lambishness.'

. . .

[Meeting 23: Thursday, 9 October 3.00–4.30 p.m.]

EB, *Friday, 10–Saturday, 11 October 1845*

Dear Mr. Kenyon has been here again & talking so (in his kindness too) about the probabilities as to Pisa being against me .. about all depending 'on one throw' & the 'dice being loaded' &c. .. that I looked at him aghast as if he looked at the future through the folded curtain & was licensed to speak oracles:—& ever since I have been out of spirits . . .

Well—George will probably speak before *he* leaves town, which will be on monday!—and now that the hour approaches, I do feel as if the house stood upon gunpowder, & as if I held Guy Fawkes's lantern in my right hand. And no! I shall not go. The obstacles will not be those of Mr. Kenyon's finding—and what their precise character will be I do not see distinctly. Only that they will be sufficient, & thrown by one hand just where the wheel sh^d turn, .. *that*, I see—& you will, in a few days. . . .

To show the significance of the omission of those evening or rather night visits of Papa's .. for they came sometimes at eleven, and sometimes at twelve, .. I will tell you that he used to sit & talk in them, & then *always* kneel & pray with me & for me—which I used of course to feel as a proof of very kind & affectionate sympathy on his part, & which has proportionably pained me in the withdrawing. They were no ordinary visits, you observe, .. & he could not well throw me further from him than by ceasing to pay them—the thing is quite expressively significant. Not that I pretend to complain, nor to have reason to complain. One should not be grateful for kindness, only while it lasts: *that* would be a short-breathed gratitude. I just tell you the fact, .. proving that it cannot be accidental.
. . .

RB, *Sunday 12 October 1845*

. . .
If after all you do *not* go to Pisa,—why, we must be cheerful and wise, and take courage and hope: I cannot but see with

your eyes and from your place, you know,—and will let this
all be one surprizing and deplorable mistake of mere love and
care .. but no such another mistake ought to be suffered, if
you escape the effects of this—I will not cease to believe in a
better event, till the very last, however, and it is a deep
satisfaction that all has been made plain and straight up to
this strange and sad interposition like a bar—you have done
your part, at least—with all that forethought and counsel from
friends and adequate judges of the case—so, if the bar *will*
not move, you will consider,—will you not, dearest?—where
one may best encamp in the unforbidden country and wait
the spring and fine weather—would it be advisable to go
where Mr Kenyon suggested? or elsewhere—Oh, these vain
wishes .. the will here, and no means!

. . .

EB, *Saturday, 11–Monday, 13 October 1845*

[Monday]

. . . Do not be angry with me—do not think it my fault ..
but I *do not go to Italy* .. it has ended as I feared. What passed
between George & Papa there is no need of telling: only the
latter said that I 'might go if I pleased, but that going it
would be under his heaviest displeasure.' George, in great
indignation, pressed the question fully ... but all was vain ..
& I am left in this position .. to go, if I please, with his
displeasure over me, (which after what you have said & after
what Mr. Kenyon has said, & after what my own conscience
& deepest moral convictions say aloud, I would unhesitat
ingly do at this hour!) and necessarily run the risk of exposing
my sister and brother to that same displeasure .. from which
risk I shrink & fall back & feel that to incur it, is impossible.
Dear Mr. Kenyon has been here & we have been talking—&
he sees what I see .. that I am justified in going myself, but
not in bringing others into difficulty. The very kindness &
goodness with which they desire me (both my sisters) 'not to
think of them,' naturally makes me think more of them—.
And so, tell me that I am not wrong in taking up my chain

again & acquiescing in this hard necessity. The bitterest 'fact' of all is, that I had believed Papa to have loved me more than he obviously does—: but I never regret knowledge .. I mean I never would *un*know anything .. even were it the taste of the apples by the Dead sea—& this must be accepted like the rest.

. . .

RB, *Tuesday, 14 October 1845*

Be sure, my own, dearest love, that this is for the best,— will be seen for the best in the end. It is hard to bear now— but *you* have to bear it; any other person could not,—and you will, I know, knowing you—*will* be well this one winter if you can, and then—& since I am *not* selfish in this love to you, my own conscience tells me,—I desire, more earnestly than I ever knew what desiring was, to be yours and with you and, as far as may be in this life & world, YOU—and no hindrance to that, but one, gives me a moment's care or fear,—but that one is just your little hand, as I could fancy it raised in any least interest of yours—and before that, I am, and would ever be, still silent. But now—what is to make you raise that hand? I will not speak *now*,—not seem to take advantage of your present feelings,—we will be rational, and all-consider- ing, and weighing consequences, and foreseeing them—but first I will prove .. if *that* has to be done, ⟨why⟩ but I begin speaking—and I should not, I know.

. . .

EB, *Wednesday, 15 October 1845*

. . .

What am I to say but this .. that I know what you are .. & that I know also what you are to *me*,—& that I should accept that knowledge as more than sufficient recompense for worse vexations than these late ones. Therefore let no more be said of them: & no more *need* be said, .. even if they were not likely to prove their own end good, as I believe with you. You may be quite sure that I shall be well this winter, if in any way it should be possible,—& that I *will not* be beaten down, if the will can do anything. I admire how .. if all had happened so but a year ago, .. (yet it could not have happened quite *so!*), I should certainly have been beaten down—& how it is different now, .. & how it is only gratitude to you, to *say* that it is different now—My cage is not worse but better since you brought the green groundsel to it—& to dash oneself against the wires of it will not open the door .. We shall see .. & God will oversee.

. . .

[Meeting 24: Thursday, 16 October 3.00–4.30 p.m.]

EB, *Friday, 17 October 1845*

. . .

Your beautiful flowers!—none the less beautiful for waiting for water yesterday. As fresh as ever, they were; & while I was putting them into the water, I thought that your visit went on all the time. Other thoughts too I had, which made me look down blindly, quite blindly, on the little blue flowers, .. while I thought what I could not have said an hour before without breaking into tears which would have run faster then. To say now that I never can forget,—that I feel myself bound to you as one human being cannot be more bound to another .. & that you are more to me at this moment than all the rest of the world,—is only to say in new words that it would be a wrong against *myself*, to seem to risk your happiness & abuse your generosity. For *me* .. though you threw out words yesterday about the testimony of a 'third person,' .. it would be monstrous to assume it to be necessary to vindicate my trust of you—*I trust you implicitly*—& am not too proud to owe all things to you. But now let us wait & see what this winter does or undoes—while God does His part for good, as we know—I will never fail to you from any human influence whatever—*that*, I have promised—but you must let it be different from the other sort of promise which it would be a wrong to make. My God bless you—you, whose fault it is, to be too generous. You *are* not like other men, as I could see from the beginning—no— ...

And if you like to come on monday rather than tuesday, I do not see why there should be a 'no' to that. Only we must be wise in the general practice, & abstain from too frequent meetings, for fear of difficulties—. I am Casandra you know, & smell the slaughter in the bathroom.° It would make no difference in fact,—but in comfort, much.

Ever your own—

[Meeting 25: Tuesday, 21 October 3.00–4.30 p.m.]

EB, *Tuesday, 21–Wednesday, 22 October, 1845*

Even at the risk of teazing you a little I must say a few words, that there may be no misunderstanding between us—& this, before I sleep tonight. Today & before today you surprised me by your manner of receiving my remark about your visits, for I believed I had sufficiently made clear to you long ago how certain questions were ordered in this house & how no exception was to be expected for my sake or even for yours. Surely I told you this quite plainly long ago. I only meant to say in my last letter, in the same track .. (fearing in the case of your wishing to come oftener that you might think it unkind in me not to seem to wish the same) .. that if you came too often & it was *observed*, difficulties & vexations w^d follow as a matter of course, & it would be wise therefore to run no risk. That was the head & front of what I meant to say. The weekly one visit is a thing established & may go on as long as you please—& there is no objection to your coming twice a week *now & then* .. if now & then merely .. if there is no habit .. do you understand. I may be prudent in an extreme perhaps—& certainly everybody in the house is not equally prudent!—but I did shrink from running any risk with that calm & comfort of the winter as it seemed to come on. . . . Still I do perfectly see that whether new or old, what it INVOLVES may well be unpleasant to you—& that (however old) it may be apt to recur to your mind with a new increasing unpleasantness. We have both been carried too far perhaps, by late events & impulses—but it is never too late to come back to a right place, & I for my part come back to mine, & entreat you my dearest friend, first, *not to answer this*, & next, to weigh & consider thoroughly 'that particular contingency' which (I tell you plainly, I who know) the tongue of men & of angels would not modify so as to render less full of vexations to you. Let Pisa prove the excellent hardness of some marbles!—Judge. From motives of selfrespect, you may well walk an opposite way .. *you!* .. When I told you once .. or twice .. that 'no human influence should' &c &c, .. I spoke for myself, quite overlooking you—& now that I turn & see you, I am surprised that I did not see you *before* .. *there*. I ask you therefore to consider 'that contingency' well—not forgetting the other obvious evils, which the late decision about Pisa has aggravated beyond calculation .. for as the smoke rolls off we see the harm done by the fire. And so, and now .. is it not advisable for you to go abroad at once .. as you always intended, you know .. now that your book is through the press? What if you go next week? I leave it to you. In any case, *I entreat you not to answer this*—neither let your thoughts be too hard on me for what you may call perhaps vacillation— only that I stand excused (I do not say justified) before my own moral sense.

. . .

RB, *Thursday, 23 October 1845*

But I *must* answer you, and be forgiven, too, dearest. I was (to being at the beginning) surely not '*startled*' .. only properly *aware* of the deep blessing I have been enjoying this while, and not disposed to take its continuance as pure matter of course, and so treat with indifference the first shadow of a threatening intimation from without, the first hint of a possible obstruction from the quarter to which so many hopes

& fears of mine have gone of late: in this case, knowing you, I was sure that if any imaginable form of displeasure could touch you without reaching me, I should not hear of it too soon—so I spoke—so *you* have spoken—and so now you get—'excused'?—No—wondered at, with all my faculty of wonder for the strange exalting way you will persist to think of me; now, once for all, I *will* not pass for what I make no least pretence to: I quite understand the grace of your imaginary self-denial, and fidelity to a given word, and noble constancy,—but it all happens to be none of mine, none in the least. I love you because I *love* you; I see you 'once a week' because I cannot see you all day long; I think of you all day long, because I most certainly could not think of you once an hour less, if I tried, or went to Pisa, or 'abroad' (in every sense) in order to 'be happy' .. a kind of adventure which you seem to suppose you have in some way interfered with: do, for this once, think, and never after, on the impossibility of your ever .. (you know I must talk your own language, so I shall say ..) hindering any scheme of mine, stopping any supposeable advancement of mine: do you really think that before I found you, I was going about the world seeking whom I might devour,—° that is, be devoured by, in the shape of a wife .. do you suppose I ever dreamed of marrying?—what would it mean for me, with my life I am hardened in,—considering the rational chances,—how the land is used to furnish its contingent of Shakespeare's-women: or by 'success,' 'happiness' &c &c you never never can be seeing for a moment with the world's eyes and meaning 'getting rich' & all that?—Yet, put that away, and what do you meet at every turn, if you are hunting about in the dusk to catch my good, but *yourself*?

I know who has got it, caught it, & means to keep it on his heart—the person most concerned—*I*, dearest, who cannot play the disinterested part of bidding *you* forget your 'protestation' .. what should I have to hold by, come what will, thro' years, thro' this life, if God shall so determine, if I were not sure, *sure* that the first moment when you can suffer me with you 'in that relation,' you will remember and act accordingly—I will, as you know, conform my life to *any* imaginable rule which shall render it possible for your life to move with it and possess it, all the little it is worth—

For your friends .. whatever can be 'got over,' whatever opposition may be rational, will be easily removed, I suppose: you know when I spoke lately about the 'selfishness' I dared believe I was free from, I hardly meant the low faults of .. I shall say, a different organization to mine—which has vices in plenty, but not those: beside half a dozen scratches with a pen make one stand up an apparent angel of light, from the lawyer's parchment,—and Doctors' Commons° is one bland smile of applause. The selfishness I deprecate is one which a good many women & men, too, call 'real passion'—under the influence of which, I ought to say 'be mine, what ever happens to *you*'—but I know better, and you know best—and you know me, for all this letter, which is no doubt in me, I feel, but dear entire goodness and affection, of which God knows whether I am proud or not—and now you will 'let me be,' will not you? Let me have my way, live my life, love my love

Whose I am, praying God to bless her ever

RB

EB, *Thursday, 23 October 1845*

'*And be forgiven*' .. yes! and be thanked besides—if I knew how to thank you worthily & as I feel .. only that I do not know it, & cannot say it. And it was not indeed 'doubt' of you (.. oh no!—) that made me write as I did write: it was rather because I felt you to be surely noblest, .. & therefore fitly dearest, ... that it seemed to me detestable & intolerable to leave you on this road where the mud must splash up against you, & never cry 'gare' [beware]. Yet I was quite enough unhappy yesterday, & before yesterday .. I will confess today, .. to be too gratefully glad to 'let you be' .. to 'let you have your way'—you who overcome always! Always, but where you tell me not to think of you so & so!—as if I could help thinking of you *so*, & as if I should not take the liberty of persisting to think of you just so. 'Let me be'—'Let me have

my way'. I am unworthy of you perhaps in everything except
one thing—& *that*, you cannot guess. May God bless you—

Ever I am yours.

. . .

EB, *Friday, 24 October 1845*

I wrote briefly yesterday not to make my letter longer by
keeping it; & a few last words which belong to it by right,
must follow after it .. must—for I want to say that you need
not indeed talk to me about squares being not round, and of
YOU being not 'selfish'! You know it is foolish to talk such
superfluities, & not a compliment, .. I wont say to my
knowledge of you & faith in you .. but to my understanding
generally. Why should you say to me at all .. much less for
this third or fourth time .. 'I am not selfish'?—to *me* who
never .. when I have been deepest asleep & dreaming, .. never
dreamed of attributing to you any form of such a fault?
Promise not to say so again .. now promise. Think how it
must sound to my ears, when really & truly I have sometimes
felt jealous of myself .. of my own infirmities, .. and thought
that you cared for me only because your chivalry touched
them with a silver sound—& that, without them, you would
pass by on the other side:—why twenty times I have thought
that & been vexed—ungrateful vexation!—In exchange for
which too frank confession, I will ask for another silent
promise .. a silent promise—no, but first I will say another
thing.

First I will say that you are not to fancy any .. the least, ..
danger of my falling under displeasure through your visits—
there is no sort of risk of it *for the present*—& if I ran the risk
of making you uncomfortable about *that*, I did foolishly, &
what I meant to do was different. I wish you also to
understand that *even if* YOU CAME HERE EVERYDAY, my
brothers & sisters would simply care to know if I liked it, &
then be glad if I was glad:—the caution refered to one person
alone. In relation to WHOM, however, there will be no '*getting*

over'—you might as well think to sweep off a third of the stars of Heaven with the motion of your eye-lashes—this, for matter of fact & certainty—& this, as I said before, the keeping of a general rule and from no disrespect towards individuals—: a great peculiarity *in the individual* of course. But ... though I have been a submissive daughter, & this from no effort, but for love's sake .. because I loved him tenderly, (& love him), .. & hoped that he loved me back again even if the proofs came untenderly sometimes—yet I have reserved for myself ALWAYS that right over my own affections which is the most strictly personal of all things, & which involves principles & consequences of infinite importance & scope— even though I NEVER thought (except perhaps when the door of life was just about to open .. before it opened) never thought it probable or possible that I should have occasion for the exercise,—from without & from within at once. I have too much need to look up. . . .

And the silent promise I would have you make is this— that if ever you should leave me, it shall be (though you are not 'selfish') for your sake—& not for mine: for your good, & not for mine. I ask it—not because I am disinterested,—but because one class of motives would be valid, and the other void—simply for that reason. .

. . .

RB, *Monday, 27 October 1845*

How does one make 'silent promises' .. or, rather, how does the maker of them communicate that fact to whomsoever it may concern? I know, there have been many, very many unutterable vows & promises made,—that is, THOUGHT down upon, the white slip at the top of my notes,—such as of this note,—and not trusted to the pen,—that always comes in for the shame,—but given up, and replaced by the poor forms to which a pen is equal—and, a glad minute I should account *that*, in which you collected and accepted *those* 'promises'—because they would not be all so unworthy of me— much less you! I would receive, in virtue of *them*, the ascription of whatever worthiness is supposed to lie in deep, truest love, and gratitude,—

. . . Yesterday I took out 'Luria' & read it thro', the skeleton. I shall hope to finish it soon now. It is for a purely imaginary Stage,—very simple and straightforward. Would you .. no, Act by Act, as I was about to propose that you should read it,—that process would affect the oneness I most wish to preserve.

. . .

[Meeting 26: Tuesday, 28 October 3.00–4.30 p.m.]

RB, *Wednesday, 29 October 1845*

. . . I do believe that we shall be happy; that is, that *you* will be happy: you see I dare confidently expect *the* end to it all .. so it has always been with me in my life of wonders,— absolute wonders, with God's hand over all .. and this last and best of all would never have begun so, and gone on so, to break off abruptly even here, in this world, for the little time.

So try, try, dearest, every method, take every measure of hastening such a consummation—Why, we shall see Italy together! I could, would, *will* shut myself in four walls of a room with you and never leave you and be most of all *then* 'a lord of infinite space'°—but, to travel with you to Italy, or Greece—very vain, I know that, all such day dreaming! And ungrateful, too; with the real sufficing happiness here of being, and knowing that you know me to be, and suffer me to tell you I am yours, ever your own.

God bless you, my dearest—

EB, *Friday, 31 October 1845*

All today, friday, Miss Mitford has been here: she came at two & went away at seven—and I feel as if I had been making a five-hour speech on the corn laws° in Harriet Martineau's parliament; .. so tired I am. Not that dear Miss Mitford did not talk both for me & herself, .. for that, of course she did. But I was forced to answer once every ten minutes at least—& Flush, my usual companion, does not exact so much—& so I am tired & come to rest myself on this paper—Your name was not once spoken today; a little from my good fencing: when I saw you at the end of an alley of associations, I pushed the conversation up the next— because I was afraid of questions such as every moment I expected, with a pair of woman's eyes behind them; & those are worse than Mr. Kenyon's, when he puts on his spectacles. So your name was not once spoken: not thought of, I do not say . . .

. . . the truth is, that your letter went to the bottom of my heart, & that my thoughts have turned round it ever since & through all the talking today—. Yes indeed, dreams! But what *is* not dreaming is this & this—this reading of these words—this proof of this regard—all this that you are to me in fact, & which you cannot guess the full meaning of, dramatic poet as you are .. cannot .. since you do not know what my life meant before you touched it, .. o my angel at the gate of the prison!°—My wonder is greater than your wonders, .. I who sate here alone but yesterday, so weary of my own being that to take interest in my very poems I had to lift them up by an effort & separate them from myself & cast them out from me into the sunshine where I was not—feeling nothing of the light which fell on them even—making indeed a sort of pleasure & interest about that factitious personality associated with them .. but knowing it to be all far on the outside of *me .. myself* .. not seeming to touch it with the end of my finger .. & receiving it as a mockery & a bitterness when people persisted in confounding one with another. Morbid it was if you like it—perhaps very morbid—but all these heaps of letters which go into the fire one after the other, & which, because I am a woman & have written verses, it seems so amusing to the letter-writers of your sex to write & see 'what will come of it,' .. some, from kind good motives I know, .. well, .. how could it all make for me even such a narrow strip of sunshine as Flush finds on the floor sometimes, & lays his nose along, with both ears out in the shadow? It was not for *me .. me ..* in any way!—it was not within my reach—I did not seem to touch it as I said. Flush came nearer, & I was grateful to him .. yes, grateful .. for not being tired! I have felt grateful & flattered .. yes flattered .. when he has chosen rather to stay with me all day than go down stairs. Grateful too, with reason, I have been & am to my own family for not letting me see that I was a burthen. Those are facts. And now how am I to feel when you tell me what you have told me—& what you 'could would & will' do, & SHALL NOT do? .. but when you tell me .. ?

Only remember that such words make you freer & freer— if you can be freer than free—just as every one makes me happier & richer—too rich by you, to claim any debt. May God bless you always—When I wrote that letter to let you come the first time, do you know, the tears ran down my cheeks .. I could not tell why: partly it might be mere nervousness. And then, I was vexed with you for wishing to come as other people did, & vexed with myself for not being able to refuse you as I did them.

. . .

[Meeting 27: Monday, 3 November 3.00–4.30 p.m.]

EB, *Wednesday, 5 November 1845*

. . .

And now—not to make any more fuss about a matter of simple restitution—may I have my letter back? .. I mean the letter which if you did not destroy .. did not punish for its sins long & long ago .. belongs to me—which, if destroyed, I must lose for my sins, .. but, if undestroyed, which I may have back,—may I not? is it not my own? must I not?—that letter I was made to return & now turn to ask for again in further expiation. Now do I ask humbly 'nough? And send it at once, if undestroyed—do not wait till saturday.

I have considered about Mr. Kenyon & it seems best, in the event of a question or of a remark equivalent to a question, to confess to the visits 'generally once a week' .. because he may hear, one, two, three different ways . . . I fear that he . . . will wonder a little—& he has looked at me with scanning spectacles already & talked of its being a mystery to him how you made your way here; & *I*, who though I can *bespeak* selfcommand, have no sort of presence of mind (not so much as one would use to play at Jack straws) did not help the case at all. Well—it cannot be helped. Did I ever tell you what he said of you once—'that you *deserved to be a poet*—being one in your heart and life:' he said *that* of you to me, & I thought it a noble encomium & deserving its application.

. . .

RB, *Thursday, 6 November 1845*

Just arrived .. (mind, the *silent writing* overflows the page, and laughs at the black words for Mr. Kenyon to read!)—°
But your note arrived earlier——more of that, when I write after this dreadful dispatching-business that falls on me— friend A. & B. & C. must get their copy, and word of regard, all by next post!—

Could you think that *that* untoward letter lived ONE MOMENT after it returned to me? I burned it and cried 'serve it right'! Poor letter!—yet I should have been vexed & offended *then* to be told I *could* love you better than I did already. 'Live and *learn*!' Live and love you .. dearest, as loves you

RB

. . .

[Meeting 28: Saturday, 8 November 3.00–4.05 p.m.]

RB, *Sunday, 9 November 1845*

When I come back from seeing you, and think over it all, there never is a least word of yours I could not occupy myself with, and wish to return to you with some .. not to say, all .. the thoughts & fancies it is sure to call out of me:—there is nothing in you that does not draw out all of me:—you possess me, dearest .. and there is no help for the expressing it all, no voice nor hand, but these of mine which shrink and turn away from the attempt: so you must go on, patiently, knowing me, more and more, and your entire power on me, and I will console myself, to the full extent, with your knowledge,— penetration, intuition .. *somehow* I must believe you can get to what is here, in me,—without the pretence of my telling or writing it. But, because I give up the great achievements, there is no reason I should not secure any occasion of making clear one of the less important points that arise in our intercourse .. if I fancy I can do it with the least success: for instance, it is on my mind to explain what I meant yesterday by trusting that the entire happiness I feel in the letters, and the help in the criticising might not be hurt by the surmise, even, that those labours to which you were born, might be suspended, in any degree, thro' such generosity to *me*: dearest, I believed in your glorious genius and knew it for a true star from the moment I saw it,—long before I had the blessing of knowing it was MY star, with my fortune and futurity in it— and, when I draw back from myself, and look better and more clearly, then I *do* feel, with you, that the writing a few letters more or less, reading many or few rhymes of any other person, would not interfere in any material degree with that power of yours—that you might easily make one so happy and yet go on writing 'Geraldines' and 'Berthas'—but—how can I, dearest, leave my heart's treasures long, even to look at your genius? .. and when I come back and find all safe, find the comfort of you, the traces of you .. *will* it do,—tell me— to trust all that as a light effort, an easy matter?

Yet, if you can lift me with one hand, while the other suffices to crown you—there is queenliness in *that*, too!

. . .

EB, *Monday, 10 November 1845*

If it were possible that you could do me harm in the way of work, (but it isn't) it would be possible, not through writing letters & reading manuscripts, but because of a reason to be drawn from your own great line

'What man is strong until he stands alone?'°

What man .. what woman? For have I not felt twenty times the desolate advantage of being insulated here & of not minding anybody when I made my poems?—of living a little like a disembodied spirit, & caring less for supposititious criticism than for the black fly buzzing in the pane?—*That* made me what dear Mr. Kenyon calls 'insolent,'—untimid, & unconventional in my degree; & not so much by strength, you see, as by separation. *You* touch your greater ends by mere strength,—breaking with your own hands the hampering threads which, in your position, w^d have hampered *me*.

Still .. when all is changed for me now, & different, it is not possible, .. for all the changing, .. nor for all your line & my speculation, .. that I should not be better & stronger for being within your influences & sympathies, in this way of writing as in other ways. We shall see—you will see. Yet I have been idle lately I confess,—leaning half out of some turret-window of the castle of Indolence & watching the new sunrise—as why not?—Do I mean to be idle always?—no!—and am I not an industrious worker on the average of days? Indeed yes! Also I have been less idle than you think perhaps, even this last year, though the results seem so like trifling: and I shall set about the prose papers for the New York people, and the something rather better besides we may hope .. may *I* not hope, if *you* wish it? Only there is no 'crown' for me, be sure, except what grows from this letter & such letters .. this sense of being anything to *One!* there is no room for *another* crown. Have I a great head like Goethe's that there should be room? . . .

[Meeting 29: Thursday, 13 November, 3.00–4.30 p.m. The following letter was begun the day before this meeting took place and resumed after it.]

EB, *Wednesday, 12–Friday, 14 November, 1845*

Two letters in one—*Wednesday*.

I shall see you tomorrow & yet am writing what you will have to read perhaps. When you spoke of 'stars' & 'geniuses' in that letter, I did not seem to hear,—I was listening to those words of the letter which were of a better silver in the sound than even your praise could be: and now that at last I come to hear them in their extravagance (oh such pure extravagance about 'glorious geniuses'—) I cant help telling you they were heard last, & deserved it.

Shall I tell you besides?—The first moment in which I seemed to admit to myself in a flash of lightning the *possibility* of your affection for me being more than dream-work .. the first moment was *that* when you intimated (as you have done since repeatedly) that you cared for me not for a reason, but because you cared for me.° Now such a 'parceque' which reasonable people w^d take to be irrational, was just the only one fitted to the uses of my understanding on the particular question we were upon .. just the 'woman's reason' suitable to the woman .. : for I could understand that it might be as you said, &, if so, that it was altogether unanswerable .. do you see?—If a fact includes its own cause .. why there it stands for ever—one of 'earth's immortalities'°—*as long as it includes it.*

And when unreasonableness stands for a reason, it is a promising state of things, we may both admit, & proves what it would be as well not too curiously to enquire into. But then .. to look at it in a brighter aspect, .. I do remember how, years ago, when talking the foolishness which women will talk when they are by themselves, & not forced to be sensible, .. one of my friends thought it 'safest to begin with a little aversion,' & another, wisest to begin with a great deal of esteem, & how the best attachments were produced so & so, .. I took it into my head to say that the best was where there was no cause at all for it, & the more wholly unreasonable, the better still, .. that the motive sh^d lie in the feeling itself & not in the object of it—& that the affection which could (if it could) throw itself out on an idiot with a goître would be more admirable than Abelard's—Whereupon everybody laughed, & some one thought it affected of me & no true opinion, & others said plainly that it was immoral, and somebody else hoped, in a sarcasm, that I meant to act out my theory for the advantage of the world. To which I replied quite gravely that I had not virtue enough—& so, people laughed as it is fair to laugh when other people are esteemed

to talk nonsense.° And all this came back to me in the south
wind of your 'parceque', & I tell it as it came .. now .. . . .

Friday evening.

Shall I send this letter or not?—I have been 'tra 'l si e 'l no'
[between yes and no], & writing a new beginning on a new
sheet even—but after all you ought to hear the remote echo
of your last letter :. far out among the hills, .. as well as the
immediate reverberation, & so I will send it,—& what I send
is not to be answered, remember!——

I read Luria's first act twice through before I slept last
night, & feel just as a bullet might feel, not because of the
lead of it but because shot into the air and suddenly arrested
& suspended. It ('Luria') is all life, & we know (that is, the
reader knows) that there must be results here & here. How
fine that sight of Luria is upon the lynx hides—how you see
the Moor in him just in the glimpse you have by the eyes of
another—& that laugh when the horse drops the forage, what
wonderful truth & character you have in *that!*—And then,
when *he* is in the scene—! 'Golden-hearted Luria' you called
him once to me,° & his heart shines already .. wide open to
the morning sun. The construction seems to me very clear
everywhere—the rhythm, even over-smooth in a few verses,
where you invert a little artificially—but *that* shall be set
down on a separate strip of paper: & in the meantime I am
snatched up into 'Luria' & feel myself driven on to the ends
of the poet, just as a reader should. . . .

When you write will you say exactly how you are?—and
will you write?—And I want to explain to you that although
I dont make a profession of equable spirits, (as a matter of
temperament, my spirits were always given to rock a little, up
& down) yet that I did not mean to be so ungrateful & wicked
as to complain of low spirits now & to you. It would not be
true either: & I said 'low' to express a merely bodily state.
My opium comes in to keep the pulse from fluttering &
fainting .. to give the right composure & point of balance to
the nervous system. I dont take it for 'my spirits' in the usual
sense,—you must not think such a thing. The medical man
who came to see me made me take it the other day when he
was in the room, before the right hour & when I was talking

quite cheerfully, just for the need he observed in the pulse—
'It was a necessity of my position,' he said. Also I do not
suffer from it in any way, as people usually do who take
opium. I am not even subject to an opium-headache.—As to
the low spirits I will not say that mine *have not* been low
enough & with cause enough; but *even then*, .. why if you were
to ask the nearest witnesses, .. say, even my own sisters, ..
everybody would tell you, I think, that the 'cheerfulness' even
then, was the remarkable thing in me .. certainly it has been
remarked about me again and again. Nobody has known that
it was an effort (a habit of effort) to throw the light on the
outside . . . yet I may say that for three years I never was
conscious of one movement of pleasure in anything. Think if
I could mean to complain of 'low spirits' now, and to you!
Why it would be like complaining of not being able to see at
noon—which would simply prove that I was very blind . . .
May God bless you long after you have done blessing me!

your own
EBB

. . .

RB, *Sunday, 16 November 1845*

At last your letter comes—and the deep joy—(I know and
use to analyse my own feelings, and be sober in giving
distinctive names to their varieties; this is *deep* joy—)—the
true love with which I take this much of you into my heart ..
that proves what it is I wanted so long, and find at last, and
am happy for ever. I must have more than 'intimated'—I
must have spoken plainly out the truth, if I do myself the
barest justice, and told you long ago that the admiration at
your works went *away*, quite another way and afar from this
hope of you: if I could fancy some method of what I shall say
happening without all the obvious stumbling-blocks of falseness, &c which no foolish fancy dares associate with you .. if
you COULD tell me when I next sit by you—'I will undeceive
you,—I am not *the* Miss B.—she is upstairs and you shall see

her—I only wrote those letters, and am what you see, that is all now left you'—(all the misapprehension having arisen from *me*, in some inexplicable way) .. I should .. not begin by *saying* anything, dear, dearest—but *after that*, I should assure you—soon make you believe that I did not much wonder at the event, for I have been all my life asking what connection there is between the satisfaction at the display of power, and the sympathy with—ever-increasing sympathy with—all imaginable weakness? . . . And now—here I refuse to fancy .. you KNOW whether, if you never write another line, speak another intelligible word, recognize me by a look again— whether I shall love you less or *more* .. MORE,—having a right to expect more strength with the strange emergency. And it is because I know this, build upon this entirely, that as a reasonable creature I am bound to look first to what hangs farthest and most loosely from me .. what *might* go from you to your loss, and so to mine, to say the least .. because I want ALL of you, not just so much as I could not live without— and because I see the danger of your entirely generous disposition and cannot quite, yet, bring myself to profit by it in the quiet way you recommend. Always remember, I never wrote to you, all the years, on the strength of your poetry .. tho' I constantly heard of you thro' Mr K., and was near seeing you once, and might have easily availed myself of his intervention to commend any letter to your notice, so as to reach you out of the foolish crowd of rushers-in upon genius .. who come and eat their bread and cheese on the high-altar—and talk of reverence without one of its surest instincts—never quiet till they cut their initials on the cheek of the Medicean Venus to prove they worship her. My admiration, as I said, went its natural way in silence—but when on my return to England in December, late in the month, Mr. K. sent those Poems to my sister, and I read my name there—and when, a day or two after, I met him and, beginning to speak my mind on them, and getting on no better than I should now, said quite naturally—'if I were to *write* this, now?'—and he assured me with his perfect kind-ness, you would be even 'pleased' to hear from me under those circumstances .. nay,—for I will tell you all, in this, in everything—when he wrote me a note soon after to re-assure me on that point .. THEN I *did* write, on *account of my purely personal obligation*, tho' of course taking that occasion to allude to the general and customary delight in your works: I did write, on the whole, UNWILLINGLY .. with consciousness of having to *speak* on a subject which I *felt* thoroughly concerning, and could not be satisfied with an imperfect expression of: as for expecting THEN what has followed .. I shall only say I was scheming how to get done with England and go to my heart in Italy. And now, my love—I am round you .. my whole life is wound up and down and over you .. I feel you stir everywhere: I am not conscious of thinking or feeling but *about* you, with some reference to you—so I will live, so may I die! And you have blessed me *beyond* the *bond*, in more than in giving me yourself to love,—inasmuch as you believed me from the first .. what you call 'dream-work' *was* real of its kind, did you not think? and now you believe me, *I* believe and am happy, in what I write with my heart full of love for you: why do you tell me of a doubt, as now, and bid me not clear it up, 'not answer you?'—Have I done wrong in thus answering? Never, never do *me* direct *wrong* and hide for a moment from me what a word can explain as now: you see, you thought, if but for a moment, I loved your intellect,—or what predominates in your poetry and is most distinct from your heart,—better, or as well as you—did you not? and I have told you every thing,—explained everything .. have I not? And now I will dare .. yes, dearest, kiss you back to my heart again,—my own. There—and there!

And since I wrote what is above, I have been reading among other poems that sonnet—'Past and Future'°—which affects me more than any poem I ever read. How can I put your poetry away from you, even in these ineffectual attempts to concentrate myself upon, and better apply myself to, what remains?—poor, poor work it is,—for is not that sonnet to be loved as a true utterance of yours? I cannot attempt to put down the thoughts that rise;—may God bless me, as you pray, by letting that beloved hand shake the less .. I will only ask, *the less* .. for being laid on mine thro' this life! And, indeed, you write down, for me to calmly read, that I make

you happy! Then it is—as with all power—God thro' the
weakest instrumentality .. and I am past expression proud
and grateful—

My love, I am your
R. B.

. . .

EB, *Monday, 17 November 1845*

How you overcome me as always you do°—& where is the
answer to anything except too deep down in the heart for
even the pearl-divers? But understand .. what you do not
quite .. that I did not mistake you as far even as you say here
& even 'for a moment.' I did not write any of that letter in a
'doubt' of you—not a word .. I was simply looking back in it
on my own states of feeling, .. looking back from that point of
your praise to what was better .. (or I should not have looked
back)—and, so, coming to tell you, by a natural association,
how the completely opposite point to that of any praise was
the one which struck me first & most, viz. the no-reason of
your reasoning .. acknowledged to be yours. Of course I
acknowledge it to be yours, .. that high reason of no reason—
I acknowledged it to be yours (didn't I?) in acknowledging
that it made an impression on me. And then, referring to the
traditions of my experience such as I told them to you, I
meant, so, farther to acknowledge that I would rather be
cared for in *that* unreasonable way, than for the best reason in
the world. But all *that* was history & philosophy simply—was
it not?—& not *doubt of you*.

The truth is .. since we really are talking truths in this
world .. that I never have doubted you—ah, you *know!*—I
felt from the beginning so sure of the nobility & integrity in
you that I would have trusted you to make a path for my
soul—*that*, you *know*. I felt certain that you believed of yourself
every word you spoke or wrote—& you must not blame me if
I thought besides sometimes (it was the extent of my thought)
that you were selfdeceived as to the nature of your own

feelings. If you could turn over every page of my heart like the pages of a book, you would see nothing there offensive to the least of your feelings .. not even to the outside fringes of your man's vanity .. should you have any vanity like a man,— which I DO doubt.—I never wronged you in the least of things—never .. I thank God for it. But 'selfdeceived,' it *was* so easy for you to be!—see how on every side & day by day, men are—& women too .. in this sort of feelings. 'Self-deceived,' it was so possible for you to be, & while I thought it possible, could I help thinking it *best* for you that it should be so—& was it not right in me to persist in thinking it possible?—It was my reverence for you that made me persist!—What was *I* that I should think otherwise? I had been shut up here too long face to face with my own spirit, not to know myself, &, so, to have lost the common illusions of vanity. All the men I had ever known could not make your stature among them. So it was not distrust, but reverence rather. I sate by while the angel stirred the water, & I called it *Messiah.*° Do not blame me now, .. *my* angel!

Nor say that I 'do not lean' on you with all the weight of my 'past' .. because I do!—You cannot guess what you are to me—you cannot—it is not possible:—&, though I have said *that* before, I must say it again .. for it comes again to be said. It is something to me between dream & miracle,—as if some dream of my earliest brightest dreaming-time had been lying through these dark years to steep in the sunshine, returning to me in a double light. *Can* it be, I say to myself, that *you* feel for me *so?*—can it be meant for me?—this from YOU?

. . . And now I must say this besides. When grief came upon grief, I never was tempted to ask 'How have I deserved this of God,' as sufferers sometimes do: I always felt that there must be cause enough .. corruption enough, needing purification .. weakness enough, needing strengthening .. *nothing* of the chastisement could come to me without cause & need. But in this different hour, when joy follows joy, & God makes me happy, as you say, *through* you .. I cannot repress the .. 'How have I deserved THIS of Him'?—I know I have not—I know I do not.

. . .

[Meeting 30: Wednesday, 19 November 3.00–4.30 p.m.]

RB, *Sunday, 23 November 1845*

. . . Give me, dearest beyond expression, what I have always dared to think I would ask you for .. one day! Give me .. wait—for your own sake, not mine who never, never dream of being worth such a gift .. but for your own sense of justice, and to *say*, so as my heart shall hear, that you were wrong and are no longer so, give me so much of you—all precious that you are—as may be given in a lock of your hair—I will live and die with it, and with the memory of you—this *at the worst!* If you give me what I beg,—shall I say next Tuesday .. when I leave you, I will not speak a word:—if you do not, I will not think you unjust, for all my light words but I will pray you to wait and remember me one day—when the power to deserve more may be greater .. never the will. God supplies all things: may he bless you, beloved! So I can but pray, kissing your hand.

RB

Now pardon me, dearest, for what is written .. what I cannot cancel, for the love's sake that it grew from.

. . .

EB, *Monday, 24 November 1845*

. . . I never gave away what you ask me to give *you*, to a human being, except my nearest relatives & once or twice or thrice to female friends,° .. never, though reproached for it!— and it is just three weeks since I said last to an asker that I was 'too great a prude for such a thing'! .. it was best to anticipate the accusation!—And, prude or not, I could not— I never could—*something* would not let me. And now .. what am I to do .. 'for my own sake and not yours'—? Should you have it, or not? Why I suppose .. YES. I suppose that 'for my own sense of justice & in order to show that I was wrong' (which is wrong—you wrote a wrong word there .. 'right,' you meant!) 'to show that I was *right* & am no longer so', .. I suppose you must have it, 'oh, YOU,' .. who have your way in everything!

. . .

[Meeting 31: Tuesday, 25 November 3.15–4.30 p.m. The following letter was begun the day before this meeting took place and resumed after it.]

EB, *Monday, 24–Wednesday, 26 November 1845*

Monday evening.

Now you must not blame me—you must not. To make a promise is one thing, & to keep it, quite another . . . I *never can* nor *will give you this thing*;—only that I will, if you please, exchange it for another thing—you understand. *I* too will avoid being 'assuming'; I will not pretend to be generous, no, nor 'kind.' It shall be pure merchandise° or nothing at all— Therefore determine! . . .

Then there is another reason for me, entirely mine. You have come to me as a dream comes, as the best dreams come .. dearest—& so there is need to me of 'a sign' to know the difference between dream & vision—And *that* is my comple-test reason, my own reason—you have none like it,—none. A ticket to know the horn-gate from the ivory,° .. ought I not to have it? Therefore send it to me before I send you anything, & if possible by that Lewisham post which was the most frequent bringer of your letters until these last few came, & which reaches me at eight in the evening when all the world is at dinner & my solitude most certain. Everything is so still then, that I have heard the footsteps of a letter of yours ten doors off .. or more, perhaps. Now beware of imagining from this which I say, that there is a strict police for my correspon-dence .. (it is not so—) nor that I do not like hearing from you at any & every hour: it *is* so. Only I would make the smoothest & sweetest of roads for .. & you *understand*, & do not *imagine* beyond. . . .

[Wednesday.]

Do not fancy, in the meantime, that you stay here 'too long' for any observation that can be made. In the first place there is nobody to 'observe'—everybody is out till seven, except the one or two who will not observe if I tell them not. My sisters are glad when you come, because it is a gladness of mine, .. they observe. I have a great deal of liberty, to have so many chains,—we all have, in this house: & though the liberty has melancholy motives, it saves some daily torment, & *I* do not complain of it for one.

. . .

RB, *Friday, 28 November 1845*

Take it, dearest,—what I am forced to think you mean—and take *no more* with it—for I gave all to give long ago—I am all yours—and now, *mine*,—give me *mine* to be happy with! . . .

Shall I dare ⟨speak⟩ write down a grievance of my heart, and not offend you?—Yes, trusting in the right of my love. You tell me, sweet, here in the letter, 'I do not look so well'—and sometimes, I 'look better' .. *how do you know?* When I first saw you—*I saw your eyes*—since then, *you*, it should appear, see mine—but I only *know* yours are there, and have to use that memory as if one carried dried flowers about when fairly inside the garden-enclosure: and while I resolve, and hesitate, and resolve again to complain of this,—(kissing your foot .. not boldly complaining, nor rudely)—while I have this on my mind, on my heart, ever since that May morning .. can it be

—No, nothing *can be* wrong now—you will never call me 'kind' again, in that sense, you promise! Nor think 'bitterly' of my kindness, that word!

. . .

EB, *Friday, 28–Saturday, 29 November 1845*°

It comes at eight oclock—the post says eight .. *I* say nearer half past eight .. : it *comes*—and I thank you, thank you, as I can. Do you remember the purple lock of a king on which hung the fate of a city?° *I* do! And I need not in conscience—because this one here did not come to me by treason—'ego et rex meus',° on the contrary, do fairly give & take.

. . . I meant at first to send you only what was in the ring: but your fashion is best so you shall have it both ways. Now dont say a word on monday .. nor at all. As for the ring, recollect that I am forced to feel blindfold into the other world, & take what is nearest .. by chance, not choice .. or it might have been better—a little better perhaps. The *best* of it is that it's the colour of your blue flowers. Now you will not say a word—I trust to you.

It is enough that you should have said these others I think. Now *is* it just of you? isn't it hard upon me? And if the charge is true, whose fault is it, pray?—I have been ashamed & vexed with myself fifty times for being so like a little girl, .. for seeming to have 'affectations'; & all in vain: 'it was stronger than I,' as the French say. And for *you* to complain!—As if Haroun Alraschid° after cutting off a head, should complain of the want of an obeisance!—Well!—I smile notwithstanding. Nobody could help smiling—both for my foolishness which is great I confess, though somewhat exaggerated in your statement—(because if it was quite as bad as you say, you know, I never should have *seen you* .. & *I have!*—) & also for yours .. because you take such a very preposterously wrong way for overcoming anybody's shyness. Do you know, I have laughed .. really laughed at your letter—No—it has not been so bad. I have seen you at every visit, as well as I could with both eyes wide open—only that by a supernatural influence they won't stay open with *you* as they are used to do with other people .. so now I tell you. And for the rest I promise nothing at all—as how can I, when it is quite beyond my controul—& you have not improved my capabilities .. do you think you have?—Why what nonsense we have come to .. we, who ought to be 'talking Greek'! said Mr. Kenyon .. !!

. . .

[Meeting 32: Monday, 1 December 1845, 3.00–4.30 p.m.]

RB, *Tuesday, 2 December 1845*

I was happy, so happy before! But I am happier and richer now—My love—no words could serve here, but there is life before us, and to the end of it the vibration now struck will extend—I will live and die with your beautiful ring, your beloved hair—comforting me, blessing me—

. . .

EB, *Thursday, 4 December 1845*

. . . It seems to me (as I say over & over .. I say it to my own thoughts oftenest) it seems to me still a dream how you came here at all, .. the very machinery of it seems miraculous. Why did I receive you & only you? Can I tell? no, not a word.

Last year I had such an escape of seeing Mr. Horne; and in this way it was. He was going to Germany, he said, for an indefinite time, and took the trouble of begging me to receive him for ten minutes before he went. I answered with my usual 'no,' like a wild Indian—whereupon he wrote me a letter so expressive of mortification & vexation .. 'mortification' was one of the words used, I remember, .. that I grew ashamed of myself & told him to come any day (of the last five or six days he had to spare) between two & five. Well!—he never came. Either he was overcome with work & engagements of various sorts & had not a moment, (which was his way of explaining the matter & quite true I dare say) or he was vexed & resolved on punishing me for my caprices. If the latter was the motive, I cannot call the punishment effective, .. for I clapped my hands for joy when I felt my danger to be passed—& now of course, I have no scruples .. I may be as capricious as I please, .. may I not?—Not that I ask you. It is a settled matter. And it is useful to keep out Mr. Chorley with Mr. Horne, & Mr. Horne with Mr. Chorley, & the rest of the world with those two. Only the miracle is that *you* should be behind the enclosure—within it .. & so!—

That is *my* side of the wonder! of the machinery of the wonder, .. as *I* see it!—But there are greater things than these—

Speaking of the portrait of you in the 'Spirit of the age'° .. which is not like .. no!—which has not your character, in a line of it .. something in just the forehead & eyes & hair, .. but even *that*, thrown utterly out of your order, by another bearing so unlike you .! speaking of that portrait .. shall I tell you?—Mr. Horne had the goodness to send me all those portraits, & I selected the heads which, in right hero-worship, were anything to me, & had them framed after a rough fashion & hung up before my eyes,—Harriet Martineau's .. because she was a woman & ⟨amiable⟩ admirable, & had written me some kind letters—& for the rest, Wordsworth's, Carlyle's, Tennyson's & yours. The day you paid your first visit here, I, in a fit of shyness not quite unnatural, .. though I have been cordially laughed at for it by everybody in the house .. pulled down your portrait, .. (there is the nail, under Wordsworth!—) & then pulled down Tennyson's in a fit of justice,—because I would not have his hung up & yours away. It was the delight of my brothers to open all the drawers & the boxes & whatever they could get access to, & find & take those two heads & hang them on the old nails & analyze my 'absurdity' to me, day after day,—but at last I tired them out, being obstinate; & finally settled the question one morning by fastening the print of you inside your Paracelsus. Oh no, it is not like—& I knew it was not, before I saw you, though Mr. Kenyon said, 'Rather like!'

. . .

[Meeting 33: Saturday, 6 December. There is no record of this meeting, the only one which Browning omitted to note in his usual manner (see p.55); hence there is no indication of its length. That the meeting did take place

is confirmed by references to it in both Browning's and
Elizabeth Barrett's letters of the following day (Sunday,
7 December), not included in this edition.
Meeting 34: Thursday, 11 December, 3.00–4.45 p.m.]

RB, *Friday, 12 December 1845*

And now, my heart's love, I am waiting to hear from
you,—my heart is *full* of you: when I try to remember what I
said yesterday, *that* thought, of what fills my heart,—only *that*
makes me bear with the memory .. I know that even such
imperfect, poorest of words *must* have come *from* thence if not
bearing up to you all that is there—and I know you are ever
above me to receive, and help, and forgive, and *wait* for the
one day which I will never say to myself cannot come, when
I shall speak what I feel—more of it—or *some* of it—for now
nothing is spoken.

My all-beloved—

Ah, you opposed very rightly, I dare say, the writing that
paper I spoke of!° The process should be so much simpler! I
most earnestly EXPECT of you, my love, that in the event of
any such necessity as was then alluded to, you accept at once
in my name *any* conditions possible for a human will to submit
to—there is no imaginable condition to which you allow me
to accede that I will not joyfully bend all my faculties to
comply with—And you know this—but so, also do you know
more .. and yet 'I may tire of you'—'may forget you'!

. . .

EB, *Friday, 12 December 1845*

. . .

As to unfavourable influences, .. I can speak of them
quietly, having forseen them from the first, .. & it is true, I
have been thinking since yesterday, that I might be prevented
from receiving you here, & *should*, if all were known: but with

that act, the adverse power would end. It is not my fault if I
have to choose between two affections,—only my pain: & I
have not to choose between two duties, I feel, .. since I am
yours, while I am of any worth to you at all. For the plan of
the sealed letter it would correct no evil,—ah, you do not see,
you do not understand. The danger does not come from the
side to which a reason may go. Only one person holds the
thunder—& I shall be thundered at; I shall not be reasoned
with—it is impossible. I could tell you some dreary chronicles
made for laughing & crying over; and you know that if I once
thought I might be loved enough to be spared above others, I
cannot think so now. In the meanwhile we need not for the
present be afraid—Let there be ever so many suspectors,
there will be no informers .. I suspect the suspectors, but the
informers are out of the world I am very sure:—and then, the
one person, by a curious anomaly, *never* draws an inference of
this order, until the bare blade of it is thrust palpably into his
hand, point outwards. So it has been in other cases than
our's—& so it is, at this moment in the house, with others
than ourselves.

I have your letter to stop me—. If I had my whole life in
my hands with your letter, could I thank you for it, I wonder,
at all worthily?—I cannot believe that I could. Yet in life &
in death I shall be grateful to you ..

But for the paper—no. Now, observe, that it would seem
like a prepared apology for something wrong. And besides, ..
the apology would be nothing but the offence in another form
.. unless you said it was all a mistake .. (*will* you, again?) ..
that it was all a mistake & you were only calling for your
boots!°—Well, if you said THAT, it would be worth writing,—
but anything less would be something worse than nothing—,
& would not save me .. which you were thinking of, I know,—
would not save me the least of the stripes. For 'conditions' ..
now I will tell you what I said once in a jest ..

'If a prince of Eldorado should come, with a pedigree of
lineal descent from some signory in the moon in one hand, &
a ticket of good-behaviour from the nearest Independent
chapel, in the other'...

'Why even *then*,' said my sister Arabel, 'it would not *do*.'

And she was right, & we all agreed that she was right. It is an obliquity of the will—& one laughs at it till the turn comes for crying.

. . .

EB, *Monday, 15 December 1845*

. . .

When I had sent away my last letter I began to remember .. & could not help smiling to do so, .. that I had totally forgotten the great subject of my 'fame,' & the oath you administered about it ... totally!!—Now how do you read that omen? If I forget myself, who is to remember me, do you think? .. except *you* ..? which brings me where I would stay. Yes—'yours' it must be—but *you*, it had better be!—But, to leave the vain superstitions, let me go on to assure you that I did mean to answer that part of your former letter, & do mean to behave well & be obedient. Your wish would be enough, even if there could be likelihood without it of my doing nothing ever again. Oh, certainly I have been idle—it comes of lotos-eating .. &, besides, of sitting too long in the sun. Yet 'idle' may not be the word—: silent I have been, through too many thoughts to speak .. just *that!* As to writing letters & reading manuscripts filling all my time, why I must lack 'vital energy' indeed .. you do not mean seriously to fancy such a thing of me!—For the rest ...

Tell me—Is it your opinion that when the apostle Paul saw the unspeakable things,° being snatched up into the third Heavens 'whether in the body or out of the body he could not tell,' ... is it your opinion that, all the week after, he worked particularly hard at the tent-making? For my part, I doubt it.

I would not speak profanely or extravagantly—it is not the best way to thank God. But to say only that I was in the desert & that I am among the palm-trees, is to say nothing ... Because it is easy to *understand how*, after walking straight on .. on .. furlong after furlong .. dreary day after dreary day, .. one may come to the end of the sand & within sight of the fountain:—there is nothing miraculous in *that*, you know!——

Yet even in that case .. to doubt whether it may not all be *mirage*, would be the natural first thought .. the recurring dream-fear! .. now would it not? And you can reproach me for *my* thoughts, .. as if *they* were unnatural!

. . .

[Meeting 35: Wednesday, 17 December 3.15–4.30 p.m.]

EB, *Thursday, 18–Friday, 19 December 1845*

Thursday evening.

Dearest you know how to say what makes me happiest, you who never think, you say, of making me happy! For my part I do not think of it either—I simply understand that you *are* my happiness, & that therefore you could not make another happiness for me, such as would be worth having— not even *you!* Why, how could you?—*That* was in my mind to speak yesterday, but I could not speak it—to write it, is easier.

Talking of happiness, .. shall I tell you? Promise not to be angry & I will tell you. I have thought sometimes that, if I considered my self wholly, I should choose to die this winter .. now .. before I had disappointed you in anything. But because you are better & dearer & more to be considered than I, I do *not* choose it. I CANNOT choose to give you any pain, even on the chance of its being a less pain, a less evil, than what may follow perhaps, (who can say?) if I should prove the burden of your life.

For if you make me happy with some words, you frighten me with others .. as with the extravagance yesterday—& seriously *too* seriously, when the moment for smiling at them is past, .. I am frightened .. I tremble! When you come to know me as well as I know myself, what can save me, do you think, from disappointing & displeasing you? I ask the question, & find no answer— . . .

As your letter does not come it is a good opportunity for asking what sort of ill humour, or (to be more correct,) bad temper, you most particularly admire?—sulkiness? .. the divine gift of sitting aloof in a cloud like any god for three weeks together perhaps—? pettishness .. which will get you up a storm about a crooked pin or a straight one either? obstinacy .. which is an agreeable form of temper I can assure you, & describes itself?—or the good open passion which lies on the floor & kicks, like one of my cousins?—Certainly I prefer the last, & should I think, prefer it, (as an evil) even if it were not the born weakness of my own nature—though I humbly confess (to *you*, who seem to think differently of these things) that never since I was a child, have I upset all the chairs & tables & thrown the books about the room in a fury—I am afraid I do not even 'kick' .. like my cousin, now. Those demonstrations were all done by the 'light of other days' .. not a very full light, I used to be accustomed to think:—but *you*, .. *you* think otherwise .. *you* take a fury to be the opposite of 'indifference' .. as if there could be no such thing as self-controul! .. Now for my part, I do believe that the worst tempered persons in the world, are less so through sensibility than selfishness—they spare nobody's heart, on the ground of being themselves pricked by a straw. Now see if it isn't so. What, after all, is a good temper but generosity in trifles—& what without it, is the happiness of life?—we have only to look round us. I *saw* a woman, once, burst into tears, because her husband cut the bread & butter too thick. I saw *that* with my own eyes. Was it *sensibility*, I wonder!— They were at least real tears & ran down her cheeks. 'You ALWAYS do it'! .. she said. . . .

But I must say, though in ever such an ill temper (which you know is just the time to select for writing a panegyric upon good temper) that I am glad you do not despise my own right name too much, because I never was called Elizabeth by any one who loved me at all, & I accept the omen—So little it seems my name that if a voice said suddenly 'Elizabeth,' I should as soon turn round as my sisters would .. no sooner. Only, my own right name has been complained of for want of euphony .. *Ba* .. now & then it has—& Mr. Boyd makes a compromise & calls me *Elibet* .. because nothing could induce him to desecrate his organs accustomed to Attic harmonies, with a *Ba*—So I am glad, & accept the omen.

. . .

RB, *Friday, 19 December 1845*

. . . you never before heard me love and bless and send my heart after .. 'Ba'—did you? Ba .. and that is you!° I TRIED—(more than *wanted*—) to call you *that*, on Wednesday! I have a flower here—rather, a star, a mimosa,—which must be turned and turned, the side to the light changing in a little time to the *leafy* side, where all the fans lean and spread .. so I turn your name to me, that side I have not last seen: you cannot tell how I feel glad that you will not part with the name—Barrett—seeing you have two of the same—and must always, moreover, remain my EBB!

. . .

RB, *Saturday, 20 December 1945*

I do not, nor will not think, dearest, of ever 'making you happy'—I can imagine no way of working to that end, which does not go straight to my own truest, only true happiness: yet in every such effort there is implied some distinction, some supererogatory grace, or why speak of it at all? *You* it is, are my happiness, and all that ever can be: YOU—dearest!

But never, if you would not .. what you will not do I know,—never revert to *that* frightful wish.—'Disappoint me?'—'I speak what I know and testify what I have seen'°—you shall say 'mystery' again & again—I do not dispute that, but do not *you* dispute, neither, that mysteries *are*: but it is simply because I do most justice to the mystical part of what I feel for you .. because I consent to lay most stress on that fact of facts that I love you, beyond admiration, and respect, and esteem and affection, even—and do not adduce any reason which stops short of accounting for *that*, whatever else it would account for .. because I do this, in pure logical justice—*you* are able to turn and wonder (.. if you *do* .. *now*) what causes it all! My love, only wait, only believe in me— and it cannot be but I shall, little by little, become known to you—after long years, perhaps, but still one day—I *would* say *this* now—but I will write more to-morrow. God bless my sweetest—

ever, love, I am your
RB

. . .

EB, *Saturday, 20 December 1845*

I have your letter now, & now I am sorry I sent mine. If I wrote that you had 'forgotten to write,' I did not mean it,— not a word!—If I had meant it I should not have written it. But it would have been better for every reason to have waited just a little longer before writing at all. A besetting sin of mine is an impatience which makes people laugh when it does not entangle their silks, pull their knots tighter, & tear their books in cutting them open. . . .

My true initials are *E B M B*—my long name, as opposed to my short one, being: .. Elizabeth Barrett Moulton Barrett!—there's a full length to take away one's breath!— Christian name .. Elizabeth Barrett:—surname, Moulton Barrett. So long it is, that to make it portable, I fell into the habit of doubling it up & packing it closely, .. & of forgetting that I was a *Moulton*, altogether. One might as well write the alphabet as all four initials. Yet our family-name is *Moulton Barrett*, & my brothers reproach me sometimes for sacrificing the governorship of an old town in Norfolk with a little honorable verdegris from the Heralds' Office—As if I cared for the *Retrospective Review*! Nevertheless it is true that I would give ten towns in Norfolk (if I had them) to own some purer lineage than that of the blood of the slave!—Cursed we are

from generation to generation!—I seem to hear the 'Commination Service'.° . . .

You do not say how you are—not a word!—And you are
wrong in saying that you 'ought to have written'—as if
'ought' could be in place *so*!—You *never 'ought' to write to me
you know!*—or rather .. if you ever think you ought, you ought
not!—Which is a speaking of mysteries on my part!—°

RB, *Sunday, 21 December 1845*

Sunday Night.

Now, *'ought'* you to be 'sorry you sent that letter,' which
made, & makes me so happy—so happy—can you bring
yourself to turn round and tell one you have so blessed with
your bounty that there was a mistake, and you meant only
half that largess? If you are not sensible that you *do* make me
most happy by such letters, and do not warm in the reflection
of your own rays, then I *do* give up indeed the last chance of
procuring *you* happiness,—My own 'ought,' which you object
to, shall be withdrawn—being only a pure bit of selfishness; I
felt, in missing the letter of yours, next day, that I *might* have
drawn it down by one of mine,—if I had begged never so
gently, the gold would have fallen—*there* was my omitted duty
to myself—which you properly blame—I should stand
silently and wait and be sure of the ever-remembering
goodness.

Let me count my gold now—and rub off any speck that
stays the full shining. First—*that thought* .. I told you; I pray
you, pray you, sweet—never that again—or what leads never
so remotely or indirectly to it! On *your own fancied ground*—the
fulfilment would be of necessity fraught with every woe that
can fall in this life. I am yours for ever—if you are not *here*,
with me—what then? Say, you take all of yourself away but—
just enough to live on,—then, *that* defeats every kind purpose
.. as if you cut away all the ground from my feet but so much
as serves for bare standing room .. why still, I *stand* there—
and is it the better that I have no broader space, when off *that*
you cannot force me? I have your memory, the knowledge of

you, the idea of you printed into my heart and brain,—on that, I can live my life—but it is for you, the dear, utterly generous creature I know you, to give me more and more beyond mere life—to extend life and deepen it—as you do, and will do. Oh, *how* I love you when I think of the entire truthfulness of your generosity to me—how, meaning, and willing to *give*, you gave *nobly*! Do you think I have not seen in this world how women who *do* love will manage to confer that gift on occasion? And shall I allow myself to fancy how much alloy such pure gold as *your* love would have rendered endurable?—Yet it came, virgin ore, to complete my fortune! And what but this makes me confident and happy? *Can* I take a lesson by your fancies, and begin frightening myself with saying .. 'but if she saw all the world—the worthier, better men there .. those who would' &c &c. No, I think of the great, dear *gift* that it was,—how I *'won'* NOTHING (the hateful word, and *French* thought)—did nothing by my own arts or cleverness in the matter .. so what pretence have the *more* artful or more clever for—but I cannot write out this folly—I am yours for ever, with the utmost sense of grati- tude—to say I would give you my life joyfully is little .. I would, I hope, do that for two or three other people—but I am not conscious of any imaginable point in which I would not implicitly devote my whole self to you—be disposed of by you as for the best. There! It is not to be spoken of—let me *live* it into proof, beloved!

. . .

[Meeting 36: Tuesday, 23 December 3.00–4.45 p.m. The following letter was begun two days before this meeting took place and resumed the day after it; the latter part is not included here.]

EB, *Saturday, 21–Wednesday, 24 December 1845*

Sunday Night.
But did I 'dispute?' Surely not. Surely I believe in you and in 'mysteries.' Surely I prefer the no-reason to ever so much rationalism .. (rationalism & infidelity go together they say!).

All which I may do, & be afraid sometimes notwithstanding—& when you overpraise me (*not* over*love*) I must be
frightened as I told you.

It is with me as with the theologians. I believe in you &
can be happy & safe *so*: but when my 'personal merits' come
into question in any way, even the least, .. why then the
position grows untenable:—it is no more 'of grace'.° . . .

                                                    Monday

For my part, you must admit it to be too possible that you
may be, as I say, 'disappointed' in me—it *is* too possible.
And if it does me good to say so, even now perhaps .. if it is
mere weakness to say so & simply torments you, why do *you*
be magnanimous & forgive *that* .. let it pass as a weakness &
forgive it *so*. Often I think painful things which I do not tell
you & ....

While I write, your letter comes. Kindest of you it was, to
write me such a letter, when I expected scarcely the shadow
of one!—this makes up for the other letter which I expected
unreasonably & which you '*ought not*' to have written, as was
proved afterwards. And now why should I go on with that
sentence?—What had I to say of 'painful things,' I wonder?
All the painful things seem gone .. vanished—I forget what I
had to say. Only do you still think of this, dearest beloved,—
that I sit here in the dark but for *you*, & that the light you
bring me (from *my* fault!—from the nature of *my* darkness!) is
not a settled light as when you open the shutters in the
morning, but a light made by candles which burn some of
them longer & some shorter, & some brighter & briefer, at
once, being 'double-wicks,' & that there is an intermission for
a moment now & then between the dropping of the old light
into the socket & the lighting of the new—Every letter of
yours is a new light which burns so many hours .. & *then*!—I
am morbid, you see—or call it by what name you like .. too
wise or too foolish. 'If the light of the body is darkness, how
great is that darkness!'° Yet even when I grow too wise, I
admit always that while you love me it is an answer to all.
And I am never so much too foolish as to wish to be worthier
for my own sake—only for yours!—not for my own sake,
since I am content to owe all things to you.

So often as I have said, (it reminds me) that in this situation I should be more exacting than any other woman— so often I have said it!—& so different everything is from what I thought it would be! Because if I am exacting it is for *you* & not for *me*—it is altogether for *you*—you understand *that*, dearest of all .. it is for YOU *wholly*. It never crosses my thought, in a lightning even, the question whether I may be happy so & so—*I*. It is the other question which comes always—too often for peace.

People used to say to me, 'You expect too much—you are too romantic—' And my answer always was that 'I could not expect too much when I expected nothing at all' .. which was the truth—for I never thought (& how often I have SAID *that!*) I never thought that anyone whom *I* could love, would stoop to love ME .. the two things seemed clearly incompatible to my understanding.

And now when it comes in a miracle, you wonder at me for looking twice, thrice, four times, to see if it comes through ivory or *horn*. You wonder that it should seem to me at first all illusion—illusion for you, .. illusion for me as a consequence. But how natural—

It is true of me .. very true .. that I have not a high appreciation of what passes in the world . . . under the name of love; & that a distrust of the thing had grown to be a habit of mind with me when I knew you first. It has appeared to me, through all the seclusion of my life & the narrow experience it admitted of, that in nothing, men .. & women too! .. were so apt to mistake their own feelings, as in this one thing. Putting *falseness* quite on one side, .. quite out of sight & consideration, .. an honest mistaking of feeling appears wonderfully common—& no mistake has such frightful results—none can. Selflove & generosity, a mistake may come from either—from pity, from admiration, from any blind impulse—oh, when I look at the histories of my own female friends .. to go no step further!—And if it is true of the *women*, what must the other side be?—To see the marriages which are made every day!—worse than solitudes & more desolate! In the case of the two happiest I ever knew, one of the husbands said in confidence, to a brother of mine—not much in confidence or I should not have heard it, but in a sort of smoking frankness, .. that he had 'ruined his prospects by marrying'; & the other said to myself at the very moment of professing an extraordinary happiness, ... 'But I should have done as well if I had not married *her*.'

Then for the falseness——the first time I ever, in my own experience, heard that word which rhymes to glove & comes as easily off and on, (on some hands!) .. it was from a man of whose attentions to another woman I was at that *time her confidante*. I was bound so to silence for her sake, that I could not even speak the scorn that was in me—and in fact my uppermost feeling was a sort of horror .. a terror—for I was very young then, & the world did, at the moment, look ghastly!

The falseness & the calculations!—why how can you, who are *just, blame women* .. when you must know what the 'system' of men is towards them,—& of men not ungenerous otherwise? Why are women to be blamed if they act as if they had to do with swindlers?—is it not the mere instinct of preservation which makes them do it? Men make women what they are. And your 'honorable men,' the most loyal of them, .. (for instance) .. is it not a rule with them (unless when taken unaware through a want of selfgovernment) to force a woman (trying all means) to force a woman to stand committed in her affections .. (they with their feet lifted all the time to trample on her for want of delicacy—) before *they* risk the pin-prick to their own personal pitiful vanities? Oh—to see how these things are set about by *men*! to see how a man carefully holding up on each side the skirts of an embroidered vanity to keep it quite safe from the wet, will contrive to tell you in so many words that he ... might love you if the sun shone! And women are to be blamed!—Why there are, to be sure, cold & heartless, light & changeable, ungenerous & calculating women in the world!—that is sure. But for the most part, they are only what they are made .. & far better than the nature of the making .. of that I am confident. The loyal make the loyal, the disloyal the disloyal. And I give no more discredit to those women you speak of, than I myself can take any credit in this thing—I. Because who could be disloyal with YOU .. with whatever corrupt inclination? *you*, who are the noblest of all? If you judge me so, .. it is my privilege rather than my merit .. as I feel of myself.

. . .

RB, *Thursday, 25 December 1845*

My dear Christmas gift of a letter! I will write back a few lines, (all I can, having to go out now)—just that I may forever,—certainly during our mortal 'forever'—mix my love for you, and, as you suffer me to say, your love for me .. dearest! .. these shall be mixed with the other loves of the day and live therein—as I write, and trust, and know—forever! While I live I will remember what was my feeling in reading, and in writing, and in stopping from either .. as I have just done .. to kiss you and bless you with my whole heart—Yes, yes, bless you, my own!

All is right, all of your letter .. admirably right and just in the defence of the women I *seemed* to speak against,—and only seemed—because that is a way of mine which you must have observed,—that foolish concentrating of thought and feeling, for a moment, on some one little spot of a character or anything else indeed, and—in the attempt to do justice and develop whatever may seem ordinarily to be overlooked in it,—that over vehement *insisting* on, and giving an undue prominence to, the same—which has the effect of taking away from the importance of the rest of the related objects which, in truth, are not considered at all .. or they would also rise proportionally when subjected to the same (.. that is, corre-spondingly magnified and dilated ..) light and concentrated feeling: so, you remember, the old divine, preaching on 'small sins,' in his zeal to expose the tendencies & consequences usually made little account of, was led to maintain the said small sins to be 'greater than great ones.' *But then* .. if you look on the world *altogether*, and accept the small natures, in their usual proportion, with the greater .. things do not look *quite* so bad; because, the conduct which *is* atrocious in those higher cases, of proposal and acceptance, *may* be no more than the claims of the occasion justify—(wait and hear!)—in certain other cases where the thing sought for and granted is avowedly less by a million degrees; it shall all be traffic, exchange—(counting spiritual gifts as only coin, for our purpose)—but surely the formalities and policies and decencies all vary with the nature of the thing trafficked for—a man makes up his mind during half his life to acquire a Pitt-diamond or a Pilgrim-pearl°—and gets witnesses and testimony and soforth—but, surely, when I pass a shop where oranges are ticketed up seven for sixpence I offend no law by sparing all words and putting down the piece with a certain authoritative ring on the counter: if instead of diamonds you want—(being a King or Queen)—provinces with live men on them .. there is so much more diplomacy required; new interests are appealed to .. high motives *supposed*, at all events—whereas, when, in Naples, a man asks leave to black your shoe in the dusty street 'purely for the honor of serving your Excellency' you laugh and would be sorry to find yourself without a 'grano' or two—(six of which, about, make a farthing)—Now do you not see! Where so little is to be got, why offer much more? If a man knows that .. but I am teaching you! All I mean is, that, in Benedick's phrase, 'the world must go on.'° He who honestly wants his wife to sit at the head of his table and carve .. that is be his *help-meat*, not 'help mete for him'—he shall assuredly find a girl of his degree who wants the table to sit at—

. . .

[Meeting 37: Monday, 29 December 3.00–4.45 p.m.]

EB, *Tuesday, 30 December 1845*

When you are gone I find your flowers; & you never spoke of nor showed them to me—so instead of yesterday I thank you today—thank you. Count among the miracles, that your flowers live with me°—I accept *that* for an omen, dear—

dearest! Flowers in general, all other flowers, die of despair when they come into the same atmosphere .. used to do it so constantly & observably that it made me melancholy & I left off for the most part having them here. Now, you see how they put up with the close room, & condescend to me & the dust—it is true and no fancy! To be sure they know that I care for them & that I stand up by the table myself to change their water & cut their stalks freshly at intervals—*that* may make a difference perhaps. Only the great reason must be that they are yours, & that you teach them to bear with me patiently. . . .

What a *misomonsism*° you fell into yesterday, you who have so much great work to do which no one else can do except just yourself!—& you, too, who have courage & knowledge, & must know that every work, with the principle of life in it, *will* live, let it be trampled ever so under the heel of a faithless & unbelieving generation—yes, that it will live like one of your toads, for a thousand years in the heart of a rock. All men can teach at second or third hand, as you said .. by prompting the foremost rows .. by tradition & translation:— all, *except poets*, who must preach their own doctrine & sing their own song, to be the means of any wisdom or any music, & therefore have stricter duties thrust upon them, & may not lounge in the στοά° like the conversation-teachers. So much I have to say to you, till we are in the Siren's island—& *I*, jealous of the Siren!—

'The Siren waits thee singing song for song,'

says Mr. Landor.° A prophecy which refuses to class you with the 'mute fishes,' precisely as I do.

. . .

RB, *Wednesday, 31 December 1845*

. . . Dearest, whatever change the new year brings with it, we are together—I can give you no more of myself—indeed, you give me now—(back again if you choose, but changed and renewed by your possession—) the powers that seemed most properly mine: I could only mean that, by the expressions to which you refer—only could mean that you were my crown and palm branch, now and for ever, and so, that it was a very indifferent matter to me if the world took notice of that fact or no—Yes, dearest—that *is* the meaning of the prophecy—which I was stupidly blind not to have read and taken comfort from long ago—You ARE the veritable Siren—and you 'wait me,' and will sing 'song for song'—And this is my first song, my true song—this love I bear you—I look into my heart and then let it go forth under that name—love—I am more than mistrustful of many other feelings in me: they are not earnest enough; so far, not true enough—but this is all the flower of my life which you call forth and which lies at your feet.

Now let me say it .. what you are to remember: that if I had the slightest doubt, or fear, I would utter it to you on the instant—secure in the incontested stability of the main *fact*, even though the heights at the verge in the distance should tremble and prove vapour—and there would be a deep consolation in your forgiveness—indeed, yes,—but I tell you, on solemn consideration, it does seem to me that,—once take away the broad & general words that admit in their nature of any freight they can be charged with,—put aside love, and devotion, and trust—and *then* I seem to have said *nothing* of my feeling to you—nothing whatever.

⟨Indeed I so far conform myself to your pleasure, as I understand it, as never to *try*, even, to express⟩ I will not write more now—on this subject—believe you are my blessing and infinite reward beyond possible desert in intention,— my life has been crowned by you, as I said.

. . .

EB, *Thursday 1 January 1846*

How good you are—how best! it is a favorite play of my memory to take up the thought of what you were to me (to my mind gazing!) years ago, as the poet in an abstraction .. then the thoughts of you .. a little clearer, in concrete personality, as Mr. Kenyon's friend, who had dined with him on such a day, or met him at dinner on such another, & said some great memorable thing 'on wednesday last', & enquired kindly about *me* perhaps on thursday, .. till I was proud! .. & so, the thoughts of you .. nearer & nearer (yet still far!) as the Mr. Browning who meant to do me the honor of writing to me, & who did write; & who asked me once in a letter (does he remember?) 'not to lean out of the window while his foot was on the stair'!° .. to take up all those thoughts, & more than those, one after another, & tie them together with all *these*, which cannot be named so easily—which cannot be classed in botany & Greek. It is a nosegay of mystical flowers, looking strangely & brightly, .. & keeping their May-dew through the Christmases—better even than *your* flowers!— And I am not 'ashamed' of mine, .. be very sure! no!

. . .

[Meeting 38: Saturday, 3 January 3.00–5.00 p.m.]

RB, *Sunday, 4 January 1846*

Yesterday, nearly the last thing, I bade you 'think of me'— I wonder if you could misunderstand me in that?—As if my words or actions or any of my ineffectual outside-self *should* be thought of, unless to be forgiven! But I do—dearest—feel confident that while I am in your mind,—cared for, rather than thought about,—no great harm can happen to me—and as, for great harm to reach me, it must pass thro' you,—you will care for yourself; *my*self, best self!

. . . I suspect . . . you have found out by this time my odd liking for 'vermin'—you once wrote '*your* snails'—and certainly snails are old clients of mine—but efts! . . . But never try and catch a speckled gray lizard when we are in Italy, love—and you see his tail hang out of the chink of a wall, his winter-house—because the strange tail will snap off, drop from him and stay in your fingers—and tho' you afterwards learn that there is more desperation in it and glorious determination to be free, than positive pain—(so people say who have no tails to be twisted off)—and tho', moreover, the tail grows again after a sort—*yet* .. don't do it, for it will give you a thrill! What a fine fellow our English water-eft is; 'Triton paludis Linnaei'—*e come guizza* [and how it darts] (*that* you can't say in another language; cannot preserve the little in-and-out motion along with the straightforwardness!)—I always loved all those wild creatures God '*sets up for themselves*' so independently of us, so successfully, with their strange happy minute inch of a candle, as it were, to light them; while we run about and against each other with our great cressets and fire-pots. I once saw a solitary bee nipping a leaf round till it exactly fitted the front of a hole; his nest, no doubt; or tomb, perhaps . . . Well, it seemed awful to watch that bee—he seemed so *instantly* from the teaching of God!° . . .

My best, dear, dear one,—may you be better, less *depressed*, .. I can hardly imagine frost reaching you if I could be by you. Think what happiness you mean to give me,—what a life,—what a death! 'I may change'—too true,—yet, you see, as an eft was to me at the beginning so it continues—I *may* take up stones and pelt the next I see—but—do you much fear that?—Now, *walk*, move, *guizza, anima mia dolce* [dart, my sweet soul].

. . .

EB, *Sunday, 4–Monday, 5 January 1846*

. . .

You never guessed perhaps .. what I look back to at this moment in the physiology of our intercourse, ... the curious double feeling I had about you .. you personally, & you as the writer of these letters, .. & the crisis of the feeling, when I was positively vexed & jealous of *myself* for not succeeding better in making a unity of the two. I could not!—And moreover I could not help but that the writer of the letters seemed nearer to me, long .. long .. & in spite of the postmark .. than did the personal visitor who confounded me, & left me constantly under such an impression of its being all dreamwork on his side, that I have stamped my feet on this floor

with impatience to think of having to wait so many hours
before the 'candid' closing letter c^d come with its confession
of an illusion. 'People say,' I used to think, 'that women
always know .. & certainly I do not know .. & therefore ..
therefore'—The logic crushed on like Juggernaut's car. But
in the letters it was different—the dear letters took me on the
side of my own ideal life where I was able to stand a little
upright & look round.—I could read such letters for ever &
answer them after a fashion .. that, I felt from the beginning.
But you—! . . .

I have this moment a parcel of books° via Mr. Moxon—
Miss Martineau's two volumes—& Mr. Bailey sends his
'Festus' very kindly, .. And 'Woman in the nineteenth century' from America from a Mrs. or a Miss Fuller. How I hate
those 'Women of England' 'Women & their mission' & the
rest. As if any possible good were to be done by such
expositions of rights & wrongs.

Your letter would be worth them all, if *you* were less *you!* I
mean, just this letter, .. all alive as it is with crawling buzzing
wriggling coldblooded warmblooded creatures .. as all alive
as your own pedant's book in the tree.° And do you know, I
think I like frogs too—particularly the very little leaping
frogs, which are so highhearted as to emulate the birds. I
remember being scolded by my nurses for taking them up in
my hands & letting them leap from one hand to the other.
But for the toad!—why, at the end of the row of narrow beds
which we called our gardens when we were children, grew an
old thorn, & in the hollow of the root of the thorn, lived a
toad, a great ancient toad, whom I, for one, never dared
approach too nearly. That he 'wore a jewel in his head'° I
doubted nothing at all. You might see it glitter if you stooped
& looked steadily into the hole. And on days when he came
out & sate swelling his black sides, I never looked steadily,—
I would run a hundred yards round through the shrubs,
deeper than knee-deep in the long wet grass & nettles, rather
than go past him where he sate; being steadily of opinion in
the profundity of my natural history-learning, that if he took
it into his toad's head to spit at me I should drop down dead
in a moment, poisoned as by one of the Medici.

Oh—and I had a field-mouse for a pet once, & should have

joined my sisters in a rat's nest if I had not been ill at the time: (as it was, the little rats were tenderly smothered by over-love!) & blue-bottle flies I used to feed, & hated your spiders for them,—yet no, not much. My aversion proper .. call it horror rather .. was for the silent, cold, clinging, gliding *bat*,—& even now, I think, I could not sleep in the room with that strange bird-mouse-creature, as it glides round the ceiling silently, silently as its shadow does on the floor—If you listen or look, there is not a wave of the wing—the wing never waves!—A bird without a feather! a beast that flies!—and so cold!—as cold as a fish!—It is the most supernatural-seeming of natural things. And then to see how when the windows are open at night those bats come sailing .. without a sound—& go .. you cannot guess where!—fade with the night-blackness!

You have not been well—which is my first thought if not my first word. Do walk, & do not work,—& think .. what I could be thinking of, if I did not think of *you* .. dear—dearest!—'As the doves fly to the windows,'° so I think of you! As the prisoners think of liberty, as the dying think of Heaven, so I think of you. When I look up straight to God .. nothing, no one, used to intercept me—now there is *you*—only you under Him!

. . .

RB. *Tuesday, 6–Wednesday, 7 January 1846°*

But, my sweet, there is safer going in letters than in visits, do you not see? In the letter, one may go to the utmost limit of one's supposed tether without danger—there is the distance so palpably between the most audacious step *there*, and the next .. which is no where, seeing it is not in the letter: quite otherwise in personal intercourse, where any indication of turning to a certain path, even, might possibly be checked not for its own fault but lest, the path once reached and proceeded in, some other forbidden turning might come into sight, we will say: in the letter, all ended *there*, just there .. and you may think of that, and forgive; at all events, may avoid speaking irrevocable words—and when, as to me, those words are intensely *true, doom-words*—think, dearest! Because, as I told you once, what most characterizes my feeling for you is the perfect *respect* in it, the full *belief* .. (I shall get presently to poor Robert's very avowal of 'owing you all esteem'!)°—It is on that I build, and am secure—for how should I know, of myself, how to serve you and be properly yours if it all was to be learnt by my own interpreting, and what you professed to dislike you were to be considered as wishing for, and what liking, as it seemed, you were loathing at your heart, and if so many 'noes' made a 'yes,' and 'one refusal no rebuff' and all that horrible bestiality which stout gentlemen turn up the whites of their eyes to, when they rise after dinner and, pressing the right hand to the left side say, 'The toast be dear woman!' Now, love, with this feeling in me from the beginning,—I do believe,—*now*, when I am utterly blest in this gift of your love and least able to imagine what I should do without it,—I cannot but believe, I say, that had you given me once a 'refusal'—clearly derived from your own feelings, and quite apart from any fancied consideration for my interests,—had this come upon me, whether slowly but inevitably in the course of events, or suddenly as precipitated by any step of mine,—I should, *believing you*, have never again renewed directly or indirectly such solicitation,—I should have begun to count how many other ways were yet open to serve you and devote myself to you .. but *from the outside*, now, and not in your livery! Now, if I should have acted thus under *any* circumstances, how could I but redouble my endeavours at precaution after my own foolish .. you know, and forgave long since, and I, too, am forgiven in my own eyes, for the cause, tho' not the manner—but could I do other than keep 'farther from you' than in the letters, dearest? For your own part in that matter, seeing it with all the light you have since given me (and *then*, not inadequately by my own light) I could,—I *do*—kiss your feet, kiss every letter in your name, bless you with my whole heart and soul if I could pour them out, from me, before you, to stay and be yours,—when I think on your motives and pure perfect generosity—It was the plainness of *that* which determined me to wait and be patient and grateful and your own for ever in any shape or capacity you might please to accept. Do you think that because I am so rich now, I could not have been most rich, too, *then*—in what would seem little only to *me*, only with this great happiness? I should have been proud beyond measure & happy past all desert, to call and be allowed to see you simply, speak with you and be spoken to—what am I more than others? Don't think this mock-humility—*it is not*—you take me in your mantle, and we shine together, but I know my part in it! All this is written breathlessly on a sudden fancy that you *might* .. if not now, at some future time,—give other than this, the true reason, for that discrepancy you see, that nearness in the letters, that early farness in the visits! And, love, all love is but a passionate *drawing closer*—I would be one with you, dearest,—let my soul press close to you, as my lips, dear life of my life—

. . .

[Meeting 39: Thursday, 8 January 3.00–5.00 p.m.]

EB, *Saturday, 10 January 1846*

. . . Shall I tell you?—it seems to me, to myself, that no man was ever before to any woman what you are to me—the fulness must be in proportion, you know, to the vacancy .. & only *I* know what was behind .. the long wilderness *without* the 'footstep', .. without the blossoming rose .. & the capacity for happiness, like a black gaping hole, before this silver flooding.° Is it wonderful that I should stand as in a dream, & disbelieve .. not *you*—but my own fate? Was ever any one taken suddenly from a lampless dungeon & placed upon the pinnacle of a mountain, without the head turning round & the heart turning faint, as mine do? And you love me MORE, you say?—Shall I thank you or God?—Both, .. indeed—& there is no possible return from me to either of you!—I thank you as the unworthy may .. & as we all thank God. How shall I ever prove what my heart is to you? how will you ever see it as I feel it? I ask myself in vain.

. . .

RB, *Sunday, 11 January 1846*

. . .

Must you see 'Pauline'? At least then let me wait a few days,—to correct the misprints which affect the sense, and to write you the history of it,—° what is necessary you should know before you see it. . . .

I was out last night—to see the rest of Frank Talfourd's theatricals°—, and met Dickens and his set—so my evenings go away! If I do not bring the *Act*° you must forgive me—yet I shall .. I think,—the roughness matters little in this stage. Chorley says very truly that a tragedy implies as much power *kept back* as brought out—very true that is—I do not, on the whole, feel dissatisfied .. as was to be but expected .. with the effect of this last—the *shelve* of the hill, whence the end is seen, you continuing to go down to it .. so that at the very last you may pass off into a plain and so away—not come to a stop like your horse against a church wall. It is all in long speeches—the *action, proper*, is in them—they are no descriptions, or amplifications—but here .. in a drama of this kind, all the *events*, (and interest,) take place in the *minds* of the actors .. somewhat like Paracelsus in that respect: you know, or don't know, that the general charge against me, of late, from the few quarters I thought it worth while to listen to, has been that of abrupt, spasmodic writing—they will find some fault with this, of course. . . .

And now, my Audience, my crown-bearer, my path-preparer°—I am with you again and out of them all—there, *here*, in my arms, is my *proved, palpable success!*—my life, my poetry,—gained nothing, oh no!—but this found them, and blessed them.

. . .

[Meeting 40: Tuesday, 13 January 3.30–5.30 p.m.]

EB, *Tuesday, 13–Wednesday, 14 January 1846*

Ah Mr. Kenyon!—how he vexed me today. To keep away all the ten days before, & to come just at the wrong time after all! It was better for you .. I suppose .. I believe .. to go with him down stairs—yes, it certainly was better: it was disagreeable enough to be very wise! Yet I, being addicted to every sort of superstition turning to melancholy, did hate so breaking off in the middle of that black thread .. (do you remember what we were talking of when they opened the door?) that I was on the point of saying 'Stay one moment,' which I should have repented afterwards for the best of good reasons. Oh, I *should* have liked to have 'fastened off' that black thread, and taken one stitch with a blue or a green one!—

You do not remember what we were talking of? What *you*, rather, were talking of?—And what *I* remember, at least, because it is exactly the most unkind & hard thing you ever said to me .. ever dearest—so I remember it by that sign!— That you should say such a thing to me—! think what it was, for indeed I will not write it down here ... Only the foolishness of it (I mean, the foolishness of it alone) saves it, smooths it to a degree!—the foolishness being the same as if you asked a man where he would walk when he lost his head ...

And you!—you, who talk so finely of never, never doubting,—of being such an example in the way of believing & trusting—! it appears, after all, that you have an imagination apprehensive (or comprehensive) of 'glass bottles' like other sublunary creatures, & worse than some of them. For mark, that I never went any farther than to the stone-wall-hypothesis of your forgetting me!—*I* always stopped there—& never climbed to the top of it over the broken-bottle fortification, to see which way you meant to walk afterwards. And you, to ask me so coolly—think what you asked me. That you should have the heart to ask such a question!—

And the reason—! And it could seem a reasonable matter of doubt to you whether I would go to the south for my health's sake—And I answered quite a common 'no' I believe—for you bewildered me for the moment—& I have had tears in my eyes two or three times since, just through thinking back on it all .. of your asking me such questions. Now did I not tell you when I first knew you, that I was leaning out of the window?° True, *that* was—I was tired of living .. unaffectedly tired. All I cared to live for was to do better some of the work which, after all, was out of myself & which I had to reach across to do. But I told you. Then, last year, .. for duty's sake I would have *consented* to go to Italy!— but if you really fancy that I would have struggled in the face of all that difficulty—or struggled, indeed, anywise, to compass such an object as *that* .. except for the motive of your caring for it & me .. why you know nothing of me after all— nothing!—And now, take away the motive .. & I am where I was .. leaning out of the window again. To put it in plainer words .. (as you really require information ..) I should let them do what they liked to me till I was dead—only I *wouldn't go to Italy* .. if anybody proposed Italy out of contradiction. In the meantime I do entreat you never to talk of such a thing to me any more. . . .

Wednesday.

For '*Pauline*' .. when I had named it to you I was on the point of sending for the book to the booksellers—then suddenly I thought to myself that I would wait & hear whether you very, very much would dislike my reading it. See now! Many readers have done virtuously, but *I*, (in this virtue I tell you of) surpassed them all!°—And now, because I *may*, I '*must* read it'—: & as there are misprints to be corrected, will you do what is necessary, or what you think is neccessary, & bring me the book on monday?

. . .

RB, *Wednesday, 14 January 1846*

Was I in the wrong, dearest, to go away with Mr. Kenyon? I *well knew and felt* the price I was about to pay .. but the thought *did* occur that he might have been informed my probable time of departure was that of his own arrival—and that he would not know how very soon, alas, I should be *obliged* to go—so .. to save you any least embarrassment in the world, I got—just that shake of the hand, just that look—and no more! And was it all for nothing, all needless after all? So I said to myself all the way home.

When I am away from you—a crowd of things press on me for utterance .. 'I will say them, not write them,' I think:—when I see you—all to be said seems insignificant, irrelevant,—'they can be written, at all events'—I think *that* too. So, feeling so much, I say so little!

. . .

RB, *Thursday, 15 January 1846*

Dearest, dearer to my heart minute by minute, I had no wish to give you pain, God knows. No one can more readily consent to let a few years more or less of life go out of account,—be lost—but as I sate by you, you so full of the truest life, for this world as for the next,—and was struck by that possibility, all that might happen were I away, in the case of your continuing to acquiesce—dearest, it *is* horrible,—I could not but speak—if in drawing you, all of you, closer to my heart, I hurt you whom I would—*outlive* .. yes,—I cannot speak here—forgive me, Ba.

My Ba, you are to consider now for me: your health, your strength—it is all wonderful,—that is not my dream, you know—but what all see: now, steadily care for us both—take time, take counsel if you choose; but at the end tell me what you will do for your part—thinking of me as utterly devoted, soul and body, to you, living wholly in your life, seeing good and ill, only as you see,—being yours as your hand is,—or as your Flush, rather. Then I will, on my side, prepare. When I say 'take counsel'—I reserve my last right, the man's right of first speech. *I* stipulate, too, and require to say my own speech in my own words or by letter, remember! But this living without you is too tormenting now. So begin thinking—, as for Spring, as for a New Year, as for a New Life. . . .

Will you, and must you have 'Pauline'? If I could pray you to revoke that decision! For it is altogether foolish and *not* boylike—and I shall, I confess, hate the notion of running over it—yet commented it must be; more than mere correction! I was unluckily *precocious*—but I had rather you saw real infantine efforts .. (verses at six years old,—and drawings still earlier)—than this ambiguous, feverish—Why not wait? When you speak of the 'Bookseller'—I smile, in glorious security—having a whole bale of sheets at the house-top: he never knew my name even!—and I withdrew these after a very little time.

. . .

EB, *Thursday, 15 January 1846*

. . . How am I? But I am too well to be asked about. Is it not a warm summer? The weather is as 'miraculous' as the rest, I think. It is you who are unwell & make people uneasy, .. dearest—Say how you are, & promise me to do what is right & try to be better. The walking, the changing of the air, the leaving off Luria .. do what is right, I earnestly beseech you. The other day, I heard of Tennyson being ill again, .. too ill to write a simple note to his friend Mr. Venables who told George. A little more than a year ago, it would have been no worse a thing to me to hear of your being ill than to hear of his being ill!—How the world has changed since then! To *me*, I mean. . . .

May God bless you!—Did I ever say that I had an objection to read the verses at six years old .. or see the drawings either? I am reasonable, you observe!—Only, 'Pauline' I must have *some day*—why not without the emendations? But if you insist on them, I will agree to wait a little .. if you promise *at last* to let me see the book which I will not show .. Some day, then!—you shall not be vexed nor hurried for the day—some day—Am I not generous? And *I* was 'precocious' too, & used to make rhymes over my bread & milk when I was nearly a baby .. only really it was mere echo-verse, that of mine, & had nothing of mark or of indication, such as I do not doubt that yours had. I used to write of virtue with a large 'V,' & 'Oh Muse' with a harp—, & things of that sort. At nine years old I wrote what I called 'an epic'—& at ten various tragedies, French & English, which we used to act in the nursery. . . . And these were my 'maturer works,' you are to understand, .. and 'the moon was bright at ten oclock at night' years before. As to the gods & goddesses, I believed in them all quite seriously, & reconciled them to Christianity, which I believed in too after a fashion, as some greater philosophers have done—& went out one day with my pinafore full of little sticks, (& a match from the housemaids' cupboard) to sacrifice to the blue eyed Minerva who was my favorite goddess on the whole because she cared for Athens. As soon as I began to doubt about my goddesses, I fell into a vague sort of general scepticism, .. & though I went on saying 'the Lord's prayer' at nights & mornings, & the 'Bless all my kind friends' afterwards, by the childish custom .. yet I ended this liturgy with a supplication which I found in 'King's memoirs'° & which took my fancy & met my general views exactly .. 'O God, if there be a God, save my soul, if I have a soul.' Perhaps the theology of many thoughtful children is scarcely more orthodox than this: but indeed it is wonderful to myself sometimes how I came to escape, on the whole, as well as I have done, considering the commonplaces of education in which I was set, with strength & opportunity for breaking the bonds all round into liberty & license. Papa used to say .. 'Dont read Gibbon's history—it's not a proper book. Dont read "Tom Jones"—& none of the books on *this* side, mind.' So I was very obedient & never touched the books on *that* side, & only read instead, Tom Paine's Age of Reason, & Voltaire's Philosophical Dictionary, & Hume's Essays, & Werther,° & Rousseau, & Mary Wollstonecraft .. books, which I was never suspected of looking towards, & which were not 'on *that* side' certainly, but which did as well.

. . .

EB, *Thursday, 15–Friday, 16 January 1846°*

. . .

For the rest, I will think as you desire: but I have thought a great deal, & there are certainties which I know; & I hope we *both* are aware that nothing can be more hopeless than our position in some relations & aspects, though you do not guess perhaps that the very approach to the subject is shut up by dangers, & that from the moment of a suspicion entering *one mind*, we should be able to meet never again in this room, nor to have intercourse by letter through the ordinary channel. I mean, that letters of yours, addressed to me here, would infallibly be stopped & destroyed—if not opened. Therefore it is advisable to hurry on nothing—on these grounds it is advisable. What should I do if I did not see you nor hear from you, without being able to feel that it was for your happiness? What should I do for a month even? And then, I might be thrown out of the window or its equivalent—I look back shuddering to the dreadful scenes in which poor Henrietta was involved who never offended as I have offended .. years ago which seem as present as today. She had forbidden the subject to be referred to until that consent was obtained—& at a word she gave up all—at a word. In fact she had no true attachment, as I observed to Arabel at the time: a child never submitted more meekly to a revoked holiday. Yet how she was made to suffer—Oh, the dreadful scenes!—and only because she had seemed to feel a little. I told you, I think, that there was an obliquity .. an eccentricity—or something beyond .. on one class of subjects. I hear how her knees were made to ring upon the floor, now! —she was carried out of the room in strong hysterics, & I, who rose up to follow her, though I was quite well at that time & suffered only by sympathy, fell flat down upon my face in a fainting-fit. Arabel thought I was dead.

I have tried to forget it all—but now I must remember—& throughout our intercourse I *have remembered*. It is necessary to remember so much as to avoid such evils as are evitable, & for this reason I would conceal nothing from you. Do *you* remember, besides, that there can be no faltering on my

'part,' & that, if I should remain well, which is not proved
yet, I will do for you what you please & as you please to have
it done. But there is time for considering!

Only .. as you speak of 'counsel,' I will take courage to tell
you that my SISTERS KNOW—. Arabel is in most of my
confidences, & being often in the room with me, taxed me
with the truth long ago—she saw that I was affected from
some cause—& I told her. We are as safe with both of them
as possible—& they thoroughly understand that if *there should
be any change it would not be* YOUR FAULT .. I made them
understand that thoroughly. From themselves I have received
nothing but the most smiling words of kindness & satisfaction
(—I thought I might tell you so much,—) they have too
much tenderness for me to fail in it now. My brothers, it is
quite necessary not to draw into a dangerous responsibility: I
have felt that from the beginning & shall continue to feel it—
though I hear, & can observe that they are full of suspicions
& conjectures, which are never unkindly expressed. I told you
once that we held hands the faster in this house for the weight
over our heads. But the absolute *knowledge* would be dangerous for my brothers: with my sisters it is different, & I could
not continue to conceal from *them* what they had under their
eyes—and then, Henrietta is in a like position—It was not
wrong of me to let them know it?—no?—

Yet of what consequence is all this to the other side of the
question? What, if *you* should give pain & disappointment
where you owe such pure gratitude—But we need not talk of
these things now. Only you have more to consider than *I*, I
imagine, while the future comes on. . . .

My life was ended when I knew you, & if I survive myself
it is for your sake:—*that* resumes all my feelings & intentions
in respect to you. No 'counsel' could make the difference of a
grain of dust in the balance. It *is so*, & not otherwise. If you
changed towards me, it would be better for you I believe—&
I should be only where I was before. While you do *not* change,
I look to you for my first affections & my first duty—&
nothing but your bidding me, could make me look away.

. . .

RB, *Sunday, 18 January 1846*

. . .

On the saddest part of all,—silence. You understand, and I can understand thro' you. Do you know, that I never *used* to dream unless indisposed, and rarely then—(of late I dream of you, but quite of late)—and *those* nightmare dreams have invariably been of *one* sort—I stand by, (powerless to interpose by a word even) and see the infliction of tyranny on the unresisting—man or beast (generally the last)—and I wake just in time not to die: let no one try this kind of experiment on me or mine! Tho' I have observed that by a felicitous arrangement, the man with the whip puts it into use with an old horse commonly: I once knew a fine specimen of the boilingly passionate, desperately respectable on the Eastern principle that reverences a madman—and this fellow, whom it was to be death to oppose, (some bloodvessel was to break)—he, once at a dinner party at which I was present, insulted his wife, (a young pretty simple believer in his awful immunities from the ordinary terms that keep men in order)—brought the tears into her eyes and sent her from the room .. purely to 'show off' in the eyes of his guests .. (all males, law-friends &c he being a lawyer.) This feat accomplished, he, too, left us with an affectation of compensating relentment, to 'just say a word and return'—and no sooner was his back to the door than the biggest, stupidest of the company, began to remark 'what a fortunate thing it was that Mr So-&-so had such a submissive wife—not one of the women who would resist—that is, attempt to resist,—and so exasperate our gentleman into .. Heaven only knew what!'— I said it *was*, in one sense, a fortunate thing,—because one of those women, without necessarily being the lion-tressed Bellona,° would richly give him his desert, I thought—'Oh, indeed? No—*this* man was not to be opposed—wait, you might, till the fit was over, and then try what kind argument would do'—and so forth to unspeakable nausea. Presently we went upstairs—there sate the wife with dried eyes, and a smile at the tea table—and by her, in all the pride of conquest, with her hand in his, our friend—disposed to be very good-

natured of course. I listened *arrectis auribus* [with ears
pricked]—and in a minute he said he did not know somebody
I mentioned—I told him, *that* I easily conceived—such a
person would never condescend to know *him*, &c, and treated
him to every consequence ingenuity could draw from that
text—and at the end marched out of the room,—and the
valorous man, who had sate like a post, got up, took a candle,
followed me to the door, and only said in unfeigned wonder,
'What *can* have possessed you, my *dear* B?'—All which I as
much expected beforehand, as that the above mentioned man
of the whip keeps it quiet in the presence of an ordinary-
couraged dog—All this is quite irrelevant to *the* case .. indeed,
I write to get rid of the thought altogether: but do hold it the
most stringent duty of all who can, to stop a condition, a
relation of one human being to another which God never
allowed to exist between Him and ourselves—*Trees* live and
die, if you please, and accept will for a law—but with us, all
commands surely refer to a previously-implanted conviction
in ourselves of their rationality and justice—Or why declare
that 'the Lord *is* holy, just and good'° unless there is recognised and independent conception of holiness and goodness,
to which the subsequent assertion is referable? 'You know
what *holiness* is, what it is to be good? Then, He *is* that'—Not,
'*that* is so—because he is that',—tho' of course, when once the
converse is demonstrated, this, too, follows, and may be urged
for practical purposes—All God's urgency, so to speak, is on
the *justice* of his judgments, *rightness* of his rule: yet why? one
might ask—if one *does* believe that the rule *is* his; why ask
further?—Because, his is a 'reasonable service,'° once for all.

Understand why I turn my thoughts in this direction—if it
is indeed as you fear—and no endeavour, concession, on my
part will avail, under any circumstances—(and by endeavour,
I mean all heart & soul could bring the flesh to perform)—in
that case, you will not come to me with a shadow past hope
of chasing——

The likelihood is—I over frighten myself for you, by the
involuntary contrast with those here—you allude to them—if
I went with this letter downstairs and said simply 'I want this
taken to the direction tonight—and am unwell & unable to
go—will you take it now?'—My father would not say a

word,—or rather would say a dozen cheerful absurdities about his 'wanting a walk,' 'just having been wishing to go out' &c—At night he sits studying my works—illustrating them (I will bring you drawings to make you laugh)—and *yesterday* I picked up a crumpled bit of paper .. 'his notion of what a criticism on this last number ought to be—, none, that have appeared, satisfying him!'—So judge of what he will say!—(And my mother loves me just as much more as must of necessity be—)

. . .

EB, *Sunday, 18 January 1846*

. . .

Now, shall I tell you what I did yesterday. It was so warm, so warm, the thermometer at 68 in this room, that I took it into my head to call it April instead of January, & put on a cloak & walked down stairs into the drawing room .. walked, mind!—Before, I was carried by one of my brothers, .. even to the last autumn-day when I went out ... I never walked a step for fear of the cold in the passages. But yesterday it was so wonderfully warm, & I so strong besides—it was a feat worthy of the day—& I surprised them all as much as if I had walked out of the window instead. That kind dear Stormie who with all his shyness & awkwardness has the most loving of hearts in him, said that he was '*so* glad to see me'! . . .

A hundred letters I have, by this last, .. to set against Napoleon's Hundred Days—did you know *that*?

. . .

RB, *Monday, 19 January 1846*

Love, if you knew but how vexed I was, so very few minutes after my note left last night, how angry with the unnecessary harshness into which some of the phrases might be construed—you would forgive me, indeed. But, when all is confessed and forgiven, the fact remains—that it would be the one trial I *know* I should not be able to bear,—the repetition of those 'scenes'—intolerable—not to be written of, even—my mind *refuses* to form a clear conception of them—

_____

My own loved letter is come—and the news ... I fancy myself meeting you on 'the stairs'—stairs and passages generally, and galleries, (ah, those indeed!)—all, with their picturesque *accidents*, of landing-places, and spiral heights & depths, and sudden turns and visions of half open doors into what Quarles calls 'mollitious chambers'°—and above all, *landing-places*—they are my heart's delight—I would come upon you unaware on a landing-place in my next dream! One day we may walk in the galleries round and over the inner-court of the Doges' Palace at Venice,—and read, on tablets against the wall, how such an one was banished for an 'enormous dig (intacco) into the public treasure'—another for .. what you are not to know because his friends have got chisels and chipped away the record of it—underneath the 'giants' on their stands, and in the midst of the *cortile* [courtyard] the bronze fountains whence the girls draw water . . .

Now to you—Ba! When I go thro' sweetness to sweetness, at 'Ba' I stop last of all, and lie and rest. That is the quintessence of them all,—they all take colour and flavour from that. So, dear, dear Ba, be glad as you can to see me to morrow—God knows how I embalm every such day,—I do not believe that one of the *forty* is confounded with another in my memory. So, *that* is gained and sure for ever. And of letters, this makes my 104th and, like Donne's Bride, 'I take, /My jewels from their boxes,—call / My Diamonds, Pearls, and Emeralds, and make / Myself a constellation of them all!'° Bless you, my own Beloved!

. . .

[Meeting 41: Tuesday, 20 January 3.00–5.00 p.m.]

EB, *Wednesday, 21 January 1846*

. . . I want to ask *you* something—I have had it in my head a long time, but it might as well have been in a box—& indeed if it had been in the box with your letters, I should have remembered to speak of it long ago. So now, at last, tell me— how do you write, o my poet? with steel pens, or Bramah pens,° or goosequills or crowquills?—Because I have a pen-holder which was given to me when I was a child, & which I have used both then & since in the production of various great epics & immortal 'works,' until in these latter years it has seemed to me too heavy & I have taken into service, instead of it, another two-inch-long instrument which makes Mr. Kenyon laugh to look at—& so, my fancy has run upon your having the heavier holder, which is not very heavy after all, & which will make you think of me whether you choose it or not, besides being made of a splinter from the ivory gate of old, & therefore not unworthy of a true prophet. Will you have it .. dearest? Yes—because you can't help it. When you come .. on saturday!—

And for 'Pauline', .. I am satisfied with the promise to see it some day .. when we are in the isle of the sirens, or ready for wandering in the Doges' galleries ... I seem to understand that you would really rather wish me not to see it now .. & as long as I *do* see it ..! So *that shall* be!—Am I not good now, & not a teazer? If there is any poetical justice in 'the seven worlds,' I shall have a letter tonight.

By the way you owe me two letters by your confession. A hundred & four of mine you have, I, only a hundred & two of yours .. which is a 'deficit' scarcely creditable to me, (— now is it? ..) when according to the law & ordinance, a woman's hundred & four letters would take two hundred & eight at least, from the other side, to justify them—Well—I feel inclined to wring out the legal per centage to the uttermost farthing,—but fall into a fit of gratitude, notwithstanding, thinking of monday, & how the second letter came beyond hope. Always better, you are, than I guess you to be,—& it was being *best*, to write, as you did, for me to hear twice on one day!—best & dearest!—

But the first letter was not what you feared—I know you too well not to know how that letter was written & with what intention. Do *you*, on the other hand, endeavour to comprehend how there may be an eccentricity & obliquity in certain relations & on certain subjects, while the general character stands up worthily of esteem & regard .. even of yours. Mr. Kenyon says broadly that it is monomania .. neither more nor less. Then the principle of passive filial obedience is held .. drawn (& quartered) from Scripture. He *sees* the law & the gospel on his side. Only the other day, there was a setting forth of the whole doctrine, I hear, down stairs—'passive obedience, & particularly in respect to marriage.' One after the other, my brothers all walked out of the room, & there was left for sole auditor, Captain Surtees Cook, who had especial reasons for sitting it out against his will,°—so he sate and asked 'if children were to be considered slaves' as meekly as if he were asking for information. I could not help smiling when I heard of it. He is just *succeeding* in obtaining what is called an 'adjutancy,' which, with the half pay, will put an end to many anxieties—

Dearest—when, in the next dream, you meet me in the 'landing-place,' tell me why I am to stand up to be reviewed again. What a fancy, *that* is of yours, for 'full-lengths'—& what bad policy, if a fancy, to talk of it so!—because you would have had the glory & advantage, & privilege, of seeing me on my feet twenty times before now, if you had not impressed on me, in some ineffable manner, that to stand on my head w^d scarcely be stranger. Nevertheless you shall have it your own way, as you have everything—which makes you so very, very, exemplarily submissive, you know!—

. . .

RB, *Thursday, 22 January 1846*

. . .

And do you think, sweet, that there *is* any free movement of my soul which your pen-holder is to secure? Well, try!—it will be yours by every right of discovery—and I, for my part,

will religiously report to you the first time I think of you
'which, but for your present I should not have done'—or is it
not a happy, most happy way of ensuring a better fifth act to
Luria than the foregoing? See the absurdity I write—when it
will be more probably the ruin of the whole—for was it not
observed in the case of a friend of mine once,—who wrote his
own part in a piece for private theatricals, and had ends of
his own to serve in it,—that he set to work somewhat after
this fashion: Scene 1st. A breakfast chamber—Lord & Lady
A. at table. Lady A. / 'No more coffee, my dear?—Lord A. /
One more cup! (*Embracing her*). Lady A. / I was thinking of
trying the ponies in the Park—are you engaged? Lord A. /
Why, there's that bore of a Committee at the House till 2.
(*Kissing her hand*)'—And so forth, to the astonishment of the
auditory, who did not exactly see the 'sequitur' in either
instance—Well, dearest—whatever comes of it, the 'aside,'
the bye-play, the digression, will be the best, and only true
business of the piece. And tho' I must smile at your notion of
securing *that* by any fresh appliance,—mechanical or spiritual, yet I do thank you, dearest, thank you from my heart
indeed—(and I write with Bramahs *always*,—not being able
to make a pen!)

. . .

[Meeting 42: Saturday, 24 January 3.05–5.15 p.m.]

RB, *Sunday, 25 January 1846*

. . .

That remark of your sister's delights me—you remember?—that the anger would not be so formidable. I have
exactly the fear of encountering *that*, which the sense of having
to deal with a ghost would induce: there's no striking at it
with one's partizan°—Well, God is above all! It is not my
fault if it so happens that by returning my love you make me
exquisitely blessed; I believe—more than hope, I am *sure* I
should do all I ever *now* can do, if you were never to know
it—that is, my love for you was in the first instance its own

reward—if one must use such phrases—and if it were possible
for that .. not *anger*, which is of no good, but that *opposition*—
that adverse will—to show that your good would be attained
by the—

But it would need to be *shown* to me. . . .

I believe—first of all, *you*—but when that is done, and I
am allowed to call your heart *mine*,—I cannot think you
would be happy if parted from me—and that belief, coming
to add to my own feeling in *that* case—So, this will *be*—I trust
in God.

. . .

EB, *Monday, 26–Tuesday, 27 January 1846*

. . .

Henrietta, say that the 'anger' would not be so formidable
after all!'! Poor dearest Henrietta, who trembles at the least
bending of the brows .. who has less courage than I, & the
same views of the future!! What she referred to, was simply
the infrequency of the visits .. 'Why was I afraid,' she said—
'where was the danger? who would be the *informer*'?—Well! I
will not say any more. It is just natural that you, in your
circumstances & associations, should be unable to see what I
have seen from the beginning—only you will not hereafter
reproach me, in the most secret of your thoughts, for not
having told you plainly. If I could have told you with greater
plainness I should blame myself (& I do not:) because it is
not an opinion I have, but a perception. I see, I know. The
result .. the end of all .. perhaps now and then I see *that* too ..
in the 'lucid moments' which are not the happiest for anybody. Remember, in all cases, that I shall not repent of any
part of our past intercourse,—& that, therefore, when the
time for decision comes, you will be free to look at the
question as if you saw it then for the first moment, without
being hampered by considerations about 'all those
yesterdays.'

For *him* .. he would rather see me dead at his foot than

yield the point: & he will say so, & mean it, & persist in the meaning.

Do you ever wonder at me .. that I should write such things, & have written others so different? *I have thought* THAT *in myself very often*. Insincerity & injustice may seem the two ends, while I occupy the straight betwixt two—& I should not like you to doubt how this may be!—Sometimes I have begun to show you the truth, & torn the paper,—I *could* not— yet now again I am borne on to tell you, .. to save you from some thoughts which you cannot help perhaps—

There has been no insincerity .. nor is there injustice. I believe, I am certain, I have loved him better than the rest of his children .. I have heard the fountain within the rock, & my heart has struggled in towards him through the stones of the rock .. thrust off .. dropping off .. turning in again & clinging! Knowing what is excellent in him well, loving him as my only parent left, & for himself dearly, notwithstanding that hardness, & the miserable 'system' which made him appear harder still—I have loved him & been proud of him for his high qualities, for his courage & fortitude when he bore up so bravely years ago under the wordly reverses which he yet felt acutely .. more than you & I could feel them—but the fortitude was admirable. Then came the trials of love— then, I was repulsed too often, .. made to suffer in the suffering of those by my side .. depressed by petty daily sadnesses & terrors, from which it is possible however for an elastic affection to rise again as fast .. Yet my friends used to say 'You look broken-spirited'—& it was true. In the midst, came my illness,—and when I was ill he grew gentler & let me draw nearer than ever I had done—& after that great stroke .. you *know* .. though *that* fell in the middle of a storm of emotion & sympathy on my part, which drove clearly against him, ... God seemed to strike our hearts together by the shock,—& I was grateful to him for not saying aloud what I said to myself in my agony, '*If it had not been for* YOU' ..! And comparing my selfreproach to what I imagined his selfreproach must certainly be, (for if *I* had loved selfishly, *he* had not been kind) I felt as if I could love & forgive him for two .. (I knowing that serene generous departed spirit, & seeming left to represent it—) .. & I did love him better than

all those left to ME to love in the world here. I proved a little
my affection for him, by coming to London at the risk of my
life rather than diminish the comfort of his home by keeping
a part of my family away from him. And afterwards for long
& long, he spoke to me kindly & gently, & of me affectionately
& with too much praise,—& God knows that I had as much
joy as I imagined myself capable of again, in the sound of his
footstep on the stairs, & of his voice when he prayed in this
room,—my best hope, as I have told him since, being, to die
beneath his eyes. Love is so much to me naturally—it is, to
all women!—& it was so much to *me* to feel sure at last that
he loved me—to forget all blame .. to pull the weeds up from
that last illusion of life—& this, till the Pisa-business, which
threw me off, far as ever, again—farther than ever—when
George said 'he could not flatter me' & I dared not flatter
myself. But do *you* believe that I never wrote what I did not
feel: I never did. And I ask one kindness more .. do not notice
what I have written here. Let it pass—We can alter nothing
by ever so many words. After all, he is the victim. He isolates
himself—& now and then he feels it .. the cold dead silence
all round, which is the effect of an incredible system. If he
were not stronger than most men, he could not bear it as he
does. With such high qualities too!—so upright & honorable—you would esteem him, you would like him, I think.
And so .. dearest .. let *that* be the last word.

I dare say you have asked yourself sometimes, why it was
that I never managed to draw you into the house here, so that
you might make your own way. Now *that* is one of the things
impossible to me. I have not influence enough for *that*. George
can never invite a friend of his even. Do you see? The people
who do come here, come by particular license & association
.. Capt. Surtees Cook being one of them. Once .. when I was
in high favour too .. I asked for Mr. Kenyon to be invited to
dinner—he an old college friend, & living close by & so
affectionate to me always—I felt that he must be hurt by the
neglect, & asked. *It was in vain*. Now, you see—!

May God bless you always!—I wrote all my spirits away
in this letter yesterday, and kept it to finish to-day .. being
yours everyday, glad or sad, ever beloved!—

                                        Your Ba

RB, *Wednesday, 28 January 1846*

Ever dearest—I will say, as you desire, nothing on that subject—but this strictly for myself: you engaged me to consult 'my own good' in the keeping or breaking our engagement; not *your* good as it might even seem to me; much less seem to another: my only good in this world,—that against which all the world goes for nothing—is to spend my life with you, and be yours. You know that when I *claim* anything, it is really yourself in me—you *give* me a right and bid me use it, and I, in fact, am most obeying you when I appear most exacting on my own account—so, in that feeling, I dare claim, once for all, and in all possible cases, (except that dreadful one of your becoming worse again .. in which case I wait till life ends with both of us ..)—I claim your promise's fulfilment—say, at the summer's end: it cannot be for your good that this state of things should continue. We can go to Italy for a year or two and be happy as day & night are long. For me, I adore you. This is all unnecessary, I feel as I write: but you will think of the main fact as *ordained*, granted by God, will you not, dearest?—so, not to be put in doubt *ever again*—Then, we can go quietly thinking of after matters. Till to-morrow, and ever after, God bless my heart's own, own Ba. All my soul follows you, love!—encircles you—and I live in being yours.

R.

[Meeting 43: Thursday, 29 January 3.00–5.00 p.m.]

EB, *Friday, 30 January 1846*

Friday Morning.

Let it be this way, ever dearest. If in the time of fine weather, I am not ill, .. THEN .. *not now* .. you shall decide, & your decision shall be duty & desire to me, both—I will make no difficulties. Remember, in the meanwhile, that I *have* decided to let it be as you shall choose .. *shall* choose. That I love you enough to give you up 'for your good', is proof (to myself at least) that I love you enough for any other end:— but you thought *too much of* ME *in the last letter*. Do not mistake me. I believe & trust in all your words—only you are generous unawares, as other men are selfish. . . .

For Italy .. you are right—we should be nearer the sun, as you say, & further from the world, as I think—out of hearing of the great storm of gossiping . . . Even if you liked to live altogether abroad, coming to England at intervals, it would be no sacrifice for me—and whether in Italy or England, we should have sufficient or more than sufficient means of living, without modifying by a line that 'good free life' of yours which you reasonable praise—which, if it had been necessary to modify, *we must have parted*, .. because I could not have borne to see you do it,—though, that you once offered it for my sake, I never shall forget.
  . . .

RB, *Saturday, 31 January 1846*

It is a relief to me this time to obey your wish, and reserve further remark on *that* subject till by and bye.—And, whereas some people, I suppose, have to lash themselves up to the due point of passion, and choose the happy minutes to be as loving in as they possibly can .. (that is, in *expression*; the just correspondency of word to fact & feeling; for *it*,—the love,— may be very truly *there*, at the bottom, when it is got at, and spoken out)—quite otherwise, I do really have to guard my tongue and set a watch on my pen .. that so I may say as little as can well be likely to be excepted to by your generosity: dearest, *love* means *love* certainly, and adoration carries its sense with it—and *so*, you may have received my feeling in that shape—but when I begin to hint at the merest putting into practice one or the other profession, you 'fly out'— instead of keeping your throne— . . .

I must think that Mr Kenyon sees, and knows, and .. in his goodness .. hardly disapproves—he knows I could not avoid,—escape you—for he knows, in a manner, what you are . . . and, early in our intercourse, he asked me (—did I tell you?)—'what I thought of his young relative'—and I considered half a second to this effect—'if he asked me what I thought of the Queen-diamond they showed me in the crown of the Czar°—, and I answered truly—he would not return,—"then of course you mean to try and get it to keep"—' So I *did* tell the truth in a very few words—Well, it is no matter.

   . . .

EB, *Friday, 30 January–Sunday, 1 February 1846°*

Friday evening.

  Something, you said yesterday, made me happy—'that your liking for me did not come & go'—do you remember? Because there was a letter, written at a crisis long since,° in which you showed yourself awfully, as a burning mountain, & talked of 'making the most of your fire-eyes,' & of having at intervals 'deep black pits of cold water'!—and the lava of that letter has kept running down into my thoughts of you too much, until quite of late—while even yesterday I was not too well instructed to be 'happy,' you see!—Do not reproach me! I would not have 'heard your enemy say so'—it was your own word!—And the other long word *idiosyncrasy* seemed long enough to cover it; and it might have been a matter of temperament, I fancied, that a man of genius, in the mystery of his nature, should find his feelings sometimes like dumb notes in a piano .. should care for people at half past eleven on tuesday, and on wednesday at noon prefer a black beetle— How you frightened me with your 'fire-eyes!—' 'making the most of them' too!—& the 'black pits,' which gaped .. *where* did they gape?—who could tell?—Oh—but lately I have not been crossed so, of course, with those fabulous terrors—lately that horror of the burning mountain has grown more like a superstition than a rational fear!—and if I was glad .. happy .. yesterday, it was but as a tolerably sensible nervous man might be glad of a clearer moonlight, showing him that what he had half shuddered at for a sheeted ghoule, was only a white horse on the moor. . . .

                                                    Saturday.

Well—I have your letter—& I send you the postscript to my last one, written yesterday you observe .. & being simply a postscript in some parts of it, *so* far it is not for an answer. Only I deny the 'flying out'—perhaps you may do it a little more .. in your moments of starry centrifugal motion.

So you think that dear Mr. Kenyon's opinion of his 'young relative' .. (neither young nor his relative .. not very much of either!) is to the effect that you couldn't possibly 'escape' her—? It looks like the sign of the Red Dragon, put *so* .. & your burning mountain is not too awful for the scenery.

Seriously .. gravely .. if it makes me three times happy that you should love me, yet I grow uneasy & even saddened when you say infatuated things such as this & this .. unless after all you mean a philosophical sarcasm on the worth of Czar diamonds——! No—do not say such things!—If you do, I shall end by being jealous of some ideal Czarina who must stand between you & me .. I shall think that it is not *I* whom you look at .. & *pour cause*. 'Flying out,' *that* w^d be!

And for Mr. Kenyon, I only know that I have grown the most ungrateful of human beings lately, & find myself almost glad when he does not come, certainly uncomfortable when he does—yes, REALLY I would rather not see him at all & when you are not here. The sense of which & the sorrow for which, turn me to a hypocrite, & make me ask why he does not come &c .. questions which never came to my lips before .. till I am more & more ashamed & sorry. Will it end, I wonder, by my ceasing to care for any one in the world, except .. except ..? or is it not rather that I feel trodden down by either his too great penetration or too great unconsciousness, both being overwhelming things from him to me. From a similar cause I hate writing letters to any of my old friends— I feel as if it were the merest swindling to attempt to give the least account of myself to anybody, & when their letters come & I know that nothing very fatal has happened to them, scarcely I can read to an end afterwards through the besetting care of having to answer it all. Then I am ignoble enough to revenge myself on people for their stupidities .. which never in my life I did before nor felt the temptation to do .. & when they have a distaste for your poetry through want of understanding, I have a distaste for *them*° .. cannot help it—& you need not say it is wrong, because I know the whole iniquity of it, persisting nevertheless.

. . .

[Meeting 44: Tuesday, 3 February 3.00–5.00 p.m.]

RB, *Wednesday, 4 February 1846*

You ought hardly—, ought you, my Ba?—to refer to *that* letter or any expression in it—I had .. and *have*, I trust .. your forgiveness for what I wrote, meaning to be generous or at least just, God knows: that, and the other like exaggerations were there to serve the purpose of what you properly call a *crisis*. I *did* believe, .. taking an expression, in the note that occasioned mine, in connection with an excuse which came in the postscript for not seeing me on the day previously appointed, I did fully believe that you were about to deny me admittance again unless I blotted out,—not merely softened down,—the past avowal. All was wrong, foolish, but from a good motive, I dare to say. And then, that particular exaggeration you bring most painfully to my mind—*that* does not, after all, disagree with what I said and you repeat—does it, if you will think? I said my other '*likings*' (as you rightly set it down) *used* to 'come & go, & and that my love for you *did not*, and that is true, the first clause as the last of the sentence, for my sympathies are very wide and general,—always have been—and the natural problem has been the giving unity to their object, concentrating them instead of dispersing. I seem to have foretold, *foreknown* you in other likings of mine—now here .. when the liking '*came*' .. and now elsewhere .. when as surely the liking '*went*': and if they had stayed before the time would that have been a comfort to refer to? . . .

And as you amuse me sometimes, as now, by seeming surprised at some chance expression of a truth which is grown

a veriest commonplace to *me* . . . so I will make you laugh at
me, if you will, for *my* inordinate delight at hearing the success
of your experiment with the opium,—I never dared, nor shall
dare inquire into your use of that—for, knowing you utterly
as I do, I know you only bend to the most absolute necessity
in taking more or less of it—so that increase of the quantity
must mean simply increased weakness, illness—and diminution, diminished illness—And now there *is* diminution! Dear,
dear Ba—you speak of my silly head and its ailments .. well,
and what brings on the irritation? A wet day or two spent at
home,—and what ends it all directly?—just an hour's walk!
So with *me*: now,—fancy me shut in a room for seven years ..
it is—no, *don't* see, even in fancy, what is left of me then! But
you, at the end; this is *all* the harm! I wonder .. I confirm my
soul in its belief in perpetual miraculousness .. I bless God
with my whole heart that it is thus with you!

. . .

EB, *Wednesday, 4 February 1846*

. . .

And that you should care so much about the opium—!
Then *I* must care, & get to do with less .. at least. On the
other side of your goodness & indulgence (a very little way
on the other side, ..) it might strike you as strange that I who
have had no pain .. no acute suffering to keep down from its
angles .. should need opium in any shape. But I have had
restlessness till it made me almost mad—at one time I lost
the power of sleeping quite .. and even in the day, the
continual aching sense of weakness has been intolerable ..
besides palpitation .. as if one's life, instead of giving movement to the body, were imprisoned undiminished within it, &
beating & fluttering impotently to get out, at all the doors &
windows. So the medical people gave me opium .. a preparation of it, called morphine, & ether—& ever since I have
been calling it my amreeta draught, my elixir .. because the
tranquillizing power has been wonderful. Such a nervous
system I have .. so irritable naturally, & so shattered by

various causes .. that the need has continued in a degree until now—& it would be dangerous to leave off the calming remedy, Mr. Jago° says, except very slowly & gradually. But slowly & gradually something may be done—& you are to understand that I never *increased* upon the prescribed quantity .. prescribed in the first instance—no!—Now think of my writing all this to you!—

And after all the lotus-eaters are blessed beyond the opium-eaters, & the best of lotuses are such thoughts as I know.
. . .

[Meeting 45: Monday, 9 February 3.00–5.15 p.m.]

EB, *Tuesday, 10 February 1846*

Ever dearest, I have been possessed by your Luria just as you would have me, & I should like you to understand, not simply how fine a conception the whole work seems to me, so developed, but how it has moved & affected me, without the ordinary means & dialect of pathos, by that calm attitude of moral grandeur which it has—it is very fine. For the execution, *that* too is worthily done .. although I agree with you, that a little quickening & drawing in closer here & there, especially toward the close where there is no time to lose, the reader feels, would make the effect stronger—but you will look to it yourself—and such a conception *must* come in thunder & lightning, as a chief god would—*must* make its own way .. & will not let its poet go until he speaks it out to the ultimate syllable. Domizia disappoints me rather. You might throw a flash more of light on her face .. might you not? But what am I talking? I think it a magnificent work—a noble exposition of the ingratitude of men against their 'heroes', & (what is peculiar) an *humane* exposition .. not misanthropical, after the usual fashion of such things: for the return, the remorse, saves it—& the 'Too late' of the repentance & compensation covers with its solemn toll, the fate of persecutors & victim—we feel that Husain himself could only say afterward .. '*That is done*.' And now .. surely you think well of the work as a whole?

. . .

RB, *Wednesday, 11 February 1846*

. . .

And now, Luria, so long as the parts cohere and the whole is discernible, all will be well yet. I shall not look at it, nor think of it, for a week or two, and then see what I have forgotten.—Domizia is all wrong—I told you I knew that her special colour had faded,—it was but a bright line, and the more distinctly deep that it was so narrow—One of my half-dozen words on my scrap of paper 'pro memoriâ' was, under the 'Act V,' '*she loves*'—to which I could not bring it, you see! Yet the play requires it still,—something may yet be effected, though: I meant that she should propose to go to Pisa with him, and begin a new life. But there is no hurry—I suppose it is no use publishing much before Easter—I will try and remember what my whole character *did* mean—it was, in two words, understood at the time by 'panther's-beauty'—on which hint I ought to have spoken!—But the work grew cold, and you came between, and the sun put out the fire on the hearth—'nec vult panthera domari!' [nor would the panther be tamed!]

For the Soul's Tragedy—*that* will surprise you, I think—there is no trace of you there,—you have not put out the black face of *it*—it is all sneering and *disillusion*—and shall not be printed but burned if you say the word—now wait and see and then say! I will bring the first of the two parts next Saturday.

. . .

RB, *Friday, 13 February 1846*

Two nights ago I read the 'Soul's Tragedy' once more—
and though there were not a few points which still struck me
as successful, in design & execution yet on the whole I came
to a decided opinion—that it will be better to postpone the
publication of it for the present: it is not a good ending—, an
auspicious wind-up of this series,—subject-matter & style are
alike unpopular even for the literary *grex* [herd] that stands
aloof from the purer *plebs*, and uses that privilege to display
& parade an ignorance which the other is altogether incons-
cious of—so that, if Luria is clear*ish*, the Tragedy would be
an unnecessary troubling the waters: whereas, if I printed it
first in order, my readers, according to custom, would make
the (comparatively) little they did not see into, a full excuse
for shutting their eyes at the rest—and we may as well part
friends, so as not to meet enemies: but, at bottom, I believe
the proper objection is to the immediate, *first* effect of the
whole,—its moral effect,—which is dependent on the contrary supposition of its being really understood, in the main
drift of it—yet I don't know,—for I wrote it with the intention
of producing the best of all effects—perhaps the truth is, that
I am tired, rather, and desirous of getting done, and Luria
will answer my purpose so far: will not the best way be to
reserve this unlucky play and, in the event of a second
edition,—as Moxon seems to think such an apparition possible,—might not this be quietly inserted?—in its place, too,
for it was written two or three years ago. I have lost, of late,
interest in dramatic writing, as you know—and, perhaps,
occasion. And, dearest, I mean to take your advice and be
quiet awhile and let my mind get used to its new medium of
sight—, seeing all things, as it does, thro' you: and then, let
all I have done be the prelude and the real work begin—I felt
it would be so before, and told you at the very beginning—do
you remember?

. . .

[Meeting 46: Saturday, 14 February 3.00–5.05 p.m.]

EB, *Monday, 16 February 1846°*

. . . Now ought I not to know about letters, I who have had so many .. from chief minds too, as society goes in England & America? And *your* letters began by being first to my intellect, before they were first to my heart. All the letters in the world are not like yours .. & I would trust them for that verdict with any jury in Europe, if they were not so far too dear!— Mr. Kenyon wanted to make me show him your letters—I did show him the first, & resisted gallantly afterwards, which made him say what vexed me at the moment, .. 'oh—you let me see only *women's* letters!'—till I observed that it was a breach of confidence, except in some cases, .. & that *I* should complain very much, if anyone, man or woman, acted so by myself. But nobody in the world writes like you .. not so *vitally*—and I have a right, if you please, to praise my letters, besides the reason of it which is as good.

. . .

[Meeting 47: Wednesday, 18 February 3.00–5.15 p.m.]

RB, *Thursday, 19 February 1846*

. . .

One thing vexed me in your letter—I will tell you,—the praise of *my* letters: now, one merit they *have*—in language mystical—that of having *no* merit. If I caught myself trying to write finely, graphically &c &c nay, if I found myself conscious of having in my own opinion, so written—all would be over! yes, over! I should be respecting you inordinately, paying a proper tribute to your genius, summoning the necessary collectedness,—plenty of all that!—But the feeling with which I write to you, not knowing that it *is* writing,— with *you*, face and mouth and hair and eyes opposite me, touching me, knowing that all *is* as I say, and helping out the imperfect phrases from your own intuition—*that* would be gone—and *what* in its place?

. . .

EB, *Thursday, 19 February 1846(2)*

And I offended you by praising your letters .. or rather *mine*, if you please .. as if I had not the right!—Still, you shall not, shall not fancy that I meant to praise them in the way you seem to think .. by calling them 'graphic,' 'philosophic', .. why did I ever use such words? I agree with you that if I could play critic upon your letters, it would be an end!—but no, no .. I did not, for a moment. In what I said I went back to my first impressions—& they were *vital* letters, I said— which was the resumé of my thoughts upon the early ones you sent me .. because I felt your letters to be *you* from the very first, & I began, from the beginning, to read every one several times over—nobody, I felt, nobody of all these writers, did write as you did—.

. . .

RB, *Saturday, 21 February 1846*

. . .

Now to these letters! I do solemnly, unaffectedly wonder how you can put so much pure felicity into an envelope so as that I shall get it as from the fount head. This to-day, those yesterday—there is, I see, and know, thus much goodness in line after line, goodness to be scientifically appreciated, *proved there*—but over and above, is it in the writing, the dots and traces, the seal, the paper,—where does the subtle charm lie beyond all rational accounting for? The other day I stumbled on a quotation from J. Baptista Porta°—wherein he avers that any musical instrument made out of wood possessed of medicinal properties retains, being put to use, such virtues undiminished,—and that, for instance, a sick man to whom you should pipe on a pipe of elder-tree would so receive all the advantage derivable from a decoction of its berries. From whence, by a parity of reasoning, I may discover, I think, that the very ink and paper were .. ah, what were they? Curious thinking won't do for me and the wise head which is mine, so I will lie and rest in my ignorance of content and understand that without any magic at all you simply wish to make one person—, which of your free goodness proves to be your R.B,—to make me supremely happy, and that you have your wish—you *do* bless me! More and more—for the old treasure is piled undiminished and still the new comes glittering in—dear, dear heart of my heart, life of my life, *will this last*, let *me* begin to ask? Can it be meant I shall love thee to the end? Then, dearest, care also for the life beyond, and put in my mind how to testify *here* that I have felt, if I could not deserve that a gift beyond all gifts! I hope to work hard, to prove I do feel, as I say—it would be terrible to accomplish nothing now.

. . .

[Meeting 48: Monday, 23 February 3.00–5.30 p.m.]

EB, *Monday, 23 February 1846*

. . .

I was thinking the other day that certainly & after all (or rather before all) I had loved you all my life unawares .. that is, the idea of you. Women begin for the most part, (if ever so very little given to reverie) by meaning, in an aside to themselves, to love such & such an ideal, seen sometimes in a dream & sometimes in a book .. & forswearing their ancient faith as the years creep on . . . and *this* being otherwise with *me*, is miraculous compensation for the trials of many years, .. though such abundant, overabundant compensation, that I cannot help fearing it is too much .. as I know that you are too good & too high for me, & that by the degree in which I am raised up you are let down, for us two to find a level to meet on. One's ideal must be above one, as a matter of course, you know. It is as far as one can reach with one's eyes (soul-eyes) not reach to touch. And here is mine .. shall I tell you? .. even to the visible outward sign of the black hair & the complexion—(why you might ask my sisters!—) yet I would not tell you, if I could not tell you afterwards that, if it had been red hair quite, it had been the same thing—only I prove the coincidence out fully & make you smile half—

Yet indeed I did not fancy that *I* was to love *you* when you came to see me—no indeed .. any more than I did your caring on your side. My ambition when we began our correspondence, was simply that you should forget I was a woman (being weary & blasée of the empty written gallantries, of which I have had my share & all the more perhaps from my peculiar position which made them so without consequence) that you should forget *that* & let us be friends, & consent to teach me what you knew better than I, in art & human nature, & give me your sympathy in the meanwhile. I am a great hero-worshipper & had admired your poetry for years, & to feel that you liked to write to me & be written to was a pleasure & a pride, as I used to tell you I am sure .. & then your letters were not like other letters .. as I must not tell you again. Also you *influenced* me, in a way in which no one else did. For instance, by two or three halfwords you made me see you, & other people had delivered orations on the same subject quite without effect. I surprised everybody in this house by consenting to see you—Then, when you came, .. you never went away—I mean I had a sense of your presence constantly. Yes .. & to prove how free that feeling was from the remotest presentiment of what has occurred .. I said to Papa in my unconsciousness the next morning .. 'it is most extraordinary how the idea of Mr. Browning does beset me— I suppose it is not being used to see strangers, in some degree—but it haunts me .. it is a persecution'. On which he smiled & said that 'it was not grateful to my friend to use such a word.' When the letter came ...

Do you know that all that time I was frightened of you? frightened in this way. I felt as if you had a power over me & meant to use it, & that I could not breathe or speak very differently from what you chose to make me. As to my thoughts I had it in my head somehow that you read *them* as you read the newspaper—examined them, & fastened them down writhing under your long entomological pins—ah, do you remember the entomology of it all?°

But the power was used upon *me*—& I never doubted that you had mistaken your own mind, the strongest of us having some exceptional weakness. Turning the wonder round in all lights, I came to what you admitted yesterday .. yes, I saw *that* very early .. that you had come here with the intention of trying to love whomever you should find, .. & also that what I had said about exaggerating the amount of what I could be to you, had just operated in making you more determined to justify your own presentiment in the face of mine. Well—& if that last clause was true a little, too .. why should I be sorry now .. & why should you have fancied for a moment, that the first could make me sorry. At first & when I did not believe that you really loved me .. when I thought you deceived yourself .. *then*, it was different. But now .. now .. when I see & believe your attachment for me .. do you think that any cause in the world (except what diminished it) could render it less a source of joy to me?—I mean as far as I myself am considered. Now if you ever fancy that I am *vain* of your love for me .. you will be unjust, remember. If it were less dear, & less above me, I might be vain perhaps. But I may say *before* God & you, that of all the events of my life .. inclusive of its afflictions, .. nothing has humbled me so much as your love. Right or wrong it may be, but true it *is* .. & I tell you. Your love has been to me like God's own love, which makes the receivers of it kneelers.

. . .

RB, *Wednesday 25 February 1846*

Once you were pleased to say, my own Ba, that 'I made you do as I would'—I am quite sure, you make me *speak* as you would, and not at all as I mean—and for one instance, I never surely spoke anything half so untrue as that 'I came with the intention of loving whomever I should find'—No!— wreathed shells, and hollows in ruins, and roofs of caves may transform a voice wonderfully, make more of it or less, or so change it as to almost alter .. but turn a 'no' into a 'yes' can no echo, (except the Irish one)—and I said 'no' to such a charge, and still say 'no'—I *did* have a presentiment—and tho' it is hardly possible for me to look back on it now without lending it the true colours given to it by the event, yet I *can* put them aside, if I please, and remember that I not merely hoped it would not be so—(*not* that the effect I expected to be produced would be *less* than in anticipation,—certainly I did not hope *that*—but that it would range itself with the old feelings of simple reverence and sympathy and friendship— that I should love you as much as I supposed I *could* love, and no more)—but in the confidence that nothing could occur to divert me from my intended way of life, I made .. went on making arrangements to return to Italy—you know—did I not tell you I wished to see you before I returned?—And I had heard of you just so much as seemed to make it impossible such a relation could ever exist: I know very well, if you choose to refer to my letters you may easily bring them to bear a sense, in parts, more agreeable to your own theory than to mine, the true one—but that was instinct, Provi-dence—anything rather than foresight: now I will convince you! yourself have noticed the difference between the *letters* and the *writer*—the greater 'distance of the latter from you'— why was that? Why if not because the conduct *begun* with *him*, with one who had now seen you,—was no continuation of the conduct, as influenced by the feeling, of the letters—else, they, if *near*, should have enabled him,—if but in the natural course of time and with increase of familiarity,—to become *nearer*—but it was not so! The letters began by loving you after their way—but what a world-wide difference *that* love and the true, the love from seeing and hearing and feeling .. since you make me resolve, what now lies blended so harmo-niously, into its component parts—. . . I looked yesterday over the 'Tragedy'—and think it will do after all. I will bring one part at least next time,—and 'Luria' take away, if you let me,—so all will be off my mind—and April and May the welcomer! Don't think I am going to take any extraordinary pains—there are some things in the 'Tragedy' I should like to preserve and print now—leaving the future to spring as it likes, in any direction,—and these half-dead, half-alive works fetter it, if left behind—

. . .

EB, *Thursday, 26 February 1846 (1)*

I confess that while I was writing those words I had a thought that they were not quite yours as you said them. Still it comes to something in their likeness, .. but we will not talk of it . . . I agree that it is best not to talk—I 'gave it up' as a riddle long ago. . . . I have my own thoughts of course .. & you have yours .. & the worst is that a third person looking down on us from some snow-capped height, & free from personal influences, would have *his* thoughts too, .. & *he* would think that if you had been reasonable as usual you would have gone to Italy—I have by heart (or by head at least) what the third person would think. The third person thundered to me in an abstraction for ever so long, & at intervals I hear him still ..

. . .

RB, *Thursday, 26 February 1846*

As for the 'third person,' my sweet Ba, he was a wise speaker from the beginning; and in our case he will say, turning to me—'the late Robert Hall,°— when a friend admired that one with so high an estimate of the value of intellectuality in woman should yet marry some kind of cook maid-animal, as did the said Robert,—wisely answered— "you can't kiss Mind"! May *you* not discover eventually,' (this is to me) .. 'that mere intellectual endowments,—tho' incontestably of the loftiest character,—mere Mind, tho' that Mind be Miss B's—cannot be *kissed*—nor, repent too late the absence of those humbler qualities, those softer affections which, like flowerets at the mountain's foot, if not so proudly soaring as, as—as' .. and so on, till one of us died, with laughing or being laughed at! So judges the third person! and if, to help him, we let him into your room at Wimpole St., suffered him to see with Flush's eyes, he would say with just as wise an air—'True, mere personal affections may be warm enough .. but does it augur well for the durability of an attachment that it should be *wholly, exclusively* based on such perishable attractions as the sweetness of a mouth, the beauty of an eye? I could wish, rather, to know that there was something of less transitory nature co-existent with this— some congeniality of Mental pursuit, some—' Would he not say that? But I can't do his platitudes justice because here is our post going out and I have been all the morning walking in the perfect joy of my heart—with your letter—and under its blessing—dearest, dearest Ba—let me say more to-morrow—only this now, that you—ah, what are you not to me! My dearest love, bless you—till to-morrow when I will strengthen the prayer; (no, *lengthen* it!)

Ever your own
RB

'Hawthorn'—to show how Spring gets on!°

EB, *Thursday, 26 February 1846 (2)*

Thursday evening.

If all third persons were as foolish as this third person of yours, ever dearest, first & second persons might follow their own devices without losing much in the way of good counsel. But you are unlucky in your third person as far as the wits go—he talks a great deal of nonsense .. & Flush, who is sensible, will have nothing to do with him, he says . . . he is quite a third person *singular* for the nonsense he talks!—. . .

Ah my hawthorn spray!—Do you know, I caught my self pitying it for being gathered, with that green promise of leaves on it!—there is room too on it for the feet of a bird!—Still I shall keep it longer than it would have stayed in the hedge .. *that* is certain!

The first you ever gave me was a yellow rose sent in a letter°—and shall I tell you what *that* means—the yellow rose ..? '*Infidelity*', says the dictionary of flowers. You see what an omen, .. to begin with!—

. . .

[Meeting 49: Saturday, 28 February 3.00–5.15 p.m.]

EB, *Sunday, 1 March 1846*

You never could think that I meant any insinuation against you by a word of what was said yesterday, or that I sought or am likely to seek a 'security' ... do you know it was not right of you to use such an expression—indeed no. You were angry with me for just one minute, or you would not have used it—and why? Now what did I say that was wrong or unkind even by construction? If I did say anything, it was three times wrong, & unjust as well as unkind, & wronged my own heart & consciousness of all that you are to me—, more than it could *you*. But you began speaking of yourself just as a woman might speak under the same circumstances .. you remember what you said .. & then *I*, remembering that all the men in the world would laugh such an idea to scorn, said something to that effect .. you *know*. I once was in company with a man, however, who valued himself very much on his constancy to a woman who was so deeply affected by it that she became his wife at last .. & the whole neighbourhood came out to stare at him on that ground as a sort of monster. And can you guess what the constancy meant? Seven years before, he loved that woman, he said, & she repulsed him .. 'And in the meantime—*how many?*' I had the impertinence to ask a female friend who told me the tale. 'Why,' she answered with the utmost simplicity, 'I understand that Miss A & Miss B & Mrs. C would not listen to him, but he took Miss D's rejection most to heart.' That was the head & front of his 'constancy' to Miss E, who had been loved she boasted, for seven years .. that is, once at the beginning & once at the end. It was just a coincidence of the 'premier pas' & the 'pis aller' [first attempt and last resort].

Beloved, I could not mean this for you—you are not made of such stuff—, as we both know.

And for myself, it was my compromise with my own scruples, that you should not be 'chained' to me .. not in the merest metaphor .. that you should not seem to be bound, in honour or otherwise, .. so that if you stayed with me it should be your free choice to stay, not the *consequence* of a choice so many months before. That was my compromise with my

scruples .. & not my doubt of your affection—& least of all,
was it an intention of trifling with you sooner or later that
made me wish to suspend all *decisions* as long as possible. I
have decided (for me) to let it be as you shall please—now I
told you that before. Either we will live on as we are .. until
an obstacle arises, .. for indeed I do not look for a 'security'
where you suppose .. & the very appearance of it THERE is
what most rebuts me; or I will be yours in the obvious way,
& go out of England the next half hour if possible. As to the
steps to be taken (or not taken) before the last step, we must
think of those—The worst is that the only question is about a
form. Virtually the evil is the same all round, whatever we do.
Dearest, it was plain to see yesterday evening when he came
into this room for a moment at seven oclock, before going to
his own to dress for dinner .. plain to see, that he was not
altogether pleased at finding you here in the morning.° There
was no pretext for objecting gravely—but it was plain that he
was not pleased. Do not let this make you uncomfortable .. he
will forget all about it, & I was not *scolded*, do you understand—It was mere manner: but my sisters thought as I did
of the significance:—& it was enough to prove to me (if I had
not known) what a desperate game we should be playing if
we depended on a yielding nerve *there*.

. . .

RB, *Tuesday, 3 March 1846*

. . . what I meant by charging you with *seeing*, (not, *not*
'*looking* for')—*seeing* undue 'security' in *that*, in the form,—I
meant to say 'you talk about me being "free" now, free till
then .. and I am rather jealous of the potency attributed to the
form, with all its solemnity, because it *is* a form, and no
more—yet you frankly agree with me that *that* form complied
with, there is no redemption; yours I am *then* sure enough, to
repent at leisure &c. &c.' So I meant to ask, 'then, all *now*
said, all short of that particular form of saying it, all goes for
comparatively nothing'? Here it is written down—you 'wish
to *suspend* all decisions as long as possible'—*that* form effects
the decision, then,—till then, 'where am I'?

. . . You tell me what was observed in the 'moment's' visit; by you, and (after, I suppose) by your sisters. First, I *will* always see with your eyes *there*—next, what I see I will *never* speak, if it pain you; but just this much truth I ought to say, I think. I always give myself to you for the worst I am,—full of faults as you will find, if you have not found them: but I *will* not affect to be so bad, so wicked, as I count wickedness, as to call that conduct other than intolerable—*there*, in my conviction of *that*, is your real 'security' and mine for the future as the present. That a father choosing to give out of his whole day some five minutes to a daughter, supposed to be prevented from participating in what he, probably, in common with the whole world of sensible men, as distinguished from poets and dreamers, consider *every* pleasure of life,—by a complete foregoing of society—that he, after the Pisa business and the enforced continuance, and as he must believe, permanence of this state in which any other human being would go mad,—I do dare say, for the justification of God, who gave the mind to be *used* in this world,—where it saves us, we are taught, or destroys us,—and not to be sunk quietly, overlooked, and forgotten,—that, under these circumstances, finding .. what, you say, unless he thinks he *does* find, he would close the door of his house instantly,—a mere sympathizing man, of the same literary tastes, who comes goodnaturedly, on a proper and unexceptionable introduction, to chat with and amuse a little that invalid daughter, once a month, so far as is known, for an hour perhaps,—that such a father should show himself '*not pleased* plainly,' at such circumstance ... my Ba, it is SHOCKING! See, I go *wholly* on the supposition that the real relation is not imagined to exist between us. I so completely could understand a repugnance to trust you to me were the truth known, that, I will confess, I have several times been afraid the very reverse of this occurrence would befall,—that your father would have at some time or other thought himself obliged, by the usual feeling of people in such cases, to see me for a few minutes and express some commonplace thanks after the customary mode .. (just as Capt. Domett sent a heap of unnecessary thanks to me not long ago for sending now a letter now a book to his son in New Zealand—keeping up the spirits of

poor dear Alfred now he is cut off from the world at large)—
and if *this* had been done, I shall not deny that my heart
would have accused me .. unreasonably I *know* but still,
suppression, and reserve, and apprehension .. the whole of
that is horrible always! But this way of looking on the
endeavour of anybody, however humble, to just preserve your
life, remedy in some degree the first .. if it *was* the first ..
unjustifiable measure,—this being 'displeased'—is exactly
what I did *not* calculate upon. Observe, that in this *only*
instance I am able to do as I shall be done by;—to take up
the arms furnished by the world, the usages of society—this
is monstrous on the *world's* showing! I say this now that I
may never need recur to it—that you may understand why I
keep *such* entire silence henceforth.

Get but well, keep but *as* well, and all is easy now. This
wonderful winter—the spring—the summer—you will take
exercise, go up and down stairs, get strong. I PRAY YOU, AT
YOUR FEET, TO DO THIS, DEAREST! Then comes Autumn,
with the natural expectation, as after *rouge* one expects *noir*:°
the LIKELIHOOD of a *severe* winter after this mild one, which
to prevent, you reiterate your demand to go and save your life
in Italy .. ought you not to do that? And the matter brought
to issue, (with even, if possible, less shadow of ground for a
refusal than before, if you are *well*, plainly well enough to
bear the voyage)—*there* I *will* bid you 'be mine in the obvious
way'—if you shall preserve your belief in me—and you *may*
in much, in all important to you.

. . .

EB, *Tuesday, 3 March 1846*

Yes, but, dearest, you mistake me, or you mistake yourself.
I am sure I do not over-care for forms—it is not my way to
do it—& in this case .. no. Still you must see that there is a
fact as well as a form, & involving a frightful quantity of
social inconvenience (to use the mildest word) if too hastily
entered on. I deny altogether looking for, or 'seeing' any

'security' in it for myself—it is a mere form for the heart &
the happiness: illusions may pass after as before. Still the
truth is that if they were to pass with you now, you stand free
to act according to the wide-awakeness of your eyes, & to
reform your choice .. see!—whereas afterward you could not
carry out such a reformation while I was alive, even if I
helped you. All I could do for you would be to walk away—
And you pretend not to see this broad distinction?—ah! ..
For me I have seen just this & no more, & have felt averse to
forstall, to seem to forstall even by an hour, or a word, that
stringency of the legal obligation from which there *is* in a
certain sense no redemption. . . .

You do not see aright what I meant to tell you on another
subject. If he was displeased .. (& it was expressed by a
shadow, a mere negation of pleasure ..) it was not with you as
a visitor & my friend—you must not fancy such a thing. It
was a sort of instinctive indisposition towards seeing you
here—unexplained to himself, I have no doubt—of course
unexplained, or he would have desired me to receive you
never again .. *that* would have been done at once & unscru-
pulously. But without defining his own feeling, he rather
disliked seeing you here—it just touched one of his vibratory
wires .. brushed by & touched it—oh, we understand in this
house. He is not a nice observer, but, at intervals very wide,
he is subject to lightnings ..—call them fancies, sometimes
right, sometimes wrong. Certainly it was not in the character
of a 'sympathising friend' that you made him a very little
cross . . . And yet you never were nor will be in danger of
being *thanked* .. he would not think of it. For the reserve, the
apprehension .. dreadful those things are, & desecrating to
one's own nature—but we did not make this position .. we
only endure it. The root of the evil is the miserable misconcep-
tion of the limits & character of parental rights—it is a
mistake of the intellect rather than of the heart. Then, after
using one's children as one's chattels for a time, the children
drop lower & lower toward the level of the chattels, & the
duties of human sympathy to them become difficult in proportion. And, (it seems strange to say it, yet it is true) *love*, he
does not conceive of at all. He has feeling .. he can be moved

deeply .. he is capable of affection in a peculiar way—but *that*, he does not understand, .. any more than he understands Chaldee, respecting it less of course.

. . .

RB, *Wednesday, 4 March 1846*

. . .

I dare say I am unjust,—hasty certainly, in the other matter—but all faults are such inasmuch as they are 'mistakes of the intellect'—toads may spit or leave it alone,—but if I ever see it right, exercising my intellect, to treat any human beings like my 'chattels,'—I shall pay for that mistake one day or another, I am convinced—and I very much fear that you would soon discover what one fault of mine is, if you were to hear anyone assert such a right in my presence—

. . .

[Meeting 50: Thursday, 5 March 3.15–5.45 p.m.]

EB, *Friday, 6 March 1846*

. . .

Because it is colder today I have not been down-stairs, but let to-morrow be warm enough & 'facilis descensus'.° There's something infernal to me really, in the going down,—& now too that our cousin is here! Think of his beginning to attack Henrietta the other day .. '*So* Mr. C. has retired & left the field to Surtees Cook. Oh .. you needn't deny .. it's the news of all the world except your father. And as to *him*, I don't blame you—he never will consent to the marriage of son or daughter. Only you should consider, you know, because he wont leave you a shilling, &c &c ...'—You hear the sort of man. And then in a minute after .. 'And what is this about Ba?' 'About Ba' said my sisters, 'why who has been persuading you of such nonsense?'—'Oh—my authority is very good,—perfectly unnecessary for you to tell any stories, Arabel!—a literary friendship, is it?' ... and so on .. after that fashion! This comes from my brothers of course, but we need not be afraid of its passing *beyond*, I think, though I was a good deal vexed when I heard first of it last night . . .

[Meeting 51: Monday, 9 March 3.30–6.15 p.m.]

EB, *Tuesday, 10 March 1846 (1)*

Now I shall know what to believe when you talk of very bad & very indifferent doings of yours. Dearest, I read your 'Soul's tragedy' last night & was quite possessed with it, & fell finally into a mute wonder how you could for a moment doubt about publishing it. It is very vivid, I think, & vital, & impressed me more than the first act of 'Luria' did .. though I do not mean to compare such dissimilar things, .. & for pure nobleness 'Luria' is unapproachable .. will prove so, it seems to me ... But this 'tragedy' shows more heat from the first .. & then, the words beat down more closely .. well! I am struck by it all as you see. If you keep it up to this passion .. if you justify this high key-note, .. it is a great work, & worthy of a place next Luria. Also do observe how excellently balanced the two will be, & how the tongue of this next silver Bell will swing from side to side. And *you* to frighten me about it—!—Yes!—and the worst is (because it was stupid in me) the worst is that I half believed you & took the manuscript to be something inferior .. for YOU .. & the adviseableness of its publication, a doubtful case. And yet, after all, the really worst is, that you should prove yourself such an adept at deceiving!
    . . .

EB, *Tuesday 10 March 1846 (2)*

. . . You mean, you say, to run all risks with me, & I don't mean to draw back from my particular risk of .. what am I to do to you hereafter to make you vexed with me?—What is

there in marriage to make all these people on every side of us
.. (who all began, I suppose, by talking of love ..) look askance
at one another from under the silken mask .. & virtually hate
one another through the tyranny of the stronger & the
hypocrisy of the weaker party. It never could be so with *us*—
I know that. But you grow awful to me sometimes with the
very excess of your goodness & tenderness .. & still, I think
to myself, if you do not keep lifting me up quite off the ground
by the strong faculty of love in you, I shall not help falling
short of the hope you have placed in me—it must be
'supernatural' of you, to the end! .. or I fall short & disappoint
you. Consider this, beloved. Now if I could put my soul out
of my body, just to stand up before you & make it clear!—
. . .

RB, *Wednesday, 11 March 1846*

. . . Oh, my love—why .. what is it you think to do, or
become 'afterward,' that you may fail in and so disappoint
me? It is not very unfit that you should thus punish yourself
and that sinning by your own ambition of growing something
beyond my Ba even, you should 'fear' as you say! For, sweet,
why wish, why think to alter ever by a line, change by a
shade, turn better, if that were possible, and so only rise the
higher above me, get further from instead of nearer to my
heart? What I expect, what I build my future on, am quite,
quite prepared to 'risk' *everything* for,—is that one belief that
you *will not alter*, will just remain as you are—meaning by
'*you*,' the love in you, the qualities I have *known* .. (for you will
stop me, if I do not stop myself)—what I have evidence of in
every letter, in every word, every look. Keeping these, if it be
God's will that the body passes—what is that?—Write no
new letters, speak no new words, look no new looks,—only
tell me, years hence, that the present is alive, that what was
once, still is—and I am, must needs be, blessed as ever! You
speak of my feeling as if it were a pure speculation—as if
because I *see somewhat* in you I make a calculation that there
must be more to see somewhere or other—where bdellium is

found, the onyx-stone may be looked for in the mystic land of the four rivers!°

. . .

[Meeting 52: Saturday, 14 March 3.00–5.45 p.m.]

RB, *Sunday, 15 March 1846*

How will the love my heart is full of for you, let me be silent? Insufficient speech is better than no speech, in one regard—the speaker had *tried* words, and if they fail, hereafter he needs not reflect that he did not even try—so with me now, that loving you, Ba, with all my heart and soul,—all my senses being lost in one wide wondering gratitude and veneration, I press close to you to say so, in this imperfect way, my dear dearest beloved! Why do you not help me, rather than take my words, my proper words, from me and call them yours, when yours they are not? You said lately love of you 'made you humble'—just as if to hinder *me* from saying that earnest truth!—entirely true it is, as I feel ever more convincingly. You do not choose to understand it should be so—nor do I much care—for the one thing you must believe, must resolve to believe in its length and breadth, is that I do love you and live only in the love of you—

I will rest on the confidence that you do so believe! You *know* by this that it is no shadowy image of you and *not* you, which having attached myself to in the first instance, I afterward compelled my fancy to see reproduced, so to speak, with tolerable exactness to the original idea, in you, the dearest real *you* I am blessed with—you *know* what the eyes are to me, and the lips and the hair—And I, for my part, know *now*, while fresh from seeing you, certainly *know*, whatever I may have said a short time since, that *you* will go on to the end, that the arm round me will not let me go,—over such a blind abyss—I refuse to think, to fancy, *towards* what it would be to lose you now! So I give my life, my soul into your hand—the giving is a mere form too, it is yours, ever yours from the first—but ever as I see you, sit with you, and come away to think over it all, I find more that seems mine to give,—you give me more life and it goes back to you.

. . .

EB, *Monday, 16 March 1846*

. . .

Other human creatures (how often I do think it to myself!) have their good things scattered over their lives, sown here & sown there, down the slopes, & by the waysides. But with me .. I have mine all poured down on one spot in the midst of the sands!—if you knew what I feel at moments, & at half-hours, when I give myself up to the feeling freely & take no thought of red eyes. A woman once was killed with gifts, crushed with the weight of golden bracelets thrown at her:° &, knowing myself, I have wondered more than a little, how it was that I could *bear* this strange & unused gladness, without sinking as the emotion rose. Only I was incredulous at first, & the day broke slowly .. & the gifts fell like the rain .. softly:—& God gives strength, by His providence, for sustaining blessings as well as stripes. Dearest!—— . . .

But where, pray, did I say .. & when, .. that 'everything would end well'?—Was *that* in the dream, when we two met on the stairs?° I did not really say so I think. And 'well' is how you understand it. If you jump out of the window you succeed in getting to the ground, somehow, dead or alive .. but whether *that* means 'ending well,' depends on your way of considering matters.

. . .

RB, *Tuesday, 17 March 1846*

'Out of window' would be well, as I see the leap, if it ended (*so far as I am concerned*) in the worst way imaginable—I would 'run the risk' (Ba's other word) rationally, deliberately,—

knowing what the ordinary law of chances in this world justifies in such a case; and if the result after all *was* unfortunate, it would be far easier to undergo the extremest penalty with so litle to reproach myself for,—than to put aside the adventure,—waive the wondrous probability of such best fortune, in a fear of the barest possibility of an adverse event, and so go to my grave, Walter the Penniless,° with an eternal recollection that Miss Burdett Coutts° once offered to wager sundry millions with me that she could throw double-sixes a dozen times running—which wager I wisely refused to accept because it was not written in the stars that such a sequence might never be—I had rather, rather a thousand-fold lose my paltry stake, and be the one recorded victim to such an unexampled unluckiness that half a dozen mad comets, suns gone wrong, and lunatic moons must have come laboriously into conjunction for my special sake to bring it to pass, which were no slight honor, properly considered!

. . .

[Meeting 53: Thursday 19 March 3.15–5.15 p.m.
Meeting 54: Monday, 23 March 3.00–5.45 p.m.]

RB, *Tuesday, 24 March 1846*

My own dearest, if you *do*—(for I confess to nothing of the kind,)—but if you *should* detect an unwillingness to write at certain times, what would that prove,—I mean, what that one need shrink from avowing?—If I never had you before me except when writing letters to you—then! ..

Why, we do not even *talk* much, now! . . . Oh, how coldly I should write,—how the bleak-looking paper would seem unpropitious to carry my feeling—if all had to begin and try to find words *this* way!

Now, this morning I have been out—to town & back—and for all the walking my head aches—and I have the conviction that presently when I resign myself to think of you wholly, with only the pretext,—the make-believe of occupation, in the shape of some book to turn over the leaves of,—I shall see you and soon be well,—so soon! You must know, there is a chair (one of the kind called gondóla-chairs by upholsterers— with an emphasized o)—which occupies the precise place, stands just in the same relation to *this* chair I sit on now, that yours stands in and occupies—to the left of the fire: and, how often, how *always* I turn in the dusk and *see* the dearest real Ba with me—

. . .

EB, *Tuesday, 24 March 1846 (2)*

Ah; if I '*do*' .. if I '*should*' .. if I *shall* .. if I *will* .. if I *must* .... what can all the 'ifs' prove, but a most hypothetical state of the conscience? And in brief, I beg you to stand convinced of one thing, .. that whenever the 'certain time' comes for you to 'hate writing to me' confessedly, 'avowedly', .. (oh what words!) *I shall not like it at all*—not for all the explanations .. & the sights in gondola chairs, which the person seen is none the better for!—The εἴδωλου° sits by the fire—the real Ba is cold at heart through wanting her letter. And that's the doctrine to be preached now, .. is it? I 'shrink,' shrink from it—That's your word!—& mine! Dearest, I began by half a jest & end by half-gravity, .. which is the fault of your doctrine & not of me I think.

. . .

[Meeting 55: Saturday, 28 March 3.15–5.45 p.m.]

RB, *Monday, 30 March 1846*

. . .

How you surprize me, (what ever you may think) by liking that Tragedy! It seems as if, having got out of the present trouble, I shall never fall into its fellow—I will strike, for the future, on the glowing, malleable metal; afterward, *filing* is quite another process from hammering, and a more difficult one: note, that 'filing' is the wrong word,—and the rest of it, the wrong simile,—and all of it, in its stupid wrongness very characteristic of what I try to illustrate—oh, the better, better days are before me *there* as in all else! But, do you notice how stupid I am to-day? My head begins again—that is the fact; it is better a good deal than in the morning—its oeconomy passes my comprehension altogether, that is the other fact. With the deep joy in my heart below—this morning's letter here—what *does* the head mean by its perversity? I will go out presently and walk it back to its senses.

. . .

[Meeting 56: Thursday, 2 April 3.00–5.30 p.m.]

EB, *Sunday, 5 April 1846*

. . . Tomorrow I shall force you to tell me how you like the Tragedy NOW! For my part, it delights me—& must raise your reputation as a poet & thinker .. *must*. Chiappino is highly dramatic in that first part, & speaks so finely sometimes, that it is a wrench to one's sympathies to find him overthrown. Do you know, that, as far as the *temper* of the man goes, I am acquainted with a Chiappino° .. just such a man, in the temper, the pride & the bitterness .. not in other things. When I read your manuscript I was reminded—but here in print, it seems to grow nearer & nearer. My Chiappino has tired me out at last—I have borne more from him than women ought to bear from men, because he was unfortunate & embittered in his nature and by circumstances, & because I regarded him as a friend of many years. Yet, as I have told him, anyone, who had not such confidence in me, would think really *ill of me* through reading the insolent letters which he has thought fit to address to me on what he called a pure principle of adoration. At last I made up my mind (& shall keep it so) to answer no letter of the kind .. Men are ignoble in some things, past the conceiving of their fellows. Again & again I have said .. 'Specify your charge against me'—but there is no charge. With the most reckless & dauntless

inconsistency I am lifted halfway to the skies, & made a mark
there for mud pellets—so that I have been excited sometimes
to say quite passionately .. 'If I am the filth of the earth, tread
on me—if I am an angel of Heaven, respect me—but I cant
be both, remember'! See where your Chiappino leads you ..
& me! Though I shall not tell you the other name of mine.
Whenever I see him now, I make Arabel stay in the room—
otherwise I *am afraid*—he is such a violent man. A good man
though, in many respects, & quite an old friend. Some men
grow incensed with the continual pricks of ill-fortune, like
mad bulls: some grow tame & meek.

. . .

RB, *Sunday, 5 April 1846*

. . . There are many things in which I agree with you to
such a tremblingly exquisite exactness, so to speak, that I
hardly dare cry out lest the charm break, the imaginary
oscillation prove incomplete and your soul, *now* directly over,
pass beyond mine yet, and not *stay!* Do you understand, dear
soul of my soul, dearest Ba? Oh, how different it all *might* be!
In this House of Life—where I go, you go,—where I ascend
you run before,—where I descend, it is after you.° Now, one
might have a *piece* of Ba, but a very little of her, and make it
up into a Lady and a Mistress, and find her a room to her
mind perhaps where she should sit and sing, 'warble, eat and
dwell,' like Tennyson's blackbird°— and to visit her there
with due honor one might wear the finest of robes, use the
courtliest of ceremonies,—and then,—after a time, leave her
there and go, the door once shut, without much blame . . .
How different with us! If it were *not*, indeed—what a mad
folly would marriage be!

. . .

[Meeting 57: Monday, 6 April 3.00–5.45 p.m.]

EB, *Wednesday, 8 April 1846*

. . .

Your headache!—tell me how your headache is,—remember to tell me. When your letter came, I kissed it by a sort of instinct .. not that I do always at first sight, (please to understand) but because the writing did not look angry .. not vexed writing. Then I read .. 'First of all, kiss' ....°

So it seemed like magic.

Only I know that if I went on to write disagreeing disagreeable letters, you might not help to leave off loving me at the end. I seem to see through this crevice.

Good Heavens!—how dreadfully natural it would be to me, seem to me, if you DID leave off loving me!! How it would be like the sun's setting .. & no more wonder!—Only, more darkness, more pain—May God bless you my only dearest! & me, by keeping me

Your Ba

. . .

RB, *Thursday, 9 April 1846*

Thursday. 8 a.m.

Dearest, I have to go out presently and shall not be able to return before night .. so that the letter I expect will only be read *then*, and answered to-morrow. What will it be, the letter? Nothing but dear and kind, I know .. even, *deserve* to know, in a sense,—because I am sure all in MY letter was meant to be 'read by your light.'° I submit, unfeignedly, to you, there as elsewhere. . . .

Bless you, now, and ever, my own Ba. Do you know, next Saturday, in its position of successor to Good Friday, will be the anniversary of Mr Kenyon's asking me, some four years ago, 'if *I would like to see Miss B.*' How I remember! I was staying with him for a couple of days. Now,—I will ask myself 'would you like to kiss Ba?'

. . .

EB, *Thursday, 9 April 1846*

You are good & kind, .. *too* good & kind, .. always, always!—& I love you gratefully & shall to the end, & with an unspeakable apprehension of what you are in yourself, & towards me:—yet you cannot, you know,—you know you cannot, dearest .. 'submit' to me in an *opinion*, any more than I could to you, if I desired it ever so anxiously. We will talk no more however on this subject now—I have had some pain from it, of course .. but I am satisfied to have had the pain, for the knowledge .. which was as necessary as possible, under circumstances, for more reasons than one—. . .

I am writing as with the point of a pilgrim's staff rather than a pen. 'We are all strangers and pilgrims'.° Can you read anywise?

I think of you, bless you, love you—but it would have been better for you, never to have seen my face perhaps, though Mr. Kenyon gave the first leave. *Perhaps!!*—I 'flatter' *myself* tonight, in change for *you*.

Best beloved I am your Ba—

RB, *Friday, 10 April 1846*

Dearest, sweetest best—how can you, seeing so much, yet see that 'possibility'—*I leave off loving* you! and be 'angry' and 'vexed' and the rest! . . . I protest in the most solemn way I am capable of conceiving, that I am altogether unable to imagine how or whence or why any possible form of anger or vexation or any thing akin can or could or should or shall ever rise in me to you—it is a sense hitherto undreamed of, a new faculty—altogether an inexplicable, impossible feeling. . . . But I *can* fancy your being angry with me, very angry—and speaking the truth of the anger—that is to be *fancied*: and God knows I should in that case kiss *my* letters, here, till you pleased to judge me not unworthy to kiss the hem of your garment again. My own Ba! My election is made, or God made it for me,—and is irrevocable. I am wholly yours.—I see you have yet to understand what that implies,—but you will one day. . . .

Your note arrives here—Ba;—it would have been 'better for me,' THAT? Oh, dearest, let us marry soon, very soon, and end all this! If I could begin taking exceptions again, I might charge you with such wild conventionalism, such wondrous perversity of sight—or blindness rather! *Can* you, now, by this time, tell me or yourself that you could believe me happy with any other woman that ever breathed? I tell *you*, without affectation, that I lay the whole blame to myself, .. that I feel that if I had spoken my love out SUFFICIENTLY, all this doubt could never have been possible. You quite believe I am in earnest, know my own mind and speak as I feel, on these points we disputed about—yet *I* am far from being sure of it, or so it seems now—but, as for loving you,—*there* I mistake, or may be wrong, or may, or might or—

Now kiss me, my best—dearest beloved! It seems I am always understood *so*—the words are words, and faulty, and inexpressive, or wrongly expressive—, but when I live under your eyes, and die, you will never mistake,—you *do not* now, thank God, say to me 'you want to go elsewhere for all you say the visit seems too brief'—and, 'you would change me for another, for all you profess'—never do you *say* such things—but when I am away, all the mistaking begins—let it end soon, soon, dearest life of my life, light of my soul, heart's joy of my heart!

. . .

[Meeting 58: Saturday, 11 April 3.00–5.45 p.m.]

EB, *Sunday, 12 April 1846*

I will not speak much of the letter, as you desire that I should not. And because everything you write must be answered in some way & sense, .. must have some result, .. there is the less need of words in the present case. Let me say only then, ever dearest, dearest, that I never felt towards you as I felt when I had read that letter .. never loved you so entirely! .. that it went to my heart, & stayed there, & seemed to mix with the blood of it ... believe this of me, dear dearest beloved! For the rest, there is no need for me to put aside carefully the assumption of being didactic to *you* .. of being better than *you*, so as to teach you! ... ah, you are so fond of dressing me up in pontifical garments! ('for fun,' as the children say!)—but because they are too large for me, they drop off always of themselves, .. they do not require my pulling them off: these extravagances get righted of their own accord. After all, too, you, .. with that praeternatural submissiveness of yours, .. you know your power upon the whole, & understand, in the midst of the obeisances, that you can do very much what you please, with your High priest. . . .

Well—now I shall be good for at least a fortnight. Do I not teaze you & give you trouble? I feel ashamed of myself sometimes. Let me go away from myself to talk of Mr. Kenyon, therefore!—

For he came today, & arrived in town on friday evening— (what an escape on saturday!) & said of you, .. with those detestable spectacles .. like the Greek burning glasses,° turned full on my face .. 'I suppose now that Mr. Browning's book is done & there are no more excuses for coming, he will come *without* excuses.' Then, after talk upon other subjects, he began a long wandering sentence, the end of which I could see a mile off, about how he 'ought to know better than I, but wished to enquire of me' .... what, .. do you suppose? .. why, 'what, Mr. Browning's objects in life were. Because Mrs. Procter° had been saying that it was a pity he had not seven or eight hours a day of occupation,' &c. &c. It is a good thing to be angry, as a refuge from being confounded: I really *could* SAY something to *that*. And I did say that you 'did not *require* an occupation as a means of living .. having simple habits & desires—nor as an end of living, since you found one in the exercise of your genius! & that if Mr. Procter had looked as simply to his art as an end, he would have done better things.'

Which made Mr. Kenyon cry out .. 'Ah now! you are spiteful! and you need not be, for there was nothing unkind in what she said.' 'But *absurd*'! .. I insisted—'seeing that to put race horses into dray carts, was not usually done nor advised.'

. . .

RB, *Tuesday, 14 April 1846*

. . .

About the other,—that part which you bid me not refer to—you are obeyed now—my time will come in its turn, and I will try and speak. With respect to the immediate leaving England, you will let me say, I think, that *all* my own projects depend on that,—there will not be one least objection made to it by my father or mother, I know beforehand. You perhaps misconceived something I said last Saturday—I meant the obvious fact, however—that while there would be a *best* way of finding myself with you, still, from the WORST way (probably, of taking a house opposite Mrs Procter's!)—from *that* even, to the *best* way of any other life I can imagine,—what a descent! From the worst of roses to the most flourishing of— dandelions. But we breathe together, understand together, know, feel, live together .. I feel every day less and less need of trying to assure you *I* feel thus & thus—I seem to know that *you* must *know!*

Mrs Procter is very exactly the Mrs Procter I knew long ago. What she says is of course purely foolish. The world does seem incurably stupid on this, as other points.

. . .

[Meeting 59: Wednesday, 15 April 3.00–5.45 p.m.]

RB, *Sunday, 19 April 1846*

Just now I read again your last note for a particular purpose of thinking about the end of it .. where you say, as you have said so many times, 'that your hand was not stretched out to the good—it came to you sleeping'°etc. I wanted to try and find out and be able to explain to myself, and perhaps to you, why the *wrongness* in you should be so exquisitely dear to me, dear as the *rightness*, or dearer, inasmuch as it is the topmost grace of all, seen latest on leaving the contemplation of the others, and first on returning to them——because, Ba, that adorable spirit in all these phrases,—what I should adore without their embodiment in these phrases which fall into my heart and stay there,—that strange unconsciousness of how the love-account really stands between us,—*who* was giver altogether and *who* taker,—and, by consequence, what is the befitting virtue for each of us, a generous disposition to forgetfulness on the giver's part, as of everlasting remembrance and gratitude on the other—this unconsciousness *is wrong*, my heart's darling, strangely wrong by the contrast with your marvellous apprehension on other points, every other point I am capable of following you to: I solemnly assure you I cannot imagine any point of view wherein I ought to appear to any rational creature the benefitting party and you the benefitted—nor any matter in which I can be supposed to be even magnanimous,—(so that it might be said, '*there*, is a sacrifice'—'*that*, is to be borne with' &c)—none where such a supposition is not degrading to me, dishonouring and affronting. I *know* you, my Ba,—not because you are *my* Ba,—but thro' the best exercise of whatever power in me you too often praise, I *know*—that you are immeasurably my superior,—while you talk most eloquently and affectingly to me, I *know* and could prove you are as much my Poet as my Mistress; if I suspected it *before* I knew you,—personally,—how is it with me NOW? I feel it every day, I tell myself every day it is so. Yet you do not feel nor know it—for you write thus to me. Well,—and this is what I meant to say from the beginning of the letter, I love your inability to feel it in spite of right and justice and rationality. I would,—I *will*, at a moment's notice, give you back your golden words, and lie under your mind's supremacy as I take unutterable delight in DOing under your eye, your hand. So Shakespeare chose to 'envy this man's art and that man's scope' in the sonnets.° But I did not mean to try and explain what is unexplainable, after all—(tho' I wisely said I *would* try and explain!)

. . .

[Meeting 60: Monday, 20 April 3.00–6.45 p.m.°]

EB, *Tuesday, 21 April 1846 (1)*

I would not say to you yesterday, perhaps could not, that
you wrote ever so much foolishness to me in the morning,
dearest, & that I knew it ever so well. There is no use, no
help, in discussing certain questions: some sorts of extravagance grow by talking of: shake this elixir, & you have more
& more bubbles on the surface of it. So I would not speak—
nor will I write much. Only I PROTEST .. from my understanding .. from my heart .. and besides I do assert the truth
.. clear of any 'affectation,' this time, .. & it is that you always
make me melancholy by using such words. It seems to me as
if you were in the dark altogether, & held my hand for
another's!—let the shutter be opened suddenly, .. & the hand
.. is dropped perhaps ... must I not think such thoughts, when
you speak such words?—I ask you if it is not reasonable. No,
I do not ask you. We will not argue whether eagles creep, or
worms fly. . . . Ah—if you could know .. if you could but
know for a full moment of conviction, how you depress &
alarm me by saying such things, you would never say them
afterwards, *I* know. So trust to me, even as I trust to you .. &
do not say them ever again, .. YOU, who never flatter!—Is it
not enough that you love me? Is there anything greater? And
will you run the risk of ruining that great wonder by bringing
it to the test of an 'argumentum ad absurdum' such as I
might draw from your letter. Have pity on me my own
dearest, & consider how I must feel to see myself idealized
away, little by little, like Ossian's spirits into the mist .. till ..
'Gone is the daughter of Morven'!°—And what if it is mist or
moon-glory, if I stretch out my hands to you in vain, & must
still fade away farther? Now *you will not any more*. When the
world comes to judge between us two, or rather over us both,
the world will say (even the purblind world, as I myself with
wide-open eyes!) that I have not been generous with my
gifts—no—, you are in a position to choose .. & you might
have chosen better—.. that is my immoveable conviction. It
has been only your love for me, .. which I believe in perfectly
as love .. & which, being love, does not come by pure logic,

as the world itself may guess .. it has been only, wholly &
purely your love for me which has made a level for us two to
meet & stand together. There is my fact against your fiction!

. . .

RB, *Wednesday, 22 April 1846*

I never thought I should convince you, dearest—and I was
foolish to write *so*, since it makes you reply so: at all events, I
do not habitually offend in this kind—fortynine days out of
fifty I hear my own praises from your lips; and yet keep
silence—on the fiftieth I protest gently—is that too much?
Then I will be quiet altogether, my Ba, and get a comfort out
of the consciousness of obedience there at least. But I should
like some talking-bird to tell you the struggle there is and
what I *could* say.—Shall I idealize you into mere mist, Ba,
and see the fine, fine, last of you? Well, I cannot even play
with the fancy of *that*—so, one day, when so much is to be
cleared up between us, look for a word or two on this matter
also!

. . .

[Meeting 61: Saturday 25 April 3.15–5.45 p.m.
Meeting 62: Thursday, 30 April 3.00–5.45 p.m.]

RB, *Friday, 1 May 1846*

I go to you, my Ba, with heart *full* of love, so it seems,—
yet I come away always with a greater capacity of holding
love,—for there is more, and still more,—*that* seems too! At
the beginning, I used to say (most truly) that words were all
inadequate to express my feelings,—now, those very feelings
seem, as I see them from this present moment,—just as
inadequate in their time to represent what I am conscious of
now. I *do* feel more, widelier, strangelier .. how can I tell you?
You must *believe*,—my only, only beloved! I daresay I have

said this before, because it has struck me repeatedly,—and, judging by past experience, I shall need to say it again, and often again. Am I really destined to pass my life sitting by you? And you speak of *your* hesitation at trusting in miracles!

. . .

EB, *Friday, 1 May 1846 (2)*

How you write to me! Is there any word to answer to these words .. which, when I have read, I shut my eyes as one bewildered, & think blindly .. or do not think—some feelings are deeper than the thoughts touch. My only beloved, it is thus with me ... I stand by a miracle in your love,—& because I stand in it & it covers me, just for *that*, you cannot see me——! May God grant that you NEVER *see me*—for then, we two shall be 'happy' as you say, & I, in the only possible manner, be very sure.

. . .

[Meeting 63: Monday, 4 May 3.00–5.45 p.m.]

RB, *Tuesday, 5 May 1846*

Yes, you were right, my Ba—our meeting was on the 20th of last May: the next letter I received was the 14th° and *that* ran in my head, no doubt, yesterday. You must have many such mistakes to forgive in me when I undertake to talk and 'stare' at the same time .. well for me if they are no more serious mistakes!

I referred to my letters—and found much beside the date to reflect on. I will tell you. Would it not be perilous in some cases,—many cases—to contrast the present with the very early Past—the fruit time, even when there is abundant fruit,—with the dewy springing and blossoming? One would confess to a regret at the vanishing of that charm, at least, if it were felt to be somehow vanished out of the present. And,

looking upon our experience as if it were another's,—
undoubtedly the peril seems doubled—with that five months'
previous correspondence .. only *then*,—after all the curiosity,
and hope and fear,—the first visit to come! And after,—
shortly after,—you know—the heightened excitement that
followed .. I should not believe in the case of another,—or
should not *have* believed,—that the strange delight could last
.. no more than I should think it reasonable to wonder, or
even grieve, that it did not last—so long as other delights
came in due succession. Now, hear the truth! I never, God
knows, felt the joy of being with you as I felt it YESTER-
DAY—the fruit of my happiness has grown under the blossom, lifting it and keeping it as a coronet—not one feeling is
lost, and the new feelings are infinite. Ah, my Ba, can you
wonder if I seem less inclined to see the adorable kindness in
those provisions, and suppositions, and allowances for escape,
change of mind &c you furnish me with,—than to be struck
at the strange fancy which, as I said, insists on my being free
to leave off breathing vital air the moment it shall so please
me!

      . . .

EB, *Tuesday, 5 May 1846 (2)*

Tuesday evening.
 But, my own only beloved, I surely did not speak too
'insistingly' yesterday. I shrank from your question as you
put it, because you put it wrong. If you had asked me instead,
whether I meant to keep my promise to you, I would have
answered 'yes' without hesitation: but the form you chose,
referred to *you* more than to *me*, & was indeed & indeed a
foolish form of a question, my own dearest!—For the rest ..
ah, you do not see my innermost nature, .. *you!*—.. you are
happily too high, & cannot see into it .. cannot perceive how
the once elastic spring is broken with the long weights! .. you
wonder that it should drop, when you, who lifted it up, do
not hold it up!—you cannot understand! .. you wonder!—
And *I* wonder too .. on the other side!—*I* wonder how I can

feel happy & alive .. as I can, *through you!*—how I can turn
my face toward life again .. as I can, *for you!* .. and chiefly of
all, how I can ever imagine .. as I do, sometimes .. that such
a one as you, may be happy perhaps with such a one as *I!* ..
happy! . . .

But, no—do not, beloved, wish the first days here again.
You saw your way better in them than I did. I had too bitter
feelings sometimes:—they looked to me like an epigram of
destiny!—as if 'He who sitteth on high should laugh her to
scorn—should hold her in derision'°—as why not? My best
hope was that you should be my friend after all. We will not
have them back again .. those days! And in these, you do not
love me less but more?—Would it be strange to thank you? I
feel as if I *ought* to thank you!

  . . .

EB, *Thursday, 7 May 1846*

May 7th 1846——°
Beloved, my thoughts go to you this morning, loving &
blessing you!—May God bless you for both His worlds—not
for this alone. For me, if I can ever do or be anything to you,
it will be my uttermost blessing of all I ever knew, or could
know, as He knows. A year ago, I thought, with a sort of
mournful exultation, that I was *pure of wishes*. Now, they recoil
back on me in a spring-tide .. flow back, wave upon wave, ..
till I should lose breath to speak them!—and it is nothing, to
say that they concern another ... for they are so much the
more intensely mine, & of me. May God bless you, very dear!
dearest.

So I am to forget today, I am told in the letter. Ah!—But I
shall forget & remember what I please. In the meanwhile I
was surprised while writing thus to you this morning .. as a
good deed to begin with .. by Miss Bayley's coming°. Remembering the seventh of May, I forgot *thursday*, which she had
named for her visit, & altogether she took me by surprise. I

thought it was wednesday!—She came—& then, Mr. Kenyon came, .. and as they both went down stairs together, Mrs. Jameson came up. Miss Bayley is what is called *strong-minded*, & with all her feeling for art & Beauty, talks of utility like a Utilitarian of the highest, & professes to receive nothing without *proof*, like a reasoner of the lowest. She told me with a frankness for which I did not like her less, that she was a materialist of the strictest order, & believed in no soul & no future state. In the face of those conclusions, she said, she was calm & resigned. It is more than *I* could be, as I confessed. My whole nature would cry aloud against that most pitiful result of the struggle here—a wrestling only for the dust, & not for the crown. What a resistless melancholy would fall upon me if I had such thoughts!—& what a dreadful indifference. All grief, to have itself to end in!—all joy, to be based upon nothingness!—all love, to feel eternal separation under & over it! Dreary & ghastly, it w^d be! I should not have strength to love you, I think, if I had such a miserable creed.
. . .

[Meeting 64. Saturday, 9 May 3.00–5.45 p.m.]

RB, *Sunday, 10 May 1846*

I am always telling you, because always feeling, that I can express nothing of what goes from my heart to you, my Ba: but there is a certain choice I have all along exercised, of subjects on which I would *try* and express somewhat—while others might be let alone with less disadvantage. When we first met, it was in your thought that I loved you only for your poetry .. I think you thought that: and because one *might* be imagined to love that and not you,—because everybody must love it, indeed, that is worthy, and yet needs not of necessity love you,—yet *might* mistake, or determine to love you thro' loving *it* .. for all these reasons, there was not the immediate demand on me for a full expression of my admiration for your intellectuality,—do you see?—rather, it was proper to insist as little as possible on it, and speak to the woman, Ba, simply—and so I have tried to speak,—partly, in truth, because I love *her* best, and love her mind by the light and warmth of her heart—reading her verses, saying 'and these are Ba's,'—not kissing her lips because they spoke the verses. But it does not follow that I have lost the sense of any delight that has its source in you, my dearest, dearest—however I may choose to live habitually with certain others in preference. I would shut myself up with you, and die to the world, and live out fifty long,—long lives in bliss through your sole presence—but it is no less true that it will also be an ineffable pride,—something too sweet for the name of pride,—to avow myself, before anyone whose good opinion I am solicitous to retain, as *so* distinguished by you—it is *too* sweet, indeed,— so I guard against it,—for frequent allusion to it, might, .. (as I stammer, and make plain things unintelligible) .. might cause you to misconceive me, .. which would be dreadful .. for after all, Ba's head has given the crown its worth,— though a wondrous crown it is, too!—All this means .. the avowal we were speaking of, will be a heart's pride above every other pride whenever you decide on making such an avowal. You will understand as you do ever your own

R

. . .

EB, *Monday, 11 May 1846*

. . .

Look what is inside of this letter—look! I gathered it for you today when I was walking in the Regent's Park. Are you surprised? Arabel & Flush & I were in the carriage—& the sun was shining with that green light through the trees, as if he carried down with him the very essence of the leaves, to the ground, .. & I wished so much to walk through a half open gate along a shaded path, that we stopped the carriage & got out & walked, & I put both my feet on the grass, .. which was the strangest feeling! .. & gathered this laburnum for you. It hung quite high up on the tree, the little blossom

did, and Arabel said that certainly I could not reach it—but
you see! It is a too generous return for all your flowers: or, to
speak seriously, a proof that I thought of you & wished for
you—which it was natural to do, for I never enjoyed any of
my excursions as I did today's—the standing under the trees
& on the grass, was so delightful. It was like a bit of that
Dreamland which is your special dominion: & I felt joyful
enough for the moment, to look round for you, as for the
cause. It seemed *illogical*, not to see you close by. And you
were not far after all, if thoughts count as bringers near.
Dearest, we shall walk together under the trees some
day!——

And all those strange people ⟨flitting⟩ moving about like
phantoms of life—How wonderful it looked to me!—& only
you, .. the idea of you .. & myself seemed to be real there!
And Flush a little, too!—

. . .

[Meeting 65. Thursday, 14 May 3.00–5.45 p.m.]

EB, *Friday, 15 May 1846 (1)*

. . .

Papa brought me some flowers yesterday when he came
home .. & they went a little to my heart as I took them. I put
them into glasses near yours, & they look faded this morning
nevertheless, while your roses, for all your cruelty to them,
are luxuriant in beauty as if they had just finished steeping
themselves in garden-dew. I look gravely from one set of
flowers to the other—I cannot draw a glad omen—I wish he
had not given me these. Dearest, there seems little kindness
in teazing you with such thoughts .. but they come & I write
them: and let them come ever so sadly, I do not for a moment
doubt .. hesitate. One may falter, where one does not fail.
And for the rest, .. is it my fault, and not my sorrow rather,
that we act so? Is it by choice that we act so? If he had let me
I should have loved him out of a heart altogether open to

him—. It is not my fault that he would not let me. Now it is too late—I am not his nor my own, any more—

. . .

[Meeting 66: Monday, 18 May 3.00–5.45p.m.. Browning mistakenly numbered this meeting 65, and from here on his numbering was in error.]

EB, *Tuesday, 19 May 1846 (1)*

. . . How I shall think of you tomorrow! . . . I shall remember our first day, the only day of my life which God blessed visibly to me, the only day undimmed with a cloud .. my great compensation-day, which it was worth while being born for!——

. . .

RB, *Tuesday, 19 May 1846*

With this day expires the first year since you have been yourself to me—putting aside the anticipations, and prognostications, and even assurances from all reasons short of absolute sight and hearing,—excluding the five or six months of these, there remains a year of this intimacy: you accuse me of talking extravagantly sometimes—I will be quiet here,—is the tone *too* subdued if I say, *such* a life—made up of such years—I would deliberately take rather than any other imaginable one in which fame and worldly prosperity and the love of the whole human race should combine, excluding 'that of yours—to which I hearken'°—only wishing the rest were there for a moment that you might see and know that I did turn from them to you—My dearest, inexpressibly dearest. How can I thank you? I feel sure you *need* not have been so kind to me, so perfectly kind and good,—I should have remained your own, gratefully, entirely your own, thro' the bare permission to love you, or even without it,—seeing that

I never dreamed of stipulating at the beginning for a 'return,' and 'reward,'—but I also believe, joyfully, that no course but the course you have taken could have raised me above my very self, as I feel on looking back,—I began by loving you in comparision with all the world,—now, I love you, my Ba, in the face of your past self, as I remember it. ⟨And the⟩
.. All words are foolish—but I kiss your feet and offer you my heart and soul, dearest, dearest Ba—

I left you last evening without the usual privilege .. you did not rise, Ba! But,—I don't know why—, I got nervous of a sudden,—it seemed late,—and I remembered the Drawing-room & its occupants.

EB, *Tuesday, 19 May 1846 (2)*

Tuesday evening.

Do you remember how, when poor Abou Hassan, in the Arabian story, awakens from sleep in the Sultan's chamber, to the sound of instruments of music, & is presently complimented by the grand vizier on the royal wisdom displayed throughout his reign .. do you remember? Because just as he listened, do *I* listen, when you talk to me about 'the course I have taken'.... *I*, who have just had the wit to sit still in my chair with my eyes half shut, & dream .. dream!—Ah, whether I am asleep or awake, what do I know .. even now?— As to the 'course I have taken,' it has been somewhere among the stars .. or under the trees of the Hesperides, at lowest. ..

Why how can I write to you such foolishness? Rather I should be serious, grave, & keep away from myths & images, & speak the truth plainly. And speaking the truth plainly, I, when I look back, dearest beloved, see that you have done for me everything, instead of my doing anything for you—that you have lifted me ... Can I speak? Heavens!,—how I had different thoughts of you & of myself & of the world & of life, last year at this hour!° The spirits who look backward over the grave, cannot feel much otherwise from my feeling as I look back. As to *your* thanking *me, that* is monstrous, it seems to me. It is the action of your own heart alone, which has appeared to do you any good. For myself, if I do not spoil your life, it is the nearest to deserving thanks that I can come. Think what I was when you saw me first .. laid there on the sofa as an object of the merest compassion! & of a sadder spirit than even the face showed! .. & then think of all your generosity & persistence in goodness. Think of it!—shall I ever cease? Not while the heart beats, which beats for you.

And now as the year has rounded itself to 'the perfect round,' I will speak of that first letter, about which so many words were, .. just to say, this time, that I am glad now, yes, glad, .. as we were to have a miracle, .. to have it *so*, a born-miracle from the beginning. I feel glad, now, that nothing was *between* the knowing & the loving .. & that the beloved eyes were never cold discerners & analyzers of me at any time. I am glad & grateful to you, my own altogether dearest!—Yet the letter was read in pain & agitation, & you have scarely guessed how much. I could not sleep night after night,—c^d not,—& my fear was at nights, lest the feverishness should make me talk deliriously & tell the secret aloud. Judge if the deeps of my heart were not shaken. From the first you had that power over me, notwithstanding those convictions which I also had & which you know.

For it was not the character of the letter apart from you, which shook me,—I could prove that to you. I received & answered very calmly,—with most absolute calmness,—a letter of the kind last summer .. knowing in respect to the writer of it, (just as I thought of *you*), that a moment's enthusiasm had carried him a good way past his discretion. I am sure that he was perfectly satisfied with my way of answering his letter .. as I was myself. But *you* .. *you* .. I could not escape so from *you*. You were stronger than I, from the beginning, & I felt the mastery in you by the first word & first look.

Dearest & most generous.—No man was ever like you, I know! May God keep me from laying a blot on one day of yours!—on one hour!—& rather blot out mine!

. . .

[Meeting 67: Saturday, 23 May 3.00–5.45 p.m.]

RB, *Sunday, 24 May 1846*

. . . To-morrow I will send you the Review and some of the other books you have spoken of from time to time—but, I almost dare to keep the 'Statesmen',° spite of your positive request. Why, dear, want to see what I desire to forget altogether? So of my other poems, 'Sordello' &c.—I most unaffectedly shudder at the notion of your reading them, as I said yesterday. *My* poetry is far from the 'completest expression of my being'°—I hate to refer to it, or I could tell you why, wherefore, .. *prove* how imperfect (for a mild word), how unsatisfactory it must of necessity be. Still, I should not so much object, if, such as it is, it were the best, the flower of my life .. but that is all to come, and thro' you, mainly, or more certainly. So will it not be better to let me write one last poem this summer,—quite easily, stringing every day's thoughts instead of letting them fall,—and laying them at the dear feet at the summer's end for a memorial?° I have been almost determining to do this, or try to do it, as I walked in the garden just now. A poem to publish or not to publish,—but a proper introduction to the after-work. What do you think, my Ba, my dearest siren, and muse, and Mistress, and .. something beyond all, above all and better .. shall I do this?
. . .

EB, *Sunday, 24 May 1846*

. . .

In the midst I had to hold my sunday-levee, when for the only day in the week & for one half hour I have to see all my brothers and sisters at once: on the week days, one being in one place & one in another, & the visits to me only coming by twos & threes. Well, & Alfred, who never had said a word to me before, gave me the opportunity of saying '*no, no, it is not true*'°—followed hard by a remark from somebody else, that 'of course Ba must know, as she & Mr. Browning are such VERY intimate friends,' & a good deal of laughter on all sides: on which, without any transition & with an exceeding impertinence, Alfred threw himself down on the sofa & declared that he felt inclined to be very ill, .. for that then perhaps (such things being heard of) some young lady might come to visit *him*, to talk sympathetically on the broad & narrow guage!°—Altogether, I shall leave you for the future to ... contradict yourself! I did not mean to do it this time, only that Alfred forced me into it.

. . .

EB, *Monday, 25 May 1846*

My beloved I scarcely know what to say about the poem. It is almost profane & a sin to keep you from writing it when your mind goes that way,—yet I am afraid that you cannot begin without doing too much & without suffering as a consequence in your head. Now if you make yourself ill, what will be the end? So you see my fears!—Let it be however as it must be! Only you will promise to keep from all excesses, & to write very very gently .... Ah—can you keep such a promise, if it is made ever so? There, are the fears again.

You are very strange in what you say about my reading your poetry—as if it were not my peculiar gladness & glory!— my own, which no man can take from me. And not *you*, indeed!—Yet I am not likely to mistake your poetry for the flower of your nature, knowing what that flower is, knowing something of what that flower is without a name, & feeling something of the mystical perfume of it—When I said, or when others said for me, that my poetry was the flower of me, was it praise, did you think, or blame? might it not stand for a sarcasm? It might,—if it were not true, miserably true after a fashion.

Yet something of the sort is true, of course, with all poets who write directly from their personal experience & emotions—their ideal rises to the surface & floats like the bell of the waterlily. The roots & the muddy water are *subaudita* [understood], you know .. as surely there, as the flower.

But *you* .. you have the superabundant mental life &

individuality which admits of shifting a personality & speaking the truth still. *That* is the highest faculty, the strongest & rarest, which exercises itself in Art,—we are all agreed there is none so great faculty as the dramatic. Several times you have hinted to me that I made you care less for the drama, & it has puzzled me to fancy how it could be, when I understand myself so clearly both the difficulty & the glory of dramatic art. Yet I am conscious of wishing you to take the other crown besides—& after having made your own creatures speak in clear human voices, to speak yourself out of that personality which God made, & with the voice which He tuned into such power & sweetness of speech. I do not think that, with all that music in you, only your own personality should be dumb, nor that having thought so much & deeply on life & its ends, you should not teach what you have learnt, in the directest & most impressive way, the mask thrown off, however moist with the breath. And it is not, I believe, by the dramatic medium, that poets teach most impressively .. I have seemed to observe *that!* .. it is too difficult for the common reader to analyze, & to discern between the vivid & the earnest—also he is apt to understand better always, when he *sees the lips move*. Now, here is yourself, with your wonderful faculty!—it is wondered at & recognised on all sides where there are eyes to see—it is called wonderful & admirable! Yet, with an inferior power, you might have taken yourself closer to the hearts & lives of men, & made yourself dearer, though being less great. Therefore I do want you to do this with your surpassing power—it will be so easy to you to speak, & so noble, when spoken.

Not that I usen't to fancy I could see you & know you, in a reflex image, in your creations! I used, you remember. How those broken lights & forms look strange & unlike now to me, when I stand by the complete idea. Yes, *now* I feel that no one can know you worthily by those poems. Only .. I guessed a little. *Now* let us hear your own voice speaking of yourself— if the voice may not hurt the speaker. Which is my fear.

. . .

[Meeting 68: Wednesday, 27 May 3.00–5.45 p.m.]

EB, *Friday, 29 May 1846*

I have your letter .. you who cannot write!—The contrariety is a part of the 'miracle'. After all it seems to me that you can write for yourself pretty well—rather too well I used to think from the beginning. But if you persist in the proposition about my doing it for you, leaving room for your signature ... shall it be this way?

Show me how to get rid of you.

(signed) *RB*

Now isn't it *I* who am .. not 'balancing my jewel'° over the gulph .. but actually tossing it up in the air out of sheer levity of joyousness?—Only it is not perhaps such dangerous play as it looks: there may be a little string perhaps, tying it to my finger. Which, if it is not imprudence in act, is impudence in fact, you see!—

Dearest, I committed a felony for your sake today—so never doubt that I love you. We went to the Botanical Gardens, where it is unlawful to gather flowers, & I was determined to gather this for you, & the gardeners were here & there .. they seemed everywhere .. but I stooped down & gathered it—Is it felony, or burglary on green leaves—or what is the name of the crime? would the people give me up to the police I wonder? *Transie de peur* [overcome with fear], I was, .. listening to Arabel's declaration that all gathering of flowers in those gardens is highly improper,—and I made her finish her discourse, standing between me & the gardeners .. to prove that I was the better for it.

How pretty those gardens are, by the way! We went to the summerhouse & sate there, & then on, to the empty seats where the band sit on your high days. What I enjoy most to see, is the green under the green .. where the grass stretches under trees. *That* is something unspeakable to me, in the beauty of it. And to stand under a tree & feel the green shadow of the tree! I never knew before the difference of the *sensation* of a green shadow & a brown one—I seemed to feel that green shadow through & through me, till it went out at the soles of my feet & mixed with the other green below.

. . .

RB, *Saturday, 30 May 1846*

Oh, yes, do 'show me how to get rid of you', my best Ba,—
for so I shall have the virtuous delight of deciding to keep
you, instead of being wholly kept by you; it is all out of my
head, now, how I used to live when I was my own: and if you
can, by one more witchery, give me back that feeling for once
.. Ba, I have no heart to write more nonsense, when I can
take your dearest self into my arms; yet I shall never quite lie
quiet and happy, I do think .. I shall be always wishing you
would be angry, and cruel, and unjust, for a moment,—for
my love overflows the bounds, needs to prove itself—all
which is foolish, I know.

. . .

[Meeting 69: Monday, 1 June 3.00–5.45 p.m.]

RB, *Wednesday, 3 June 1846*

I will tell you, dearest: your good is my good, and your will
mine; if you were convinced *that* good would be promoted by
our remaining as we are for twenty years instead of one, I
should endeavour to submit in the end .. after the natural
attempts to find out and remove the imagined obstacle: if,—
as you seem to do here,—you turn and ask about *my* good,—
yours being supposed to be uninfluenced by what I answer ..
then, here is my TRUTH on that subject, in that view,—my
good for *myself*: Every day that passes before *that day* is one
the more of hardly endurable anxiety and irritation, to say
the least; and the thought of another year's intervention of
hope deferred—altogether intolerable! Is there anything I
can do in that year—or that you can do—to forward our
object? Anything impossible to be done sooner? If not—

. . .

EB, *Wednesday, 3 June 1846 (2)*

. . .

For me I agree with your view—I never once thought of
proposing a delay on my own account—We are standing on
hot scythes, & because we do not burn in the feet, by a
miracle, we have no right to count on the miracle's prolonga-
tion. Then nothing is to be gained—& everything may be
lost—& the sense of mask-wearing for another year, would
be suffocating—This for *me*. And for yourself, I shall not be
much younger or better otherwise, I suppose, next year. I
make no motion, then, for a delay, further than we have
talked of, .. to the summer's end.

My good .. happiness!—Have I any that did not come
from you, that is not *in* you, that you should talk of my good
apart from yours? I shudder to look back to the days when
you were not for me. Was ever life so like death before? My
face was so close against the tombstones, that there seemed
no room even for the tears. And it is unexampled generosity
of yours, that, having done all for me, you should write as you
always do, about *my giving* .. giving!—Among the sons of men
there is none like you as I believe & know, .. & every now &
then declare to my sisters.

. . .

[Meeting 70: Saturday, 6 June 3.00–5.45 p.m.]

RB, *Monday, 8 June 1846*

. . . Mrs. Jameson told me she called the other day on Miss
Barrett and was informed that lady was 'walking before her
door'—for I went last night, and deserved to be amused,
perhaps, for the effort, .. and so I was: I never liked our friend
as I now like her,—I more than like the goodnature and good
feeling and versatility of ready intelligence and quick general
sympathy—She is to see you to-day. She told this to a Miss
Kindersley who had been reading the Drama of Exile to her

complete delight—but in listening silently;—and after, when Mrs. J. obligingly turned and said 'How I should like to introduce YOU to Miss Barrett .. did you ever see her?' .. to which I answered in the old way, 'that nobody, as she knew, saw you.' At all these times did not I feel the 'mask' you speak of! I am, fortunately, out of the way of enquirers .. but if the thing were of constant occurrence, it would be intolerable. Shall it indeed end soon? May I count by months, by weeks? It is not safe—beginning to write on this subject—I can do nothing moreover.

. . .

[Meeting 71: Thursday, 11 June 3.00–5.45 p.m.]

RB, *Friday, 12 June 1846*

. . . I believe you to be the one woman in the world I am able to marry because able to love—I wish, on some accounts, I had forseen the contingency of such an one's crossing my path in this life—but I did not,—and on all ordinary grounds preferred being free and poor, accordingly. All is altered now. Does anybody doubt that I can by application in proper quarters obtain quite enough to support us both in return for no extraordinary expenditure of such faculties as I have? If is *is* to be doubted, I have been greatly misinformed, that is all. Or, setting all friends and their proposals and the rest of the hatefulness aside—I should say that so simple a procedure as writing to anybody .. Lord Monteagle,° for instance, who reads and likes my works, as he said at Moxon's two days ago on calling there for a copy to give away .. surely to write to him, 'when you are minister next month, as is expected, will you give me for my utmost services about as much as you give Tennyson for nothing?'°—*this* would be rational and as easy as all rationality: *let me do so, and at once, my own* Ba! And do you, like the unutterably noble creature I know you, transfer your own advantages to your brothers or sisters .. making if you please a proper reservation in the case of my own exertions failing, as failure comes everywhere—So shall the one possible occasion of calumny be removed and all other charges go for the simple absurdities they will be—I am entirely in earnest about this, and indeed had thought for a moment of putting my own share of the project into immediate execution—but on consideration,—no! *So* I will live and so die with you: I will not be poorly endeavouring to startle you with unforeseen generosities, catch you in pretty pitfalls of magnanimities, be always surprising you, or trying to do it—No, I resolve to do my best, *thro'* you—by your counsel, with your help, under your eye .. the most strenuous endeavour will only approximate to an achievement of *that*,— and to suppose a superfluousness of devotion to you (as all these surprises do) would be miserably foolish. So, dear, dear Ba, understand and advise me: I took up the paper with ordinary feelings .. but the absurdity and tyranny suddeny flashed upon me .. it *must* not be borne—indeed its only safety in this instance is in its impotency. I am not without fear of some things in this world—but the 'wrath of man,'° all the men living put together, I fear as I fear the fly I have just put out of the window—but I fear *God*—and am ready, he knows, to die this moment in taking his part against any piece of injustice & oppression—*So* I aspire to die!

. . .

EB, *Friday, 12 June 1846 (2)*

. . .

For the rest .. you are generous & noble as always—but, no, .. I shall refuse steadily for reasons which are plain, to put away from me God's gifts .. given perhaps in order to this very end .. & apart from which, I should not have seen myself justified, .. even as far as now I vaguely, dimly seem .. to cast the burden of me upon you. *No.* I care as little for money as you do—but this thing I will not agree to, because I ought not. At the same time, you shall be at liberty to arrange that after the deaths of us two, the money should return to my family .. this, if you choose—for it shall be by your own act hereafter, that they may know you for what you are—. In the

meanwhile, I should laugh to scorn all *that* sort of calumny ..
even if I could believe it to be possible. Supposing that you
sought *money*, you would not be quite so stupid, the world
may judge for itself, as to take hundreds instead of thousands,
& pence instead of guineas. To do the world justice, it is not
likely to make a blunder on such a point as this. . . .

And do you think that because this may be done, or not
done .. & because *that* ought *not* to be borne .. we can make
any change .. act any more openly .. face to face, perhaps—
voice to voice? Alas, no!—You said once that women were as
strong as men, .. unless in the concurrence of physical force.
Which is a mistake. I would rather be kicked with a foot, ..
(I, for one woman! ..) than be overcome by a loud voice
speaking cruel words. I would not yield before such words—
I would not give you up if they were said .. but, being a
woman & a very weak one, (in more senses than the bodily, ..)
they would act on me as a dagger would, .. I could not help
dropping, dying before them—I say it that you may understand. Tyranny? Perhaps. Yet in that strange, stern nature,
there is a capacity to love—& I love him—& I shall suffer,
in causing him to suffer. May God bless you. You will scarcely
make out these hurried straggling words—& scarcely do they
carry out my meaning. I am for ever

your Ba.

[Meeting 72: Monday, 15 June 3.00–5.45 p.m.]

EB, *Tuesday, 16 June 1846 (1)*

. . .
Shall I tell you? I repented yesterday .. I repented last
night .. I repent today, having made the promise you asked
of me. I could scarcely sleep at all last night, through thinking
that I ought not to have made it. Be generous, & free me from
that promise. To be true to you in the real right sense, I need
no promises at all—& if an argument were addressed to me
in order to separate us, I should see through the piteous ingenuity
of it I think, whatever ground it took, & admit no judgement

& authority over your life to be higher than your own. But I
have misgivings about that promise, because I can conceive
of circumstances .. Loose me from my promise, & let me be
grateful to you, my beloved, in all things & ways, & hold you
to be generous in the least as in the greatest. What *I* asked of
you, was as different as our positions are—different beyond
what you see or can see. No third person can see,—no second
person can see .. what my position is & has been .. I do not
enter on it here. But there is just & only *one* way in which I
may be injured by you, .. & *that* is, in being allowed to *injure
you* .. so remember, remember, .. to the last available moment.
    . . .

RB, *Tuesday, 16 June 1846*

. . . Do you remember that the first word I ever wrote to
you was 'I love you, dear Miss Barrett'? It was so,—could
not but be so—and I always loved you, as I shall always—
    . . .

EB, *Tuesday, 16 June 1846 (3)*

    . . .

Do I remember? Yes indeed, I remember. How I recalled
and wondered afterwards, though at the moment it seemed
very simple & what was to be met with in our philosophy
every day. But there, you see, there's the danger of using *mala
verba* [bad words]! The Fates catch them up & knit them into
the web!—Then I remember all the more (though I should at
any rate) through an impudence of my own (or a piece of ill-
luck rather .. it shall not be called an impudence—) of which
I will tell you. I was writing to Miss Mitford & of you—we
differed about you often,—because she did not appreciate you
properly, & was fond of dwelling on the 'obscurity' when I
talked of the light,—& I just then writing of you, added in
my headlong unreflecting way that I had had a real letter

from you which said that you loved me—'Oh—but,' I wrote on, 'you are not to mistake this, not to repeat it—for of course, it is simply the purest of philanthropies ...' ... some words to that effect°—and if yours was the purest of philan-thropies, mine was the purest of innocences, as you may well believe, .. for if I had had the shadow of a foresight, I should not have fallen into the snare. So vexed I was afterwards!— Not that she thought anything at the time, or has referred to it since, or remembers a word now. Only I was vexed in my innermost heart .. & *am* .. do you know? .. that I should have spoken lightly of such an expression of yours—though you meant it lightly too. Dearest!—It was a disguised angel & I should have known it by its wings though they did not fly.

. . .

RB, *Wednesday, 17 June 1846*

My own Ba, I release you from just as much as you would easily dispense me from observing in that mutual promise: indeed, it has become one unnecessary for our present relation and knowledge: it was right at the beginning for either to say to the other, using calm words, 'it is your good I seek, not mine' and as, if it were demonstrated that I should secure yours at the expense of mine by leaving you I would endea-vour to do it: so, you assure me, you would act by me. The one point to ascertain, therefore, is—what will amount to a demonstration—and I, for my part, apprize you that no other person in the world can by any possibility know so much of me as to be entitled to pronounce in the matter—to say 'it is for good or for evil'—. . . Just this, so rational and right, I understood you to bid me promise—and so much you have promised me, a proper precaution for the earlier time when the friend might seem to argue with some plausibility 'really I understand my friends interests better than you can'—But now, who dares assure me that? I disbelieve it: one only knows better, can ever know better—yourself: and I will obey yourself. So with me—I know better my own good than you do yet, I think—when I tell you that good requires such a step as you speak of, you shall acquiesce; I will tell you on the instant—as you, in your own case, should tell me on the instant. I needed not ask you to promise, as I foolishly did, that you would not act in the saddest of ways—professing to see what could never be, and believe what must be untrue.

. . .

[Meeting 73: Saturday, 20 June 3.00–5.45 p.m.
Meeting 74: Thursday, 25 June 3.00–6.00 p.m.]

RB, *Friday, 26 June 1846*

Friday Morning.

I drew the table to the fire before I wrote this. Here is cool weather, grateful to those overcome by last week's heat, I suppose!—much as one conceives of a day's starvation being grateful to people who were overfeasted some time back. But the coolness—(that is, piercing cold as the north wind can make)—sets me to ponder on what you said yesterday,—of considering summer as beginning next Wednesday, or thereabout, and ending by consequence with September. Our time is 'at the Summer's end': and it does strike me that there may be but too many interpositions beside that of 'my own will' .. far too many! If those equinoctial winds disturb the sea, and the cold weather adds to the difficulties of the land-journey .. *then* the will may interpose or stand aloof .. I cannot take you and kill you .. really, inevitably kill you! As it is .. or rather, as it might be, I should feel during a transit under the most favorable circumstances possible, somewhat as the performer of that trick by which a full glass of water resting on the open hand is made to describe a circle from above to below and back without spilling a drop .. thro' some good natured suspension, in the operator's interest, of just a fundamental law of the universe, no more! Therefore if any September weather shall happen in September .. let us understand and wait .. another year! and another, and another.

Now, have I ever, with all those askings, asked you once

too often,—that is, unnecessarily—'*if* this should be,'—or 'when this should be?' What is my 'will' to do with it? Can I keep the winds away, alas? My own will has all along been annihilated before you,—with respect to you—I should never be able to say 'she shall dine on fish, or fruit,'—'she shall wear silk gloves or thread gloves'—even to exercise in fancy that much 'will OVER YOU' is revolting—I *will* THIS, never to be 'over you' if I could!

So, you decide here as elsewhere—but *do* decide, Ba, my own only Ba—do *think*, to decide: I *can* know nothing here as to what is gained or lost by delay or anticipation—I only refer to the few obvious points of the advantage of our 'flight not being in the winter'°—and the consideration that the difficulty in another quarter will never be less nor more,—therefore is out of the question.

. . .

[Meeting 75: Monday 29 June 3.00–6.00 p.m.]

EB, *Tuesday, 30 June 1846 (1)*

The gods & men call you by your name, but I never do—never dare. In case of invocation, tell me how you should be called by such as I? not to be always the 'inexpressive *He*'° which I make of you. In case of courage for invocation!—
. . .

RB, *Tuesday, 30 June 1846*

. . .

I think my head is dizzy with reading the debates this morning—Peel's speech and farewell.° How exquisitely absurd, it just strikes me, would be any measure after Miss Martineau's own heart, which should introduce women to Parliament as we understand its functions at present—how essentially retrograde a measure! Parliament seems no place for originating, creative minds—but for second-rate minds influenced by and bent on working out the results of these—and the most efficient qualities for such a purpose are confessedly found oftener with men than with women—physical power having a great deal to do with it beside—. So why shuffle the heaps together which, however arbitrarily divided at first, happen luckily to lie pretty much as one would desire,—here the great flint stones, here the pebbles .. and diamonds too.

. . .

EB, *Tuesday, 30 June 1846 (2)*

. . .

Right you are, I think, in opposition to Miss Martineau, though your reasons are too gracious to be right .. except indeed as to the physical inaptitude, which is an obvious truth. Another truth (to my mind) is, that women, as they *are*, (whatever they *may be*) have not mental strength any more than they have bodily,—have not instruction, capacity, wholeness of intellect enough. To deny that women, as a class, have defects, is as false I think, as to deny that women have wrongs.

. . .

RB, *Wednesday, 1 July 1846*

Dearest—dearest, you *did* once, one time only, call me by my name—Robert; and tho' it was to bid 'R. not talk extravagances' (your very words) still the name so spoken became what it never had been before to me. I never am called by any pet-name, nor abbreviation, here at home or elsewhere .. Oh, best let it alone .. it is one of my incommunicable advantages to have a Ba of my own, and call her so—

indeed, yes, my Ba! I write 'dearest,' and 'most dearest,' but it all ends in—'Ba,' and the 'my' is its framework,—its surrounding arm—Ba—my own Ba! 'Robert' is in Saxon, (*ni fallor* [if I am not mistaken]), 'famous in counsel'° . . .

EB, *Wednesday, 1 July 1846*

No, no!—indeed I never did. If you heard me say 'Robert,' it was on a stair landing in the House of Dreams—never anywhere else! Why how could you fancy such a thing? Wasn't it rather your own disquieted Conscience which spoke instead of me, saying 'Robert, dont be extravagant'. Yes— just the speech THAT IS, for a 'good *un*easy,' discerning conscience—& you took it for my speech!

'Dont be extravagant' I may certainly have said. Both I & the Conscience might have said so obvious a thing.

Ah—& now I have got the name, shall I have courage to say it? tell me, best councillor! I like it better than any other name, though I never spoke it with my own lips—I never called any one by such a name .. except once when I was in the lane with Bertha.°

. . .

RB, *Thursday, 2 July 1846*

Dear, you might as well imagine you had never given me any other of the gifts, as that you did not call me, as I tell you: you spoke quickly, interrupting me, and, for the name, 'I can hear it, 'twixt my spirit and the earth-noise intervene'°: do you think I forget one gift in another, even a greater? I should still taste the first freshness of the vinegar, (or whatever was the charm of it)—tho' Cleopatra had gone on dissolving pearl after pearl in it: I love you for these gifts to me now— hereafter, it seems almost as if I must love you even better, should you choose to continue them to me in spite of complete knowledge: I feel this as often as I think of it, which is not seldom.

. . .

EB, *Thursday 2 July 1846*

. . .

In the meanwhile,—quite you make me laugh by your positiveness about the name-calling. Well—if ever I did such a thing, it was in a moment of unsconsciousness all the more surprising, that, even to my own soul, in the lowest spirit-whisper, I have not been in the *habit* of saying 'Robert,' speaking of you. You have only been The One. No word ever stood for you. The Idea admitted of no representative—the words fell down before it & were silent. Still such very positive people must be right of course—they always are. At any rate it is only one illusion more—and some day I expect to hear you say & swear that you saw me fly out of one window & fly in at another. So much for your Cleopatra's Roman pearls, oh my famous in council!—& appreciation of sour vinegar!

. . .

[Meeting 76: Wednesday, 8 July 3.00–6. ? p.m. Browning's '6' is followed by an unfinished fraction, which may indicate a quarter or half an hour, or which may be a slip of the pen.]

EB, *Thursday, 9 July 1846 (1)*

. . .

Ah Flush, Flush!—he did not hurt you really? You will forgive him for me? The truth is that he hates all unpetti-coated people, & that though he does not hate *you*, he has a certain distrust of you, which any outward sign, such as the

umbrella, reawakens—But if you had seen how sorry &
ashamed he was yesterday!—I slapped his ears & told him
that he never should be loved again: and he sate on the sofa
(sitting, not lying) with his eyes fixed on me all the time I did
the flowers, with an expression of quiet despair in his face. At
last I said, 'If you are good, Flush, you may come & say that
you are sorry' .. on which he dashed across the room &,
trembling all over, kissed first one of my hands & then
another, and put up his paws to be shaken, & looked into my
face with such great beseeching eyes, that you would certainly
have forgiven him just as I did. It is not savageness—If he
once loved you, you might pull his ears & his tail, & take a
bone out of his mouth even, & he would not bite you. He has
no savage caprices like other dogs & men I have known.
  . . .

RB, *Friday, 10 July 1846*

  . . .
  Oh, poor Flush,—do you think I do not love and respect
him for his jealous supervision,—his slowness to know
another, having once known you? All my apprehension is
that, in the imaginations downstairs, he may very unconsciously play the part of the dog that is heard to 'bark
violently' while something dreadful takes place: yet I do not
sorrow over his slapped ears, as if they ever pained him very
much—you dear Ba!
  . . .

[Meeting 77: Saturday, 11 July 3.10–6.00 p.m.
Meeting 78: Tuesday, 14 July 3.05–6.00 p.m.]

EB, *Wednesday, 15 July 1846 (1)*

  . . .
  At dinner my aunt° said to Papa .. 'I have not seen Ba all
day—and when I went to her room, to my astonishment a

gentleman was sitting there.' 'Who was *that*' said Papa's eyes to Arabel—'Mr. Browning called here today,' she answered—'And Ba bowed her head,' continued my aunt, 'as if she meant to signify to me that I was not to come in'— 'Oh,' cried Henrietta, '*that* must have been a mistake of yours. Perhaps she meant just the contrary'—'You should have gone in,' Papa said, '& seen the *poet*.' Now if she really were to do that the next time!—Yet I did not, you know, make the expelling gesture she thought she saw. Simply I was startled. As to Saturday we must try whether we cannot defend the position .. set the guns against the approaches to right & left .. we must try.

In speaking too of your visit this morning, Stormy said to her .. 'Oh Mr. Browning is a *great* friend of Ba's! He comes here twice a week—is it twice a week or once, Arabel?'

While I write, the Hedleys come—& Mrs. Hedley is beseeching me into seeing Mr. Bevan whom perhaps I must see, notwithstanding Flush's wrongs—

By the way, I made quite clear to Flush that you left the cakes, & they were very graciously received indeed—

Dearest, since the last word was written, Mrs. Hedley came back leading Mr. Bevan, & Papa who had just entered the room found the door shut upon him .. I was nervous .. oh, so nervous! & the six feet, & something more, of Mr. Bevan seemed to me as if they never would end, so tall the man is. . . .

My aunt (Mrs. Hedley) said when she introduced him— 'You are to understand this to be a great honour—for she never lets anybody come here except Mr. Kenyon, .. & a few other gentlemen' ... (laughing). Said Papa—'Only ONE other gentleman, indeed. Only Mr. Browning, the poet—the man of the pomegranates.' Was *that* likely to calm me, do you think? How late it is—I must break off.

Tonight I shall write again°—Dearest beloved

I am your own always.

RB, *Thursday, 16 July 1846*

. . .

I think your Father's words on these two occasions, very kind,—very! They confuse,—perhaps humble me .. that is not the expression, but it may stay. I dare say he is infinitely kind at bottom—I think so, that is, on my own account,—because, come what will or may, I shall never see otherwise than with your sight. If he could know me, I think he would soon reconcile himself to all of it,—know my heart's purposes toward you: but that is impossible. And with the sincere will to please him by any exertion or sacrifice in my power, I shall very likely never have the opportunity of picking up a glove he might drop. In old novels, the implacable father is not seldom set upon by a round dozen of ruffians with blacked faces, from behind a hedge,—and just as the odds prove too many, suddenly a stranger (to all save the reader) leaps over an adjacent ditch, &c 'Sir, under Providence, I owe you my life!' &c &c How does Dumas improve on this in 'Monte Cristo'°—are there 'new effects?'

Absurdity! Yet I would fain .. fain!—you understand.

. . .

EB, *Thursday, 16 July 1846*

Dearest, if *you* feel *that*, must I not feel it more deeply? Twice or three times lately he has said to me 'my love,' and even 'my puss,' his old words before he was angry last year, .. & I quite quailed before them as if they were so many knife-strokes. Anything, but his *kindness*, I can bear now.

Yet I am glad that you feel *that* .. The difficulty, (almost the despair!) has been with me, to make you understand the two ends of truth .. both that he is *not* stone .. and that he *is* immoveable *as* stone. Perhaps only a very peculiar nature could have held so long the position he holds in his family—. His hand would not lie so heavily, without a pulse in it—. Then he is upright—faithful to his conscience. You would respect him, .. & love him perhaps in the end. For me, he might have been king & father over me *to* the end, if he had thought it worth while to love me openly enough—yet, even *so*, he should not have let you come too near. And you could not (so) have come too near—for he would have had my confidence from the beginning, & no opportunity would have been permitted to you of proving your affection for me, and I should have thought always what I thought at first. So the nightshade & the eglantine are twisted, twined, one in the other, .. & the little pink roses lean up against the pale poison of the berries—we cannot tear this from that, let us think of it ever so much!

We must be humble & beseeching *afterwards* at least, & try to get forgiven—Poor Papa!—I have turned it over & over in my mind, whether it would be less offensive, less *shocking* to him, if an application were made first—. If I were strong, I think I should incline to it at all risks—but as it is, .. it might .. would, probably, .. take away the power of action from me altogether. We should be separated you see, from *that moment*, .. hindered from writing .. hindered from meeting .. & I could evade nothing, as I am—not to say that I should have fainting fits at every lifting of his voice—through that inconvenient nervous temperament of mine which has so often made me ashamed of myself. Then .. the positive disobedience might be a greater offence than the unauthorised act—I shut my eyes in terror sometimes—May God direct us to the best—

Oh—do not write about this, dearest, dearest!—I throw myself out of it into the pure, sweet, deep thought of you .. which is the love of you always. I am yours .. your own. I never doubt of being yours. I feel too much yours. It is might & right together. You are more to me, beside, than the whole world—

. . .

[Meeting 79: Saturday, 18 July 3.00–6.00 p.m.
Meeting 80: Tuesday, 21 July 3.00–6.00 p.m.]

RB, *Wednesday, 22 July 1846*

. . .

Will you let me write something, and forgive me?—
Because it is, I know, quite unnecessary to be written, and,
beside, may almost seem an interference with your own
delicacy,—teaching it its duty! However, I will venture to
go on, with your hand before my two eyes. Then,—you
remember what we were speaking of yesterday,—house-rents
and styles of living?—You will never overlook, thro' its very
obviousness, that to consult my feelings on the only point in
which they are sensitive to the world, you must endeavour
to live as simply and cheaply as possible, down to my own
habitual simplicity and cheapness . . . You see, Ba, if you
have more money than you want, you shall save it or spend
it in pictures or parrots or what you please .. you avoid all
offence to *me* who never either saved money nor spent it—
but the large house, I should be forced to stay in,—the
carriage, to enter, I suppose. And you see too, Ba, that the
one point on which I desire the world to be informed
concerning our future life, will be that it is ordered *so*—I
wish they could hear we lived in one room like George Sand
in 'that happy year—'°

No,—*there* I have put down an absurdity—because, I shall
have to confess a weakness, at some time or other, which is
hardly reconcileable to that method of being happy—why
may I not tell you now, my adored Ba, to whom I tell
everything as it rises in me? Now put the hand on my eyes
again .. now that I have kissed it: I shall begin by begging a
separate room from yours—I could never brush my hair and
wash my face, I do think, before my own father: I could not,
I am sure, take off my coat before you *now*—why should I
ever? 'The Kitchen' is an unknown horror to me,—I come to
the dining room for whatever repast there may be,—nor
willingly stay too long there,—and on the day on which poor
Countess Peppa° taught me how maccaroni is made,—*then*
began a quiet revolution, (indeed a rapid one) against 'tag-
liolini,' 'fettucce,' 'lasagne' etc, etc, etc.—typical, typical!

What foolishness .. spare me, my own Ba, and don't answer

one word,—do not even laugh,—for I *know* the exceeding, unnecessary foolishness of it!

. . .

EB, *Wednesday, 22 July 1846*

Dearest, what you say is unnecessary for you to say—it is, in everything, *so* of course & obvious! You must have an eccentric idea of *me* if you can suppose for a moment such things to be necessary to say. If they had been *unsaid*, it would have been precisely the same, believe me, in the event.

As to the way of living—now you shall arrange *that* for yourself—You shall choose your own lodging, order your own dinner .. & if you choose to live on locusts & wild honey,° I promise not to complain .. I shall not indeed be *inclined* to complain .. having no manner of ambition about carriages & large houses, even if they were within our possibilities . . . The more simply we live, the better for *me!*—So you shall arrange it for yourself, lest I should make a mistake! .. which, in THAT question, is a just possible thing.

One extravagance I had intended to propose to you .. but it shall be exactly as you like, and I hesitate a little as I begin to speak of it. I have thought of taking Wilson with me, .. for a year, say, if we returned then—if not, we might send her home alone .. & by that time, I should be stronger perhaps & wiser .. rather less sublimely helpless & impotent than I am now. My sisters have urged me a good deal in this matter— but if you would rather it were otherwise, be honest & say so, & let me alter my thoughts at once—There is one considera- tion which I submit to yours, .. that I cannot leave this house with the necessary number of shoes & pocket handkerchiefs, without help from somebody. Now whoever helps me, will suffer through me. If I left her behind she would be turned into the street before sunset. Would it be right & just of me, to permit it? Consider! I must manage a sheltering ignorance for my poor sisters, at the last, .. & for all our sakes. And in order to *that*, again, I must have some one else in my confidence. Whom again, I would unwillingly single out for an absolute *victim*.

Wilson is attached to me, I believe—and, in all the discussions about Italy, she has professed herself willing to 'go anywhere in the world with me'. Indeed I rather fancy that she was disappointed bitterly last year, & that it would not be a pure devotion. She is an expensive servant—she has sixteen pounds a year, .. but she has her utilities besides,—& is very amiable & easily satisfied, & would not add to the expenses, or diminish from the economies, even in the matter of room—I would manage *that* for her. Then she would lighten your responsibilities . . .

RB, *Thursday, 23 July 1846*

. . .

My dearest—dearest,—you might go to Pisa without shoes,—or feet to wear them, for aught I know, since you may have wings, only folded away from me—but without your Wilson, or some one in her capacity, you .. no, I will not undertake to speak of *you*; then, *I*, should be simply, exactly, INSANE to move a step; I would rather propose, let us live on bread and water, and sail in the hold of a merchant-ship; THIS CANNOT be dispensed with!—It is most fortunate, most providential, that Wilson is inclined to go—I am *very* happy: for a new servant, with even the best dispositions, would never be able to anticipate your wants & wishes during the voyage, at the very beginning. Yet you write of this to me *so*, my Ba! I think I will, in policy, begin the anger at a good place. Yes, all the anger I am capable of descends on the head—(not in kisses, whatever you may fancy)—

And so poor Flush suffered after all! Dogs that are dog-like would be at no such pains to tell you they would not see you with comfort approached by a stranger who might be—! A 'muzzle'? Oh, no—but suppose you have him removed next time, and perhaps the next, till the whole occurrence is out of his mind as the fly bite of last week—because, if he sees me and begins his barking and valiant snapping, and gets more and heavier vengeance down stairs, perhaps,—his transient suspicion of me, will confirm itself into absolute dislike—, hatred! Whereas, after an interval, we can renew acquaintance on a better footing.°

. . .

[Meeting 81: Saturday, 25 July 3.00–6.00 p.m.]

EB, *Sunday, 26 July 1846*

. . .

I will write the paper as you bid me. Only, in the face of all that is to come, I solemnly tell you that neither I nor mine .. certainly not I .. will consent to an act of injustice, disinheriting my last hours (whenever they shall come) of a natural satisfaction. You are noble in all things—but this will not be in your power—I will not discuss it so as to teaze you—. Your reputation is dear to me of course .. the thoughts which men shall have of you in the least matter, I would choose to keep clean .. free from every possible taint. But it will be obvious to all, that if you pleased, you might throw out of the windows everything called mine, the moment after our marrige—interest & principal—why not? And if you abstain from this, & after your own death allow the sum which originally came from my family, to relapse there .. why it is all of pure generosity on your part—& they will understand it as I do, as generosity .. as more than justice. . . .

Is this what is called a *document?* It seems to me that I have a sort of legal genius—& that I should be on the Woolsack in the Martineau-Parliament. But it seems, too, rather *bold* to attach such a specification to your name—Laugh & pardon it all!—°

In compliance with the request of Robert Browning, who may possibly become my husband, that I would express in writing my wishes respecting the ultimate disposal of whatever property I posses at this time, whether in the funds or elsewhere, .. I here declare my wishes to be .. that he, Robert Browning, .. having, of course, as it is his right to do, first held & used the property in question for the term of his natural life, .. should bequeath the same, by an equal division, to my two sisters, or, in the case of the previous death of either or both of them, to such of my surviving brothers as most shall need it by the judgement of my eldest surviving brother.

Elizabeth Barrett Barrett.

Wimpole Street, July—1846—

RB, *Monday, 27 July 1846*

That is sufficient, ever dearest; now dismiss the matter from your thoughts, as I shall—having forced myself once to admit that most dreadful of possibilities and to provide for it, I need not have compunction at dwelling on the brighter, better chances which God's previous dispensations encourage me to expect. There may be even a *claimant*, instead of a recipient, of whatever either of us can bequeath—who knows? For which reason, but most of all for the stronger yourself adduce,—the contingency of your illness,—I do *not* ask you to 'relinquish a part'—not as our arrangements now are ordered; for I have never been so foolish as to think we could live without money, if not of my obtaining, then of your possessing—and though, in certain respects I should have preferred to try the first course,—at the beginning at least, when my faculties seemed more my own and that 'end of summer' had a less absorbing interest (as I perceive now)— yet, as that is not to be, I have only to be thankful that you are not dependent on my exertions,— which I could not be *sure* of,—particularly with this uncertain head of mine. I hope when we once are together, the world will not hear of us again until the very end—it would be horrible to have to come back to it and ask its help.

. . .

[Meeting 82: Tuesday, 28 July 3.00–5.15 p.m. The meeting was cut short by the arrival of Mr Kenyon.]

RB, *Wednesday, 29 July 1846*

. . . Oh, how *can* you, blessing me so, speak as you spoke yesterday,—for the *first* time! I thought you would only write such suppositions, such desires—(for it was a desire) .. and that along with you I was safe from them,—yet you are adorable amid it all—only I *do* feel such speaking, Ba, lightly as it fell—no, not *now* I feel it,—this letter is before my heart like the hand on my eyes. I feel this letter, only. How good, good, good of you to write it! . . .

And—now! now, Ba, to the subject-matter: whatever you decide on writing to Mrs Jameson will be rightly written—it seems to me *nearly* immaterial,—(putting out of the question the confiding the whole secret, which, from its responsibility, as you feel, must not be done,—) whether you decline her kindness for untold reasons which two months (Ba?) will make abundantly plain,—or whether you further inform her that there *is* a special secret—of which she must bear the burthen, even in that mitigated form, for the same two months,—as I say, it seems immaterial—but it is most material that you should see how the ground is crumbling from beneath our feet, with its chances & opportunities—do not talk about 'four months,'—till December, that is—unless you mean what *must* follow as a consequence.

EB, *Wednesday, 29 July 1846*

. . .

Let it be september then, if *you* do not decide otherwise. I w^d not lean to dangerous delays which are unnecessary—I wish we were at Pisa, rather!—

. . .

RB, *Thursday, 30 July 1846*

Now you are my very own best, sweetest, dearest Ba—Do you think after such a letter as mine any amount of confidence in my own intentions, or of the reasonableness of being earnest on such a subject, can avail to save me from mortal misgivings? I should not have said those words, certainly I should not—but you forgive them and me, do you not? . . .

And we will 'decide' on nothing, being sure of the *one* decision—I mean, that if the summer *be* long, and likely to lead in as fine an Autumn, and if no new obstacles arise,—September shall go as it comes, and October too, if your convenience is attained thereby in the least degree,—afterward, you will be all my own, all your days and hours and minutes . . .

[Meeting 83: Saturday, 1 August 3.00–6.05 p.m. Elizabeth Barrett alludes in the following letter to a violent thunderstorm, the worst since 1809, which occurred in the afternoon. Mr Barrett, anxious about his daughter because of her fear of thunder (see p. 82), returned early from the City; he was, of course, unaware of the frequency and length of Browning's visits.]

EB, *Sunday, 2 August 1846*

Ever dearest, you were wet surely? The rain came before you reached the front door; & for a moment (before I heard it shut) I hoped you might return. Dearest, how I blame myself for letting you go—for not sending for a cab in despite of you! I was frightened out of all wisdom by the idea of who was down stairs & listening perhaps, & watching—as if the cab would have made you appear more emphatically *you!*— And then you said 'the rain was over'—and I believed you as usual. If this isn't a precedent of the evils of too much belief ....!!

Altogether, yesterday may pass among the 'unsatisfactory

days,' I think—for if I was not frightened of the storm, (&
indeed I was not, much!) of the state of affairs down in the
provinces, I was most sorely frightened—uneasy the whole
time. I seem to be with you, Robert, at this moment, more
than yesterday I was .. though if I look up now, I do not see
you sitting there!—But when you sate there yesterday, I was
looking at Papa's face as I saw it through the floor, & now I
see only yours——.

Dearest, he came into the room at about seven, before he
went to dinner. I was lying on the sofa & had on a white
dressing gown, to get rid of the strings .. so oppressive the air
was,—for all the purifications of lightning. He looked a little
as if the thunder had passed into him, & said, 'Has this been
your costume since the morning, pray?' 'Oh no'—I
answered—'only just now,. because of the heat.' 'Well,' he
resumed, with a still graver aspect .. (*so* displeased, he looked,
dearest!) 'it appears, Ba, that *that man* has spent the whole
day with you.' To which I replied as quietly as I could, that
you had several times meant to go away, but that the rain
would not let you,—& there, the colloquy ended. Brief
enough!—but it took my breath away .. or what was left, by
the previous fear. And think how it must have been a terrible
day, when the lightning of it, made the *least* terror ..

I was right too about the message. He took up the fancy
that I might be ill perhaps with fear .. '& only Mr. Browning
in the room'!!!—which was not to be permitted. He was
peremptory with Arabel, she told me.

Well—we need not talk any more of it—it has made one of
us uncomfortable long enough. Shall you dare come on
tuesday after all?—He will be out—If he is not .. if my aunt
should not be .. if a new obstacle should occur .. why you
shall hear on tuesday. At any rate I shall write, I think. He
did not see you go yesterday—he had himself preceded you
by an hour .. at five oclock .. which if it had been known,
would have relieved me infinitely. Yet it did not prevent.. you
see .. the appalling commentary at seven!—no.

. . .

RB, *Monday, 3 August 1846*

Oh, the comfort you are to me, Ba—the perpetual blessing and sustainment! And what a piece of you, how instinct with you, this letter is! I will not try to thank you, but my whole life shall.

See! *Now* talk of 'three or four months'! And is not the wonder, that this should wait for the eighty-second visit to happen? Or could anything be more fortunate, more *mitigating* than the circumstances under which it *did* happen at last? The rain & the thunder (see the accounts—nothing like it has been known, for years),—the *two* hours, at most, *proved* against us,—the ignorance of the visits last week—in spite of all which, see what comes and is likely to come!

Let me say at once that, at the worst, it *may* come! You have had time to know enough for me, my Ba,—and I, who from the first knew you, have taken one by one your promises from your lips,—I *believe* what you write here; I accept it as the foundation of all my future happiness—'you will never fail me'—I will never fail you, dearest dearest.

How you have mistaken my words, whatever they may have been, about the 'change' to be expected in my life! I have, most sincerely I tell you, no one habit nor manner to change or persevere in,—if you once accept the general constitution of me as accordant to yours in a sufficient degree,—my incompleteness with your completeness, dearest,—there is no further difficulty. I want to be a Poet—to read books which make wise in their various ways, to see just so much of nature and the ways of men as seems necessary—and having done this already in some degree, I can easily and cheerfully afford to go without any or all of it for the future, if called upon,—and so live on, and 'use up,' my past acquisitions such as they are. I will go to Pisa and learn,—or stay here and learn in another way—putting, as I always have down [sic], my whole pride, if that is the proper name, in the being able to work with the least possible materials. There is my scheme of life *without* you, *before* you existed for me; prosecuted hitherto with every sort of weakness, but always kept in view and believed in: now then, please to introduce Ba, and say what is the habit she changes? But do not try to say what divinest confirmation she brings to 'whatever is good and holy and true' in this scheme, because even She cannot say that!

. . . My presentiment is that suddenly you will be removed to Devonshire or Sussex or—In which case, our difficulties will multiply considerably—be prepared for such events! . . .

Do *re*consider, Ba,—had I better stay away to-morrow? You cannot misunderstand me,—I ONLY think of you—any man's anger to me is Flush's barking, without the respectability of motive,—but, once the door shut on me, if he took to biting *you!*—Think for us both! Is there any possibility of a suspicious sudden return *because* of the facilities of the day?— Or of the servant being desired to mention my visits—or to 'deny you,' as unwell &c? All my soul revolts at the notion of a scene in your presence—my own tied tongue, and a system of patience I can well *resolve* upon, but not be *sure* of, as experience makes sure.

EB, *Monday, 3 August 1846*

. . .

For the rest, dearest, do not exaggerate to yourself my report of what passed on saturday. It was an unpleasant impression, & that is all, .. & nothing, I believe, has been thought of it since. Once before, remember, your apparition made an unpleasant impression,° which was perfectly transitory then as now. Now as then, do not suffer such things to vex you beyond their due import. There will be no coming back, no directions to servants, nothing of the sort. Only it would not do to deepen saturday's impression with tomorrow's—we must be prudent a little.

And you see me, my prophet, sent to Sussex or Devonshire, in a flash of lightning? That is your presentiment, do you say? Well!—Sussex is possible, Kent is not impossible—This house, .. vox populi clamat [the popular voice cries out],— wants cleaning, painting, papering—the inhabitants thereof, too, cry aloud for fresh air. Nevertheless, summer after

summer, there have been the same reasons for going, &
nobody goes. We shall see—

. . .

[Meeting 84: Tuesday, 4 August 3.00–4.15 p.m.
Meeting 85. Saturday, 8 August 3.05–6.05 p.m.]

EB, *Monday, 10 August 1846*

. . .

Dearest, no, indeed!—there is nothing for your goodness to
do in that badness I told you of, & which you describe so
precisely in your word, 'drunkenness' of mind—It is precisely
that, & no more nor less—a throwing off of moral restraint ..
a miserable degradation.° One may get angry, frightened,
disgusted—but, after all, compassion comes in:—& who
would think of fighting a delirious man with a sword? It
would be a cruelty, like murder. There is a fine nature too,
under these ruins of the will; and a sensibility which strikes
inwards & outwards—(no one else should have any sensibility, within a thousand miles.) Think of a sort of dumb
Rousseau,—with the Confessions *in* him, pining evermore to
get out! . . . An old, old friend, too!—known as a friend these
twelve or thirteen years! And then,—men are nearly all the
same in the point of *wanting generosity to women*. It is a sin of
sex, be sure—& we have our counter-sins & should be
merciful. So I have been furiously angry, & then relented—
by turns; as I could. Oh yes—it was he who followed you up
stairs. There was an explosion that day among the many—
and I had to tell him as a consequence, that if he chose to
make himself the fable & jest of the whole house, he was the
master, but that I should insist upon his not involving my
name in the discussion of his violences. Wilson said he was
white with passion as he followed you, & that she in fear
trembled so she could scarcely open the door. He was a little
ashamed afterwards, & apologized in a manner for what
sufficiently required an apology—. Before a servant too!—
But that is long ago—& at that time, he knew nothing for a

certainty. Is it possible to be continuously angry with any one who proves himself so *much the weaker?* The slave of himself .. of his own passions .. is too unhappy for the rod of another— man or woman.

. . .

[Meeting 86: Tuesday, 11 August 3.00–6.00 p.m.]

EB, *Wednesday 12 August 1846 (2)*

. . .

Always I know, my beloved, that I am unworthy of your love in a hundred ways—yet I do hold fast my sense of advantage in one,—that, as far as I can see, I see after you .. understand you, divine you .. call you by your right name. Then it is something to be able to look at life itself as you look at it—(I quite *sigh* sometimes with satisfaction at that thought!—) there will be neither hope nor regret away from your footsteps. Dearest—I feel to myself sometimes. 'Do not move, do not speak—or the dream will vanish'! So fearfully like a dream it is! Like a reflection in the water, of an actual old, old dream of my own, too, .. touching which, .. now silent voices used to say 'That romantic child'!—

. . .

RB, *Thursday, 13 August 1846*

. . .

When I have chosen to consider the circumstances of the altered life I am about to lead with you (.. 'chosen,' because you have often suggested drawbacks, harms to my interest &c which I have really been forced to take up and try to think over seriously, lest I should be unawares found treating what had undoubtedly come from you, with disrespect),—I never, after all the considering in my power, was yet able to *fancy* even the possibility of their existence. I will not revert to them now—nor to the few *real* inconveniences which I *did* apprehend at the beginning, but which never occured to *you*: at present I take you, and with you as much happiness as I seem fit to bear in this world,—the one shadow being the fear of its continuance. Or if there is one thing I shall regret .. it is just that which I should as truly lose if I married any Miss Campbell° of them all—rather, *then* should *really* lose, what now is only modified,—transferred partly and the rest retainable. There was always a great delight to me in this prolonged relation of childhood almost .. nay altogether—with all here. My father and I have not one taste in common, one artistic taste .. in pictures, he goes, 'souls away,' to Brauwer, Ostade, Teniers° .. he would turn from the Sistine Altar piece° to these,—in music he desiderates a tune 'that has a story connected with it' . . . what I mean is, that the sympathy has not been an intellectual one—I hope if you want to please me especially, Ba, you will always remember I have been accustomed, by pure choice, to have another will lead mine in the little daily matters of life. If there are two walks to take (to put the thing at simplest) you must say, '*This* one' and not 'either' .. because though they were before indifferently to be chosen,—after *that* speech, one is altogether better than the other, to *me* if not to you. When you have a real preference which I can discern, you will be good enough to say nothing about it, my own Ba! Now, do you not see how, with this feeling, which God knows I profess to be mine without the least affectation,—how much my happiness would be disturbed by allying myself with a woman to whose intellect, as well as goodness, I could *not* look up?—in an obedience to whose desires, therefore, I should not be justified in indulging? It is pleasanter to lie back on the cushions inside the carriage and let another drive—but if you suspect he cannot drive?—

. . .

[Meeting 87: Friday, 14 August 3.00–6.00 p.m.]

EB, *Sunday, 16 August 1846*

. . . I have had a letter from that poor Chiappino,° to desire a 'last interview' .. which is promised to be 'pacific'. —— Oh—such stuff!! Am I to hold a handkerchief to my eyes & sob a little? . . . And I forgot to tell you that there were TWO things in which I had shown great want of feeling—one, the venturing to enclose your verses—the other .. (now listen!) the other .. the having said that 'I was sincerely sorry for all his real troubles'. Which I do remember having said once, when I was out of patience—as how can any one be patient continually?—& how was I especially to condole with him in lawn & weepers, on the dreadful fact of your existence in the world? Well—he has real troubles unfortunately, & he is going away to live in a village somewhere. Poor Chiappino! A little occupation would be the best thing that could happen for him: it would be better than prosperity without it. When a man spins evermore on his own axis, like a child's toy I saw the other day, .. what is the use of him but to make a noise? No greater tormentor is there, than selflove, .. even to self. And no greater instance of this, than *this!*
. . .

[Meeting 88: Thursday, 20 August 3.10–5.55 p.m.]

EB, *Friday, 21 August 1846*

. . .
Oh, to look back! It is so wonderful to me to look back on my life & my old philosophy of life, made of the necessities of sorrow & the resolution to attain to something better than a perpetual moaning & complaint,—to that state of neutralized emotion to which I did attain—that serenity which meant the failure of hope! *Can* I look back to such things, & not thank you next to God? For you, who had the *power*, to stoop to having the will,—is it not worthy of thanks? So I thank you & love you & shall always, however it may be hereafter. I

could not feel otherwise to you, I think, than by my feeling at this moment.

How Papa has startled me—He came in while I was writing .. (I shut the writing case as he walked over the floor—) & then, after the usual talk of the weather, & how the nights 'were growing cold,' ... he said suddenly .. looking to the table .. 'What a beautiful colour those little blue flowers have—' Calling them just *so*, .. 'little blue flowers'. I could scarcely answer I was so frightened—but he observed nothing & turned and left the room with his favorite enquiry 'pour rire' [for a laugh], as to whether he 'could do anything for me in the city'—

Do anything for *me* in the city!—Well—do you do something for me, by thinking of me & loving me, Robert. Dear you are, never to be tired of me, with so much reason for it as I know. May God bless you, very dear!—& ever dearest! I am your own too entirely to need

to say so.
Ba.

EB, *Sunday 23 August 1846*

. . .

While I write comes in Arabel with such a face!—My brothers had been talking, talking of me. Stormie suddenly touched her & said 'Is it true there is an engagement between Mr. Browning & Ba—'? she was taken unaware, but had just power to say 'You had better ask them, if you want to know—What nonsense, Storm.' 'Well!—' he resumed, 'I'll ask Ba when I go up stairs'. George was by, looking as grave as if antedating his judgeship—Think how frightened I was, Robert .. expecting them up stairs every minute—for all my brothers come here on sunday, all together. But they came, & not a single word was said—not on that subject .. & I talked on every other in a sort of hurried way—I was so frightened—

. . .

RB, *Monday 24 August 1846*

My own dearest, let me say the most urgent thing first. You hear these suspicions of your Brothers. Will you consider if, during this next month, we do not risk too much in seeing each other as usual? We risk everything .. and what do we gain, in the face of that? I can learn no more about you, be taught no new belief in your absolute peerlessness—I have taken my place at your feet for ever: all my use of the visits is, therefore, the perfect delight of them .. and to hazard a whole life of such delight for the want of self denial during a little month,—that would be horrible. I altogether sympathize with your brothers' impatience, or curiosity, or anxiety, or 'graveness'—and am prepared for their increasing and growing to heights difficult or impossible to be borne. But do you not think we may avoid compelling any premature crisis of this kind? I am guided by your feelings, as I seem to perceive them, in this matter; the harm to be apprehended is *through* the harm to *them*; to your brothers. If they determine on avowedly *knowing* what we intend, I do not see which to fear most,—the tacit acquiescence in our scheme which may draw down a vengeance on them without doing us the least good,— or the open opposition which would bring just so much additional misfortune. I *know*, now, your perfect adequacy to any pain and danger you will incur for our love's sake—I believe in you as you would have me believe: but give yourself to me, dearest dearest Ba, the entire creature you are, and not a lacerated thing only reaching my arms to sink there. Perhaps this is all a sudden fancy, not justified by circumstances, arising from my ignorance of the characters of those I talk about; that is for you to decide,—your least word reassures me, as always.

. . .

EB, *Monday 24 August 1846*

. . . I agree with you that for this interval it will be wise for us to set the visits, .. 'our days' .. far apart, .. nearly a week apart, perhaps, so as to escape the dismal evils we apprehend. I agree in all you say—in all. At the same time, the cloud has passed for the present—nothing has been said more, & not a word to me,—& nobody appears out of humour with me. They will be displeased of course, in the first movement .. we must expect *that* .. they will be vexed at the occasion given to conversation & so on. But it will be a passing feeling, & their hearts & their knowledge of circumstances may be trusted to justify me thoroughly. I do not fear offending them—there is no room for fear. At this point of the business too, you place the alternative rightly—their approbation or their disapprobation is equally to be escaped from. Also, we may be certain that they would press the applying for permission—& I might perhaps, in the storm excited, among so many opinions & feelings, fail to myself & you, through weakness of the body. Not of the will!—And for my affections & my conscience, they turn to you—& untremblingly turn.

. . .

RB, *Wednesday 26 August 1846*

. . .

And now, dearest, I will revert, in as few words as I can, to the account you gave me, a short time since, of your income.° At the beginning, if there had been the necessity I supposed, I should have proposed to myself the attainment of something like such an amount, by my utmost efforts, before we could marry. We could not under the circumstances begin with less—so as to be free from horrible contingencies,—not the least of which would be the application for assistance afterward .. after we marry, nobody must hear of us. In spite of a few misgivings at first I am not proud, or rather, am proud in the right place. I am utterly, exclusively proud of you: and though I should have gloried in working myself to death to prove it, and shall be as ready to do so at any time a necessity shall exist, yet at present I shall best serve you, I think, by the life by your side, which we contemplate. I hope and believe, that by your side I shall accomplish something to justify God's goodness and yours: and, looking at the matter in a worldly light, I see not a few reasons for thinking that— unproductive as the kind of literature may be, which I should aim at producing, yet, by judicious management, and profiting by certain favorable circumstances,—I shall be able to realize an annual sum quite sufficient for every purpose .. at least in Italy.

As I never calculated on such a change in my life, I had the less repugnance to my father's generosity, that I knew that an effort at some time or other might furnish me with a few hundred pounds which would soon cover my very simple expenses. If we are poor, it is to my father's infinite glory, who, as my mother told me last night, as we sate alone, 'conceived such a hatred to the slave-system in the West Indies,' (where his mother was born, who died in his infancy,) that he relinquished every prospect,—supported himself, while there, in some other capacity, and came back, while yet a boy, to his father's profound astonishment and rage—one proof of which was, that when he heard that his son was a suitor to *her*, my mother—he benevolently waited on her Uncle to assure him that his niece 'would be thrown away on a man so evidently born to be hanged'!—those were his very words. My father on his return, had the intention of devoting himself to art, for which he had many qualifications and abundant love—but the quarrel with his father,—who married again and continued to hate him till a few years before his death,—induced him to go at once and consume his life after a fashion he always detested. You may fancy, I am not ashamed of him.

I told my mother, who told *him*. They have never been used to interfere with, or act for me—and they trust me. If you care for any love, *purely* love,—you will have theirs—they give it you, whether you take it or no. You will understand, therefore, that I would not *accept* even the £100 we shall want: I said 'you shall lend it me—I will pay it back out of my first literary earnings: I take it, because I do not want to sell my copyrights, or engage myself to write a play, or any other nuisance'—Surely I can get fifty pounds next year, and the other fifty in due course!

. . .

EB, *Wednesday, 26 August 1846*

. . .

For the rest of what you tell me, it is all the purest kindness—and you were perfectly, perfectly right in taking so, & as a loan, what we ought, I think, to return when our hands are free, without waiting for the completion of other projects. By living quietly & simply, we shall surely have enough—& more than enough. Then among other resources, is Blackwood. I calculated once that without unpleasant labour, with scarcely an effort, I could make a hundred a year by magazine-contributions,—& this, without dishonor either. It does 'fugitive poems', observe, no harm whatever, to let them fly through a periodical before they alight on their tree to sing. Then *you* will send perhaps the sweepings of your desk to Blackwood, to alternate with my sendings!—Shall we do *that*, when we sit together on the ragged edge of earthquake chasms, in the midst of the 'sulphurous vapour.'° *I* afraid? No indeed. I think I should never be afraid if you were near enough. Only that you never must go away *in boats*°—But there is time enough for such compacts.

. . . if I am to think & decide, I have decided .. let us go through France. And let us go quick, quick, & not stop anywhere within hearing of England .. not stop at Havre, nor at Rouen, nor at Paris—*that* is how *I* decide. May God help us, & smooth the way before & behind. May your father indeed be able to love me a little, for *my* father will never love me again.

. . .

RB, *Thursday 27 August 1846*

. . .

I used those words you object to—(in your true way,) because you shall love nothing connected with me, for conventional reasons: and if I under-stated the amount of kind feeling which you might be led to return for theirs, be assured that I also expressed in the simplest and coldest terms possible my father & mother's affection for you. I told you, they *believe* me .. therefore, know in some measure what you are to me. They are both entirely affectionate and generous. My father is tender-hearted to a fault. I have never known much more of those circumstances in his youth than I told you, in consequence of his invincible repugnance to allude to the matter—and I have a fancy, to account for some peculiarities in him, which connects them with some abominable early experience. Thus,—if you question him about it, he shuts his eyes involuntarily and shows exactly the same marks of loathing that may be noticed if a piece of cruelty is mentioned .. and the *word* 'blood,' even, makes him change colour. To all women and children *he* is 'chivalrous' .. as you called his unworthy son! There is no service which the ugliest, oldest, crossest woman in the world might not exact of him. But I must leave off—tomorrow I do really see you at last, dearest!

. . .

EB, *Thursday, 27 August 1846 (2)*

Thurs night.

Here is the bad news going to you as fast as bad news *will* go! for you 'do really (NOT) see me tomorrow,' Robert,—there is no chance of it for such 'too, two' wise people as we are!—In the first place, Mr. Kenyon never paid his visit today & will do it tomorrow instead:—and secondly, & while I was gloomily musing over this 'great fact,' arrives the tiding of my uncle & aunt Hedley's being at Fenton's Hotel for two days from this evening .. so that not only friday perishes, but even saturday, unless there should be a change in their plans. We shall have them here continually,—& there would neither be safety nor peace if we attempted a meeting. So let us take patience, dearest beloved, & let me feel you loving me through the distance. . . .

Your father is worthy to be your father, let you call yourself his 'unworthy son' ever so. The noblest inheritance of sons, is to have such thoughts of their fathers, as you have of yours—the privilege of such thoughts, the faith in such virtues & the gratitude for such affection. You have better than the silver or the gold, & you can afford to leave those to less happy sons. And your mother:—Scarcely I was woman when I lost *my* mother .. dearest as she was, & very tender, .. (as yours even could be,—) but of a nature harrowed up into some furrows by the pressure of circumstances: for we lost more in Her than She lost in life, my dear dearest mother. A sweet, gentle nature, which the thunder a little turned from its sweetness—as when it turns milk—One of those women who never can resist,—but, in submitting & bowing on themselves, make a mark, a plait, within, .. a sign of suffering. Too womanly she was—it was her only fault—Good, good, & dear—& refined too! She would have admired & loved you,—but I can only tell you so, for she is gone past us all into the place of the purer spirits. God had to take her, before He could bless her enough.

. . .

RB, *Friday 28 August 1846*

I was beginning to dress, hours before the proper time, thro' the confidence of seeing you *now*,—after the letter which came early in the morning, when this new letter changes everything. It just strikes me, what a comfort it is that whenever such a disappointment is inevitable, *your* hand or voice announces it, and not anothers—no second person bids me stay away for good reasons I must take in trust, leaving me to deal with the innumerable fancies that arise: on the contrary, you contrive that with the one misfortune, twenty

...ndnesses shall reach me: can I be very sorry *now*, for instance, that you tell me *why* it is, and how it affects you, and how it will affect me in the end? Dear Ba, if you will not believe in the immortality of love, do think the poor thought that when love shall end, gratitude will begin!

I altogether agree with you .. it is best to keep away: we cannot be too cautious now at the 'end of things'—I am prepared for difficulties enough, without needing to cause them by any rashness or wilfulness of my own. I really expect, for example, that out of the various plans of these sympathizing friends and relations some one will mature itself sufficiently to be directly proposed to you, for your acceptance or refusal, contingent on your father's approbation; the shortness of the remaining travelling season serving to compel a speedy development. Or what if your father, who was the first to propose, or at least talk about, a voyage to Malta or elsewhere, when you took no interest in the matter comparatively,—and who perhaps chiefly found fault with last year's scheme for its not originating with himself .. what if he should again determine on some such voyage now that you are apparently as obedient to his wishes as can be desired? Would it be strange, not to say improbable, if he tells you some fine morning that your passage is taken to Madeira, or Palermo? Because, all the attempts in the world cannot hide the truth from the mind, any more than all five fingers before the eyes keep out the sun at noonday: you see a *red* thro' them all—and your father *must* see your improved health and strength, and divine the opinions of everybody round him as to the simple, proper course for the complete restoration of them. Therefore be prepared, my own Ba!

. . . I rejoice in your desire (by the way) of going rapidly on, stopping nowhere, till we reach our appointed place—because that spirit *helps* the body wonderfully—and, in this case, exactly corresponds with mine. Above all, I should hate to be seen at Paris by anybody a few days only after our adventure—

. . .

EB, *Friday 28 August 1846*

. . .

Dearest, I have had all your thoughts by turns, or most of them .. & each one has withered away without coming to bear fruit. Papa seems to have no more idea of my living beyond these four walls, than of a journey to Lapland. I confess that I thought it possible he might propose the country for the summer, or even Italy for the winter—in a 'late remorse'—but no, 'nothing' & there is not a probability of either now as I see things. My brothers 'wish that something could be arranged'—a wish which I put away quietly as often as they bring it to me. And for my uncle & aunt, they have been talking to me today—& she with her usual acuteness in such matters, observing my evasion, said, 'Ah Ba, you have arranged your plans more than you would have us believe. But you are right not to tell us—Indeed I would rather not hear. Only *dont be rash—that* is my only advice to you.'

I thought she had touched the truth, & wondered—but since then, from another of her words, I came to conclude that she imagined me about to accept the convoy of Henrietta & Captain Cook!—. . .

While we were talking, Papa came into the room. My aunt said, 'How well she is looking'—'Do you think so?' he said. 'Why, .. do not *you* think so? Do you pretend to say that you see no surprising difference in her?'—'Oh, I dont know,' he went on to say .. 'She is mumpish, I think.' Mumpish!

'She doesn't talk,' resumed he—

'Perhaps she is nervous' .. my aunt apologized—I said not one word .. When birds have their eyes out, they are apt to be mumpish.

Mumpish!—The expression proved a displeasure—Yet I am sure that I have shown as little sullenness as was possible—To be very talkative & vivacious under such circumstances as these of mine, would argue insensibility, & was certainly beyond my power.

I told her gently afterwards that she had been wrong in speaking of me at all—a wrong with a right intention,—as all her wrongings must be. She was very sorry to have done it, she said, & looked sorry.

Poor Papa!—Presently I shall be worse to him than 'mumpish' even. But *then*, I hope, he will try to forgive me, as I have forgiven HIM, long ago. . . .

Our adventure, indeed!—But it is *you* who are adventurous in the matter,—& as any Red Cross Knight of them all, whom you exceed in their chivalry proper.

Chiappino little knew how right he was, when he used to taunt me with my 'New Cross Knight.' He did—Ah! Even if he had talked of 'Rosie Cross,'° he would not have been so far wide—the magic 'saute aux yeux' [leaps to the eye].

. . .

[Meeting 89: Saturday 29 August 3.05–5.00 p.m.]

EB, *Sunday 30 August 1846*

. . .

Think of our waiting day after day to fall into the net so, yesterday! How I was provoked & vexed—but more for you, dearest dearest, than for me—much more for you. As for me I *saw you*, which was joy enough, let the hours be ever so clipped of their natural proportions—& then, you know, you were obliged to go soon, whether Mr. Kenyon had come or not come. After you were gone, nothing was said, & nothing asked—and it is delightful to have heard of those intended absences one upon another till far into October, which will secure us from future embarrassments. See if he means to put us to the question!—not such a thing is in this thoughts.

And I said what you 'would not have believed of me'—! Have you forgiven me, beloved—for saying what you would not have believed of me,—understanding that I did not mean it very seriously, though I proved to be capable of saying it? Seriously, I dont want to make unnecessary delays—It is a horrible position, however I may cover it with your roses & the thoughts of you—& far worse to myself than to you, inasmuch that what is painful to you once a week, is to me so continually—To hear the voice of my father & meet his eye, makes me shrink back—to talk to my brothers, leaves my nerves all trembling .. & even to receive the sympathy of my sisters turns into sorrow & fear, lest they should suffer through their affection for me. How I can look & sleep as well as I do, is a miracle exactly like the rest—or would be, if the love were not the deepest & strongest thing of all, & did not hold & possess me overcomingly.

. . .

RB, *Sunday 30 August 1846*

I wonder what I shall write to you, Ba—I could suppress my feelings here, as I do on other points, and say nothing of the hatefulness of this state of things which is prolonged so uselessly. There is the point—show me one good reason, or show of reason, why we gain anything by deferring our departure till next week instead of to-morrow, and I will bear to perform yesterday's part for the amusement of Mr Kenyon a dozen times over without complaint. But if the cold plunge *must* be taken, all this shivering delay on the bank is hurtful as well as fruitless. I *do* understand your anxieties, dearest— I take your fears and make them mine, while I put my own natural feeling of quite another kind away from us both .. succeeding in *that* beyond all expectation. There is no amount of patience or suffering I would not undergo to relieve you from these apprehensions. But if, on the whole, you really determine to act as we propose in spite of them,—why, a new leaf is turned over in our journal, an old part of our adventure done with, and a new one entered upon, altogether distinct from the other: having once decided to go to Italy with me, the next thing to decide is on the best means of going: or rather, there is just this connection between the two measures, that by the success or failure of the last, the first will have to be justified or condemned. You tell you have decided to go— then, dearest, you will be prepared to go earlier than you promised yesterday—by the end of September at very latest. In proportion to the too probable excitement and painful circumstances of the departure, the greater amount of advantages should be secured for the departure itself. How can I take you away in even the beginning of October? We shall be a fortnight on the journey—with the year, as everybody sees and says, a full month in advance .. cold mornings and dark evenings already. Everybody would cry on such folly when it was found that we let the favourable weather escape, in full assurance that the autumn would come to us unattended by any one beneficial circumstance.

My own dearest, I am wholly your own, for ever, and under every determination of yours. If you find yourself unable, or unwilling to make this effort, tell me so and plainly and at once—I will not offer a word in objection: I will continue our present life, if you please, so far as may be desirable, and wait till next autumn, and the next and the next, till providence end our waiting. It is clearly not for me to pretend to instruct you in your duties to God & yourself .. enough, that I have long ago chosen to accept your decision. If, on the other hand, you make your mind to leave England now, you will be prepared by the end of September.

I should think myself the most unworthy of human beings if I could employ any arguments with the remotest show of a tendency to *frighten* you into a compliance with any scheme of mine. Those methods are for people in another relation to you. But you love me, and, at lowest, shall I say, wish me well—and the fact is too obvious for me to commit any indelicacy in reminding you, that in any dreadful event to our journey, of which I could accuse myself as the cause,—as of this undertaking to travel with you in the worst time of year when I could have taken the best,—in the case of your health being irretrievably shaken, for instance .. the happiest fate I should pray for would be to live and die in some corner where I might never hear a word of the English language, much less a comment in it on my own wretched imbecility .. to disappear and be forgotten.

So that must not be, for all our sakes. My family will give me to you that we may be both of us happy .. but for such an end—no! . . .

My friend Pritchard tells me that Brighton is not to be thought of under ordinary circumstances as a point of departure for Havre. Its one packet a week, from Shoreham, cannot get in if the wind & tide are unfavorable. There is the greatest uncertainty in consequence .. as I have heard before: while, of course, from Southampton, the departures are calculated punctually. He considers that the least troublesome plan, and the cheapest, is to go from London to Havre .. the voyage being so arranged that the river passage takes up the day and the sea-crossing the night—you reach Havre early in the morning and get to Paris by four oclock, perhaps, in the afternoon .. in time, to leave for Orleans and spend the night there, I suppose.

Do I make myself particularly remarkable for silliness when confronted by our friend as yesterday?—And the shortened visit,—and comments of everybody. Oh, Mr Hunter, methinks you should be of some use to me with those amiable peculiarities of yours if you would just dye your hair black, take a stick in your hand, sink the clerical character you do such credit to, and have the goodness just to deliver yourself of one such epithet as *that* pleasant one, the next time you find me on the steps of No. 50, with Mr Kenyon somewhere higher up in the building! It is delectable work this having to do with relatives and 'freemen who have a right to beat their own negroes,' and father Zeus with his paternal epistles, and peggings to the rock, and immense indignation at 'this marriage you talk of' which is to release his victim . . .°

EB, *Monday 31 August 1846*

. . . That you should endure painfully & impatiently a position unworthy of you, is the natural consequence of the unworthiness—& I do hold that you would be justified at this moment, on the barest motive of selfrespect, in abandoning the whole ground & leaving me to Mr. Kenyon & others. What I might complain of, is another thing—what I might complain of is, that I have not given you reason to *doubt me* or my inclination to accede to any serious wish of yours relating to the step before us. One the contrary I told you in so many words in July, that, if you really wished to go in August rather

than in September, I would make no difficulty—to which you
answered, remember, that *october or november would do as well*.
Now is it fair, ever dearest, that you should turn round on
me so quickly, & call in question my willingness to keep my
engagement for years, if ever? Can I help it, if the circumstances around us are painful to both of us?—Did I not keep
repeating, from the beginning, that they *must* be painful? . . .
As to a light word ... why now, dear, judge me in justice! If I
had written it, there might have been more wrong in it—But
I spoke it lightly to show it was light, & in the next breath I
told you that it was a jest. Will you not forgive me a word so
spoken, Robert? will you rather set it against me as if
habitually I threw to you levities in change for earnest
devotion?—you imply *that* of me. Or you *seem* to imply it—
you did not mean, you could not, a thought approaching to
unkindness,—but it looks like *that* in the letter, or *did*, this
morning. And all the time, you pretended not to know very
well, .. (dearest! ..) that what you made up your mind to wish
& ask of me, I had not in my power to say 'no' to—Ah, you
knew that you had only to make up your mind—, & to see
that the thing was possible. So if September shall be possible,
let it be September. I do not object nor hold back. To sail
from the Thames has not the feasibility—& listen why! All
the sailing or rather steaming from London, begins *early*,—&
I told you how out of the question it was, for me to leave this
house early. I could not, without involving my sisters. Arabel
sleeps in my room, on the sofa, & is seldom out of the room
before nine in the morning—& for me to draw her into a
ruinous confidence, or to escape without a confidence at that
hour, would be equally impossible. Now see if it is my fancy,
my whim! . . . You are not angry with me, dearest, dearest? I
did not mean any harm.

May God bless you always—*I* am not angry either, understand, though I did think this morning that you were a little
hard on me, just when I felt myself ready to give up the whole
world for you at the holding up of a finger. And now say
nothing of this. I kiss the end of the dear finger; & when *it* is
ready, *I* am ready; I will not be reproached again.

. . .

RB, *Tuesday, 1 September 1846*

Tuesday—3 p.m.

Dearest, when your letter kept away, all this morning, I never once fancied you might be angry .. I knew you must feel the love which produced the fear. And I will lay to my heart the little, gentlest blame that there is, in the spirit which dictated it,—I know, my own Ba, your words have given me the right to doubt nothing from your generosity—but it is not the mere bidding .. no, at the thousandth repetition, .. which can make me help myself to all that treasure which you please to call mine: I shall perhaps get used to the generosity and readier to profit by it.

I have not time to write much: all is divinely kind of you, and I love you for forgiving me.

. . .

EB, *Tuesday, 1 September 1846*

Here is a distress for me, dearest! I have lost my poor Flush—*lost* him!—You were a prophet when you said 'Take care'.

This morning Arabel & I, & he with us, went in a cab to Vere Street where we had a little business, & he followed us as usual into a shop & out of it again, & was at my heels when I stepped up into the carriage. Having turned, I said 'Flush', & Arabel looked round for Flush—there was no Flush!—He had been caught up in that moment, from *under* the wheels, do you understand? & the thief must have run with him & thrown him into a bag perhaps—It was such a shock to me—think of it!—losing him in a moment, *so!* No wonder if I looked white, as Arabel said! So she began to comfort me by showing how certain it was that I should recover him for ten pounds at most, & we came home ever so drearily—. Because *Flush* doesn't know that we can recover him, & he is in the extremest despair all this while, poor darling Flush, with his fretful fears, & pretty whims, & his

fancy of being near me. All this night he will howl & lament,
I know perfectly,—for I fear we shall not ransom him tonight.
Henry went down for me directly to the Captain of the
banditti, who evidently knew all about it, said Henry,—&
after a little form of consideration & enquiry, promised to let
us hear something this evening, but has not come yet. In the
morning perhaps he will come. Henry told him that I was
resolved not to give much—but of course they will make me
give what they choose—I am not going to leave Flush at their
mercy, & they know that as well as I do. My poor
Flush!—— ...

If we go to Southampton, we go straight from the railroad
to the packet, without entering any hotel—and if we do *so, no*
greater expense is incurred than by the long water-passage
from London. Also, we reach Havre alike in the morning, &
have the day before us for Rouen, Paris, & Orleans. Therefore
nothing is lost by losing the early hour for the departure—
Then, if I accede to your 'idée fixe' about the marriage!—
Only do not let us put a long time between that & the setting
out, & do not you come here afterwards—let us go away as
soon as possible afterwards, at least. You are afraid for me of
my suffering from the autumnal cold when it is yet far off—
while *I* (observe this!) while *I* am afraid for myself, of breaking
down under quite a different set of causes, in nervous excitement & exhaustion. I belong to that pitiful order of weak
women who cannot command their bodies with their souls at
every moment, & who sink down in hysterical disorder when
they ought to act & resist. Now I think & believe that I shall
take strength from my attachment to you, & so go through to
the end what is before us,—but at the same time, knowing
myself & fearing myself, I do desire to provoke the 'demon'
as little as possible, & to be as quiet as the situation will
permit.

. . .

RB, *Wednesday, 2 September 1846*

Poor Flush—how sorry I am for you, my Ba! But you will
recover him, I dare say .. not, perhaps directly,—the delay
seems to justify their charge at the end: poor fellow—was he

no better than the rest of us, and did all that barking and fanciful valour spend itself on such enemies as Mr Kenyon and myself, leaving only blandness and waggings of the tail for the man with the bag? I am sure you are grieved and frightened for our friend and follower, that was to be, at Pisa—will you not write a special note to tell me when you get him again?

For the rest—I will urge you no more by a single word— you shall arrange everything henceforward without a desire on my part,—an expressed one at least. Do not let our happiness be caught up from us, after poor Flush's fashion— there may be no redemption from *that* peril.

There can hardly be another way of carrying our purpose into effect than by that arrangement you consent to—except you choose to sacrifice a day and incur all sorts of risk. Of course, the whole in the way and with the conditions that you shall determine.

. . .

EB, *Wednesday, 2 September 1846*

'Our friend & follower, that *was* to be'—is *that*, then, your opinion of my poor darling Flush's destiny—? Ah—I should not have been so quiet if I had not known differently & better—. I 'shall not recover him directly,' you think!—But, dearest, I am *sure* that I *shall*. I am learned in the ways of the Philistines—I knew from the beginning where to apply & how to persuade. The worst is poor Flush's fright & suffer- ing—And then, it is inconvenient just now to pay the ransom for him—But we shall have time tomorrow if not tonight. Two hours ago the chief of the Confederacy came to call on Henry & to tell him that the 'society had the dog,' having done us the honour of tracking us into Bond Street & out of Bond Street into Vere Street where he was kidnapped—Now he is in Whitechapel (poor Flush,)—And the great man was going down there at half past seven to meet other great men in council & hear the decision as to the ransom exacted, & would return with their *ultimatum*. Oh, the villainy of it, is excellent, & then the humiliation of having to pay for your own vexations & anxieties!—*Will* they have the insolence, now, to make my pay ten pounds, as they said they would? But I must have Flush, you know—I cant run any risk, & bargain & haggle—There is a dreadful tradition in this neighbourhood, of a lady who did so, having her dog's head sent to her in a parcel. So I say to Henry—'Get Flush back, whatever you do'—for Henry is angry as he may well be, & as *I* should be if I were not too afraid .. & talks police-officers against the thieves, & finds it very hard to attend to my instructions & be civil & respectful to their Captain. There, he found him, smoking a cigar in a room with pictures!— They make some three or four thousand a year by their honorable employment. As to Flush's following anyone 'blandly,' never think it!—He was caught up & gagged .. depend upon *that*. If he could have bitten, he would have bitten—if he could have yelled, he would have yelled. Indeed on a former occasion the ingenuous thief observed, that he 'was a difficult dog to get, he was so distrustful'. They had to drag him with a string & put him into a cab, they said, before. Poor Flush!——

. . .

RB, *Thursday, 3 September 1846 (1)*

I am rejoiced that poor Flush is found again, dearest— altogether rejoiced.

And now that you probably have him by your side, I will tell you what I should have done in such a case, because it explains our two ways of seeing & meeting oppression lesser or greater. I would not have given five shillings on that fellow's application. I would have said,—and in entire earnestness,—'*You* are responsible for the proceedings of your gang, and *you* I mark—don't talk nonsense to me about cutting off heads or paws—be as sure as that I stand here and tell you, I will spend my whole life in putting you down, the nuisance you declare yourself—and by every imaginable means I will be the death of you and as many of your

accomplices as I can discover—but *you* I *have* discovered and
will never lose sight of—now try my sincerity, by delaying to
produce the dog tomorrow. And for the ten pounds—see!'
Whereupon, I would give them to the first beggar in the
street. You think I should receive Flush's head? perhaps .. *so*
God allows matters to happen!—on purpose, it may be, that
I should vindicate him by the punishment I would exact.

Observe, Ba, this course ought not to be yours, because it
could not be .. it would not suit your other qualities. But all
religion, right and justice, with me, seem implied in such a
resistance to wickedness, and refusal to multiply it a hundredfold—for from this prompt payment of ten pounds for a few
minutes act of the easiest villainy, there will be encouragement to .. how many similar acts in the course of next month?
And how will the poor owners fare who have not money
enough for their dogs' redemption? I suppose, the gentleman,
properly disgusted with such obstinancy, will threaten roast-
ing at a slow fire to test the sincerity of attachment! No—the
world would grow too detestable a den of thieves & oppressors
that way!

And this is too great a piece of indignation to be expressed
when one has the sick vile headache that oppresses me this
morning, dearest—I am not inclined to be even as tolerant as
usual. Will *you* be tolerant, my Ba, and forgive me—till
tomorrow at least—when, what with physic, what with
impatience, I shall be better one way or another?

Ever your own
R

EB, *Thursday, 3 September 1846*

Ever dearest, you are not well—that is the first thing!—
And that is the thing I saw first, when, opening your letter,
my eyes fell on the ending sentence of it,—which disen-
chanted me in a moment from the hope of the day. Dearest—
you have not been well for two or three days, it is plain,—&
now you are very, very unwell—tell me if it is not so? I

beseech you to let me hear the exact truth about you, for I am very uneasy, & it is dreadful to doubt about knowing the exact truth in all such cases. How everything goes against me this week! I cannot see you—I cannot comfort myself by knowing that you are well. And then poor Flush!—You must let him pass as one of the evils, & you *will*, I know,—for I have not got him back yet—no, indeed—

I should have done it. The archfiend, Taylor, the man whom you are going to spend your life in persecuting, (the life that belongs to me, too!) came last night to say that they would accept six pounds, six guineas, with half a guinea for himself, considering the trouble of the mediation,—& Papa desired Henry to refuse to pay, & not to tell me a word about it——all which I did not find out till this morning. Now it is less, as the money goes, than I had expected, and I was very vexed & angry, & wanted Henry to go at once & conclude the business—only he wouldn't, talked of Papa, & persuaded me that Taylor would come today with a lower charge—He has not come—I knew he would not come,—& if people wont do as I choose, I shall go down tomorrow myself & bring Flush back with me—All this time he is suffering & I am suffering. It may be very foolish—I do not say it is not—or it may even be 'awful sin,' as Mr. Boyd sends to assure me— but I cannot endure to run cruel hazards about my poor Flush for the sake of a few guineas, or even for the sake of abstract principles of justice—I cannot—*You* say that *I* cannot, .. but that *you would*. You would!—Ah dearest—most pattern of citizens, but you WOULD *not*—I know you better. Your theory is far too good not to fall to pieces in practice— A man may love justice intensely; but the love of an abstract principle is not the strongest love—now is it? Let us consider a little, putting poor Flush out of the question. (You would bear, you say, to receive his head in a parcel—it would satisfy you to cut off Taylor's in return)—Do you mean to say that if the banditti came down on us in Italy & carried me off to the mountains, & sending to you one of my ears, to show you my probable fate if you did not let them have ... how much may I venture to say I am worth? .. five or six scudi,—(is THAT reasonable at all?) .. would your answer be 'Not so many crazie,—'° & would you wait, poised upon abstract

principles, for the other ear, & the catastrophe, as was done
in Spain not long ago? Would you, dearest? Because it is as
well to know beforehand, perhaps——

. . .

RB, *Friday, 4 September 1846*

. . .

Dear Ba, I wrote under the notion (as I said) that poor
Flush was safe by your side; and only took that occasion to
point at what I must still consider the wrongness of the whole
system of giving way to, instead of opposing, such proceedings. I think it lamentable weakness .. though I can quite
understand and allow for it in you—, but weakness it
essentially *is, as you* know perfectly. For see, you first put the
matter in the gentlest possible light .. 'who would give much
time and trouble to the castigation of such a fellow as *that!*'
you ask: and immediately after, for another purpose, you very
rightly rank this crime with that other enormous one, of the
Spanish Banditti—nay, you confess that, in this very case,
any such injury to Flush as you dread, would give you
inexpressible grief—is the threatening this outrage then so
little a matter? Am I to think it a *less* matter if the same
miscreant should *strike* you in the street, because you would
probably suffer less than by this that he *has* done? There is
the inevitable inconsistency of wrong reasoning in all this—
say, as I told you on another subject,—'I determine to resist
no injury whatever, to be at the disposal of any villain in the
world, trusting to God for protection here or recompense
hereafter'—or take my course; *which* is the easier,—and in
the long run, however strangely it may seem, the more
profitable, no one can doubt—but I take the harder—in all
but the responsibility—which, without any cant, would be
intolerable to me. Look at this 'society' with its 'four thousand
a year'—which unless its members are perfect fools they will
go on to double & treble: would this have existed if a proper
stand had been made at the beginning? The first silly man,
woman or child who consented to pay five shillings, beyond

the mere expense of keeping the dog, (on the supposition of its having been found, *not* stolen,) is responsible for all the harm: what could the thief do but go and steal another, and ask double for its ransom? . . .

To all of which you have a great answer—'what should I do if *you* were to be the victim?'—That my note yesterday, the second one, told you. I sacrifice *myself* .. all that belongs *to me*—but there are some interests which *I* belong to—I have no right, no more than inclination, in such a case, to think of myself if your safety is concerned: and as I could cut off a limb to save my head, so my head should fall most willingly to redeem yours—I would pay every farthing I had in the world, and shoot with my own hand the receiver of it after a chase of fifty years—esteeming *that* to be a very worthy recompense for the trouble . . .

Ah, but here all the fuss is just about stealing a dog—two or three words, and the matter becomes simply ludicrous—very easily got rid of! One cannot take vengeance on the 'great man' with his cigar & room of pictures, and burlesque dignities of mediation! . . . Well, enough of sermonizing for the present: it is impossible for me to differ with you and treat *that* as a light matter—or, what on earth would have been so little to wonder at, as that, loving Flush, you should determine to save him at any price? If 'Chiappino' were to assure you, in terms that you could not disbelieve, that in the event of your marrying me he would destroy himself,—would you answer, as I should, 'Do so, and take the consequences,'—and think no more about the matter? I should absolutely leave it, as not my concern but God's—nor should blame myself any more than if the poor man, being uncertain what to do, had said 'if a man first passes the window—yes—if a woman—no'—and I, a total stranger, had passed.

One word more—in all this, I labour against the execrable policy of the world's husbands, fathers, brothers, and domineerers in general: I am about to marry you .. 'how wise, then, to encourage such a temper in you! such was that divine Griselda's—a word rules the gentle nature—"Do this, or" ... '

My own Ba, if I thought you could *fear* me, I think *I* should have the courage to give you up to-morrow!

. . .

EB, *Friday, 4 September 1846*

. . .

I have not Flush yet. I am to have him tomorrow morning—

And for the Flush-argument, dear dearest, I hold that your theory is entirely good & undeniable. . . .

But Flush, poor Flush, Flush who has loved me so faithfully,—have I a right to sacrifice *him* in his innocence, for the sake of any Mr. Taylor's guilt in the world? Does not Flush's condition assimilate to my own among the banditti?—for you agree that you would not, after all, leave me to the banditti—and I, *exactly on the same ground*, will not leave Flush. It seems to me that you and I are *at one* upon the whole question,—only that *I* am *your* Flush, & *he* is mine. You, if you were 'consistent' .. dearest! .. would not redeem me on any account—You do ever so much harm by it, observe—you produce catastrophe on catastrophe, just for the sake of my two ears without earrings!—Oh, I entirely agree with your principle—Evil should be resisted that it may fly from you.

But Flush is not to be sacrificed—nor even is Ba, it appears. So our two weaknesses may pardon one another—yours & mine!

. . .

EB, *Saturday, 5 September 1846*

Dearest, I write just a few lines that you may know me for thinking of you tomorrow. Flush has not come & I am going on a voyage of discovery myself,—Henry being far too lukewarm. He says I may be robbed & murdered before the time for coming back, in which case remember that it is not my fault that I do not go with you to Pisa. . . .

And if I shall not be slain by the 'society', you shall be written to again tonight. Ah—say in the letter *I* am to have,

that you are better!—And you are to come on monday—
dear, dearest! mind *that!*

                                        Your Ba—

Come back safe, but without Flush——I am to have him
tonight though.

EB, *Sunday, 6 September 1846*

Not well—not well!—But I shall see you with my own eyes
soon after you read what I write today,—so I shall not write
much—. Only a few words to tell you that Flush is found, &
lying on the sofa, with one paw & both ears hanging over the
edge of it. Still my visit to Taylor was not the successful one.
My hero was not at home—

I went, you know, .. did I tell you? .. with Wilson in the
cab. We got into obscure streets,—& our cabman stopped at
a public house to ask his way. Out came two or three men, ..
'Oh, you want to find Mr. Taylor, I dare say'! (mark that no
name had been mentioned!) & instantly an unsolicited philanthropist ran before us to the house, & out again to tell me
that the great man 'wasn't at home!—but wouldn't I get out?'
Wilson, in an aside of terror, entreated me not to think of
such a thing—she believed devoutly in the robbing & mur-
dering, & was not reassured by the gang of benevolent men
& boys who 'lived but to oblige us' all round the cab. 'Then
wouldn't I see Mrs. Taylor,' suggested the philanthropist:—
and, notwithstanding my negatives, he had run back again
and brought an immense feminine bandit, .. fat enough to
have had an easy conscience all her life, .. who informed me
that 'her husband might be in, in a few minutes, or in so
many hours—wouldn't I like to get out & wait—' (Wilson
pulling at my gown) (—The philanthropist echoing the
invitation of the feminine Taylor.)—'No, I thanked them
all—it was not necessary that I should get out, but it *was*,
that Mr. Taylor should keep his promise about the restoration
of a dog which he had agreed to restore—& I begged her to
induce him to go to Wimpole Street in the course of the day,

& not defer it any longer'—To which, replied the lady, with
the most gracious of smiles—'Oh yes certainly!—and indeed
she *did* believe that Taylor had left home precisely on that
business'——poising her head to the right & left with the
most easy grace—'she was sure that Taylor w^d give his very
best attention' ....

So, in the midst of the politeness, we drove away, & Wilson
seemed to be of opinion that we had escaped with our lives
barely. Plain enough it was, that the gang was strong there.
The society .. the 'Fancy' .. had their roots in the ground.
The faces of those men!—

I had not been at home long, when Mr. Taylor did actually
come—desiring to have six guineas confided to his honour!! ..
& promising to bring back the dog. I sent down the money,
& told them to trust the gentleman's honour, as there seemed
no other way for it—: & while the business was being
concluded, in came Alfred, & straightway called our 'honour-
able friend' (meeting him in the passage) a swindler and a
liar & a thief. Which no gentleman could bear, of course.
Therefore with reiterated oaths he swore, 'as he hoped to be
saved, we should never see our dog again'—& rushed out of
the house. Followed a great storm. I was very angry with
Alfred, who had no business to risk Flush's life for the sake of
the satisfaction of trying on names which fitted. Angry I was
with Alfred, & terrified for Flush,—seeing at a glance the
probability of his head being cut off as the proper vengeance!—& down stairs I went with the resolution of going
again myself to Mr. Taylor's in Manning Street, or Shoreditch
wherever it was, & saving the victim at any price. It was the
evening, getting dusk—& everbody was crying out against
me for being 'quite mad' & obstinate, & wilful—I was called
as many names as Mr. Taylor. At last, Set said that *he* would
do it, promised to be as civil as I could wish, & got me to be
'in a good humour & go up to my room again'. And he went
instead of me, & took the money & fair words, & induced the
'man of honour' to forfeit his vengeance & go & fetch the dog.
Flush arrived here at eight oclock, (at the very moment with
your letter, dearest!—) & the first thing he did was to dash
up to this door, & then to drink his purple cup full of water,
filled three times over. He was not so enthusiastic about

seeing me, as I expected—he seemed bewildered & frightened—and whenever anyone said to him 'Poor Flush, did the
naughty men take you away?' he put up his head & moaned
& yelled. He has been very unhappy certainly. Dirty he is, &
much thinner, & continually he is drinking. Six guineas, was
his ransom—& now I have paid twenty for him to the dog-
stealers.

. . .

RB, *Sunday, 6 September 1846*

No, dearest, I am not to see you tomorrow for all the
happiness of the permission! It seems absurd, but perhaps the
greater absurdity would be a refusal to submit, under circumstances. You shall hear—I got up with the old *vertiginousness*,
or a little worse—and so, as I had in that case determined,
went to consult my Doctor. He thinks he finds the root of the
evil and can remove it, 'if I have patience enough.' So I
promised .. expecting something worthy that preamble—
whereas I am bidden go to bed and keep there for a day or
two—from this Sunday till Wednesday morning—taking
nothing but a sip of medicine I can't distinguish from water,
thrice a day—and *milk* at discretion—no other food! The
mild queerness of it is amusing, is it not? 'And for this fine
piece of self denial,' says he 'you shall be quite well by the
week's end.' 'But may I go to town on Wednesday?'—'Yes.'

Now, Ba, my own Ba, you know how often I have to
sorrowfully disclaim all the praises your dearest kindness
would attach to me; this time, if you will praise me a little for
obeying you, I will take the praise .. for the truth of truths is,
that I said at once to myself—'have I a right to avoid
anything which promises to relieve Her from this eternal
account of aches and pains'? So here am I writing, leaning on
my elbow, in bed,—as I never wrote before I think—and
perhaps my head is a little better, or I fancy so.

. . .

EB, *Monday, 7 September 1846 (1)*

Monday morning.

Ever, ever dearest, how was it that without presentiment of evil I got up this morning in the good spirits of '*our* days', hoping to see you, believing to see you, & feeling that it would be greater happiness than usual?—The sight of your letter, even, did not provoke the cloud—*that* was only the lesser joy, I thought, preceding the greater! ... How am I to be comforted, my own dearest?— No way, except by your being really better, really well—in order to which I shall not let you come as soon as wednesday: it will not be wise for you to leave your bed for a journey into London!—Rather you should be very quiet, & keep in the garden at farthest. Take care of yourself, dearest dearest, & if you think of me & love me, show it in that best way. And I praise you, praise you,— nay, I thank you & am grateful to you for every such proof of love, more than for *other* kinds of proof,—I will love you for it, my beloved! Now judge—shall I be able to help thinking of you every moment of the day? Could I help it, if I tried? In return, therefore, you will attend to the orders, submit to the discipline——ah but, will not the leaving off all food but milk, weaken you out of measure? I am uneasy about that milk-diet for *you*, who always seem to me to want support, & something to stimulate—You will promise to tell me *every-thing*—will you, dearest?—whether better or worse, stronger or weaker, you will tell me? And if you should be too unwell to write, as may God forbid, your sister will write—she will have that great goodness?—Let it be so, I beseech you.

. . .

RB, *Monday, 7 September 1846*

. . .

I am delighted to know Flush is with you, if I am not. Did you remember my petition about him? But, dearest, it *was*

very imprudent to go to those disgusting wretches yourself—
they have had a pretty honor without knowing it!

Here I lie with a dizzy head—unable to read more than a
page or two .. there is something in the unwonted position
that tires me—but whenever the book is left off, I turn to the
dark side of the room and see you, my very own Ba,—and so
I am soon better and able to try again—

How hot, and thunder-like,—this oppressive air! And you
who are affected by such weather? Tell me, my dearest
dearest, all you can tell me—since the real lips and eyes are
away—

. . .

EB, *Monday, 7 September 1846 (2)*

Monday Night.

How unwell you are, dearest beloved!—Ah no! It is not
'the position that tires you', it is the illness that incapacitates
you. And *you* to think of getting up & coming here .. you!—
Now, for my sake, for both our sakes, you *must* & *shall* be
patient & quiet, & remember how my thoughts are with you
conjuring you continually to quiet.

. . .

RB, *Tuesday, 8 September 1846*

Do you think your wishes, much less your blessings, fall to
the ground, my own Ba? Here is your letter, and here am I
writing to you, 'clothed and in my proper' room.° My doctor
bade me 'get up and do as I pleased'—and the perfect
pleasure is to say, I may indeed see you tomorrow, dearest
dearest! Can you look as you look in this letter?—So entirely
my own, and yet,—what should never be my own, by right ..
such a treasure to one so little worthy!

I have only a few minutes to say this,—the dressing and talking having taken up the time. Tomorrow shall repay me!
. . .

[Meeting 90: Wednesday, 9 September 3.00–5.45 p.m. The time of Browning's arrival is conjectural, because the envelope of the letter on which he recorded this visit is damaged.]

EB, *Wednesday, 9 September 1846*

Wednesday night

Dearest, you are a prophet, I suppose—there can be no denying it. This night, an edict has gone out, and George is tomorrow to be on his way to take a house for a month either at Dover, Reigate, Tunbridge, .. Papa did 'not mind which,' he said, & 'you may settle it among you' .. but he 'must have this house empty for a month in order to its cleaning'—we are to go therefore & not delay.

Now!—what *can* be done? It is possible that the absence may be longer than for a month, indeed it is probable—for there is much to do in painting & repairing, here in Wimpole Street, more than a month's work they say. Decide, after thinking. I am embarrassed to the utmost degree, as to the best path to take. If we are taken away on monday .. what then?

Of course I decline to give any opinion & express any preference,—as to places, I mean. It is not for my sake, that we go:—if *I* had been considered at all, indeed, we should have been taken away earlier, .. & not certainly now, when the cold season is at hand—And so much the better it is for me, that I have not, obviously, been thought of.

Therefore decide!—It seems quite too soon & too sudden for us to set out on our Italian adventure now—& perhaps even we could not compass—

Well—but you must think for both of us—It is past twelve

& I have just a moment to seal this & entrust it to Henrietta
for the morning's post.

More than ever beloved, I am
Your own Ba

I will do as you wish—understand.

RB, *Thursday, 10 September 1846 (1)*

What do you expect this letter will be about, my own dearest?
Those which I write on the mornings after our days seem
naturally to *answer* any strong point brought out in the
previous discourse and not *then* completely disposed of .. so
they generally run in the vile fashion of a disputatious 'last
word'; 'one word yet'—do not they? Ah, but you should
remember that never does it feel so intolerable,—the barest
fancy of a possibility of losing you,—as when I have just seen
you and heard you and, alas—left you for a time; on these
occasions, it seems so horrible—that if the least recollection
of a fear of yours, or a doubt .. anything which might be
nursed, or let grow quietly, into a serious obstacle to what we
desire .. if *that* rises up threateningly,—do you wonder that I
begin by attacking *it?* There are always a hundred deepest
reasons for gratitude and love which I could write about but
which my after life shall prove I never have forgotten .. still,
that very after-life depends perhaps on the letter of the
morning reasoning with you, teazing, contradicting .. Dearest
Ba, I do not tell you that I am justified in plaguing you thus,
at any time .. only to get your pardon, if I can, on the
grounds—the true grounds—

And this pardon, if you grant it, shall be for the past
offences, not for any fresh one I mean to commit now. I will
not add one word to those spoken yesterday about the extreme
perilousness of delay. You *give* me yourself. Hitherto, from the
very first till this moment, the giving hand has been advancing
steadily—it is not for me to grasp it lest it stop within an inch
or two of my forehead with its crown.

I am going to town this morning, and will leave off now.

What a glorious dream,—thro' nearly two years—without a single interval of blankness,—much less, bitter waking!

I may say THAT, I suppose, safely thro' whatever befalls!

Also I will ever say, God bless you, my dearest dearest,— my perfect angel you have been! While I am only your

R

My mother is deeply gratified at your present.

12 O^ck. On returning I find your note.

'I will do as you wish—understand'—then I understand you are in earnest. If you *do* go on Monday, our marriage will be impossible for another year—the misery! You see what we have gained by waiting. We must be *married directly* and go to Italy—I will go for a licence today and we can be married on Saturday. I will call to-morrow at 3 and arrange everything with you. We can leave from Dover &c *after* that,—but otherwise, impossible! Inclose the ring, or a substitute—I have not a minute to spare for the post.

Ever your own

R

RB, *Thursday, 10 September 1846*

4 p.m. Thursday.

I broke open my sealed letter and added the postscript just now. The post being thus saved, I can say a few words more leisurely.

I will go to-morrow, I think, and not to-day for the licence—there are fixed hours, I fancy, at the office—and I might be too late. I will also make the arrangement with my friend° for Saturday, if we should want him,—as we shall, in all probability—it would look suspiciously to be unaccompanied—We can arrange to-morrow.

Your words, first & last have been that you 'would not fail me'—you will not—

And the marriage over, you can take advantage of circumstances and go early or late in the week, as may be practicable. There will be facilities in the general packing &c—your own measures may be taken unobserved—Write short notes to the proper persons,—promising longer ones, if necessary.

See the *tone* I take, the way I write to *you* .. but it is all thro' you, in the little brief authority you give me,—and in the perfect belief of your truth and firmness—Indeed, I do not consider this an extraordinary occasion for proving those qualities. This conduct of your Father's is quite characteristic ..

Otherwise, too, the departure with its bustle is not unfavorable. If you hesitated, it would be before a little hurried shopping and letter-writing! I expected it, and therefore spoke as you heard yesterday—now *your* part must begin.—It may as well begin and end, both, *now* as at any other time. I will bring you every information possible to-morrow.

It seems as if I should insult you if I spoke a word to confirm you, to beseech you,—to relieve you from your promise, if you claim it.

God bless you prays your own

R

EB, *Thursday, 10 September 1846*

Dearest I write one word, & have one will, which is yours. At the same time, do not be precipitate—we shall not be taken away on monday, no, nor for several days afterward. George has simply gone to look for houses—going to Reigate first.

Oh yes—come tomorrow. And then, you shall have the ring .. soon enough, & safer.

Not a word of how you are!—*you* so good as to write me that letter beyond compact, yet not good enough, to say how you are! Dear, dearest—take care, & keep yourself unhurt & calm. I shall not fail to you—I do not—I will not. I will act by your decision, & I wish you to decide. I was yours long ago, & though you give me back my promise at this eleventh hour, .. you generous, dear unkind! ... You know very well that you can do as well without it—So take it again for my sake & not your own—

I cannot write, I am so tired, having been long out—. Will not this dream break on a sudden? Now is the moment for the breaking of it—surely.

But come tomorrow, come. Almost everybody is to be away at Richmond, at a picnic, & we shall be free on all sides—

Ever & ever your Ba—

[Meeting 91: Friday, 11 September 3.00–4.30 p.m. This was the last time Browning and Elizabeth Barrett met in Wimpole Street. Underneath his note of this meeting, Browning recorded his marriage to Elizabeth Barrett in St Marylebone Church:

+++ Sat. Sepr 12, 1846.
¼11–11¼ a.m. (91.)

The '91' is underlined three times; it is of course an error for '92' (see p.250).]

RB, *Saturday, 12 September 1846*

1 p.m. Saturday.

You will only expect a few words—what will those be?

When the heart is full it may run over, but the real fulness stays within.

You asked me yesterday 'if I should repent'? Yes—my own Ba,—I could wish all the past were to do over again, that in it I might somewhat more, never so little more,—conform in the outward homage to the inward feeling: what I have professed .. (for I have performed nothing—) seems to fall short of what my first love required even—and when I think of *this* moment's love .. I could repent, as I say.

Words can never tell you, however,—form them, transform them anyway,—how perfectly dear you are to me—perfectly dear to my heart and soul.

I look back, and in every one point, every word and gesture, every letter, every *silence*—you have been entirely perfect to me—I would not change one word, one look—

My hope and aim are to preserve this love, not to fall from

it—for which I trust to God who procured it for me, and doubtlessly can preserve it.

Enough now, my dearest, dearest, own Ba! You have given me the highest, completest proof of love that ever one human being gave another. I am all gratitude—and all pride, (under the proper feeling which ascribes pride to the right source—) all pride that my life has been so crowned by you.

God bless you prays your very own

R

I will write to-morrow of course. Take every case of *my life* which is in that dearest little hand; try and be composed, my beloved.

Remember to thank Wilson for me.

EB, *Saturday, 12 September 1846*

Saturday. Sept 12.

p.m. 4 1/2

Ever dearest, I write a word that you may read it & know how all is safe so far, & that I am not slain downright with the day—oh, such *a day!*—I went to Mr. Boyd's directly, so as to send Wilson home the faster—and was able to lie quietly on the sofa in his sitting room down stairs, before he was ready to see me, being happily engaged with a medical councillor. Then I was made to talk & take Cyprus wine,— &, my sisters delaying to come, I had some bread & butter for dinner, to keep me from looking too pale in their eyes— At last they came, & with such grave faces! Missing me & Wilson, they had taken fright,—& Arabel had forgotten at first what I told her last night about the fly. I kept saying, 'What nonsense, .. what fancies you do have to be sure,' .. trembling in my heart with every look they cast at me. And so, to complete the bravery, I went on with them in the carriage to Hampstead .. as far as the heath,—& talked & looked——now you shall praise me for courage—or rather you shall love me for the love which was the root of it all. How necessity makes heroes—or heroines at least!—For I did not sleep all last night, & when I first went out with

Wilson to get to the flystand in Marylebone Street I staggered so, that we both were afraid for the fear's sake,—but we called at a chemist's for salvolatile° & were thus enabled to go on. I spoke to her last night, & she was very kind, very affectionate, & never shrank for a moment—I told her that always I should be grateful to her.

You—how are you? how is your head, ever dearest?

It seems all like a dream! When we drove past that church again, I and my sisters, there was a cloud before my eyes—. Ask your mother to forgive me, Robert. If *I* had not been there, *she* would have been there, perhaps.

And for the rest, if either of us two is to suffer injury & sorrow for what happened there today—, pray that it may all fall upon *me!*—Nor should I suffer the most pain *that* way, as I know, & God knows.

Your own
Ba.

Was I very uncourteous to your cousin?° So kind, too, it was in him!—

Can there be the least danger of the newspapers? Are those books ever examined by penny a liners,° do you suppose?—

EB, *Sunday, 13 September 1846*

My own beloved, if ever you should have reason to complain of me in things voluntary & possible, all other women would have a right to tread me underfoot, I should be so vile & utterly unworthy. There, is my answer to what you wrote yesterday of wishing to be better to me .. you!—What could be better than lifting me from the ground & carrying me into life & the sunshine? I was yours rather by right than by gift,—(yet by gift also, my beloved!—) for what you have saved & renewed, is surely yours. All that I am, I owe you:— if I enjoy anything now & henceforth, it is through you. You know this well. Even as *I*, from the beginning, knew that I had no power against you, .. or that, if I *had*, it was for your sake.

Dearest, in the emotion & confusion of yesterday morning, there was yet room in me for one thought which was not a feeling—for I thought that, of the many, many women who have stood where I stood, & to the same end, not one of them all perhaps, not one perhaps, since that building was a church, has had reasons strong as mine, for an absolute trust & devotion towards the man she married,——not one! And then I both thought & felt, that it was only just, for them, .. those women who were less happy, .. to have that affectionate sympathy & support & presence of their nearest relations, parent or sister, .. which failed to *me*, .. needing it less thro' being happier!——

All my brothers have been here this morning, laughing & talking, & discussing this matter of the leaving town,—& in the room, at the same time, were two or three female friends of ours, from Herefordshire—and I did not *dare* to cry out against the noise, though my head seemed splitting in two, (one half for each shoulder) I had such a morbid fear of exciting a suspicion. Trippy° too being one of them, I promised to go to see her tomorrow & dine in her drawing-room if she would give me, for dinner, some bread & butter— It was like having a sort of fever. And all in the midst, the bells began to ring. 'What bells are those?' asked one of the provincials. 'Marylebone Church bells' said Henrietta, standing behind my chair.

And now .. while I write, & having escaped from the great din, sit here quietly,—comes .. who do you think?—Mr. Kenyon.

He came with his spectacles, looking as if his eyes reached to their rim all the way round,—& one of the first words was, *'When did you see Browning.'* And I think I shall make a pretension to presence of mind henceforward,—for, though *certainly* I changed colour & he saw it, I yet answered with a tolerably quick evasion, .. 'He was here on friday'—& leapt straight into another subject, & left him gazing fixedly on my face—Dearest, he saw something, but not all. . . . On rising to go away, he mentioned your name a second time .. 'When do you see Browning again?' To which I answered that I did not know—

Is not *that* pleasant? The worst is that all these combinations of things, make me feel so bewildered that I cannot make the necessary arrangements, as far as the letters go— But I must break from the dream-stupour which falls on me when left to myself a little, & set about what remains to be done.

A house near Watford, is thought of now—but, as none is concluded on, the removal is not likely to take place in the middle of the week even, perhaps.

. . .

RB, *Sunday, 13 September 1846*

Thank you a thousand times for the note, my own Ba. I welcomed it as I never yet welcomed even *your* notes; entirely kind to write, and write *so!* Oh, I know the effort you made, the pain you bore for my sake! I tell you, once and forever, your proof of love to me is *made* .. I *know* your love, my dearest dearest: my whole life shall be spent in trying to furnish such a proof of *my* affection,—such a perfect proof,—and perhaps vainly spent—but I will endeavour with God's help. Do you feel what I mean, dearest? How you have dared and done all this, under my very eyes, for my only sake? I believed you would be capable of it—When then? What is a belief? My own eyes have seen—my heart will remember!

Dearest, nothing needs *much* trouble you farther: take your own time and opportunity. I confide in your judgment—(for I am not going to profess confidence in *you!*)—I am sure you will see and act for the best. My preparations are made; I have only to wait your desires. I will not ask to see you, for instance—though of course a word brings me as usual to you—your will is altogether my will.

The first obvious advantage of our present relation, I will take. You are mine—your generosity has given to me my utmost claim upon your family—so far as I am concerned, putting aside my sympathy with you, there is nothing more they *can* give me: so, I will say, perhaps a little less reservedly than I could have brought myself to say before, that there is no conceivable submission I will refuse, nor possible satisfaction I will hesitate to make to those feelings I have been forced to offend, if by any means I may preserve, for *you*, so much of their affection as you have been accustomed to receive; I do not require anything beyond *toleration* for myself .. I will cheerfully accept as the truest kindness to me, a continuance of kindness *to you*. You know what I would have done to possess you:—now that I *do* possess you, I renew the offer, to *you* .. judge with what earnest purpose of keeping my word! I do not think .. nor do you think .. that any personal application, directly or by letter, would do any good—it might rather add to the irritation we apprehend: but my consent is given beforehand to any measure you shall ever consider proper. And your father may be sure that while I adore his daughter it will be impossible for me, under any circumstances, to be wanting in the utmost respect for, and observance of, himself. Understand, with the rest, why I write this, Ba. To your brothers and sisters I am bound for ever,—by every tie of gratitude; *they* may acquiesce more easily .. comprehending more, perhaps, of the dear treasure you are, they will forgive my ambition of gaining it. I will write to Mr Kenyon. You will probably have time to write all the letters requisite.

Do not trouble yourself with more than is strictly necessary—you can supply all wants at Leghorn or Pisa. Let us be as unencumbered with luggage as possible. . . .

I only saw my cousin for a few minutes afterward—he came up in a cab immediately—he understood all there was need he should. *You* to be 'uncourteous' to anybody! No, no—sweetest!—But I will thank him as you bid, knowing the value of Ba's thanks! For the prying penny a liners .. why, trust to Providence—we must! I do not apprehend much danger ..

Dearest, I woke this morning *quite well*—quite free from the sensation in the head—I have not woke *so*, for two years perhaps—what have you been doing to me?

My father & mother & sister love you thoroughly—my mother said this morning, in my room, 'If I were as I have been, I would try and write to her'—I said, 'I will tell her what I know you feel'. She is much better (—I hear her voice while I write .. below the open window). Poor Pritchard came home from the country on Friday *night*—late—and posted here immediately—he was vexed to be made understand that there was some way in which he might have served me and did not. It was kind, very kind of Wilson.

I will leave off—to resume tomorrow. Bless you, my very own, only Ba—my pride, and joy, and utter comfort. I kiss you and

am ever your own R

RB, *Monday, 14 September 1846*

You go on to comfort me, love—bless you for it. I collect from the letter that you are recovering from the pain & excitement: that is happy! I waited to hear from you, my own Ba, and will only write a word—then go out—I *think*.

Do you feel *so*, thro' the anxieties and trouble of this situation? You take my words from me—*I* 'exult' in the irrevocability of this precious bestowal of yourself on me: come what will, my life has borne flower, and fruit—it is a glorious, successful, felicitous life, I thank God and you!

All has been for the best, you will see, even in these apparently untoward circumstances: this particular act was *precipitated* by them, certainly—, but it is done, and well done. Does it not simplify our arrangements that this is *done?* And surely there was every justification for the precipitancy in that proposed journey, and uncertain return,—(in winter, to a freshly-painted house!) But every moment of my life brings fresh proof to me of the intervention of Providence. How the *natural* course would have embarrassed us! .. any consultation with you respecting your own feelings on a removal at present .. any desire to gratify them . . .

I confided my approaching marriage to that kind old Pritchard, lest he should be too much wounded—if his surprise was considerable, his delight kept due proportion— you may depend on his secrecy: I need not say, I mentioned the fact *simply* .. without a word about any circumstances. If your father could be brought to allow the matter to pass as *indifferent* to him .. what he did not choose to interfere with, however little he approved it,—we should be fortunate! Perhaps pride, if no kinder feeling, may induce him to that—

My family all love you, dearest—you cannot conceive my father & mother's childlike faith in goodness—and my sister is very high spirited, and quick of apprehension—so as to seize the true points of the case at once. I am in great hopes you will love them all, and understand them. Last night, I asked my father, who was absorbed over some old book, 'if he should not be glad to see his new daughter'—to which he, starting, replied 'Indeed I *shall!*' with such a fervor as to make my mother laugh—not abated by his adding, 'And how I should be glad of her seeing Sis!' his other daughter, Sarianna, to wit—who was at church.

. . .

EB, *Monday, 14 September 1846 (1)*

. . .

Your mother's goodness touches me very deeply. I am grateful to her & to all your family, beyond any power of mine to express my feelings. Let me be silent therefore, instead of trying.

. . .

EB, *Monday, 14 September 1846 (2)*

Monday evening.

First, God is to be thanked for this great joy of hearing that you are better, my ever dearest—it is a joy that floats over all the other emotions. Dearest I am so glad! I had feared that excitement's telling on you quite in another way. When the whole is done, & we have left England & the talkers thereof behind our backs, you will be well, stedfastly & satisfactory, I do trust. In the meantime, there seems so much to do, that I am frightened to look towards the heaps of it. As to

acoutrements, everything has been arranged as simply as
possible that way—but, still, there are necessities—& the
letters, the letters! I am paralysed when I think of having to
write such words as .. 'Papa, I am married,—I hope you will
not be too displeased.' Ah, poor Papa!—You are too sanguine
if you expect any such calm from him as an assumption of
indifference would imply. To the utmost, he will be angry,—
he will cast me off as far from him——Well—there is no
comfort in such thoughts. How I felt tonight when I saw him
at seven oclock, for the first time since friday, & the event of
saturday! He spoke kindly too, & asked me how I was.

Once I heard of his saying of me that I was 'the purest
woman he ever knew,'—which made me smile at the moment,
or laugh, I believe, outright, because I understood perfectly
what he meant by *that*—viz—that I had not troubled him
with the iniquity of love-affairs, or any impropriety of seeming
to think about being married. But now, the whole sex will go
down with me to the perdition of faith in any of us. See the
effect of my wickedness!—'Those women!'

But we will submit, dearest—I will put myself under his
feet, to be forgiven a little, .. enough to be taken up again into
his arms. I love him—he is my father— he has good & high
qualities after all: he is my father ABOVE all. And *you*, because
you are so generous & tender to me, will let me, you say, &
help me, to try to win back the alienated affection——for
which, I thank you & bless you,—I did not thank you enough
this morning. Surely I may say to him, too, .. 'With the
exception of this act, I have submitted to the least of your
wishes all my life long—Set the life against the act, & forgive
me, for the sake of the daughter you once loved.' Surely I
may say *that*,—& then remind him of the long suffering I
have suffered,—and entreat him to pardon the happiness
which has come at last—.

And *he* will wish in return, that I had died years ago!——
For the storm will come & endure—And at last, perhaps, he
will forgive us—it is my hope.

. . . In your ways towards me, you have acted throughout
too much 'the woman's part', as that is considered—You
loved me because I was lower than others, that you might be
generous & raise me up:—very characteristic for a woman

(in her ideal standard) but quite wrong for a man, as again & again I used to signify to you, Robert—but you went on & did it all the same. And now, you still go on—you persist— you will be the woman of the play, to the last; let the prompter prompt ever so against you. You are to do every- thing I like, instead of doing what *you* like, and to 'honour & obey' *me*, in spite of what was in the vows last saturday,—is *that* the way of it & of you?—& are vows to be kept *so*, pray? after that fashion? Then, *dont* put 'at home' at the corner of the cards,° dearest!——It is my command!

And forgive the inveterate jesting, which jests with eyes full of tears—I love you—I bless God for you—You are too good for me, as always I knew. I look up to you continually.

It is best, I continue to think, that you should not come here—best for *you* because the position, if you were to try it, would be less tolerable than ever—& best for both of us, that in case the whole truth were ever discovered (I mean, of the previous marriage) we might be able to call it simply an act in order to security—I don't know how to put my feeling into words, but I do seem to feel that it would be better, & less offensive to those whom we offend at any rate, to avoid all possible remark on this point. It seems better to a sort of instinct I have.

Then, if I see you—farewell, the letter-writing. Oh no— there will be time enough when we are on the railway!—we shall talk then.

. . .

EB, *Tuesday, 15 September 1846*

. . . Next monday is the day fixed for the general departure to a house taken at Little Bookham or Hookham .. what is it? Well—we must think. Tell me when you want me to go. I might go from the new house, perhaps. But you will think, dearest, & tell me.

. . .

RB, *Wednesday, 16 September 1846*

. . .

I do not know where 'Bookham' is—you must decide .. I am sure you will be anxious to get away.

The business of the letters will grow less difficult once begun—see if it will not! and in these four or five days whole epics might be written, much more, letters. Have you arranged all with Wilson? Take, of course, the simplest possible wardrobe &c—so as to reduce our luggage to the very narrowest compass. The expense—(beside the common sense of a little luggage)—is considerable—every ounce being paid for. Let us treat our journey as a mere journey—we can return for what else we want, or get it sent, or procure it abroad—I shall take just a portmanteau and carpet bag. I think the fewer books we take the better,—they take up room—and the wise way always seemed to me to read in rooms at home, and open one's eyes and *see* abroad. . . .

Be sure, dearest, I will do my utmost to conciliate your father: sometimes I could not but speak impatiently to you of him .. that was while you were in his direct power—now there is no *need* of a word in any case .. I shall be silent if the *worst imaginable* happens; and if anything better,—most grateful. You do not need to remind me he is your father .. I shall be proud to say, *mine* too. Then, he said *that* of you—for which I love him—love the full prompt justice of that ascription of 'perfect purity'—it is another voice responding to mine, confirming mine.

Goodbye, dearest dearest,—I continue *quite* well .. I thank God, as you do, and see his hand in it. My poor mother suffers greatly, but is no worse .. rather, better I hope. They (all here) will leave town for some quiet place at the beginning of October for some three weeks at least. Dear, kind souls they arc.

Kiss me as I kiss you, dearest Ba,—I can bring you no flowers but I pluck this bud and send it with all affectionate devotion.

Your own
RB

EB, *Wednesday, 16 September 1846*

Dearest, the general departure from this house takes place on monday—& the house at Little Bookham is six miles from the nearest railroad & a mile & a half from Leatherhead where a coach runs. Now you are to judge. Certainly if I go with you on Saturday I shall not have half the letters written—you, who talk so largely of epic poems, have not the least imagination of my state of mind & spirits—I began to write a letter to Papa this morning, & could do nothing but cry, & looked so pale thereupon, that everybody wondered what could be the matter. Oh—quite well I am now, & I only speak of myself in that way to show you how the inspiration is by no means sufficient for epic poems. Still, I may certainly write the necessary letters, .. & do the others on the road .. could I, do you think? I would rather have waited—indeed rather—only it may be difficult to leave Bookham .. yet *possible*—so tell me what you would have me do.

Wilson & I have a light box & a carpet bag between us— & I will be docile about the books, dearest. Do you take a desk? Had I better not, I wonder?

Then for box & carpet bag .. Remember that we cannot take them out of the house with us. We must send them the evening before—Friday evening, if we went on saturday .. and where? Have you a friend anywhere, to whose house they might be sent, or could they go direct to the railroad office— & what office? In that case they should have your name on them, should they not?

Now think for me, ever dearest—& tell me what you do not tell me .. that you continue better. Oh no—you are ill again—or you would not wait to be told to tell me. And the dear, dear little *bud!*—I shall keep it to the end of my life, if you love me so long, .. or *not*, Sir! I thank you, dearest.

. . .

RB, *Thursday, 17 September 1846 (1)*

My only sweetest, I will write just a word to catch the earlier post,—time pressing. Bless you for all you suffer .. I *know* it though it would be very needless to call your attention to the difficulties. I know much, if not all, and can only love and admire you,—not help, alas!

Surely these difficulties will multiply, if you go to Bookham—the way will be to leave at once. . . .

Take *no* desk .. I will take a large one: take nothing you can leave—but secure letters &c. I will take out a passport. Did you not tell me roughly at how much you estimated our expenses for the journey? Because I will take about *that* much, and get Rothschild's letter of credit for Leghorn—one should avoid carrying money about with one.

. . .

[The following letter, Browning's last in the correspondence, was written after a series of mistakes about the timetables of the trains and boats which the couple were to take on the day of their elopement, hence Browning's opening remark. The letter which he enclosed was, as Kintner says, probably addressed to Kenyon; Elizabeth Barrett, in a passage (not included in this edition) from her second letter of 14 September, had suggested that they send together their separate letters to him announcing their marriage.]

RB, *Friday, 18 September 1846*

11½ Friday.

My own best Ba—How thankful I am you have seen my blunder—I took the other company's days for the South Western's—changed. What I shall write now is with the tables before me (of the Railway) and a transcript from *to-day's* advertisement in the Times.

The packet will leave tomorrow evening, from the Royal

Pier, Southampton, at *nine*. We leave Nine Elms, Vauxhall, at *five*—to arrive at *Eight*. Doors closed *five* minutes before. I will be at Hodgsons° *from* halfpast three to *four* PRECISELY when I should hope you can be ready. I shall go to Vauxhall, apprise them that luggage is coming, (yours) and send *mine* there—so that we both shall be unincumbered—& we can take a cab or coach from H's.

Never mind your scanty preparations .. we can get everything at Leghorn—and the new boats carry parcels to Leghorn on the 15th of every month, remember—so can bring what you may wish to send for.

I enclose a letter to go with yours. The cards as you choose—they are here—we can write about them from Paris or elsewhere. The advertisement, as you advise. All shall be cared for.

God bless and strengthen you, my ever dearest dearest—I will not trust myself to speak of my feelings for you—worship well belongs to such fortitude—One struggle more:—if all the kindness on your part brought a strangely insufficient return, is it not possible that this step may produce all you can hope? Write to me one word more—depend on me—I go to town about business.

Your own, own R.

EB, *Friday, 18 September 1846*

Friday night

At from half past three, to four, then—four will not, I suppose, be too late—I will not write more—I *cannot*——. By tomorrow at this time, I shall have *you only*, to love me—my beloved!——

You *only!*——As if one said *God* only—And we shall have HIM beside, I pray of Him—

I shall send to your address at New Cross your Hanmer's poems—& the two dear books you gave me,° which I do not like to leave here & am afraid of hurting by taking them with me. Will you ask *our* sister to put the parcel into a drawer, so as to keep it for us?

Your letters to me I take with me, let the 'ounces' cry out aloud, ever so. I *tried* to leave them, & I could not. That is, they would not be left: it was not my fault—I will not be scolded.

Is this my last letter to you, ever dearest?—Oh—if I loved you less .. a little, little less ..

Why I should tell you that our marriage was invalid, or ought to be—& that you should by no means come for me tomorrow. It is dreadful .. dreadful .. to have to give pain here by a voluntary act—for the first time in my life—

Remind your mother & father of me affectionately & gratefully—& your sister too! Would she think it too bold of me to say *our* Sister, if she had heard it on the last page?

Do you pray for me tonight, Robert? Pray for me, & love me, that I may have courage, feeling both—

Your own Ba—

The boxes are *safely sent*. Wilson has been perfect to me—And *I* .. calling her 'timid,' & afraid of her timidity! I begin to think that none are so bold as the timid, when they are fairly roused.

[Elizabeth Barrett and Wilson, with Flush (who obligingly did not bark), left Wimpole Street on Saturday afternoon and met Browning as arranged. They travelled to Le Havre, and then to Paris, where they found their friend Anna Jameson, in whose company they travelled south. At Orleans on 29 September Elizabeth Barrett received her father's unforgiving (and last) letter. On 14 October the Brownings arrived in Pisa, the first of their homes in the years of marriage and exile that followed. Browning published *Christmas-Eve and Easter-Day* (1850) and *Men and Women* (1855), wrote several of the poems of *Dramatis Personae* (1864), and conceived the idea of *The Ring and The Book* (1868–9); Elizabeth Barrett Browning published *Poems* (1850), including *Sonnets from the Portuguese, Casa Guidi Windows* (1851), *Aurora Leigh* (1856), and *Poems before Congress* (1860). Elizabeth Barrett Browning died in Florence in June 1861, after which Browning returned to live in England. They had one child, Robert Wiedemann Barrett Browning ('Pen'), who published the first edition of their courtship correspondence in 1899. He died without issue in 1913.]

NOTES

The Browning household at New Cross. Robert Browning (1812–89) was living at the time of the correspondence with his father, mother, and sister in New Cross, then a semi-rural suburb to the south-east of London. Robert Browning senior (1782–1866) was a clerk at the Bank of England; he had married Sarah Anna Wiedemann, the daughter of a Dundee merchant. Browning's sister Sarianna was a year and a half younger than he. For details on Browning's home life and social circumstances see Maynard, chs. 2–3.

The Barrett household at 50 Wimpole Street. Elizabeth Barrett (1806–61) was the eldest child of Edward Barrett Moulton Barrett (1785–1857) and Mary Graham-Clarke (1781–1828). In 1832, as a result of financial reverses in Jamaica, where their fortune was based, the family left their estate at Hope End in Herefordshire, first for Sidmouth and then, in 1835, London. They had been in Wimpole Street since 1837. Mr Barrett conducted business in the City. Elizabeth Barrett had eight surviving brothers and sisters: Henrietta (1809–60), who married William Surtees Cook in 1850; Arabella (1813–68), the closest to her, who slept in the same room; Charles (1814–1905), nicknamed 'Stormie'; George (1816–95), a lawyer; Henry (1818–96); Alfred (1820–1904); Septimus (1822–70); and Octavius (1824–1910). Three siblings were dead: her sister Mary (1810–14) and her two eldest brothers, Edward ('Bro', 1807–40) and Samuel (1812–40). Edward had been especially close to her (see letter EB 20–3 Aug., pp. 105–6). For further details about the family, see Kelley and Hudson, i. 285–96.

1 *your poems.* Elizabeth Barrett's two-volume *Poems* (1844), which John Kenyon (see next note) had given to Browning's sister Sarianna. Unless otherwise indicated all Browning's quotations from Elizabeth Barrett's poems in the correspondence came from this collection. Browning had been in Italy when the collection was published, and had only recently returned.

1 *Mr Kenyon.* John Kenyon (1784–1856), the son of wealthy Jamaican plantation owners, had lived for most of his life in England. He was at school with Browning's father and at Cambridge with Elizabeth Barrett's (he claimed to be a distant cousin of the Barretts, but the relationship is doubtful), and became the friend and admirer of both poets. He was a genial, cultivated, hospitable, and generous man. His legacy of £11,000, the last of many acts of kindness, made the Brownings financially secure. Browning dedicated *Dramatic Romances and Lyrics* (1845) to him, and Elizabeth Barrett *Aurora Leigh* (1856).

1 *years ago.* The episode took place in Mar. 1842. See Landis, p. 81.

2 *in women.* Lear on Cordelia: 'Her voice was ever soft, / Gentle and low, an excellent thing in woman' (*King Lear*, v. iii. 274–5).

4 *O tu.* 'To the dear memory of Torquato Tasso, Dr Bernardini offered the following Poem: *O thou*—.' Tasso (1544–95), Italian poet, author of *Gerusalemme liberata* and other influential works; famous also in popular legend because his passion for Leonora d'Este, sister of his patron Duke Alfonso II, was supposed to have led to his long imprisonment at Ferrara.

4 *Fellows.* Charles Fellows (1799–1860), archaeologist, had recently discovered the Xanthian Marbles in Lycia and brought them to the British Museum. He was knighted in May 1845.

5 *Titian's Naples Magdalen.* This painting, in the Museo di Capodimonte, is now believed to be an inferior copy, produced in Titian's workshop, of the lost original, which was sent to Philip II of Spain; the closest copy is in the Hermitage Museum, Leningrad. The Magdalen is depicted with eyes upraised, her dishevelled hair falling about her body. Browning had visited Naples during his recent trip to Italy (Aug.–Dec. 1844).

5 *I must say.* Possibly an anticipation of *Christmas-Eve*, published in *Christmas-Eve and Easter-Day*, 1850. See also p. 60 and n. *Songs of the Poets*.

6 *testa lunga.* The words do mean 'head' and 'long', but there is no such phrase in Italian.

6 *Mr Horne.* Richard Henry (or Hengist) Horne (1802–84), poet, dramatist, and man of letters, author of the 'farthing epic' *Orion* (1843) and *A New Spirit of the Age* (1844), a collection of essays on contemporary writers to which Elizabeth Barrett had anonymously contributed.

6 εἴδωλου 'Eidolon', i.e. image. See also letter EB 24 Mar., p. 233.

7 *subjective & objective.* Browning later used these terms in his essay on Shelley (1852).

8 *head aches.* This is the first of many allusions to Browning's being unwell, and especially to his head aching; the symptoms were probably those of nervous tension. For a discussion, see Karlin, pp. 73–4.

8 *Bells.* Browning published his work from 1841 to 1846 under the series title *Bells and Pomegranates*. The poems referred to here formed part of no. vii, *Dramatic Romances and Lyrics*, published in Nov. 1845.

8 *white heights.* Elizabeth Barrett's 'A Drama of Exile', ll. 660–1, Lucifer describing Eve: 'And down from her white heights of womanhood / Looks on me so amazed.'

9 *the Page.* 'Bertha in the Lane', 'A Drama of Exile', 'Rhyme of the Duchess May', 'The Romaunt of the Page'.

9 *Juliet's word.* Possibly, as Kintner suggests, 'it is an honour that I dream not of' (*Romeo and Juliet*, 1. iii. 66), Juliet's answer to the question, 'How stands your disposition to be married?' See the close of letter EB 3 Feb. (p. 13) and n. *rash & sudden*.

9 *Bradbury and Evans.* The printers employed by Browning's publisher Edward Moxon. Their reader would require legible copy.

10 *his romances.* In *A New Spirit of the Age* (see p. 6 n. *Mr Horne*), Horne stated that Elizabeth Barrett was 'in constant correspondence with many of the most eminent persons of the time'.

10 *The grand scene in Pippa Passes.* 'That great tragic scene, which you call "exquisite"—and which pants again with its own power!' (Miller, p. 80): referring to Part i, ll. 1–282, the scene between Ottima and her lover Sebald, who has just killed Ottima's husband. An introduction by John Kenyon in 1836 began Elizabeth Barrett's close literary and personal friendship with Mary Russell Mitford (1787–1855), who is best known today for the stories and sketches of *Our Village* (1832). She wrote fiction, plays and journalism, supporting her dissolute and extravagant father until his death in 1842, and then continuing a career as a professional writer. Flush, Elizabeth Barrett's spaniel, was Miss Mitford's gift in 1841. Despite the favourable comment reported here, Miss Mitford disliked Browning (whom she thought effeminate) and his work (which she thought obscure): Elizabeth Barrett had disagreed with her on the subject before she knew Browning, and was to do so again as the courtship progressed.

12 *Atalanta-ball.* In Greek myth, Atalanta raced prospective suitors and killed the losers. Hippomenes won by throwing in her path three golden apples, supplied by the goddess of love, Aphrodite, which she stopped to pick up. The story is in Ovid, *Metamorphoses*, viii.

12 *nobler sons than he.* Attributed to the mother of Brasidas, the great Spartan general in the war against Athens, after his death.

13 μηδέπω ἐν προοιμίοις. Alluding to Aeschylus, *Prometheus Bound*, ll. 740–2 (Loeb translation): '[Prometheus] As to the tale thou now hast heard—believe that it has not even reached the prelude. [Io] Ah me, ah me, alas!'

13 *rash & sudden. Romeo and Juliet*, ii. ii. 117–18; the original reads: 'I have no joy of this contract to-night. It is too rash, too unadvis'd, too sudden'.

14 *going to press.* Thomas Carlyle's edition of *Oliver Cromwell's Letters and Speeches*, published Nov. 1845. Browning had met Carlyle, whom he greatly admired, in the late 1830s. He is not known to have acted for Carlyle outside this instance. His letter was to a Mr H. W. Field: see Kelley and Hudson, *Checklist*, p. 44.

14 *masoretic.* The Masoretes were scholars who, between the 6th and 10th centuries AD, assembled and edited the now traditional text of the Hebrew Bible. Since the ancient texts had no vowels the Masoretes introduced vowel-signs to indicate pronunciation; these signs occasionally affected interpretation.

14 *Alfred over the sea.* Alfred Domett, who had emigrated to New Zealand in 1842.

15 *darling 'Luria'*. A play, published with *A Soul's Tragedy* in *Bells and Pomegranates*, no. viii (1846).

16 *Rialto where verse-merchants most do congregate.* The publisher's market; adapting *Merchant of Venice*, I. iii. 50.

16 *decamp to the crows.* A tag from Aristophanes (e.g. *Clouds*, 133), meaning 'get lost'.

17 *Cornelius Agrippa's assistance.* Heinrich Cornelius Agrippa von Nettesheim (?1486–1535), whose writings on the occult Browning knew from his father's library and quoted for the epigraph to his first published poem, *Pauline* (1833).

17 *go softly all their days.* Isaiah 38: 15: 'I shall go softly all my years in the bitterness of my soul.'

17 *does as they bid him.* Referring to Tennyson's alterations and omissions of his early work in the first volume of his 1842 collection. See Browning's letter to Domett of 13 July 1842, in F. G. Kenyon, *Robert Browning and Alfred Domett* (1906), pp. 40–1.

17 *break off in the middle.* From the 'argument' to Canto I of Samuel Butler's mock-heroic poem *Hudibras* (1663–80):
> Sir Hudibras his passing worth,
> The manner how he sally'd forth;
> His arms and equipage are shown,
> His horse's virtues, and his own.
> Th' adventure of the bear and fiddle
> Is sung, but breaks off in the middle.

18 *Mr Landor.* Walter Savage Landor (1775–1864), poet, dramatist, and man of letters, was an occasional correspondent of Elizabeth Barrett and a friend of Browning, whose poetry he admired, and who in turn said that he owed Landor more than any other contemporary writer (Kenyon, ii. 354). See also p. 179 n. *says Mr Landor.*

18 *Euripides in three days.* 'A foolish and malevolent poet once observed that he had written 100 verses in three days, while Euripides had written only three. *True*, says Euripides, *but there is this difference between your poetry and mine; yours will expire in three days, but mine shall live for ages to come*' (Lemprière's *Classical Dictionary*, 12th edn., 1823).

19 *Gr-r- you swine.* The last words of 'Soliloquy of the Spanish Cloister', published in *Dramatic Lyrics* (1842).

20 *my soul among lions.* Psalm 57: 4.

20 *Professor Wilson.* John Wilson, 'Christopher North'. He had severely criticized Tennyson's early poems.

20 *Discourse on Poetry.* Sidney's *Defence of Poesie* was written in 1579–80, before Shakespeare's literary career had started. It was published posthumously in 1595, which may account for Elizabeth Barrett's error here.

21 *Babbage.* The mathematician Charles Babbage (1792–1871), whose 'calculating machine' was the forerunner of modern computers.

22 *perverse and froward generation*. Deuteronomy 32: 20 ('a very froward generation') and Matthew 17: 17 ('O faithless and perverse generation!').

22 *prose & not verse*. Carlyle gave similar advice to other poets, including Browning.

22 *in the farm-yard*. According to legend, the cackling of the sacred geese kept in the Capitol gave the alarm and saved it from capture by the Gauls in 387 BC. Elizabeth Barrett combines this with the popular identification of critics with cackling geese. Later in life Browning kept two pet geese named, after the magazines, 'Edinburgh' and 'Quarterly'.

22 *spider-webs appertaining*. See letter RB 26 Feb., p. 24, and n. *sculls and spider webs*.

24 *enwraps a bee*. *Verse Letters to Severall Personages*, 'To the Countesse of Bedford' ['Honour is so sublime perfection'], ll. 25–6: 'This [body], as an Amber drop enwraps a Bee, / Covering discovers your quicke Soule'.

24 *Lycophron*. Greek poet and tragedian of the fourth century BC. The only extant work attributed to him, the *Alexandra*, is a dramatic monologue famous for its obscurity.

24 *sculls and spider webs*. Browning had described them in a letter to Horne, which Horne showed to Elizabeth Barrett (hence her joking statement in her next letter that Browning had told her himself). See Hood, p. 8, and Landis, p. 104.

25 *Phrenologists*. Phrenology is the 'science' of determining the nature and scope of a person's mental faculties by examining the shape of the skull. It had a great vogue in the mid-19th century; cf. such phrases in the correspondence as 'he has a great organ of order' (letter EB 2–3 July, p. 77).

25 *Polidoro's perfect Andromeda*. Polidoro de Caravaggio (*c.* 1500–43); his painting of Perseus rescuing Andromeda from the sea-monster, originally a fresco scene, was engraved by Volpato in the Piranesi series in 1772. This is almost certainly the print to which Browning refers, which hung over his desk, and which he had described in *Pauline*, ll. 656–67. See Maynard, pp. 150–1 and notes.

25 *Ostade*. Adriaen van Ostade (1610–85), Fiemish painter and print-maker; *Carousing Peasants in an Interior* (*c.* 1638) is in the Alte Pinakothek, Munich. See also letter RB 13 Aug., p. 285, and n. *Brauwer . . . Teniers*.

25 *sane human being*. J. S. Mill was sent a copy of *Pauline* (published anonymously in 1833) by Browning's friend and mentor W. J. Fox. Mill annotated the copy and returned it to Fox, who gave it to Browning. It is now in the Forster-Dyce Collection of the Victoria and Albert Museum. Mill's summary note, at the back of the volume, begins: 'With considerable poetic powers, this writer seems to me possessed with a more intense and morbid self-consciousness than I

ever knew in any sane human being.' Browning alludes to this
comment again in letter RB 24 May, p. 60.

25 *mildly sweet.* Henry Kirke White (1785–1806); 'Fragment v' ('O pale
art thou, my lamp') in *Remains of Henry Kirke White*, 2 vols. (1807), ii.
139. There is no dash between 'so' and 'mildly' in the original. 'These
fragments . . . were, for the most part, written upon the back of his
mathematical papers, during the few moments of the last year of his
life, in which he suffered himself to follow the impulse of his genius'
(ii. 136).

26 *the new 'style'.* Punning on the calendar change which in 1752 had
shifted the beginning of the year from 25 March to 1 January; pre-
1752 dates were referred to as 'old style' and 'new style'.

26 *the voice of the turtle.* Song of Solomon 2: 12. The 'turtle' is the turtle-
dove.

26 *buskin.* The high, thick-soled boot worn by actors in ancient Athenian
tragedy, hence a figure for tragic drama itself.

27 *thymele.* The altar of Dionysus in the centre of the orchestra in an
ancient Greek theatre.

27 *by your will.* Aeschylus, *Prometheus Bound*, 286–9 (Loeb translation),
Oceanus arriving on his winged sea-monster: 'I am come to the goal
of a long journey in my passage to thee, Prometheus, guiding by mine
own will, without a bit, this swift-winged bird.'

27 *judge what I say.* 1 Corinthians 10: 15.

27 *Blot on my escutcheon.* Referring to the title of Browning's play, *A Blot in
the 'Scrutcheon* (1843).

27 *Thou canst not say I did it'.* Macbeth to the ghost of the murdered
Banquo, *Macbeth*, iii. iv. 50.

28 *monologue of Aeschylus.* An unfinished poem, traditionally called 'Aeschylus' Soliloquy', corresponds to this outline. For a long time the only
known manuscript of the fragment was in Browning's hand, and
thought to be by him, but Elizabeth Barrett's draft has been found by
Barbara Rosenbaum in the Huntington Library; Browning's manuscript is a copy of this.

28 *a sort of novel-poem.* Foreshadowing *Aurora Leigh* (1856).

28 *Geraldine's Courtship.* 'Lady Geraldine's Courtship', subtitled 'A
Romance of the Age': see Introduction, pp. ix–x.

29 *cypresses grow thick and dark.* The cypress tree is an emblem of mourning.
The reference here, as in similar phrases in subsequent letters, is to the
death of Elizabeth Barrett's brother Edward ('Bro'); for her detailed
account, see letter EB 20–3 Aug., pp. 105–6.

32 *Attic.* Greek.

32 *garden of cucumbers.* Isaiah 1: 8, where the sense is not, however, idyllic:

'And the daughter of Zion is left as a cottage in a vineyard, as a lodge in a garden of cucumbers, as a besieged city.'

33 *Paracelsus*. 16th-century Swiss physician, alchemist, and mystic, subject of Browning's poem *Paracelsus* (1835).

35 *tempted me & I did eat*. Eve on the serpent, Genesis 3: 13, which has 'beguiled' for 'tempted'.

36 *Mr. Chorley*. Henry Fothergill Chorley (1808–72), writer and critic on the staff of the *Athenaeum*, a friend of Browning as well as an epistolary acquaintance of Elizabeth Barrett. He was a trustee of the Brownings' marriage.

36 *Mary Howitt's 'Improvisatore'*. Mary Howitt's translation (1845) of Hans Christian Andersen's novel (1835).

36 *a grand vision of Prometheus*. Browning had suggested, in an omitted passage of letter RB 11 Mar., that Elizabeth Barrett should write a *Prometheus Fire-bearer*, i.e. the second play in the Prometheus trilogy, to come between Aeschylus' *Prometheus Bound* and Shelley's *Prometheus Unbound*.

36 *Milton's ground*. Referring to 'A Drama of Exile', which headed the 1844 *Poems*, and which is set in Eden after the Fall, and thus in the aftermath of *Paradise Lost*.

36 *all over the field*. One of Aesop's fables relates how a farmer told his three sons that he had left them a treasure in his field. They dug up the field, thus making it fertile.

37 *Cellarius*. 'A form of waltz named for, and presumably devised by, the Austrian dancing-master who brought the polka to Paris in 1840. It had reached London by mid-November 1844 and was a sensation' (Kintner, p. 47 n. 1).

38 *the quails sing*. The 'Syrenusae' are the 'siren-isles', three small islands now known as Li Galli off the coast of Sorrento, which Browning visited in 1844; see 'The Englishman in Italy', ll. 199–228. The 'scratches' refer to a sketch in the letter, reproduced in Kintner (opposite p. 46) and Karlin (opposite p. 85). See also p. 179 n. *says Mr Landor*.

38 *Lamia*. A serpent woman; cf. Keats's poem of that name.

40 *thankful breath*. The reference is to *Vivian Grey* (1826–7), Benjamin Disraeli's first novel. The episode takes place in Bk. v, ch. xv, the last of vol. iii, which ends with the death of Violet Fane in Vivian's arms. Browning's memory is, however, creatively at fault: the incident of Violet's uncle, Mr. Sherborne, delivering his 'lecture on Gothic architecture' (*sic*), and the narrator's 'second thoughts', occur on the same page (p. 307); moreover, the incident occurs with all the characters present in the ruins of an old castle, and the 'out-of-door feast' (which no one leaves to 'catch butterflies') takes place after it, not before.

41 *Alfieri.* Vittorio Alfieri (1749–1803), Italian tragedian, poet, and radical. He wrote nineteen tragedies; *Saul* (1782) is generally thought the finest.

42 *Flush's.* Elizabeth Barrett's spaniel, given to her by Mary Russell Mitford in Jan. 1841.

42 *let us hear more of her.* The opening sections of the poem had just been published in *Hood's Magazine*: see Browning's next letter, and p. 45 n. *poor Hood in his emergency.*

42 *sound speech not to be reproved.* Titus 2: 8.

43 *Phoibos Apollon.* The allusion is to the *Iliad* (bk. 1), in which Apollo inflicts plague on the Greek camp with his bow, killing the mules and dogs first, and then the men. Elizabeth Barrett translates the beginning of the passage in a letter of 31 Mar. 1846 (not included here). Browning's spelling follows the 'phonetic' convention which he maintained throughout his career and defended in the preface to his translation of Aeschylus' *Agamemnon* (1877).

44 *bianchissimi gigli.* 'Sweet-smelling flowers, purple roses, whitest lilies.'

44 *emerald atmosphere. Marenghi*, ll. 73–5, beginning 'Whene'er he found'.

44 *Monte Calvano.* Vico Alvano, a mountain near Sorrento. See 'The Englishman in Italy', ll. 133 f.

44 *Volanti.* 'The feast of the Madonna di Piedigrotta, celebrated on 8 September at the church of that name near the Grotto of Posilipo, originated in Charles III's victory over the Austrians in 1744 . . . the Royal Family drove there in silver-gilt coaches (*volanti*) to thank the Virgin for Charles's victory' (Kintner, pp. 56–7).

45 *poor Hood in his emergency.* Browning contributed to *Hood's Magazine and Comic Miscellany* during the final illness of Thomas Hood, the poet and humorist, who died on the day this letter was written. The poems were 'The Laboratory' and 'Claret and Tokay' (later part of 'Nationality in Drinks'), June 1844; 'Garden Fancies' ('The Flower's Name' and 'Sibrandus Schafnaburgensis'), July 1844; 'The Boy and the Angel', Aug. 1844; 'The Tomb at St. Praxed's' (later 'The Bishop Orders his Tomb at Saint Praxed's Church'), Mar. 1845; and ll. 1–215 of 'The Flight of the Duchess', Apr. 1845.

46 *tongue of men & of angels.* 1 Corinthians 13: 1.

46 *red hood of poppies.* A poetic euphemism for opium or morphine. See also letter EB 4 Feb., pp. 210–11.

47 *visible darkness . . . palpable obscure.* Milton, *Paradise Lost*, i. 63 ('darkness visible'), and ii. 406.

49 *flesh shall come again like a little child's.* 2 Kings 5: 14, Elisha's cure of Naaman's leprosy.

50 *corollary.* Attributed to Armand Jean du Plessis, Cardinal and Duc de Richelieu (1585–1642), minister in the reign of Louis XIII.

51 *ashamed.* Written over 'afraid' in MS.

52 *Colburn's.* The *New Monthly Magazine*, published by Henry Colburn (d. 1855)

52 *into the Red Sea.* Exodus 10: 19, God's dispersal of the plague of locusts by 'a mighty strong west wind'.

55 *morning.* Middle-class usage at this period for 'before dinner'.

55 *deaf relative of mine.* His Uncle Reuben, whose hearing had been damaged by a cricket ball.

56 τί ἐμοὶ καὶ σοί. 'What have I to do with thee?', the cry to Jesus of the 'unclean spirit' in the man who dwelt among the tombs, Mark 5: 7.

58 *one of my aunts whom I love.* Mrs Jane Hedley, her mother's sister.

60 *Dii meliora piis.* 'May the Gods grant better things to the upright', Virgil, *Georgics*, iii. 513.

60 *spirit stirring drum.* Othello, III. iii. 353.

60 *the heart is desperately wicked.* Jeremiah 17: 9: 'The heart is deceitful above all things, and desperately wicked: who can know it?'

60 *you and—Ottima!* Edmund Kean, the great actor whose performance as Richard III in 1832, the year before his death, fired Browning's ambition (see Maynard, pp. 221–6); Father Theobald Mathew (1790–1856), an Irish Franciscan preacher who greatly impressed Browning on a visit to London in 1843; Ottima, a character in Part I of *Pippa Passes*, is guilty of adultery and murder.

60 *John Mill wondered.* See p. 25 n. *sane human being.*

60 *Songs of the Poets—No. 1. M.P.* I am unable to explain this allusion. Kintner's suggestion that it refers to *Pauline* cannot be correct, since the reference is clearly to work in progress. It may refer to the 'talking to the wind' which Browning says he has 'begun' (see letter RB 13 Jan., p. 50 and n. *I must say*, but 'Songs of the Poets' does not bring to mind *Christmas-Eve*, the poem most likely referred to there, or indeed anything else Browning is known to have been writing at the time.

60 *sleeken every word as to a bird.* Elizabeth Barrett, 'A Portrait', ll. 53–4.

61 *corvus (picus)—Mirandola!*) 'Corvus' is the Latin for carrion crow; 'picus' is the magpie, *Pica caudata*, which belongs to the family *Corvidae*; Pico della Mirandola (1463–94), Italian humanist and philosopher.

61 *Dogberry's satisfaction.* 'I hope here be truths' is spoken by Pompey in *Measure for Measure*, II. i. 136, not Dogberry in *Much Ado about Nothing*. Kintner suggests that Browning 'may have been confused by Hazlitt, who quotes this correctly as the motto for his *Character of the Country People* but also attributes it to Dogberry'.

62 *evil spirit.* The Old Testament King Saul appears in 1 Samuel; his father Kish's asses in ch. 9; and he is comforted by David playing the harp in ch. 16. Saul of Tarsus was the name of St Paul before his

conversion; the phrase 'Saul (who is also called Paul)' occurs in Acts 13: 9.

62 *R Browning*. The signature is a near-illegible scrawl.

62 *high fantastical*. Orsino in *Twelfth Night*, I. i. 14–15: 'so full of shapes is fancy, / That it alone is high fantastical.'

63 *Bootes*. The northern constellation also known as the Wagoner, which includes the bright star Arcturus.

63 *Pray do not mock me*. Lear in *King Lear*, IV. vii. 59, replying to Cordelia's 'No, sir, you must not kneel'.

64 *on the like subject*. In *A New Spirit of the Age* Horne wrote of Elizabeth Barrett's knowledge of Greek, Hebrew, and Chaldean.

64 *cothurns*. Buskins; see p. 26 n.

66 *herein enclosed*. The 'fragment' reads: 'me on Tuesday, or Wednesday? if on Tuesday, I shall come by the three o'clock train; if on Wednesday, *early* in the Morn^g, as I shall be anxious to secure rooms .. so that y^r Uncle and Arabel may come up on Thursday.'

64 *côté gauche*. 'Left side', with a pun on 'gauche', 'awkward'.

68 *dixit Casaubonus*. A saying of Casaubon', i.e. an authoritative reading, alluding to the great classical scholar Isaac Casaubon (1559–1614).

69 *the poem*. Tennyson's 'Timbuctoo', winner of the Chancellor's Medal at Cambridge in 1829. 'Oenone' and 'Morte d'Arthur', mentioned below, were first published in 1832 and 1842 respectively.

70 *bien prié*. 'Pleaded with' (lit. 'well prayed to', hence 'liturgy' further on).

71 *dismisses you*. The epigraph, attributed to Chapman by Tennyson but probably his own: 'Deep in that lion-haunted inland lies / A mystick city, goal of high emprise.' The 'good epithet of "green Europe" ' occurs in I. 3. The 'picture of a Vestal' occurs early on, in II. 32–36:

> At midnight, in the lone Acropolis,
> Before the awful Genius of the place
> Kneels the pale Priestess in deep faith, the while
> Above her head the weak lamp dips and winks
> Unto the fearful summoning without.

The poem ends (II. 246–8): 'I / Was left alone on Calpe, and the Moon / Had fallen from the night, and all was dark!'

72 *flowers be sent you in a letter*. Alluding to Elizabeth Barrett's poem, 'A Flower in a Letter'.

73 *Mr. Boyd*. The blind classical scholar Hugh Stuart Boyd (1781–1848), a friend from girlhood; see Kelley and Hudson, ii. 339–41.

75 *what vaulting Ambition once did for himself*. *Macbeth*, I. vii. 27–8: 'Vaulting ambition, which o'erleaps itself / And falls on the other.'

77 *Asolo*. A small town near Venice, where Browning had stayed in 1838,

the setting for *Pippa Passes*. The phrase means 'Alas, the evil weed flourishes!'

77 *old French friend of mine*. Kelley and Hudson, *Checklist*p. 46, records a letter of 27 June 1845 to a 'C. Caillard' in which Browning warmly anticipates a meeting.

77 *wintry chasm*. The punishment of Prometheus, chained to a rock in the Caucasus; Browning's rational arguments will pin down his friend's credulous belief in unscientific practices such as mesmerism. Denis Diderot (1713–84), mentioned below, was a leading philosopher of the Enlightenment and editor of its rationalist Bible, the *Encyclopédie*.

77 *people who don't like caviare. Hamlet*, II. ii. 465–6: 'the play, I remember, pleased not the million; 'twas caviare to the general.'

78 *son of Felicia*. Felicia Hemans (1793–1835), now remembered for a handful of anthology pieces ('Casabianca', 'The Landing of the Pilgrim Fathers'); Elizabeth Barrett's tribute to her appeared in *The Seraphim, and Other Poems* (1838). Charles (1817–76) was her youngest son. She and her husband separated for life in 1818; Elizabeth Barrett compares this to the widowhood of Vittoria Colonna (1492–1547), the poet and friend of Tasso and Michelangelo.

78 *Shelley's son*. Percy Florence, only surviving son of Shelley and Mary Shelley; he was said not to be in sympathy with his mother's devotion to his father's memory.

78 *Mrs. Jameson*. Anna Brownwell Jameson (1794–1860), writer, critic, and art historian. She was already a friend of Browning's when Elizabeth Barrett first met her in 1844. It was to Mrs Jameson that the Brownings turned for advice and help on their arrival in Paris after their elopement, and she accompanied them from there to Pisa.

78 *Miss Martineau*. Harriet Martineau (1802–76), radical and feminist writer in every genre (fiction, history, travel, philosophy, social and political polemic), began corresponding with Elizabeth Barrett in 1843. She had known Browning at the time of his *Paracelsus* (1835) and during the composition of *Sordello* (1840), but the friendship had since cooled.

78 *pro aris et focis*. Adapting a martial tag from the Roman historian Sallust (86–34 BC): 'pro patria, pro liberis, pro aris atque focis suis' ('on behalf of their country, their children, their altars, and their hearths'), to signify the virtues of domesticity for women.

79 *George Sand*. Pseudonym of Amandine-Aurore Dupin, Baroness Dudevant (1804–76), French novelist, notorious for her many liaisons (esp. with Chopin and Alfred de Musset), her political radicalism, and her 'scandalous' work, which Elizabeth Barrett had equivocally admired for several years (see e.g. her letters to Mary Russell Mitford, and the two sonnets addressed to Sand in the 1844 *Poems*). *Lélia* (*sic*, 1833) is one of a series of anti-conventional romances.

79 *hate of hate.* Tennyson, 'The Poet', 1. 3.

79 *Dr Elliotson's great boney fingers.* John Elliotson (1791–1868), physician, whose interest in unorthodox medicine led to his resignation from his post in the University of London in 1838. In 'phreno-magnetism' the practitioner exercises 'magnetic' influence over the patient by touching parts of the head whose properties are denoted by phrenology (see p. 24 n. *Phrenologists*).

80 *Mr Kenyon's door.* Kenyon lived at 40 York Terrace, about half a mile away. See also Landis, p. 134.

82 *Dr Chambers.* William Frederick Chambers (1786–1855), physician-in-ordinary to Queen Victoria and a leading London physician.

83 *Sybil.* Disraeli's novel, recently published.

86 *a great cloud of witnesses.* Hebrews 12: 1.

86 *this letter.* From the Revd George Barrett Hunter (not a relation despite the name), an Independent minister whom Elizabeth Barrett had known at Sidmouth when the Barrett family moved there from Hope End in 1832, and who was now living in London. He was a widower, several years older than she, in love with her and neurotically jealous of her success as a poet and her other friendships; for their relationship, see Karlin, pp. 156–8. Elizabeth Barrett was to nickname Hunter 'Chiappino', after the embittered 'hero' of Browning's play *A Soul's Tragedy*: see letter EB 5 Apr., pp. 234–5.

87 *Coleridge's daughter.* Sara Coleridge (1802–52). Elizabeth Barrett had recently corresponded with her, but this remark was probably relayed by Kenyon (Kintner, p. 127 n. 4).

87 *my Seraphim days.* The late 1830s: *The Seraphim, and Other Poems* was published in 1838.

88 *the Lyre & the Crown.* In Revelation 8: 10–11 the star Wormwood falls from heaven and poisons the waters. Browning's preface to the first edition of *Paracelsus* (1835) compares the scenes of the poem to stars which the reader's 'co-operating fancy' must connect 'into one constellation—a Lyre or a Crown'.

88 *Hood poems.* See p. 45 n. *poor Hood in his emergency.*

88 *18 July.* The exact date cannot be ascertained, because the letter was sent in a parcel with the manuscripts of Browning's poems from *Hood's Magazine*. The wrapper of the parcel is not extant, and the letter itself is undated.

89 *a poem you are to see.* This poem cannot be identified with certainty. Kintner (p. 129 n. 1) suggests 'Pictor Ignotus'; another possibility is that it forms part of a passage which Browning later cut from a speech by Ogniben in *A Soul's Tragedy*, and to which he alludes in his letters of 18 Mar. and 1 Apr. 1846 (not included here).

90 *as you read it.* 'The Flower's Name'; l. 20: 'Its soft meandering Spanish name'; *Sordello*, i. 909–10: 'some azure damsel-fly, / Born of the simmering quiet, there to die.'

91 *opening lines of this poem.* In *Hood's Magazine* the poem opens: 'Now I have tied thy glass mask on tightly, / May gaze thro' these faint smokes curling whitely'. Browning revised the first line for publication in *Dramatic Romances and Lyrics*: 'Now that I, tying thy glass mask tightly,'.

91 *querulous queries.* Elizabeth Barrett's critical notes on 'The Flight of the Duchess' (for the epithet 'boar-pinner' applied below to the narrator's father, see 11. 38–44 of the poem). These notes, along with her further comments on other poems of *Dramatic Romances and Lyrics*, and on *Luria* and *A Soul's Tragedy*, are now in Wellesley College Library.

94 *Now sh^d there?* The reference is to 1. 512; Browning revised it according to Elizabeth Barrett's first suggestion, ignoring her retraction.

95 *those schismatiques / of Amsterdam.* Donne, 'The Will', ll. 20–1.

96 *garrulous God-innocence.* Elizabeth Barrett, 'A Vision of Poets'. The phrase, at 1. 297, applies to Homer; Browning then refers to the description of Shelley at 11. 406–7, and that of Hesiod at 11. 310–12; 'the Moon's regality will hear no praise' comes from 11. 53–4.

96 *Anne Radcliffe.* Ann [*sic*] Radcliffe (1764–1823), author of Gothic novels such as *The Mysteries of Udolpho*.

97 *Berthas and Caterinas and Geraldines.* 'Bertha in the Lane', 'Catarina to Camoens', 'Lady Geraldine's Courtship'.

99 *Mariana in the moated Grange.* An allusion to Tennyson's poem 'Mariana', first published in 1832.

99 *what you do for me.* Referring to a further instalment of Elizabeth Barrett's notes on his poems (see p. 91 n. *querulous queries*).

100 *first season of German Opera here.* Beethoven's opera *Fidelio* was first produced in London as part of this season, at the King's Theatre in the spring of 1832.

101 *Lady Geraldine, you would!.* 'Lady Geraldine's Courtship', 1. 234. The speaker is proposing (unsuccessfully) to Lady Geraldine.

101 *Consuelo.* A novel by George Sand (see p. 79 n. *George Sand*), published 1842–3, which Browning had been reading at Elizabeth Barrett's recommendation. Below, Browning plays on two senses of 'que la Femme parle': 'let Woman speak' and 'how the woman goes on'.

105 *my brother whom I loved so.* Edward ('Bro'). The aunt with whom Elizabeth Barrett stayed in Torquay was Arabella Graham-Clarke, her mother's sister.

105 *Gismond.* 'Count Gismond', published in *Dramatic Lyrics* (1842); she quotes 11. 64–66.

106 *Wilson.* Elizabeth Wilson, who had been Elizabeth Barrett's personal maid since May 1844, and who was to witness her marriage and accompany her to Italy.

106 *an old friend in rather an ill temper.* The Revd George Barrett Hunter. See p. 86 n. *this letter* and letter EB 10 Aug., p. 283.

107 *Saul.* 'Saul' was published as a fragment of 189 lines, divided into nine sections, in *Dramatic Romances and Lyrics* (1845). It was the draft of these lines which Browning showed to Elizabeth Barrett, bringing the MS with him to the meeting on 26 Aug. at which he must have expressed his doubts about the poem, since these do not appear in a letter. Browning completed the poem for publication in *Men and Women* (1855), when the alternating long and short lines of the original were amalgamated into single long lines. The 'sixty lines thrown away' therefore probably refer, as Kintner suggests, to the thirty-one lines of the poem which in 1855 constitute the tenth section, continuing the poem from the end of the 1845 fragment.

110 *the Pisa affair.* During this period Elizabeth Barrett was seeking her father's approval for the plan (first mooted in July: see letter EB 16–17 July, p. 88) to send her abroad for the winter of 1845–6. On medical advice the destination had changed from Malta or Alexandria to Pisa, and Elizabeth Barrett would have required the escort of a brother and sister. Others besides Browning were urging her to go whether her father approved or not. The reason for Mr Barrett's reluctance to give his approval, and the consequences of the 'affair' for Elizabeth Barrett's relationship with him and with Browning, are discussed in Karlin, pp. 94–110.

110 *31 Aug.–1 Sept.* The portion of the letter printed here was written on Sunday, 31 Aug., before the meeting on Monday, 1 Sept. A postcript (not included) was added after the meeting; it does not concern the points Elizabeth Barrett is making here, which are in reply to Browning's letter of 30 Aug.

112 *happiness of your life.* Letter RB 1 Mar., p. 29.

114 βα .. ϱβαϱίζων. As Kintner argues, the evidence that Elizabeth Barrett's family nickname 'Ba' was pronounced to rhyme with 'car' is overwhelming. Kenyon's 'Ba-by' is a visual, not an aural, pun; see letter EB 7 Oct., p. 135, for another of his puns on her 'Ba-lambishness'.

116 *Fitzroy Kelly.* Fitzroy Kelly (1796–1880) became Solicitor-General on 29 June 1845. Browning is alluding to family pressure on him to study law (or a similar profession), pressure he has successfully overcome (see the close of the preceding paragraph).

116 *considering the lilies how they grow.* Matthew 6: 28: 'Consider the lilies of the field, how they grow; they toil not, neither do they spin.'

126 *as you once said.* Letter EB 17 Feb., p. 20, and see n. *my soul among lions.*

126 *Cerito.* Fanny Cerrito (*sic*) (1817–1909), Italian ballerina and choreographer, immensely successful in her London appearances at this period. She married in 1845.

133 *a boon of you*. The return of the love-letter she had sent back after their first meeting: see pp. 56 ff. She made the request nearly six weeks later: see p. 148.

134 *Duke of Palmella*. Pedro di Lonsa-Holstein, Duke of Palmella. He did not give in to George's blandishments; he and his entourage took all the cabin space for the sailing on the 20th.

134 *Your spring-song*. 'Home-Thoughts, from Abroad': Browning took Elizabeth Barrett's advice about giving the poem a title. In *Dramatic Romances and Lyrics* the poem consisted of three 'fragments': 'Oh, to be in England', 'Here's to Nelson's memory' (now part of 'Nationality in Drinks'), and 'Nobly Cape Saint Vincent' (now 'Home-Thoughts from the Sea').

140 *slaughter in the bathroom*. In Aeschylus' *Agamemnon*, Cassandra (*sic*) foretells the murder of Agamemnon in his bath by his wife Clytemnestra and her lover Aegisthus.

142 *I might devour*. 1 Peter 5: 8: 'your adversary the devil, as a roaring lion, walketh about, seeking whom he may devour'.

143 *Doctors' Commons*. The court where a matrimonial settlement would be drawn up.

146 *lord of infinite space*. *Hamlet*, II. ii. 264–6: 'I could be bounded in a nutshell, and count myself a king of infinite space, were it not that I have bad dreams'; also Donne, 'The Good Morrow', l. 11: '[Love] makes one little room, an every where'.

146 *corn laws*. Measures taxing the import of grain, which were under attack from liberals as one of the causes of famine in Ireland.

146 *Harriet Martineau's parliament*. Harriet Martineau was an advocate of women's suffrage, which neither Browning nor Elizabeth Barrett supported.

147 *gate of the prison*. Acts 5: 19, the imprisonment of the apostles: 'the angel of the Lord by night opened the prison doors, and brought them forth'.

149 *for Mr Kenyon to read!*). *Dramatic Romances and Lyrics*, published on this day, was dedicated to Kenyon.

151 *stands alone?* From Browning's play *Colombe's Birthday* (1844), III. 231: 'When is man strong until he feels alone?' referring to the heroine, Colombe.

152 *because you cared for me*. Letter RB 23 Oct., p. 142.

152 *earth's immortalities*. The title of Browning's poem, recently published in *Dramatic Romances and Lyrics*.

153 *talk nonsense*. Compare this story with 'Which?' in *Asolando* (1889), Browning's last collection. This is one of the fruits of Browning's rereading of the correspondence late in life: see McAleer, pp. 92–3.

153 *you called him once to me*. Letter RB 26 Feb., p. 26.

156 *Past and Future*. Elizabeth Barrett quotes the first line of this sonnet,

'My future will not copy fair my past', in *Sonnets from the Portuguese*, xlii, which reverses its melancholy conclusion. As Kintner points out, Sonnet xlii comes earlier in the sequence in the original manuscript (British Library Add. MS. 43487), where it is numbered xvii. See also next four notes.

157 *always you do. Sonnets from the Portuguese*, xvi, l. 1: 'And yet, because thou overcomest so'.

158 *Messiah.* Combining two texts from John: 5: 4, the healing pool of Bethesda: 'an angel went down at a certain season into the pool, and troubled the water', and 4: 25, the Samarian woman: 'I know that Messias cometh, which is called Christ'. Note also *Sonnets from the Portuguese*. xlii, l. 14: 'New angel mine'.

159 *female friends. Sonnets from the Portuguese*, xviii, ll. 1–2: 'I never gave a lock of hair away / To a man, dearest, except this to thee'.

160 *pure merchandise. Sonnets from the Portuguese*, xix, ll. 1–2: 'The soul's Rialto hath its merchandise; / I barter curl for curl upon that mart'.

160 *horn gate from the ivory.* True dreams come from the former, false from the latter: *Odyssey* xix. 562–5.

162 *Fri. 28–Sat. 29 Nov.* Only passages from the Friday section of this letter are included here.

162 *fate of a city.* Scylla, daughter of Nisus, king of Megara, cut off the lock of her father's hair, betraying the city to its besieger Minos, with whom she was in love. The story is in Ovid, *Metamorphoses*, viii.

162 *ego et rex meus.* 'I and my king', a phrase attributed to Cardinal Wolsey; see *Henry VIII*, iii. ii. 314.

162 *Haroun Alraschid.* Caliph of Baghdad (786–809) and a leading character in the *Arabian Nights*. Browning mentions him in *Sordello* (1840), v. 447.

164 *Spirit of the age.* This portrait, an engraving by J. C. Armytage of a sketch by Beard, is reproduced among other places in Kintner (facing p. 306) and Karlin (facing p. 116). See p. 6 n. *Mr Horne.*

165 *that paper I spoke of.* As Kintner suggests (p. 317 n. 1), Browning seems to have 'proposed some document to be given Mr Barrett in the event that he discovered and violently objected to the frequency of Browning's visits'.

166 *only calling for your boots!* Letter RB 24 May, p. 62.

167 *saw the unspeakable things.* 2 Corinthians 12: 2–4.

170 *Ba .. and that is you! Sonnets from the Portuguese*, xxxiii ('Yes, call me by my pet-name!').

170 *testify what I have seen.* John 3: 11.

172 *Commination Service.* In the Anglican liturgy, a recital of Divine threatenings against sinners, to be read after the Litany on Ash Wednesday and at other times. The Barrett family fortune had been founded on the slave-worked sugar plantations of the West Indies.

172 *speaking of mysteries.* 1 Corinthians 14: 8.

174 *no more 'of grace'.* Alluding to the Calvinist doctrine that salvation could not be earned by good works, but was an arbitrary gift of God's grace.

174 *how great is that darkness.* Matthew 6: 23.

178 *a Pitt-diamond or a Pilgrim-pearl.* 'The Regent or Pitt diamond, one of the French Crown Jewels, weighed 410 carats when found. The Pilgrim pearl—'La Pellegrina'—was perhaps the largest perfectly globular pearl ever found: 28 carats' (Kintner, p. 344 n. 1)

178 *the world must go on. Much Ado About Nothing,* II. iii. 262–3: 'the world must be peopled'.

178 *your flowers live with me. Sonnets from the Portuguese,* xliv ('Beloved, thou hast brought me many flowers').

179 *misomonsism.* A neologism meaning 'hatred of the world, of society'.

179 στοά. 'Stoa', portico, which gave its name to the Stoic school of philosophy. The 'conversation-teachers', however, seem more like Sophists than Stoics.

179 *says Mr Landor.* For Landor, see p. 18 n. *Mr Landor.* Browning's poem 'The Englishman in Italy', published in *Dramatic Romances and Lyrics,* contained an allusion to the 'isles of the siren': see p. 38 n. *the quails sing.* Landor's poem 'To Robert Browning', written after receiving his presentation copy of *Dramatic Romances and Lyrics,* closed with the lines: 'the breeze / Of Alpine heights thou playest with, borne on / Beyond Sorrento and Amalfi, where / The Siren waits thee, singing song for song.'

181 *while his foot was on the stair.* Letter RB 1 Mar., p. 30.

182 *teaching of God!* See *Sordello,* vi., ll. 619–26.

183 *a parcel of books.* Harriet Martineau, *Forest and Game Law Tales;* Philip James Bailey (1816–1902), founder of the 'Spasmodic School', a new edition of *Festus* (first published 1839); Margaret Fuller (1810–50) (feminist and Transcendentalist, later a friend of the Brownings in Italy), *Women* [sic] *in the Nineteenth Century.*

183 *book in the tree.* 'Sibrandus Schafnaburgensis', second section of *Garden Fancies,* recently published in *Dramatic Romances and Lyrics.*

183 *wore a jewel in his head. As You Like It,* II. i. 12–14: 'Sweet are the uses of adversity, / Which like the toad, ugly and venomous, / Wears yet a precious jewel in his head'.

184 *As the doves fly to the windows.* Isaiah 60: 8. Elizabeth Barrett had used the same image in a letter anticipating her return to Wimpole Street after Bro's death at Torquay (Kenyon, i. 88).

184 *Tues.–Wed., 6–7 Jan.* The Wednesday portion of this letter is not included here.

185 *esteem.* In Elizabeth Barrett's poem 'Bertha in the Lane' the narrator

overhears Robert, her lover, courting her younger sister: 'And he said in his deep speech / That he owed me all *esteem*' (11. 129–30).

186 *this silver flooding.* Isaiah 35: 1, 7: 'The wilderness and the solitary place shall be glad for them: and the desert shall rejoice, and blossom as the rose . . . And the parched ground shall become a pool, and the thirsty land springs of water.'

187 *the history of it. Pauline* was published anonymously in 1833. No copies were sold, and Browning became ashamed of the poem, preferring to date his literary career from *Paracelsus* (1835). In several copies of *Pauline* given privately to friends he wrote self-justifying 'prefaces'; the most famous is in the copy annotated by J. S. Mill (see p. 25 n. *sane human being*), which explains that the poem was 'written in pursuance of a foolish plan . . . which had for its object the enabling me to assume & realize I know not how many different characters;—meanwhile the world was never to guess that . . . the respective Authors of this poem, the other novel, such an opera, such a speech &c &c were no other than one and the same individual'. There is no evidence that Browning ever showed the poem to Elizabeth Barrett, though he may have done so after their marriage; he suppressed public knowledge of it until the threat of pirated publication forced him to include it in the *Poetical Works* of 1868.

187 *Frank Talfourd's theatricals.* Frank was the son of the lawyer and playwright Thomas Noon Talfourd, a friend of Browning's; the 'theatricals' were amateur performances of e.g. Ben Jonson's *Every Man in his Humour*, in which Dickens and others took part.

187 *the Act.* Act IV of *Luria*.

187 *path-preparer.* Mark 1: 3, alluding to John the Baptist: 'The voice of one crying in the wilderness, Prepare ye the way of the Lord, make his paths straight', itself quoting Isaiah 40: 3.

189 *leaning out of the window.* Letter EB 27 Feb., p. 29.

189 *surpassed them all.* Proverbs 31: 29: 'Many daughters have done virtuously, but thou excellest them all.'

192 *King's memoirs.* William King, *Political and Literary Anecdotes of his Own Times* (1818), p. 8, the prayer of a common soldier before the battle of Blenheim.

192 *Werther.* Goethe, *The Sorrows of Young Werther* (1774).

193 *Thurs–Fri., 15–16 Jan.* The Thursday portion of this letter, a short paragraph, is not included here.

195 *Bellona.* The Roman goddess of war.

196 *holy, just and good.* Romans 7: 12: 'Wherefore the law is holy, and the commandment holy, and just, and good.' See also next note.

196 *reasonable service.* Romans 12: 1: 'present your bodies a living sacrifice, holy, acceptable unto God, which is your reasonable service.'

198 *mollitious chambers.* 'Quarles uses the adjective several times but not for "chambers." Much closer . . . is Browning's own "mollitious alcoves" (*Sordello*, iii, 129)' (Kintner, p. 405 n. 1). Francis Quarles (1592–1644); his *Emblems* (1635) was a favourite book of Browning's.

198 *a constellation of them all.* 'Epithalamion . . . on St. Valentine's Day', ll. 33–6: 'Up, up, fair Bride, and call, / Thy stars, from out their several boxes, take / Thy rubies, pearls, and diamonds forth, and make / Thyself a constellation, of them all'.

199 *Bramah pens.* One of the many inventions of Joseph Bramah (1749–1814).

200 *against his will.* Captain William Surtees Cook, by reason of his distant cousinship, was one of the few people who had visiting rights in Wimpole Street; he needed to conciliate Mr Barrett in order to carry on his clandestine courtship of Henrietta Barrett, whom he eventually married in 1850. (They, like the Brownings, were cast off by Mr Barrett.)

201 *striking at it with one's partizan. Hamlet*, I. i. 140, the disappearance of the Ghost: '[Marcellus] Shall I strike at it with my partisan [spear]?'

207 *crown of the Czar.* Browning had travelled to Russia in 1834, attached to a diplomatic mission, and presumably saw the imperial crown jewels on a visit to the Kremlin.

207 *Fri.–Sun., 30 Jan.–1 Feb.* Elizabeth Barrett began this letter on Friday evening; it is placed after Browning's letter of 31 Jan., which replies to hers of Friday *morning*. Nothing from the Sunday portion of the letter is included here.

207 *a crisis long since.* Letter RB 24 May, p. 59.

209 *distaste for them.* Almost certainly, as Kintner suggests, a reference to Mary Russell Mitford.

211 *Mr. Jago.* Francis Robert Jago (d. 1862), physician, guardian, and later husband of Elizabeth Barrett's friend, Eleanor Bordman.

214 *16 Feb.* Elizabeth Barrett wrote two separate letters on this day, one in the morning and one in the evening, but sent them together. The extract here is from the first letter.

215 *J. Baptista Porta.* Giovanni Battista della Porta (*c.* 1538–1615), Italian natural philosopher; the passage is from his treatise *Magiae naturalis*, xx. vii (Kintner, p. 486 n. 1).

217 *the entomology of it all.* Letter RB 16 May, p. 52.

220 *Robert Hall.* English Baptist divine (1764–1831).

221 *Spring gets on!* A sprig of hawthorn was enclosed with the letter.

221 *a yellow rose sent in a letter.* Letter RB 14 June, p. 72.

223 *finding you here in the morning.* i.e. before dinner. It was unusual for Mr Barrett to return home in the early afternoon.

225 *after rouge one expects noir.* 'Rouge et noir' (red and black) are conventional opposites in French; Stendhal's novel *Le Rouge et le noir* was published in 1830.

227 *facilis descensus.* A tag from *Aeneid* vi. 126: 'The descent [to the Underworld] is easy.'

230 *bdellium . . . mystic land of the four rivers.* Alluding to Genesis 2: 10–14.

231 *thrown at her.* 'Tarpeia, the daughter of Tarpeius, the governor of the citadel of Rome, promised to open the gates of the city to the Sabines, provided they gave her their gold bracelets, or as she expressed it, what they carried on their left hands. Tatius, the king of the Sabines, consented, and as he entered the gates, to punish her perfidy, he threw not only his bracelet but his shield upon Tarpeia. His followers imitated his example, and Tarpeia was crushed under the weight of the bracelets and shields of the Sabine army' (*Lemprière's Classical Dictionary*, 12th ed., London, 1823).

231 *we two met on the stairs.* Letter RB 19 Jan., p. 198.

232 *Walter the Penniless.* Associate of Peter the Hermit in the 'People's Crusade', 1096.

232 *Miss Burdett Coutts.* Angela Georgina Burdett-Coutts (1814–1906), granddaughter of the banker Thomas Coutts (1735–1822).

233 εἴδωλου. 'Eidolon', image.

234 *a Chiappino.* The Revd George Barrett Hunter.

235 *after you.* See 'Life in a Love'; the phrase 'house of life' occurs in 'Transcendentalism', l. 45. Both poems were published in *Men and Women* (1855).

235 *Tennyson's blackbird.* 'The Blackbird', ll. 1–4: 'O blackbird! sing me something well: / While all the neighbours shoot thee round, / I keep smooth plats of fertile ground, / Where thou may'st warble, eat and dwell.'

236 *First of all, kiss.* In the preceding letters (not included), Browning and Elizabeth Barrett had been arguing about the morality of duelling, Elizabeth Barrett strongly disagreeing with Browning's justification of it in certain circumstances. (For a discussion of this episode, see Karlin, pp. 149–53.) Here she alludes to the fact that when Browning was ill or 'vexed' his handwriting got bigger. The letter she quotes actually begins: 'First of all, kiss me, dearest'.

236 *read by your light.* A phrase from Webster's preface to *The White Devil*, 'wishing that what I write may be read by their light', which Browning also used in his dedication to Landor of *Bells and Pomegranates*, no. viii (*Luria* and *A Soul's Tragedy*), published four days after this letter.

237 *strangers and pilgrims.* Hebrews 11: 13.

239 *Greek burning glasses.* The weapon with which Archimedes is said to have set on fire the Roman ships besieging Syracuse in 211 BC.

239 *Mrs Procter*. Anne Procter (1799–1886), hostess of a salon based around the legal and literary friends of her husband, B. W. Procter (1787–1874), a lawyer whose pen-name was 'Barry Cornwall'. The Procters were friends of Browning's, but Mrs Procter had a sharp tongue. Elizabeth Barrett, in turn, alludes to the fact that Procter's last volume had been published in 1832.

240 *it came to you sleeping*. In the closing passage of her letter of 17 April 1846 (not included here), Elizabeth Barrett wrote: 'I am glad in looking back . . . that I did not assume anything .. stretch out my hand for anything . . . It is always when one is asleep that the dream-angels come.'

241 *in the sonnets*. Sonnet xxix, l. 7: 'Desiring this man's art, and that man's scope'.

241 *6.45*. This is probably a mistake for 5.45. No other visit lasted so long; neither Browning nor Elizabeth Barrett remarked on it in subsequent letters; and the time came within fifteen minutes of Mr Barrett's return from the City.

242 *Morven*. Ossian was a legendary Celtic bard whose 'works' were fabricated by the Scottish writer James Macpherson (1736–1796); 'Morven' or Morvern, part of the Scottish Highlands.

244 *the 14th*. That is, the 14th *letter* (letter EB 21 May (p. 56) in this edition); Browning is explaining how he confused the date of the meeting with the number of Elizabeth Barrett's letters.

246 *in derision*. Psalms 2: 4.

246 *May 7th*. Browning's birthday, hence the formal date; he had told her in his letter of the same date (not included here) to 'forget' his birthday in favour of the anniversary of their first meeting: 'my day, as I told you, is the 20th—my true, happiest day!' (cf. Elizabeth Barrett in letter EB 19 May (p. 250).

246 *Miss Bayley's coming*. Sarah Bayley (d. 1868), a close friend of Kenyon's, who called her 'the deepest thinker for a woman, he ever met with'. (Kelley and Hudson, v. 141).

250 *to which I hearken*. Elizabeth Barrett's 'Catarina to Camoens', ll. 11–12: 'Other praises disregarding, / I but hearkened that of yours'.

251 *last year at this hour*. Kintner (p. 715 n. 2) compares *Sonnets from the Portuguese*, xx.

253 *the Statesmen*. Browning had helped John Forster complete his *Life of Strafford*, published in 1836 in the series *Eminent British Statesmen*.

253 *completest expression of my being*. A phrase from Elizabeth Barrett's preface to *Poems* (1844).

253 *for a memorial*. This poem is unidentified and, in the opinion of the present editor, was never written. Kintner's suggestion (p. 726 n. 5) that it is an anticipation of 'By the Fire-side' is unconvincing.

253 *it is not true*. Elizabeth Barrett had heard a rumour that Browning was engaged to be married (to someone else).

254 *broad & narrow guage*. Referring to the debate between the supporters of the broad gauge railway track, who included Brunel, and those of the narrow gauge, the system which eventually prevailed.

256 *'balancing my jewel'*. Browning had written on 28 May 1846 (letter not included): 'if my jewel must be taken from me, let some eagle stoop down for it suddenly . . . don't let me have to remember, tho' but in a minute of life afterwards, that I let it drop into the sea thro' foolishly balancing it in my open hand over the water.' See also letter RB 25 Sept., p. 129, and 27 Sept., p. 133.

259 *Lord Monteagle*. Thomas Spring-Rice, 1st Baron Monteagle (1790–1866). He had been a prominent Whig politician in the 1820s and 1830s (Chancellor of the Exchequer, 1835–9), but since his elevation to the peerage in 1839 he had retired from public life; Browning's expectation of his forming a government was unfounded.

259 *you give Tennyson for nothing*. Tennyson had been awarded a Civil List pension of £200 in September 1845.

260 *wrath of man*. James 1: 20: 'the wrath of man worketh not the righteousness of God.'

263 *some words to that effect*. 'Mr Browning and I have grown to be devoted friends I assure you—and he writes me letters praying to be let in, quite heart-moving and irresistible. . . . And then he writes letters to me with Attic contractions, saying he "*loves*" me. Who can resist *that*? But do not talk of it if you please, although it is all in the uttermost innocence' (Miller p. 239, letter of 18 Mar. 1845).

265 *flight not being in the winter*. Mark 13: 18, alluding to the Last Days.

265 *inexpressive He*. Orlando in *As You Like It*, III. ii. 9–10: 'carve on every tree / The fair, the chaste, and unexpressive she.'

265 *Peel's speech and farewell*. Sir Robert Peel resigned as Prime Minister, 29 June.

267 *famous in counsel*. 'The name is actually Old High German and means "bright in fame" ' (Kintner, p. 830).

267 *in the lane with Bertha*. See p. 185 n. *esteem*.

267 *the earth noise intervene*. Quoting Elizabeth Barrett's 'Catarina to Camoens', 11. 109–11.

270 *write again*. In her second letter, Elizabeth Barrett reported no further comments by her father.

271 *Monte Cristo*. Elizabeth Barrett had expressed her delight at Alexandre Dumas's *Le Comte de Monte Cristo* (1844–5) in a letter of 7 June 1846 (not included here).

273 *that happy year*. Alluding to her year's liaison with Jules Sandeau, described in *Lettres d'un voyageur* (1834–6).

273 *Countess Peppa.* Countess Carducci, a friend Browning had met in Rome during his 1844 visit.

274 *locusts & wild honey.* Mark 1: 6, the food of John the Baptist in the wilderness.

276 *a better footing.* Flush had bitten Browning again at the meeting on 21 July, and had been beaten by Wilson; in her letter of the following day (not included here) Elizabeth Barrett gives an account of his disgrace: 'I did not forgive him till nearly eight o'clock . . . And I have not yet given him your cakes.'

276 *pardon it all.* The following statement was written on a separate piece of paper.

282 *an unpleasant impression.* See p. 223 n. *finding you here in the morning.*

283 *a miserable degradation.* Alluding to the Revd George Barrett Hunter, who was continuing to persecute Elizabeth Barrett with unwanted attentions, and had begun to make offensive comments about Browning.

285 *Miss Campbell.* The subject of a false rumour of Browning's engagement.

285 *Brauwer . . . Teniers.* Adriaen Brouwer or Brauwer (1605/6–38), and David Teniers the Younger (1610–90), Flemish painters known for their genre scenes of common life. For Ostade, see p. 25 n. Ostade.

285 *the Sistine Altar piece.* Michelangelo's *Last Judgement.*

286 *that poor Chiappino.* The Revd George Barrett Hunter.

289 *your income.* In her letter of 5 Aug. 1846 (not included here), Elizabeth Barrett told Browning that she had £8,000 in government stocks, from which she drew a quarterly income of £40–5, and £200 p.a. from shares in the *David Lyon,* a merchant ship trading with the West Indies.

291 *sulphurous vapour.* In his letter of 25 Aug. 1846 (not included here), Browning told Elizabeth Barrett about recent earthquakes in Tuscany, after which 'great puffs of sulphureous smoke came up thro' chinks in the plains', and asked 'Do you fear, dearest?'

291 *in boats.* Because of the death by drowning of Bro.

296 *Rosie Cross.* The Revd George Barrett Hunter was punning on Browning's unfashionable address in New Cross and the 'Red Cross Knight', the hero of Book 1 of Spenser's *Faerie Queene*; the 'Rosie Cross' alludes to the occult sect of the Rosicrucians.

299 *his victim.* Browning connects the Revd George Barrett Hunter (for whose taunting 'epithet' see note above) with John Kenyon, and hence the whole Barrett family, whose fortune was founded on slave-holding in the West Indies; this image of tyranny suggests that of Mr Barrett as Zeus in Aeschylus' *Prometheus Bound*, who offers to release Prometheus from his torment if Prometheus will reveal the secret that will save Zeus from his downfall, namely the prophecy that his marriage to Thetis would produce a son greater than his father.

306 *five or six scudi . . . Not so many crazie. Scudi* and *crazie* are Italian coins; Elizabeth Barrett's expression is equivalent to saying 'five or six shillings . . . not so many pence'.

314 *my proper room.* The word 'room' was written over 'mind' in the MS.

317 *my friend.* Captain James Pritchard, an old family friend; in the event he was unable to be there, and his place was taken by Browning's cousin James Silverthorne (see p. 321 n. *your cousin*).

321 *salvolatile.* Usually two words, 'sal volatile', smelling salts (a solution of ammonium carbonate was the commonest preparation) used as a restorative in fainting fits.

321 *your cousin.* James Silverthorne (1809–52), son of Browning's maternal aunt and a companion from boyhood. Browning wrote 'May and Death' (*Men and Women*, 1855) in his memory.

321 *penny a liners.* Hack journalists, who might examine the church registers for gossip-column material.

322 *Trippy.* Mary Trepsack (*c.* 1768–1857), friend and companion of Elizabeth Barrett's paternal grandmother; for details of her relations with Elizabeth Barrett, see Kelley and Hudson, i. 301–2.

328 *at the corner of the cards.* The cards announcing their marriage, which were sent to friends and family on the day of departure. There had been much discussion about them in passages from the letters omitted here. Elizabeth Barrett jokes about not inviting wedding visits since she and Browning were fleeing abroad.

332 *Hodgsons.* A bookshop in what is now New Cavendish Street.

332 *books you gave me.* Sir John, later Lord, Hanmer (1809–81), Liberal politician; Browning knew him personally and admired his poems. He published three volumes: the one mentioned here may be *Fra Cipolla and other Poems* (1839), from which Browning used a motto in *Colombe's Birthday* (1844), or *Sonnets* (1840). The 'two dear books' are probably, as Kintner suggests, *Scholia in Aeschyli tragoedias* (1820) and a facsimile of the 1603 *Hamlet* (1825), both inscribed 'Miss Barrett from R.B.' (*Sale Catalogues of Libraries of Eminent Persons*, vi, *Poets and Men of Letters*, ed. J. Woolford (1972), pp. 94, 157).

INDEX

Note: Barrett family members are listed without the additional 'Moulton' or 'Barrett Moulton' prefixed to their surnames. See letter EB 20 Dec., p. 171.

Abelard, Peter 152
Aeschylus, *Agamemnon* 140, 349;
   Prometheus Bound 13, 27, 36, 77,
   337, 340, 341, 357
Aesop 36, 341
Agrippa, Heinrich Cornelius 17, 22, 28,
   338
Alfieri, Vittorio 41, 342
Andersen, Hans Christian, *The
   Improvisatore* 36, 40–1, 42, 341
Aristophanes 338

Babbage, Charles 21, 338
Bailey, Philip James 183, 351
Barrett, Alfred Price (EB's brother)
   253–4, 311, 335
Barrett, Arabella ('Arabel', EB's sister)
   73, 128, 193–4, 228, 248–9, 256,
   270, 280, 287, 300–1, 320–1, 335
Barrett, Charles John ('Stormie', EB's
   brother) 128, 197, 287, 335
Barrett, Edward (EB's father) x, xii,
   xiii, 27, 68, 82–3, 88, 94, 99, 103–6,
   114, 119, 123, 125, 129–30, 134,
   136, 137–8, 140–2, 144–5, 165–7,
   192, 193–4, 200, 201–4, 217,
   223–7, 249–50, 260–1, 269–72,
   280–2, 287, 291, 293–6, 297, 306,
   315, 318, 324–7, 329–30, 333, 335,
   348, 350, 353, 355, 357
Barrett, Edward ('Bro', EB's brother)
   x, 105, 340, 347, 351, 357
Barrett, Elizabeth:
  health 3, 10, 26, 29, 30, 33–4, 38, 47,
   70, 71, 73, 80, 81–2, 94, 104, 113,
   118, 124, 126, 130, 153–4, 190, 191,
   197, 210–1, 224–5, 280
  family, background, domestic and
   material circumstances x, xiii, 19,
   34, 42, 51, 68, 82–3, 95, 99, 103–6,
   119, 130, 140–1, 144, 151, 161,
   165–6, 171–2, 183–4, 192, 193–4,
   196, 206, 223–5, 253–4, 260–1,

   269–70, 274–5, 276–7, 280, 282–3,
   287–91, 294–5, 296–7, 300, 315,
   335, 350, 357
  her poetry 6–7, 12–13, 18, 34–5, 36,
   51, 67, 72–3, 87, 93, 97–8, 151–2,
   167, 191–2, 254, 267, 291
  letters and letter-writing 10–11, 13,
   17–18, 42, 64, 148, 160, 164, 182–3,
   197, 199 200, 208, 214–15, 217,
   233, 236, 252, 256, 262–3, 327–8,
   330, 333
  RB's poetry 2, 3, 7, 11, 13, 19, 21–2,
   26–7, 31, 42, 46–7, 63, 64, 70,
   72–3, 76, 77, 80, 83, 86, 88, 90–2,
   93–4, 98, 101–2, 105–6, 107–8,
   134, 150–1, 152, 153, 164, 183, 189,
   191, 192, 199, 211–12, 217, 228,
   234, 254–5
  Works:
   Aeschylus' Soliloquy' 28, 32, 58,
    340
   Aurora Leigh xiv, 28, 58, 97, 333,
    335, 340
   'Bertha in the Lane' 8, 97, 150,
    185, 267, 336, 351–2, 356
   Casa Guidi Windows 333
   'Catarina to Camoens' 97, 250,
    355, 356
   A Drama of Exile ix, 8, 16–17, 36,
    258, 336, 341
   An Essay on Mind 87, 89
   'A Flower in a Letter' 72, 73, 344
   'Lady Geraldine's Courtship' ix–x,
    28, 97, 101, 150, 340, 347
   'Past and Future' 156, 349–50
   Poems (1844) ix, 1–2, 8–9, 155,
    253, 335, 345, 355
   Poems (1850) 333
   Poems Before Congress 333
   'A Portrait' 60, 343
   Prometheus Bound (transl.) 27, 32,
    58, 67, 93, 97

Barrett, Elizabeth: Works (*cont.*)
  'Rhyme of the Duchess May' 9,
    336
  'The Romaunt of the Page' 9, 336
  The Seraphim 87, 345, 346
  Sonnets from the Portuguese 333, 350,
    351, 355
  'The Vision of Fame' 89
  'A Vision of Poets' 96, 347
  see also courtship, principal events in
Barrett, George Goodin (EB's brother)
  114, 128, 134, 136, 137, 191, 204,
  287, 315, 318, 335, 349
Barrett, Henrietta (EB's sister) 193–4,
  201–2, 227, 270, 295, 315, 320–2,
  335, 353
Barrett, Henry (EB's brother) 99,
  302–4, 306, 309, 335
Barrett, Mary (EB's sister) 335
Barrett, Mary (*née* Graham-Clarke,
  EB's mother) 293, 335
Barrett, Octavius Butler (EB's brother)
  335
Barrett, Samuel (EB's brother) 335
Barrett, Septimus James ('Set', EB's
  brother) 311, 335
Bayley, Sarah 246–7, 355
Beethoven, Ludwig van, *Fidelio* 100,
  347
Besier, Rudolf, *The Barretts of Wimpole
  Street* xiii
Bevan, James Johnstone 270
biblical quotations and allusions 17, 20,
  21, 26, 27, 32, 35, 42, 46, 49, 52,
  60, 62, 86, 88, 116, 142, 147, 158,
  170, 172, 174, 184, 186, 187, 189,
  196, 237, 246, 265, 274, 338, 339,
  340–1, 341, 342, 343, 343–4, 344,
  348, 349, 350, 351, 352, 354, 355,
  356, 357
Boccaccio, *Decameron* 36
Boyd, Hugh Stuart 73, 169–70, 306,
  320
Brauwer or Brouwer, Adriaen 285, 357
Browning, Reuben (RB's uncle) 55,
  343
Browning, Robert (RB's father) 25, 83,
  96, 196–7, 273, 290–3, 324, 326,
  333, 335, 338
Browning, Robert:
  EB's poetry 1, 4–5, 8–9, 16–17,
    31–2, 60, 71, 89, 96–7, 101, 150,
    154–6, 185, 247–8, 250, 253, 258–9

family, background, domestic and
  material circumstances ix, 96, 114,
  122, 129–30, 196–7, 239–40,
  259–60, 273, 290–1, 335, 348
health 8, 15, 25, 41, 45, 46–7, 48–9,
  50, 51, 61, 75, 76, 91, 102–3, 106,
  108–9, 191, 210, 235, 254, 305–6,
  312–4, 324, 326, 336
his poetry 5, 8, 15–16, 23, 25, 31, 32,
  45, 50, 60, 61, 71, 75, 89, 90, 92–3,
  96, 110, 146, 149, 187, 191, 201,
  212–13, 219, 233–4, 253
letters and letter-writing 1, 5, 9–10,
  14, 17, 37, 43, 62, 149, 184–6, 190,
  198, 214–15, 219, 232, 244–5,
  262–3, 329, 355
Works:
  The Agamemnon of Aeschylus (transl.)
    342
  Asolando 349
  Bells and Pomegranates ix, 8, 13, 45,
    71, 76, 88, 96, 228, 270, 336, 338,
    354
  'The Bishop Orders His Tomb at
    Saint Praxed's Church' 90, 342
  A Blot in the 'Scutcheon 27, 340
  'The Boy and the Angel' 90, 342
  'By the Fire-side' 355
  Christmas-Eve and Easter-Day 333,
    336, 343
  'Claret and Tokay' 88, 91, 342
  Colombe's Birthday 151, 349
  'Count Gismond' 105–6, 347
  Dramatic Lyrics 338, 347
  Dramatic Romances and Lyrics 23, 45,
    50, 71, 96, 149, 335, 336, 347,
    348, 349, 351
  Dramatis Personae 333
  'Earth's Immortalities' 152, 349
  'The Englishman in Italy' 341,
    342, 351
  Essay on Shelley 336
  'The Flight of the Duchess' 42, 45,
    48, 58, 70, 75, 76, 77, 80, 83, 86,
    88, 91–2, 92–3, 93–4, 342, 347
  'Garden Fancies' ('The Flower's
    Name' and 'Sibrandus
    Schafnaburgensis') 90, 183, 342,
    346, 351
  'Home-Thoughts, from Abroad'
    134–5, 349
  'The Laboratory' 90–1, 342, 347
  'Life in a Love' 354

Browning, Robert: Works (*cont.*)
  Life of Strafford (with John Forster)
    253, 355
  Luria 15, 19, 23, 26, 45, 46, 62, 65,
    71, 146, 153, 187, 191, 201,
    211–13, 219, 228, 338, 354
  'May and Death' 358
  Men and Women 333, 348, 354, 358
  Paracelsus ix, 13, 33, 47, 164, 187,
    341, 345, 346, 352
  Pauline 25, 187, 189, 191, 192, 199,
    338, 339, 343, 352
  'Pictor Ignotus' 346
  Pippa Passes 10, 19, 21–2, 25, 60,
    337, 343, 345
  The Ring and the Book 333
  'Saul' 45, 47, 58, 107–8, 110, 348
  'Soliloquy of the Spanish Cloister'
    19, 338
  Sordello ix, 90, 253, 345, 346, 351,
    353
  A Soul's Tragedy 23, 26, 70, 71, 96,
    107, 212–13, 219, 228, 233–4,
    338, 346, 347, 354
  'Transcendentalism' 354
  'Which' 349
  see also courtship, principal events in
Browning, Robert Wiedemann Barrett
  ('Pen') xi, 333
Browning, Sarah Anna (*née*
  Wiedemann, RB's mother) 76, 96,
  197, 290, 292–3, 317, 322, 324–6,
  329, 333, 335
Browning, Sarianna (RB's sister) 47,
  96, 113, 155, 324, 326, 332–3, 335
Buffon, Georges-Louis Leclerc, comte
  de 3
Bulwer (Bulwer-Lytton), Sir Edward
  Lytton ix
Burdett-Coutts, Angela Georgina 232,
  354
Butler, Samuel, *Hudibras* 17, 338
Byron, George Gordon, Lord 60, 84

Campbell, Miss 285, 357
Caravaggio, Polidoro da 25, 339
Carducci, Countess ('Countess Peppa')
  273, 356
Carlyle, Jane Welsh 24, 98
Carlyle, Thomas 14, 22, 23–4, 25, 98,
  164, 337, 339
Casaubon, Isaac 68, 344
Cerrito, Fanny 126, 348

Chambers, Dr Frederick William 82,
  83, 105, 113, 346
Chapman, George 70, 344
Chorley, Henry Fothergill 36, 96, 163,
  187, 341
Coleridge, Sara 87, 346
Colonna, Vittoria 78, 345
Cook, Captain William Surtees 200,
  204, 227, 295, 335, 353
courtship, principal events in: RB's first
  letter 1–2; first meeting 55; RB's
  abortive declaration 56ff.; the 'Pisa
  affair' 110ff.; EB acknowledges her
  love for RB 132–3; decision to live
  in Italy 205–6; decision to marry
  315–19; wedding 319–21;
  departure 331–3

Dante 41, 42, 43–4, 78; *Inferno* 53–4
Dickens, Charles ix, 187, 352
Diderot, Denis 77, 345
Disraeli, Benjamin, *Sybil* 83; *Vivian Grey*
  40, 41, 341
Domett, Alfred ix, 14, 224–5, 337, 338
Domett, Captain Nathaniel 224
Donne, John 24, 95, 198, 339, 347, 349,
  353
Dumas, Alexandre, *Le Comte de Monte
  Cristo* 271, 356
Dryden, John 20

Elliotson, John 79, 346
Euripides 18, 338

Fellows, Sir Charles 4, 336
Fielding, Henry, *Tom Jones* 192
Flush (EB's spaniel) 42, 63, 147–8,
  221, 248–9, 288–9, 275–6, 301–13,
  337, 342, 357
Forster, John 355
Franklin, Benjamin 83
Fuller, Margaret 183, 351

Gibbon, Edward, *History of the Decline
  and Fall of the Roman Empire* 192
Goethe, Johann Wolfgang von 151; *The
  Sorrows of Young Werther* 192, 352
Graham-Clarke, Arabella (EB's aunt)
  105, 347

Hall, Robert 220, 353
Hanmer, Sir John 332, 358
Haydon, Benjamin Robert xv

Hedley, Jane (EB's aunt) 114, 269–70,
    292–3, 295–6, 343
Hedley, Robert (EB's uncle) 270,
    292–3, 295
Hemans, Charles 78, 345
Hemans, Felicia 78, 345
Homer, *Iliad* 43, 342; *Odyssey* 102, 160,
    350
Hood, Thomas 45, 48, 342, 346
Horne, Richard Henry (or Hengist) 6,
    10, 24–5, 28, 64, 80, 163–4, 336,
    337, 339, 344
Howitt, Mary 36, 43, 341
Hume, David, *Essays Moral and Political*
    192
Hunt, Leigh 84
Hunter, Revd George Barrett 86, 106,
    234–5, 283–4, 286, 296, 299, 308,
    346, 348, 354, 357

Jago, Dr Francis Robert 211, 353
Jameson, Anna Brownwell 78, 97, 103,
    247, 258–9, 278, 333, 345
Johnson, Samuel, *Rasselas* xiii

Kean, Edmund 60, 343
Keats, John 12, 16, 17
Kelly, Fitzroy 116, 348
Kenyon, John 1, 3, 5, 8, 18, 37, 39, 41,
    46, 47, 48, 49, 50, 51–2, 61, 80, 81,
    86, 87, 89, 95, 96, 114, 118, 123,
    125, 135, 136, 137, 147, 148–9,
    151, 155, 163, 164, 180–1, 188,
    189–90, 199, 200, 204, 206–7, 208,
    214, 236, 237, 239, 247, 270, 292,
    296, 297, 299, 303, 322, 324, 331,
    335, 337, 346, 348, 349, 355, 357
King, William, *Political and Literary
    Anedotes of his Own Times* 192, 352

Landor, Walter Savage 18, 338; 'To
    Robert Browning' 149, 351
Lycophron 24, 339

Marlowe, Christopher 70
Martineau, Harriet 78, 146, 164, 183,
    265–6, 345, 349, 351
Mathew, Father Theobald 60, 343
Mazarin, Jules, Cardinal 50
Michaelangelo, *Last Judgement* 285, 357
Mill, John Stuart 25, 29, 60, 343, 352
Milton, John, *Paradise Lost* ix, 36, 47,
    341, 342

Mirandola, Pico della 61, 343
Mitford, Mary Russell 10, 20, 96,
    146–7, 262–3, 337, 342, 345, 353
Monteagle, Thomas Spring-Rice, 1st
    Baron 259, 356
Moxon, Edward 16, 183, 213, 259, 337

Napoleon 21, 197

Ossian 242
Ostade, Adriaen van 25, 285, 339
Ovid, *Metamorphoses* 337, 350

Paine, Thomas, *The Age of Reason* 192
Palmella, Pedro di Lonsa Holstein,
    Duke of 134, 349
Peel, Sir Robert 265, 356
Porta, Giovanni Battista della, *Magiae
    naturalis* 215, 353
Pritchard, Captain James 298–9, 317,
    325, 358
Procter, Anne 239–40, 355
Procter, Brian Waller ('Barry
    Cornwall') 239, 355

Quarles, Francis 198, 353

Radcliffe, Ann 96, 347
Richardson, Samuel 13
Richelieu, Armand Jean du Plessis,
    Cardinal and duc de 50, 342
Rogers, Samuel xv
Rousseau, Jean-Jacques 192, 283

Sallust 78, 345
Sand, George 79, 101, 102, 273, 345,
    347, 356
Shakespeare 20, 34, 61, 338; *As You Like
    It* 183, 265, 351, 356; *Hamlet* 40,
    77, 146, 201, 345, 349, 353; *Henry
    VIII* 350; *King Lear* 2, 63, 335,
    344; *Macbeth* 27, 74–5, 340, 344;
    Measure for Measure 343; *Merchant of
    Venice* 16, 338; *Much Ado About
    Nothing* 178, 343, 351; *Othello* 60,
    343; *Romeo and Juliet* 9, 13, 336,
    337; *Sonnets* 241, 355; *Twelfth Night*
    62, 344
Shelley, Percy Bysshe 44, 70, 78, 341,
    342, 345
Shelley, Percy Florence 78, 345
Sidney, Sir Philip *Defence of Poesie* 20,
    338

Silverthorne, James 321, 358
Spenser, Edmund, *Faerie Queene* 296, 357

Talfourd, Frank 187, 352
Tasso, Torquato 4, 336
Taylor, Mr 306, 309; and Mrs Taylor 310–11
Taylor, Sir Henry ix
Teniers, David, the Younger 285, 357
Tennyson, Alfred 17, 21, 69–70, 73, 164, 191, 259, 338, 356; 'The Blackbird' 235, 354; 'Mariana' 99, 347; 'Morte d'Arthur' 69; 'Oenone' 69; 'The Poet' 79, 346; 'Timbuctoo' 69–71, 344

Titian 5, 336
Trepsack, Mary ('Trippy') 322, 358

Venables, George Stovin 191
Virgil, *Georgics* 60, 343; *Aeneid* 227, 354
Voltaire, *Lettres philosophiques* 192

Walter the Penniless 232, 354
Webster, John 236, 354
White, Henry Kirke 25, 340
Wilson, Elizabeth xiii, 106, 274–5, 283, 310–11, 320–1; 325, 329, 333, 347, 357
Wilson, John ('Christopher North') 20, 338
Wollstonecraft, Mary 192
Wordsworth, William 164

OXFORD

MORE OXFORD PAPERBACKS

Details of a selection of other Oxford Paperbacks follow. A complete list of Oxford Paperbacks, including The World's Classics, Twentieth-Century Classics, OPUS, Past Masters, Oxford Authors, Oxford Shakespeare, and Oxford Paperback Reference, is available in the UK from the General Publicity Department, Oxford University Press (RS), Walton Street, Oxford, OX2 6DP.

In the USA, complete lists are available from the Paperbacks Marketing Manager, Oxford University Press, 200 Madison Avenue, New York, NY 10016.

Oxford Paperbacks are available from all good bookshops. In case of difficulty, customers in the UK can order direct from Oxford University Press Bookshop, 116 High Street, Oxford, Freepost, OX1 4BR, enclosing full payment. Please add 10 per cent of the published price for postage and packing.

THE COURTSHIP OF ROBERT BROWNING
AND ELIZABETH BARRETT

Daniel Karlin

Daniel Karlin's exciting and imaginative book gives a fresh account of one of the most celebrated romances of literary history. Based on a much closer study of the love letters than has been attempted before, shows how significant they are for an interpretation of the work of both poets.

'A well written and very perceptive study of a love affair that was as much a literary event as a private emotional experience' *New Statesman*

'A rewarding study . . . Karlin's sensitive guidance enables us to appreciate the poignancy of what Browning achieved for Elizabeth.' *Times Higher Education Supplement*

THE GREEN MAN REVISITED

Chosen by Roger Sharrock

This superb collection contains some of the best stories written in English during the 1960s and 1970s by authors living all around the world. Whether the scene of the story is an Afrikaans township, an Indian village, a synagogue in the Bronx, or a south-coast boarding-house, each piece has been chosen for its intrinsic excellence and originality.

The authors are Chinua Achebe, Kingsley Amis, George MacKay Brown, Morely Callaghan, Elsbeth Davie, Susan Hill, Dan Jacobson, Benedict Kiely, Bernard Malamud, Olivia Manning, Gordon Meyer, V. S. Naipaul, R. K. Narayan, Jean Rhys, Frank Sargeson, Elizabeth Taylor, William Trevor, Frank Tuohy, John Updike, and Patrick White.

CHARMED LIVES

Chosen by T. S. Dorsch

This collection contains stories written in the 1950s and 1960s, many of which demonstrate the impressive and accomplished skills of Commonwealth writers who began to achieve world-wide reputations during that period. The writers, chosen by T. S. Dorsch (who has also written a preface and biographical notes), come from countries as diverse as Australia, Canada, India, New Zealand, South Africa, Nigeria, and the West Indies.

The writers include Mary Lavin, Viola Meynell, Maurice Shadbolt, H. E. Bates, Bill Naughton, L. P. Hartley, Ruth Prawer Jhabvala, L. E. Jones, Peter Ustinov, May C. Jenkins, Norah Lofts, Angus Wilson, and George Lamming.

BRITISH POETRY AND PROSE 1870–1905

Edited by Ian Fletcher

This anthology of works written between 1870 and 1905 bridges the Victorian and Modernist periods. It is confined to imaginative literature, to poetry and short fiction, which together reflect an uneasy and pluralistic world, one which exerted particular pressures on the writer. Among the many authors represented are Gerard Manley Hopkins, Walter Pater, Algernon Swinburne, George Moore, Rudyard Kipling, and H. G. Wells.

LITTLE DORRIT

Charles Dickens

Edited by Harvey Peter Sucksmith

Highly regarded today as one of the greatest novels in English literature, *Little Dorrit*, first published during 1855–7, the turbulent period of the Crimean War, presents both a scathing indictment of mid-Victorian England and a devastating insight into the human condition. Examining the many social and mental prisons which incarcerate men and women, the novel also considers the nature of true spiritual freedom. Against a background of administrative and financial scandal, Dickens tells the moving story of the old Marshalsea prisoner who inherits a fortune and his devoted daughter's love for a man who believes he has done with love. He draws widely on the events of his own life and times, yet focuses a powerful imaginative vision which is as organic and universal as it is specific, immediate and intense. The author displays his characteristic mastery of irony and pathos, of satire and comedy, and the book contains some of his most mature, ambitious and effective writing.

The World's Classics

VENUS AND THE RAIN

Medbh McGuckian

This is the second collection of poems by Medbh McGuckian, one of the best known of the younger generation of Ulster poets. Her mysterious and erotic poems, sometimes puzzling, often beautiful, exercise a fascination over the reader who is willing to be beguiled as her subject-matter—domesticity, love, moving house, children—takes on an unnerving precariousness.

'a wonderfully original, bewitching collection' *London Magazine*

Oxford Poets

JOURNEY TO THE WESTERN ISLANDS OF SCOTLAND
Samuel Johnson

and

JOURNAL OF A TOUR TO THE HEBRIDES
J. Boswell

Edited by R. W. Chapman

Samuel Johnson and James Boswell spent the autumn of 1773 touring the Highlands and Western Islands of Scotland. Detailed notes of their individual impressions are now published in this volume. Johnson's *Journey to the Western Islands* records his observations on the Scottish landscape and architecture, and the traditions and character of the Scots themselves. Boswell's *Journal of a Tour to the Hebrides* is much more gossipy and circumstantial. Together, the two accounts provide a splendidly entertaining guide to Scotland.

THE NEW OXFORD BOOK OF LIGHT VERSE
Chosen by Kingsley Amis

'extremely funny and absorbing . . . a reflection, of course, of the sureness of Amis's taste' *Times Literary Supplement*

'very comprehensive and enjoyable' *Observer*

'Full of good stuff.' *New Statesman*

THE FLOWER MASTER

Medbh McGuckian

In 1979 the young Ulster poet, Medbh McGuckian, won the annual Poetry Society competition, and in 1980 she received an Eric Gregory Award.

The vivid and brilliant surface attractiveness of her style beguiles the reader into untangling the evasive meanings of her mysterious and sensual poems. Anne Stevenson, reviewing the pamphlet 'Portrait of Joanna' in *The Times Literary Supplement*, wrote: 'she is as clever (probably) as Craig Raine, as perceptive (possibly) as Elizabeth Bishop . . . Reading these poems, one senses that thoughts and perceptions make mysterious connection with a hidden terror in the poet's mind.'

Oxford Poets

THE TAIN

Translated by Thomas Kinsella

The Tain is a translation from the *Tàin Bó Cuailnge,* centrepiece of the eighth-century Ulster cycle of heroic tales, and Ireland's nearest approach to a great epic. It tells the story of a giant cattle-raid, the invasion of Ulster by the armies of Medb and Ailill, queen and king of Connacht, and their allies, seeking to carry off the great Brown Bull of Cuailnge.

'This magnificent version of the early epic . . . deserves to be as widely read for its literary significance as it is already widely coveted for its beauty as a book.' *Listener*

'Kinsella has given us something both old and new . . . a most distinguished book.' *Irish Times*

ON BALLYCASTLE BEACH
Mebdh McGuckian

This is a mature and complex collection, the third book from Mebdh McGuckian, one of the leading Ulster poets of her generation, whose mysterious and unsettling poems continue to perturb and fascinate the reader.

'one of the richest and most provocative collections of poetry to have appeared in recent years' *The Times* (of Mebdh McGuckian's first full length book, *The Flower Master*)

Oxford Poets

THE OXFORD BOOK OF VERSE IN ENGLISH TRANSLATION
Chosen and Edited by Charles Tomlinson

Our vast and often neglected literature of poetic translation is represented in this anthology by some 600 poems or extracts ranging from Gavin Douglas's *Aeneid* in the early sixteenth century to Ezra Pound's versions of classical Chinese and Elaine Feinstein's translations from the Russian of Marina Tsvetayeva.

'a treasure house packed with fresh surprises' *Books and Bookmen*

'serious, innovatory, large in its scope and meticulously edited . . . deserves high praise' *London Review of Books*

THE NEW OXFORD BOOK OF EIGHTEENTH-CENTURY VERSE

Chosen and Edited by Roger Lonsdale

'a major anthology: one of the best that Oxford has ever produced' The Times

'a major event . . . forces a reappraisal of what 18th-century poetry is' Sunday Times

'the most important anthology in recent years' The Economist

'indispensable' Kingsley Amis

THE NEW OXFORD BOOK OF LIGHT VERSE

Chosen by Kingsley Amis

'extremely funny and absorbing . . . a reflection, of course, of the sureness of Amis's taste' Times Literary Supplement

'very comprehensive and enjoyable' Observer

'Full of good stuff.' New Statesman